ALSO BY NICK SALVATORE

Eugene V. Debs: Citizen and Socialist

WE ALL GOT HISTORY

WE ALL GOT HISTORY

THE MEMORY BOOKS OF AMOS WEBBER

NICK SALVATORE

TIMES BOOKS
RANDOM HOUSE

Library of Congress Cataloging-in-Publication Data

Salvatore, Nick.

We all got history / Nick Salvatore. — 1st ed.

p.   cm.

Includes bibliographical references and index.

ISBN 0-8129-2681-1

1. Webber, Amos—Diaries.   2. Afro-Americans—Diaries.

I. Webber, Amos.   II. Title.

E185.97.W44S25   1996

973′.0496073′0092—dc20   95-20125

Manufactured in the United States of America

9   8   7   6   5   4   3   2

First Edition

Designed by Robert C. Olsson

For Ann

We all got history. Some of us just don't know it. But it's there. Just got to look for it.

—Ellen L. Hazard, eighty-three,
historian of the Hazard family,
Worcester County, Massachusetts,
January 1984

Contents

PREFACE

ON A CLEAR, WARM MORNING in early November 1985, I walked
across the Charles River from Cambridge to Boston to work in the
rich archives of the Baker Library at the Harvard University
Graduate School of Business Administration. I was just beginning to research an article on workers' control of production in
nineteenth-century America, and I hoped these archives would
help me to learn more about management perspectives of workers' shop-floor activities. Combining these accounts with comparable records of the early unions in the same industries, I hoped to
better understand the intense, alternating patterns of hostility and
accommodation that marked the nineteenth-century workplace.
But while my search produced much useful information, the close,
specific observations of those relationships over many years remained elusive.

It was with considerable excitement, then, that I noticed on my
fourth day at the library, penciled in between two lines of the
typed guide to the American Steel and Wire Collection, the notation "Amos Webber Thermometer Record and Diary." The listing
promised nine volumes, covering most of the last half of the nineteenth century, and the collection itself contained the surviving
records of Washburn and Moen, an important iron and steel firm
in Worcester, Massachusetts. Thinking that I had finally found
what I had been searching for—the temperature book clearly
referred to the furnaces, I gleefully assumed, and the diary *must*
be the work log of the foreman or department supervisor—I requested the first three volumes. I knew what I sought; but I never
anticipated what I found.

What the library staff brought to my desk was anything but what I expected. Where I yearned for a work log replete with discussions of production, comments on the workforce, and even technical discussions of furnace temperatures, I found instead a first entry describing an 1855 fire that destroyed five houses, not in Worcester, but in Philadelphia. Additional entries further confused me. Rather than discussions of the intricacies of iron production, I found a detailed account of the wedding of a wealthy young couple followed by other entries describing the rescue of a fugitive slave and an exuberant religious revival attended by both black and white Philadelphians. Toward the back of the leather- and cardboard-bound business ledgers that constituted the physical books, the pages divided into columns that recorded twice a day, every day, from December 1854 until October 1860, the temperature and wind direction, with a note on climatic conditions. The author maintained these records daily regardless of whether he recorded an entry in the diarylike first section.

By now thoroughly perplexed, and not a little impatient (would even this promising source disappoint as had the others?), I turned to the second volume. It began in 1870—there were no entries at all for the 1860s—concerned Worcester and not Philadelphia, and, while it occasionally discussed work conditions, focused far more attention on politics, natural disasters, and the issue of equal rights for black Americans. At the bottom of the first temperature page in this volume, the author referred the reader to a later entry in the volume that in turn relied on an entry he had made more than a decade earlier in the first volume. This Amos Webber obviously possessed a clear sense of history, at least concerning aspects of his own life.

Slowly, my curiosity bested my impatience and, while resigned to another disappointment concerning my initial project, I determined to make some sense out of these books before I returned them to the stacks. Two points stood foremost in my mind. First, Amos Webber not only inscribed each volume as "Amos Webber Thermometer Book," but he occasionally signed individual entries as well. What propelled him to do this? I wondered. What kind of man was he who sought self-affirmation in so private a fashion? Did he also seek a more public affirmation and, if so, in what ways? He was not a foreman in a mill, but who was he? A second point pricked the detective in me. In both volumes Webber noted as part of an entry or, more frequently, in the vertical column to the right of the day's meteorological observations, something called the "G.U.O. of O.F." Webber frequently identified himself as a participant in this group's activities and, though the initials meant nothing to me, I resolved to find out something more about them.

It took a day and a half until I came upon an entry that spelled out those initials—they stood for the Grand United Order of Odd Fellows—and appended to the title what was for me the most significant parenthesis in all of the nine volumes: "(Colored)." So intent had I been to find my white foreman that I had missed every signal Webber had provided up to that point. True, Webber rarely used the personal pronoun, and thus it was at times difficult to distinguish between his observations, often based on news reports, and his commentary on his own social and political activities. Able now to place him as a free person of color and a member of an important fraternal organization, an entirely new set of questions arose for me. The references to blacks, escaped slaves, the politics of Reconstruction, and work carried sharply different implications if written by a black man. Was he born free? If not, when and how had he achieved freedom? Was he a participant in the slave rescues he described? What kind of work did he do? And what motivated him to maintain this record for more than four decades? How did his "Thermometer Book" reflect the private self-image and public commitments of the author? With mounting excitement and not a little apprehension, I began again with the first volume, shorn this time of my original preconceptions, and read, slowly and carefully, the words of Amos Webber.

The realization grew in me that I had, without planning it, embarked on another biographical study. In my first book, a biography of Eugene V. Debs, I had explored, along with an analysis of Debs's labor and socialist activities, the question of how men and women claimed their place in a world that for the most part they did not create. As I learned more about Amos Webber, two points struck me. The question of how individuals interact with a broader, received society and culture, and from that exchange carve for themselves lives both private and public, had always been of interest to me, and the fact that Webber was a black American was also appealing. My original intellectual interest was in black history and, while my research grew in different directions, my thinking and my teaching still reflected an understanding of the centrality and complexity of race in American life.

Second, and far more problematic, was the question of the evidence available for the reconstruction of Amos Webber's life. Debs had been a public man whose own voluminous letters were augmented by thousands of others written by friends and opponents to and about him. In contrast, I discovered that with the important exception of the penciled entry in the Baker Library's guide no other known collections of Webber's work exist. His activities were not the subject of broad public debate and discussion, and letters he may have written to friends and associates have not survived. This is not unusual for individuals who were neither elites nor prominent in public life; indeed, the very presence of these journals from someone so unexceptional in society was itself rare and most extraordinary. And, I thought, it was extremely unlikely that I would discover additional information about the mysterious author. Thus the presumed joys of writing biographical history "from the bottom up," as the historical jargon refers to it, evaporated in considerable doubt and even despair over what seemed to be the intractable problem of uncovering a significant portion of this unheralded man's actual life.

Part of the problem concerned the books themselves. Webber called them his "Thermometer Book"; the guide at the Baker Library called them "Amos Webber Thermometer Record and Diary." Yet in reality they were neither. His own title provided no hint of the social and political commentary that would infuse even his temperature section. Yet his journals were not diaries. He avoided personal introspection in his entries, rarely examining his own motivations or even using the personal pronoun. His entries, moreover, did not constitute a continuous story line. A wide variety of topics vied for his attention, and discussions of political or religious themes might be followed by pages of entries devoted to natural disasters, spectacular contemporary crimes, or accounts of past history a decade or a century earlier. As Webber relied on newspapers and magazines for many of these entries, his authorial voice was not always evident.

Gradually I came to understand that these books were not diaries in any intimate sense, and certainly not solely meteorological records. Rather, Webber had maintained a chronicle, a record of events bound not by the rules of the reporter or the historian but by the scope and depth of his own interests. He discussed events that impressed him, and he occasionally allowed himself the opportunity to comment on them as well. This chronicle was no mere listing, but rather an intricate reflection of at least part of what occupied Webber's daily thoughts. When I approached the chronicle in this fashion, a framework and continuity in values and commitments across the bewildering variety of entries was revealed.

Helpful as this understanding was, Webber's chronicle proved yet more convoluted and difficult. Despite the nine volumes of almost two thousand handwritten pages, the silences in the chronicle were as noticeable as what he actually recorded. Webber's wife of more than fifty years appeared perhaps six times, his brother twice, his parents never. A deep and obvious moral vision structured many of his entries, yet only twice in all of these years did he place himself in church. His discussions of fraternal meetings, parades, and conventions were most often entered without recourse to the personal pronoun. From the chronicle it was not evident that Webber himself participated in the slave rescues he detailed, in the Civil War that he noted on occasion in the volumes after 1870, or in many of the political activities he recorded. This pointed to an even more obvious silence: he maintained no chronicle at all during the tumultuous decade of the 1860s. Civil War, the emancipation of four million slaves, the induction of black men into the Federal army, the promise and despair of early Reconstruction—on all of these topics Amos Webber was silent. In certain ways what was left out constituted a book in itself and I feared that absence would undermine any attempt to understand who Amos Webber really was.

Despite the current trend among some historians to borrow from literary theory and "read into" texts—a "text," we are told, is not complete until the reader infuses it with his own understandings— I resisted such temptations. There is an undeniable and valued autobiographical element in all historical writing, for it is historians in their present who select a particular past, from among many pasts, to explore. Yet the best historical writing seeks not to confuse one's present with another's past, and accepts the central historical challenge to engage the "otherness" of that past. To use twentieth-century political, literary, or psychological theorists to "read into"

these silences was to risk obliterating the nineteenth-century consciousness that penned the original chronicle. To say this acknowl-
edges very real limitations, for a century later it may be impossible
for anyone to fully grasp the implicit, unconscious assumptions
that created the silence itself. But a better understanding of a time
not one's own is simply not attainable if one starts with the pre-
sumption that the historian "completes" the historical text itself.
Historical objectivity may indeed be elusive, but the presence of
human subjectivity does not therefore release the historian from a
sustained effort to comprehend another's past.

Oddly enough, the very document whose silences loomed so
large also offered a partial solution. As I learned that Webber's reserved, even cryptic style contained its own patterns, I realized
that the aspects of his life he often recorded impersonally or in
curt phrases were as important as the events he chose to enter in
detail. That insight led me to a variety of other sources, including
local newspapers, military and pension records of Civil War soldiers, and the national records of the Grand United Order of Odd
Fellows. This research confirmed my suspicion that, if studied on
its own terms, the chronicle itself would reveal many of its secrets
and silences. Some silences still remain, however, testimonies to
Webber's rectitude as well as to the difficulties of human understanding. These I have noted but tried not to explain.

The particular nature of the chronicle raised two additional and
important questions that found no ready answer in Webber's own
pages. The first concerned the broad meaning of Webber's life.
Was he in any way representative of nineteenth-century northern
blacks or was he an exception, an individual who stood out from,
perhaps even above, others? Certain aspects of Webber's life suggest the latter interpretation, most obviously the nine volumes of
the chronicle. Few Americans of any race kept such detailed
records over so many decades, and even fewer did so who were not
among the educated elite. If he was unique, then how valued a
guide might his book be in understanding that nineteenth-century
world? A second question followed from this. What propelled
Webber to maintain the chronicle? Did he imagine a particular audience as he wrote?

There are no simple answers to these questions, but my reading
of the evidence, developed in the pages that follow, suggests cer-

tain responses. When Webber's personal qualities, many of which were indeed exceptional, are considered in the broader social context of his life, the question of his symbolic representativeness sharply recedes in importance. To the extent that the chronicle offers us Webber's views on a topic, he appears unique; but the same chronicle, in its own words as in the clues it left behind, amply demonstrates his rootedness in the community about him. Webber's chronicle illuminates his world, even if its light does not always reach into every corner.

As Amos Webber never discussed his reasons for keeping the chronicle, it is impossible to know for certain what motivated him. Certain entries suggest that his books provided him with the opportunity to address issues for which, as a black man living in an often inhospitable society, he lacked a more public outlet. As a chronicler, moreover, Webber took seriously his responsibility to record events he thought important. In this act there resided an implied audience, although only rarely did he acknowledge that fact. There was undoubtedly a racial dimension to this chronicle's assumed audience, for Webber pointedly recorded aspects of black collective life rarely mentioned in white newspapers and commentaries. Finally, at the core of Webber's effort lay a simple continuous assertion of the value of his own life, his actions and insights, and of those around him as well. This chronicle is his song of songs. If his prose lacks a lyrical power, it is poignant nonetheless once the melody of its patterns is unlocked. That assertion of worth, meaning, and purpose ultimately propelled the author to create his chronicle. Understanding that sheds the brightest light on Amos Webber's world.

THROUGHOUT THE BOOK I have kept Amos Webber's spelling, punctuation, and grammatical structure as he wrote it. Like most nineteenth-century records, be they private diaries or public newspapers, the spelling and punctuation in Webber's chronicle were not uniform. Semicolons, colons, and commas, as well as periods, often conclude sentences. I have also dispensed with the editorial commentary "[sic]" in the hope that the reader might engage Webber's language and ideas more directly. In a few in-

stances I have included explanatory words in brackets, necessitated by the structure of Webber's original sentence or by my selection of but a part of the entry for inclusion in the text. I have
also numbered the volumes of the chronicle in the notes in Roman
numerals I through IX. This reflects Webber's own understanding of the volumes. This numbering corresponds to volumes 118
through 126 in the American Steel and Wire Collection at the
Baker Library. In the text I use the terms "colored," "black,"
"Negro," "African" or "free African," and "free person(s)" or
"people of color" to describe people of African ancestry in the
United States. These were the terms most used by the nineteenth-
century northern descendants of those involuntary African immigrants. Webber himself favored the term "colored." Other terms,
such as "Afro-American," achieved some popularity by the last
decade of the century, and I use that term occasionally in that context. Public adoption of the term "African American" is of a much
more recent vintage.

Unfortunately, there is no known photograph of Amos Webber.

WE ALL GOT HISTORY

INTRODUCTION

ON FRIDAY, MAY, 28, 1886, at ten o'clock in the morning, Amos Webber strode to the podium at the front of the hall of the Grand Army of the Republic (GAR, the Civil War veterans' organization) in Worcester, Massachusetts. At five feet four inches and approximately 130 pounds, this sixty-year-old light-skinned Negro still looked trim and fit, the more so because he was dressed that day in the blue Federal uniform he had worn twenty-one years before as a soldier in the United States Army. The morning had already been full, greeting old comrades in arms, exchanging news, remembering a shared past. But now the moment Webber had worked toward for almost a year was at hand, as he opened the first business meeting of the Massachusetts Colored Veterans Association of Worcester.

More than 125 veterans awaited Webber's gavel. Mostly black, with but a handful of white officers who had served with black troops, the veterans came primarily from the New England and Middle Atlantic states. They represented various units that had seen action in the Civil War, although the bulk of the veterans had served in one of Massachusetts' three colored regiments: the 54th Infantry, the 55th Infantry, and Webber's own Fifth Cavalry. Webber opened the proceedings, introduced the dignitaries on the dais, and guided the rather short business meeting. The men agreed to hold a national reunion of black veterans the following year in Boston, and endorsed a motion to establish a permanent state organization for all soldiers once members of Massachusetts' Negro regiments. Former Quartermaster Sergeant Webber, former Lieutenants William H. Dupree and James Monroe Trotter of Boston, and former Sergeant William H. Carney of New Bedford, who held the congressional Medal of Honor, were among those elected to the executive committee to organize both the reunion and the state organization.

Following the business meeting these middle-aged veterans, many also in their military blues, gradually formed ranks on the street outside the hall. Their assembly was slowed by the frequent greeting of former comrades, often following years of silence, encounters that produced, the Boston *Advocate* reported, "tears [trickling] down the cheeks of men as they met." Finally, the veterans approximated their former military discipline and at one o'clock, accompanied by two bands and a cohort of aides-de-camp, Chief Marshal Amos Webber stepped off the veterans' parade through Worcester's streets. From the GAR hall on Pearl Street their line of march moved west, through a neighborhood of both well-appointed single-family homes and the stylish multiple-family dwellings ("triple-deckers" in the parlance of Worcester) of the city's skilled workers and white-collar employees. The veterans veered north to Highland Street, east to Lincoln Square, and then back down Main Street to City Hall, where the mayor formally welcomed them to the city. By the time they returned to the GAR hall some two hours later, it had been transformed into a dining hall by the caterers of the midafternoon repast.

As the veterans finished their meal, Webber again stepped to the podium, this time to introduce former Sergeant Burrill Smith, the toastmaster for the occasion. Smith, in turn, introduced the evening's main speaker, Norwood P. Hallowell, the white former colonel of the 55th Massachusetts Infantry. Following Hallowell, a number of black veterans also addressed the meeting, and Webber closed this portion of the day's activities by expressing, in the words of a local reporter, how glad he was "to have met so many of his old comrades." After the dinner, with the dishes cleared and the tables rearranged, the veterans were "tendered a promenade concert and social by their lady friends."[1]

WHO WAS THIS AMOS WEBBER who assumed such a prominent role in this public, regional celebration of the black presence in

American life? That he was a veteran was clear, but that alone did not account for his prominent position in that day's events. Certainly James Monroe Trotter, the eminent musician, author, and politician, William H. Carney, and William Dupree were all more widely known in the black North. How did a man such as Amos Webber, unknown beyond his own circle, the recipient of no awards or editorials in the local or national press, achieve such prominence in May 1886? Was this an extraordinary moment whose shining aura all but obliterated the previous sixty years of common routines? Or did his involvement that May reflect a singular role, but one that emerged from and reflected a lifetime of organizational activism and public political commitment?

Webber himself was anything but forthcoming about the meaning of this veterans' reunion. In his chronicle entry for May 28, he reported that it was partly cloudy, in the midsixties with winds from the northwest, and then added: "Re=union of Colored Veteran, 54, 55th Regiment & 5th Cavalry."[2] There was no further discussion and of his own role he remained silent. His sparse words, offered as if each were laboriously chiseled from granite and thus could be expended only with great effort, characterized many of his chronicle entries. Yet on this occasion, and on many others, Webber left a richer set of clues about his life than perhaps he ever imagined.

In the biography that follows, I have tried to explore as many of those clues as possible. In the process I have come to see that, for all of his lack of national renown, Amos Webber was a lifelong activist among the black residents he lived with in both Philadelphia and Worcester. His public commitments reflected a moral vision that insisted on both individual rectitude and social justice. Over time he claimed as his own a very specific understanding of what it meant to be an American. With fellow blacks he rescued fugitives, fought Confederates, and demanded full civil and political rights. With them he built institutions designed to provide internal structure and direction for a black population confronted with frequent, intense antagonism from whites. It was also in this collective setting that Webber struggled to understand the persistent, complex pain inherent in being both black and American.

As he matured, gained experience in the military, and resettled in Worcester, Webber emerged as a leader as well as an activist in numerous organizations central to black collective life. In this fashion his prominent role in the first meeting of the Massachusetts Colored Veterans Association was a notable but not an exceptional one. It occurred within a web of associations—fraternal, political, military, and religious—that by 1886 were more than a half century in the making. Following the clues this chronicler left reveals not only the life of this man but also the latticelike structures that crisscrossed northern black America in the nineteenth century. Largely invisible to white Americans, these dense, intermeshed collective relations provided concrete support and spiritual comfort to a significant number of individual black Americans. To understand them, and to understand the life of Amos Webber, we must go back to the beginning.

PART ONE

BECOMING AN ACTIVIST: 1826–1860

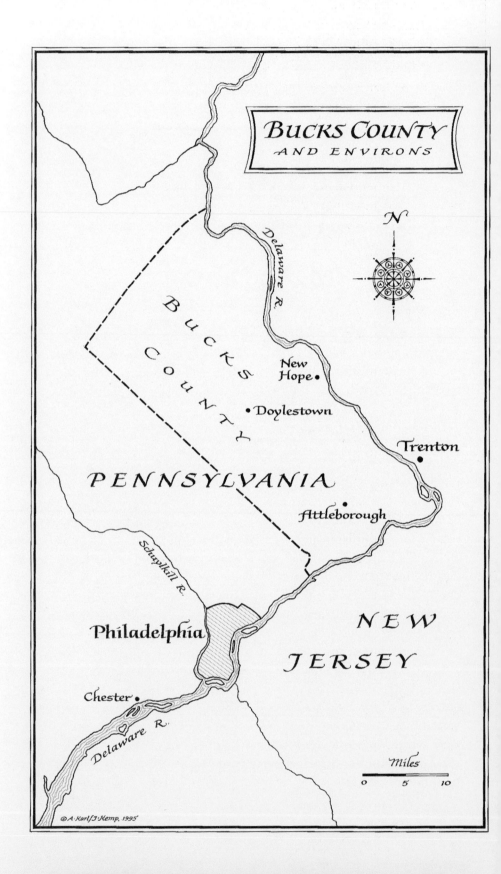

CHAPTER ONE

INTO THE CITY

Amos Webber was born in Attleborough, Bucks County, Pennsylvania, on April 25, 1826. His parents, Samuel and Fannie (Johnson) Webber, were both free people of color, born in Philadelphia. Samuel Webber died a few months before the birth of Amos, leaving behind another son, Samuel, and Amos's mother. Beyond that the history of the Webber family in the county remains hidden.[1]

The Webbers themselves were probably descendants of freed slaves, and their children grew to adulthood in a community in which slavery never sank deep roots. Although one white resident remembered, in 1845, being able as a child in the 1790s to "stand on the corner of my father's farm . . . and count sixteen farm houses, and in every house were slaves," in reality slavery was never widespread in either the county or the state. In 1790 Bucks County had ranked sixth in slave population of all counties in the state, but the nearly 600 free people of color in the county far outnumbered the 261 slaves. Thirty years later, among the almost 38,000 residents there were but two slaves in the county, both older women, while the free black population totaled more than 1,200.[2]

The free African population of Middletown Township (of which Attleborough was a division), totaling some 264 individuals, was small, well organized and relatively young. More than half were not yet twenty-four years of age. Collectively, these black men and women accounted for some 12 percent of the township's total population and for 18 percent of the entire county's black population.[3] Attleborough lay some twenty miles northeast of

Philadelphia and nine miles, across the Delaware River, from New Jersey. Bisecting the Philadelphia–Trenton road, the village was first known as Four Lanes End and was an important transportation route to and from Philadelphia. By 1830 Attleborough alone counted some 600 people, more than eighty houses, a score of shops and small businesses, and four churches.[4]

Despite the concentration of people, however, the township and the county remained largely rural. Bucks County had no mines or foundries in the 1830s and the approximately 200 flour, grist, oil, and saw mills formed a highly decentralized sector of the economy, with few units larger than a family-run business. In 1840 agriculture remained the largest single category of employment, occupying more than 70 percent of the county's workforce.[5]

From the era of the American Revolution, black Attleborough had developed strong, cohesive institutions. As early as 1784 black residents purchased lots together in the Washington Village section of Attleborough. By 1800 the settlement attracted the attention of Richard Allen, later the founder and presiding bishop of the African Methodist Episcopal (A.M.E.) Church, Philadelphia's largest independent black church. Allen, a former slave who had purchased his freedom, traveled a circuit preaching the gospel of Methodism. Following a revival meeting in Attleborough led by Allen in 1809, the town's black community formed the Colored Methodist Society. The society's membership grew as did conversions to the A.M.E. profession and, seven years later, three delegates from the society met with other black Methodists at Richard Allen's Philadelphia home to establish the A.M.E. denomination. Although the Colored Methodist Society affiliated with the new organization, the society also remained independent of it. Members proudly noted that their institutional existence predated the A.M.E.'s formation.[6]

In 1817 the members of the society, who had been conducting services in one another's houses, pooled their resources to purchase land on which to build the Bethlehem Colored Methodist Church. The Bethlehem Church (also known as Bethlehem African) grew in both size and importance over the next two decades. As the mother church for black Methodism in the county, the Attleborough congregation sponsored new churches in Bensalem in 1820 and in Buckingham in 1837. The congregation established a school almost immediately to teach black children the moral lessons of the Bible as well as reading and writing; it was in such a school in 1825 that the young Henry Highland Garnet, a future black leader, first received formal lessons while he and his family, fugitives from Maryland, briefly stayed in the community. A decade later, this same school provided young Amos with his introduction to education. The church also played an important role in fostering moral reform. Edward Jackson, one of the church's original trustees, presided over the Middletown Temperance Society (Colored), which counted twenty-six men and women in 1831, more than 10 percent of the township's adult black population. In addition, church members were central participants in the working of the Underground Railroad.[7]

The Underground Railroad passed escaped slaves from the South to the North and, in some cases, into Canada as well. Along the way men and women known as "stationmasters" transferred the fugitives, most often at night, to the next step to safety. While neither Attleborough nor Bucks County was central to the operation of the Underground Railroad in Pennsylvania (Lancaster and Chester Counties were far more active, for example), both the town and the county had a considerable number of former slaves during the 1830s and early 1840s.[8] The black church played a central role in this activity. In New Hope, Bucks County, the pastor of the Mt. Gilead A.M.E. Church, Reverend Benjamin Jones, and his congregation funneled many fugitives across the Delaware River into New Jersey. In Attleborough the Bethlehem Colored Methodist Church also actively aided fugitives on their way.[9]

Church activists worked with sympathetic whites but they also maintained a separate network within Attleborough's black community. William Bargess, the white secretary of the Anti-Slavery Society in Bucks County, recalled that on occasion during the 1840s, fugitives would arrive in Attleborough without the knowledge of the white activists. They stayed, Bargess remembered, "among some colored people," and the following day he or others might be contacted to assist in transporting the fugitives farther north.[10]

This church-driven activism significantly shaped the culture that nurtured Amos Webber into manhood. In an era when most whites thought black enslavement the natural consequence of a genetic, racial inability to achieve civilized conduct, the Bethlehem Colored Methodist Church's persistent emphasis on proper dress, conduct, and moral behavior challenged dominant white attitudes. Slaves were bound by their condition and not their color, these A.M.E. activists insisted, and in this assertion they were part of a broader moral reform effort. Influenced by the movement known as the Second Great Awakening and affected by the preaching of revivalists such as Charles Grandison Finney, who claimed the possibility of human perfectibility based on an individual's initiative and actions, Attleborough's black church activists hoped that their conduct would alter white attitudes in this life as well as assure salvation in the next.[11] This mixture of sacred and secular aspirations sparked the creation of numerous organizations by Bucks County Negroes and framed the world in which Amos Webber grew.

Yet Bucks County was no paradise for a young black boy during the 1830s and Bucks County blacks found few whites who unequivocally supported their struggle for civil and political rights. Between 1835 and 1842, as Amos grew from a nine-year-old boy into a sixteen-year-old young man, the free black population of Attleborough and the surrounding countryside suffered sustained threats to their individual and collective well-being.

Black Pennsylvanians, like other northern blacks, had long worried about white slave catchers in pursuit of fugitives. There were numerous examples of free blacks descended upon by armed whites and plucked off city streets, forced onto southern-bound ships, and then sold into slavery. Although the numbers of kidnappings gradually declined from the 1820s through the 1840s, the threat nonetheless remained.[12] Particularly difficult for Bucks County blacks was the apprehension of actual fugitives who had long resided in the community. In 1835, for example, slave catchers seized an elderly fugitive from New Jersey named Daniel, a longtime resident of the county, and within hours had returned him to New Jersey without benefit of a trial. That night his daughter, her husband, and their children, with whom Daniel had lived, left immediately for points north, as they too were fugitives. Young Amos may have known the children; undoubtedly he knew of their disappearance. Two years later, in 1837, slave catchers caught the Reverend Benjamin Jones of the New Hope church, an eleven-year resident of the county after escaping from his Maryland master. Surrounded while chopping wood, Jones gave "a stout resistance" before he was subdued and returned to Maryland. Shortly, however, a group of white citizens raised some $700 to purchase his freedom.

An even more famous case involved the four Dorsey brothers, also escaped slaves from Maryland. While three of the brothers ultimately made good their escape, Basil Dorsey was captured and held for trial at Doylestown, the county seat, before Judge John Fox, the presiding justice of the Bucks County Court. Robert Purvis, a local black landowner, secured an abolitionist lawyer from Philadelphia, David Paul Brown, to defend Dorsey, and Purvis used the two weeks between Dorsey's arrest and his trial to prepare, with other black activists, "for a forcible rescue" if Fox ruled against Dorsey. When the judge released Dorsey on a technicality, Purvis and friends immediately spirited him across the Delaware on his way to Massachusetts.[13]

The kidnapping of northern blacks gained renewed legal approval when the United States Supreme Court decided *Prigg* v. *Pennsylvania* in 1842, finding constitutional slave catcher Edward Prigg's return to slavery of a black couple who claimed they had been manumitted. The Court upheld the Fugitive Slave Act of 1793, declaring unconstitutional state laws that might interfere with that act. In writing for the majority, Justice Joseph Story of Massachusetts went even further, insisting that the owner's "right of recaption" was "self-executing"; that is, whites could accost, accuse, and remove free blacks from Pennsylvania's streets and send them into slavery without judicial review or a trial by jury. The decision all but encouraged such kidnapping and intensified the already evident sense of personal danger.[14] For young Amos, who probably heard these events discussed at home and in church gatherings, the violent images could only reinforce an adolescent's fear that his world spun dangerously out of control.

Pennsylvania's political structure created additional tensions. Although slavery was abolished in 1780 (with provisions for its gradual demise, which would take until 1827), most Pennsylvania black men were denied the right to vote during the 1830s. One of the few counties where black men voted in any appreciable numbers was indeed Bucks County, but the exercise of that right generated among whites further violence and resentment.[15]

During the spring of 1837 a state convention met in Harrisburg
to consider revisions and amendments to Pennsylvania's constitution. On the issue of Negro suffrage, the convention debate produced some intense racist rhetoric but, when it adjourned for the
long summer recess, the final clause on suffrage did not explicitly
exclude blacks from the polls. In October, before the convention
met again, Bucks County held its local elections. The Democratic
Party's candidates, strong Jacksonians all and believers in the political rights of the common man, lost five of the six contested
races to a local coalition composed of former Federalists, emerging Whigs, and anti-Masonic voters who were quite hostile to
former President Andrew Jackson's political ideas. That the Democrats lost in Bucks County was in itself not without precedent,
but in this instance two of the defeated candidates charged voting
fraud. Shortly, more than thirty white voters joined their court
suit. In the trial, again before Judge Fox, the Democrats alleged
that the presence of some thirty to forty black voters allowed, in a
close race, the more well-to-do Whig farmers, bankers, and merchants to "steal" the election. The plaintiffs claimed that blacks
were ineligible to vote in any event and that elite Whigs had paid
their taxes and thus actually controlled their votes.

Racial tensions increased as white Democrats claimed that armed
blacks, under the direction of white abolitionists, had threatened to
shoot if denied the vote. The Doylestown *Democrat* foresaw that a
black electorate would "make the very streets run with white man's
blood. They are easily excited, will lend a ready ear, to oppose the
laws of the land, and like Abolitionists and Englishmen are rife for
revolution." To further inflame racial passions, the *Democrat* listed
the names of twenty-four Middletown Township blacks who had
voted and demanded officials make public a comprehensive list of
the black electorate. The publication of the names in such an explosive climate fell just short of an open incitement to personal violence against these men and their families. As the county awaited
the judge's decision, the statewide debate that ensued guaranteed
the question of black suffrage a central place in the upcoming session of the constitutional convention. To ensure that the convention addressed the issue to their satisfaction, a mass meeting of
more than 600 Bucks County "farmers and mechanics" petitioned
the delegates to constitutionally deny blacks the vote.

In December 1837 Judge Fox delivered his opinion. The key constitutional question, he argued, was whether Negroes were legally eligible for inclusion as "freemen" under the Pennsylvania constitution. Judge Fox concluded they were not. From William Penn's time to the approval of the 1776 state constitution, the judge wrote, Pennsylvania had never accorded blacks the rights of freemen. Even the 1780 act to abolish slavery did not bestow those rights, for an act of the state assembly, in itself, could not alter a constitutional provision. As the 1790 constitutional convention made no explicit reference to this issue either, Fox held for the plaintiffs and reversed the election results, citing Chancellor Kent, a leader in New York State's 1821 constitutional convention, who had argued that "[t]he African race are essentially a *degraded caste of inferior rank and condition in society.*"

Within a month the Pennsylvania constitutional convention echoed Judge Fox's opinion and formally denied black Pennsylvanians the right to vote by a 75–45 margin. One delegate's argument captured well the central dilemma faced by the state's black population. Charles Brown, a Philadelphia delegate and Democratic politician, explained that his vote to exclude blacks from the electoral rolls was actually a vote *for* democratic egalitarian principle. Brown noted that no blacks, rich or poor, in Philadelphia could vote whereas a few black property owners in Bucks County could. He thought this unfair, as it made for distinctions based on property differences when the decision should be made as to whether "the negro . . . is a man and a citizen." That the very popular definition of democracy justified the systematic exclusion of blacks suggested just how bleak the outlook was. In the October 1838 referendum on the new constitution the state's white voters endorsed the disfranchisement of blacks, although by a smaller percentage than had the delegates to the convention.[16]

Twelve years old in 1838, Amos Webber observed and listened to the discussions as black adults in his own community, some of them congregants in the church he attended, were singled out for possible retaliation for daring to vote. Children of Amos's age could not be isolated from the fears and tensions of this adult world, even assuming a desire to do so. And the world of a black child mirrored that of an adult in more direct ways as well: as Joseph John Gurney, an English Quaker visitor to Philadelphia re-

portedly witnessed in 1838, following the state convention's decision, "a white boy . . . [seized] the marbles of a coloured boy in
one of the streets, with the words, 'you have no rights now.' " The
black youth, Gurney noted, submitted in silence.[17]

But fear and silence, however real their presence, were not the
only responses that young Amos learned during these years. In
Attleborough and throughout Bucks County there was a community of adult black activists who established a clear, forceful
response to white racism. Aiding fugitives to escape the slave
catcher was the most dramatic collective action taken, and was also
perhaps the most psychologically satisfying. A young Webber
learned of the terrors of racism, but he also came to learn from the
common courage evidenced in the responses of the adults around
him. These responses could not erase the threats themselves, but
they could indicate to a young black adolescent how he might han-
dle his fears and, in the experiences of the religious and political
activists he observed as a boy, how he might counteract these
threats in the process of developing a strong personal and collective identity.

As with most newcomers to Philadelphia, white or black, little is
known about how Amos Webber migrated to the city. Did he come
as a family member, perhaps with his mother or older brother? Was
he passed along through church connections, or encouraged by Attleborough adults to grasp the broader possibilities Philadelphia
offered? Precisely how old was he when he moved? We do not
know. Whatever the specific reasons that spurred his move, Webber became part of a migratory stream that constantly remade
black Philadelphia, the North's largest black urban center, during
the antebellum decades. By 1847, according to one contemporary
estimate, as many as 47 percent of black Philadelphians were born
outside the city. Young people, who were usually more prone to migrate than their elders, formed a majority of the community and in
1830, for example, some 50 percent of black Philadelphians were
under age twenty-four; thirty years later the federal census reported 62 percent were thirty years of age or younger. Also, black
Philadelphia remained disproportionately female during these

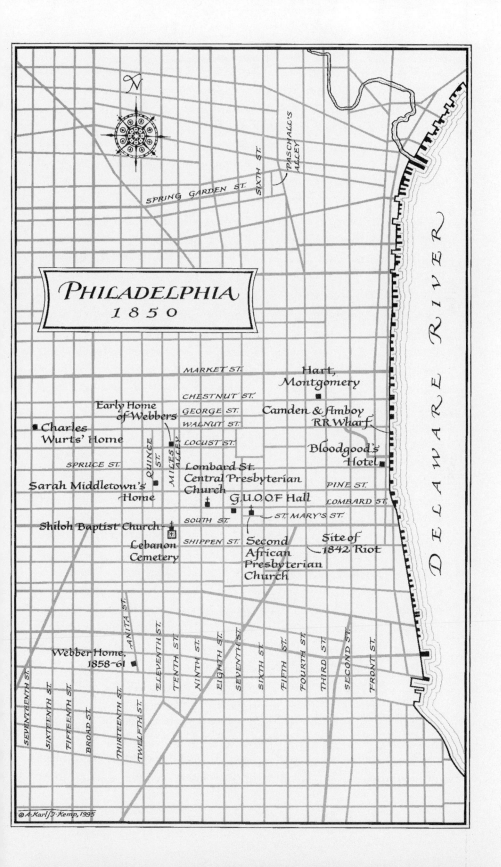

PHILADELPHIA
1850

DELAWARE RIVER

SPRING GARDEN ST.

SIXTH ST.

PASCHALL'S ALLEY

MARKET ST.

CHESTNUT ST.

Hart, Montgomery

GEORGE ST.

Early Home of Webbers

WALNUT ST.

Camden & Amboy RR Wharf

Charles Wurts' Home

LOCUST ST.

Bloodgood's Hotel

SPRUCE ST.

QUINCE ST.

MILES ALLEY

Lombard St. Central Presbyterian Church

Sarah Middletown's Home

PINE ST.

G.U.O.O.F. Hall

LOMBARD ST.

SOUTH ST.

ST. MARY'S ST.

Shiloh Baptist Church

SHIPPEN ST.

Second African Presbyterian Church

Site of 1842 Riot

Lebanon Cemetery

ANITA ST.

ELEVENTH ST.

TENTH ST.

NINTH ST.

EIGHTH ST.

SEVENTH ST.

SIXTH ST.

FIFTH ST.

FOURTH ST.

THIRD ST.

SECOND ST.

FRONT ST.

Webber Home, 1858-61

SEVENTEENTH ST.

SIXTEENTH ST.

FIFTEENTH ST.

BROAD ST.

THIRTEENTH ST.

TWELFTH ST.

© A. Karl / J. Kemp, 1995

years. Between 1820 and 1860 the percentage of women in the population remained fairly constant, at about 58 percent. This imbalance reflected both a higher mortality rate among black men and
their continued need to migrate in search of work.[18]

What is clear is that Webber found in the Philadelphia of the
1840s a sharp contrast with Attleborough. With a population of
more than a quarter of a million in 1840, the city dwarfed the
whole of Bucks County, which had but a fifth of that total. In
Philadelphia, a port city whose longshoremen unloaded new ship-
ments of southern cotton, Chinese tea, and British textiles almost
daily, domestic industry expanded enormously in the decades
prior to the Civil War. Machine shops, paper manufacturers,
clothing and shoe production, among other enterprises, proliferated and, as migrants from Europe and rural Pennsylvania
streamed into Philadelphia to work in these factories, the demand
for living space burst the boundaries of the old city's limits. This
expanding urban population filled the streets as they went about
their daily lives: storefronts offered a bewildering variety of attractive goods, from fancy imported silks to domestic, factory-
produced shoes, and the city's newspapers and street posters
proclaimed the latest in entertainment that included circuses, firemen's parades, classical concerts featuring the music of Bellini,
Haydn, and Mozart, and self-improvement lectures.[19]

Philadelphia's black world presented an equally sharp contrast
to Webber's Attleborough experience. At 20,000 people the city's
black population far eclipsed Middletown Township's 264 Negroes and, while a distinct minority of only 7.4 percent of the
city's total population, the size of this urban black population allowed for the development of a more complex and varied black social life than anything Amos Webber had previously experienced.
There were more black churches in the city than in all of Bucks
County; they included the First African Presbyterian, Bethel
A.M.E., and St. Thomas Episcopal. Black orchestras performed
public concerts of both sacred and secular music in these
churches; blacks attended the theaters and circuses, and regularly
drank with whites in the saloons and dives, such as Dandy Hall,
that so concerned religious reformers.[20]

Residential segregation was not systematic in Philadelphia at
this time. Blacks lived in all of the city's twenty-four wards in

1860, and the Quaker census of black Philadelphia of 1847 noted that as many as 18 percent of the city's black inhabitants resided with the white families for whom they worked as domestics, waiters, or handymen. Yet a pattern of residential concentration did emerge. On the eve of the Civil War four of Philadelphia's wards, all in the central city, housed 64 percent of the entire black population, even though in only one of those wards did blacks account for more than 20 percent of the population. In the central wards, as in the rest of the city, the brick homes of the wealthy abutted the crowded wood-framed homes of clerks and working people since—at a time just before public transportation transformed urban life—employers, foremen, bank tellers, and laborers all had a need to live within walking distance of their workplaces. The streets were dirty, teeming with people and horses as well as pigs, goats, and chickens, and still served for many as the only available public sewer facility.

While fewer than 10 percent of all Philadelphians owned real property during the 1850s, the figure was even lower among blacks. One 1847 survey estimated that blacks owned or held mortgages on property worth more than $500,000—but that property was held by only 315 heads of families. Further, when one adjusts for the relatively large holdings of such prominent black Philadelphians as Stephen Smith, James Forten, Robert Purvis, and Jacob C. White, Sr., it is clear that the value of the property owned by the majority of black landholders was minuscule. Returns from the 1850 federal census show that slightly more than 4 percent of all blacks held property and the mean value of that property was but $103. In both categories blacks were significantly below the Irish, German, and native-born white populations, and the gap would increase dramatically in the following decades.[21]

But property holding would not have been a very pressing need for Webber. As for most other migrants to the city, finding work was paramount for him. Despite an expanding urban economy after 1840—capital investment grew by two thirds and the workforce by 70 percent in the 1850s—Webber encountered a pervasive poverty within black Philadelphia. As a rule, black men were virtually excluded from this industrial expansion and relegated to the most menial and lowest-paying positions. An 1837 report noted that black Philadelphians were "almost altogether deprived of the opportunity of bring[ing] up their children to mechanical employments, to commercial business, or to other more lucrative occupations." Less than twenty years later a survey of more than 1,600 black adults who claimed a trade found, by a most generous standard, that fewer than two thirds were actually able to practice that trade. Perhaps more telling were the data from the 1860 census: of the 80 percent of the black male workforce that had found some work during the preceding year, laborers, waiters, or those who later became unemployed accounted for almost half. Black Philadelphia, Webber could not have helped but observe, was astonishingly poor.[22]

By far the largest economic category among Philadelphia's blacks consisted of unskilled workers. In the 1830s and 1840s, more than 60 percent of black families possessed a total wealth (including real and personal property) of less than $60. Among this number were some unskilled young people who had little connection to black institutional life. Neither church members nor active in the numerous benevolent societies, many of these young men formed a fluid subculture that possessed "a penchant for conviviality, an unrestrained display of emotions, and a desire to present oneself as individualistically as possible." Not surprisingly, given the numbing poverty, a rather close connection developed between this subculture and the world of crime. Gambling, robbery, assault, prostitution, murder—these were but a few of the criminal activities some poor blacks engaged in; yet even here, the profits from gambling and prostitution usually flowed out of the black community to whites who controlled the demimonde. But the larger part of these unskilled residents of all ages, making up as much as 80 percent of black Philadelphia in the 1850s, were workingmen and -women who despite their poverty provided the bulk of the membership in the churches and benevolent societies. Waiters, maids, laborers, and washwomen, these working poor lived in perilous conditions where the slightest economic downturn could result in disaster.[23]

Just above this group were the skilled workers, who accounted for some 16 percent of the entire black workforce. Primarily barbers, dressmakers, and shoemakers, they possessed slightly more wealth than most, although their position was not particularly secure either. The ability of this group to work at their trades had

grown more and more circumscribed over the two decades preceding the Civil War, as recent white immigrants bitterly competed for these positions. Increasingly they were hired only by
some elite whites or, more likely, by the city's few black entrepreneurs. Highly vulnerable to economic downturns, this group
nonetheless provided many of the members and effective leaders
of black organizations in the city.[24]

At the pinnacle of the social structure within the black community were the top 4 percent, the elites. Included in this group were
professionals (doctors, teachers, and some ministers), the compar-
atively few businessmen (caterers, merchants of various kinds),
and a few successful street vendors who sold food and drink. Although themselves vulnerable to economic fluctuations, the top
echelon of this group controlled some 30 percent of all black
wealth. From these men came the leaders and many of the prominent members of black organizations within the city.[25]

Despite this economic concentration at the bottom, not all black
working people were destitute. In the 1847 Quaker census, for example, the enumerators listed the occupations for those 315 heads
of families who owned real property. In the North's largest black
population, those listed as professionals accounted for some
3 percent (11 of 315) of property holders; mechanics and laborers
combined represented 38 percent (119 of 315); while waiters, hair-
dressers, coachmen, and tradesmen—occupations that involved
service to white employers or customers—totaled some 42 percent
(132 of 315). The final 17 percent were the 53 women, the great
majority of them widows, listed solely by their gender.[26]

Small as the numbers were, the distribution of property holders
nonetheless hints at the nature of the class structure young Webber encountered in black Philadelphia. With the majority of
blacks poor, and with the greater portion of black wealth concentrated in the hands of a very few, the possession of even minimal
property was significant. To work at a skill or a trade, or to secure
unskilled but steady employment even at poor wages, was to distinguish oneself from most. Those who did became in black
Philadelphia the functional equivalent of the emerging middle
class in the white world.[27]

Beyond these economic distinctions, however, there existed a
world of hierarchical social relations. An individual's family back-

ground—were they, for example, literate, freeborn Philadelphians?—influenced social standing. Similarly, the color of skin, connections with white elites, level of education, and residential
location affected one's status. As Webber soon discovered in this
complex urban society, these distinctions influenced which church
or fraternal organization one joined and the leadership positions
one attained. For a recent migrant from Bucks County who
possessed neither a skill nor a distinguished family tree, black
Philadelphia's unwritten rules may have been, at first, simply bewildering.[28]

Given the extensive exchange of news and opinion carried on
the organizational webs of the black church and fraternal lodge
between Bucks County and Philadelphia, it was likely that Webber understood the city's racial attitudes even before he migrated
there. Black adults may have told stories of the 1831 Philadelphia
riot when, during a July 4th celebration, a mob of whites attacked
blacks seeking to join the festivities, shouting that "niggers had
nothing to do with the fourth of July." Black refugees, victims of a
vicious three-day riot against black churches, associations, and
residences in August 1834, had fled to Attleborough, and they undoubtedly told how the authorities largely refused to suppress the
white mob while whites in the affected neighborhoods, following
a tradition from the American Revolution, placed lit candles in
their front windows symbolic of the candles that distinguished
American revolutionaries from those loyal to King George, and
thus exempted them from mob violence. Four years later, as white
Pennsylvanians denied blacks the ballot, another well-organized
white mob, estimated at 3,000 people, burned down Pennsylvania
Hall, an abolitionist meetinghouse, destroyed an orphanage for
black youth, and indiscriminately attacked blacks on the city's
streets. These gruesome tales, carried to Attleborough by survivors, surely became part of young Webber's consciousness.[29]

Even more immediate for Webber—he may already have moved
into the city—was the ferocious riot on the afternoon of August 1,
1842, when a group of some 1,200 black Philadelphians, marching
behind the banner of the Moyamensing Temperance Society, celebrated both the spread of temperance sentiment within their community and the anniversary of slavery's abolition in the British
West Indies. As the procession, marching from south Philadelphia

north toward City Hall, crossed Fourth and Shippen Streets in the Southward district, a large group of whites, led by an Irish mob from the neighborhood, set upon the marchers. When the marchers defended themselves, the incensed mob soon hurled "missiles of every description . . . flying about with frightful force." The mob, which quickly grew to several thousand, chased the marchers the few blocks toward St. Mary's and Lombard Streets, at the center of the black community. Whites beat individual marchers, some brutally, and clusters of rioters stormed the homes of black residents, breaking furniture and windows while beating and terrorizing the inhabitants. That evening, the mob burned Smith's Hall on Lombard Street, the site of numerous abolition and self-improvement lectures since the destruction of Pennsylvania Hall in 1838. Later that same evening, rioters torched the Second African Presbyterian Church on St. Mary's Street, a few blocks north and west of the intersection where the riot had begun.

Sunrise on August 2 brought little relief. By 6:00 A.M., a crowd estimated at over a thousand, armed with shillelaghs and clubs, again invaded the black neighborhood. Simultaneously, Irish workers attacked black workers in the coal yards along the Schuylkill River. The rioters, as Frederick Douglass described them, "marched in the very presence of the city Government, and with the ferocity of wild-beasts." The city's police stations held hundreds of blacks, including the wounded, seeking protection; hundreds more had fled the city into Bucks County and New Jersey.[30]

The catalyst for these riots explained much about Philadelphia's racial climate. According to newspaper reports, many whites believed that the banner that led the parade depicted a slave, with broken manacles still attached to his limbs, under the heading "Liberty or Death." In the background, it was thought, a burning town indicated what the price of black liberty might be for whites. Actually the banner represented an emancipated slave with one hand pointing to the manacles about his feet and the other calling attention to the sole word "Liberty," written in gold above his head. In the background a rising sun represented the hope of the emerging society and a sinking ship represented the ultimate passing of tyranny. In the heated racial atmosphere of Philadelphia, where even the newest immigrants easily adopted a virulent racism as a central component of their New World identity, such newspaper misrepresentations reflected an uglier truth. A public black presence offended many whites, violating widely held beliefs as to the proper role of free people of color. And, in fact, the grand jury that investigated the riot blamed the marchers for the violence and asked Philadelphia's white abolitionists, assumed to be the power behind the black organizations, "to discourage [blacks] from thus creating an excitement which is alike injurious to the cause of philanthropy and the objects of their care and regard."[31]

Within the black community the riot had a profound effect. Beyond the assault to person, property, and self-dignity (amazingly, no blacks were killed), the riot also underscored the crisis over programs and goals that confronted leaders and activists. Coming as it did in response to a parade that celebrated both temperance and antislavery, the twin pillars of the antebellum black reform movement, the riot created an intense self-doubt among the city's black residents, underscoring the leadership's basic inability to influence major segments of white opinion. Many, even among the leaders, questioned whether the program of evolutionary acculturation and acceptance was viable. As Robert Purvis, one of the foremost black Philadelphians, wrote some three weeks after the riot: "I am convinced of our utter and complete nothingness in public estimation . . . [and] despair black as the face of Death hangs over us—And the bloody Will is in the heart of the community to destroy us."[32]

Writing at a greater remove, Frederick Douglass nonetheless made essentially the same point. Black efforts at self-improvement had encountered "every possible hindrance" from the white community, he stated in 1846. With specific reference to the efforts of Purvis and Stephen Smith, another black leader, to encourage temperance and to the consequent destruction of Smith's Hall during the 1842 riot, Douglass continued: "The colored population cannot move through the streets of Philadelphia if they have virtue and liberty on their banners. . . . Let them go through the streets, however, poor, mean pitiful drunkards, and then the pro-slavery people will smile and say, 'Look at that poor fellow, it is very evident there is an impassible barrier between us and thou.' " Douglass's biting use of the Quaker pronoun suggested how limited was the white support upon which black Philadelphians could rely.[33]

It was a sign of the intensity of this antiblack violence that the steady increase of Philadelphia's black population ceased abruptly after 1840. Between 1790 and 1840, black Philadelphia grew from some 2,000 to almost 20,000 persons; but the organized violence, coupled with less obvious daily acts of individual terrorism, propelled many blacks to leave the city and the free black population actually decreased between 1840 and 1850, and grew at a sharply reduced rate in the following decade. By contrast, the white population of the city almost doubled in those same years, a dynamic that dropped the black proportion of the city's population from 7.4 percent to just under 4 percent.[34]

IN LIGHT OF THE VIOLENCE—experienced, threatened, or recounted by others—that permeated Webber's first twenty years, he learned while very young that to be a black activist was to test one's mettle to its very essence. As Webber began his life in Philadelphia and as he began to consider his alternatives, he would discover he already possessed within himself a moral compass that, while it would not determine his path, would provide a set of basic principles to serve as his guide.

CHAPTER TWO

Deeply Cherished Principles

On arriving in Philadelphia, Amos Webber faced a set of decisions that were, for the first time in his life, uniquely his own to make. Like so many other migrants from smaller towns or rural communities, Webber discovered in the city a peculiar freedom. The observation and even control of a young man's social activities by church elders and interested adults proved difficult to reproduce in the larger, more anonymous city. For many migrants throughout the nineteenth century, the very act of physical migration encouraged an expectation that they might remake themselves in the new environment. Many discovered, however, as Webber's early years in Philadelphia suggest, that they more closely re-created the personal and social patterns of behavior familiar from their past.

There is no record of Webber's first few years in Philadelphia, but by the late 1840s he had gained employment as a live-in servant and handyman in the household of Charles S. Wurts. A deeply religious and quite wealthy white merchant and investor, Wurts was born in Flanders, New Jersey, in 1790, the son of an iron manufacturer. The youngest of four brothers raised in a strict German Reformed family, Wurts followed his older brothers to Philadelphia in 1812, and family connections quickly landed him a position as the European agent for one of the city's leading commercial houses. By 1819, when Charles returned from Europe, his brothers were firmly ensconced among the city's leading commercial families. The foundation of the family wealth was the dry goods firm Wurts, Musgrave, & Wurts, which had obtained several lucrative government contracts for provisioning American soldiers during the War of 1812. Active in local politics and well positioned with access to both land and financing, the brothers soon expanded their interests, becoming major investors in the Delaware and Hudson Canal Company, in the promotion of anthracite coal production, and in the emerging iron (and later steel) industries. By 1824 all four brothers had focused on these investments and hired a manager to run their dry goods emporium.[1]

The Wurts household was a large one: Charles and Mary (née Vanuxem) Wurts lived with their five children, ranging in age from nine to twenty-seven, and with at least five live-in servants on a large estate at the corner of Walnut and Seventeenth Streets worth more than $8,000. Two of these servants were Irish-born women, and at least two were black men: the young Webber, then in his early twenties, and the somewhat older William Laws. Laws occupied a trusted position within the Wurts family; when, in 1854, Charles Wurts needed another servant at the family's summer home in Belvidere, New Jersey, he instructed his son to ask Laws to evaluate a prospective servant's moral character.[2]

Wurts could be a stern employer. Rules were established that ordered domestic life and established a firm religious atmosphere. "His rules were Christian-like," Webber recalled upon Wurts's death in 1859, "[e]very morning and evening we were called into worship=" A particular set of rules governed the observance of the Sabbath. As Webber remembered: "Sabbath rules-No visitors called to pay visits as it wheres [was] against his rules. No cooking—excepting cases of necessity=No cleaning of knives—Blackening boots etc if these things did not get done on Saturday they were left undone tile monday=Such was his strict rules=" Wurts's views echoed important aspects of Webber's Attleborough upbringing, and they added a new dimension as well. The daily worship services brought together family and servants, men and women, white and black, and young Amos may have experienced a recognition of a common humanity that recommended his wealthy employer to him beyond the opportunities of the position.[3]

Certainly Webber and the other servants understood that the discipline demanded of them also applied to Wurts's children. As Wurts once admonished his teenage son, before Amos joined the household, "Families are closely linked together and one member cannot err, without all being involved in the consequences."

While he served the dinner meal early in December 1850, Webber may have had an opportunity to gauge the depth of these moral rules within the family by listening to a discussion of the earnest, almost painful letter Louisa Wurts wrote her father. In Paris in the midst of a European tour, accompanied by her aunt and uncle, the twenty-one-year-old Louisa sent a long letter beseeching her father for permission to attend the opera. She knew, she wrote, that her father "did not like the Opera, in the way it was conducted, and that at home I had never asked permission to go, and would not go, because *there* it would compromise you." But she was now in Europe, with "some of the finest singers in the world" performing; unfortunately, she added, "all the concerts are given on *Sunday* night." Balancing her independence with the boundaries of her father's strictures, she concluded: "I think it is a point on which any one away from home, where the members of her own family cannot be compromised by her actions ought to be left to judge herself."[4] Her father's response remains unknown.

The particular moral code of Charles Wurts, reflecting an unreformed Calvinist orthodoxy's stress on human sinfulness, structured his philanthropic activities. For seventeen years a member of the Board of Managers of the American Sunday School Union, which encouraged participation by the city's youth in the schools, Wurts also served as the longtime president of the Union Benevolent Association, a group "instituted for the purpose of *permanently ameliorating the condition of the poor,* by teaching and encouraging the poor to supply their wants by their own efforts." Ultimately Wurts projected a stark but consistent vision of social reform that regarded the poor's "moral interests as superior to their physical." It was better for the "idle & vicious" poor "to reap to a wholesome intent, the bitter fruits of their folly and wickedness" than to receive alms too liberally dispensed; for the poor "can only be effectively helped, by elevating their character—by exercising a moral influence over them & [by motivating them] to supply their own wants." These were "the distinctive principles which have governed the U.B.A.," and which prevented it from becoming "a mere Almsgiving Society."[5]

The association implemented these guidelines throughout the city. While Wurts's Calvinist beliefs, thought by some to be too unbending, caused resignations among the "female visitors" who called on poor families, he and the male majority of the executive board persisted and, in the winter of 1848–1849, carried their principles a step further. Concerned by reports that the nondeserving poor were receiving some of the association's free distribution of coal, which resulted in "a very general dependence," Wurts persuaded the board to instead sell all of the coal at half price. "Should the experiment succeed, however, a double benefit will follow its success," he said. "The Society will have a larger supply of coal, and the poor, purchasing it, instead of procuring it for nothing, will be inspired with a disposition to exert themselves they otherwise would not have manifested."[6]

Amos Webber experienced no difficulty with the stern strictures that infused the Wurts household or Charles Wurts's charitable work. In fact Webber applauded these moral guidelines and connected them to an explicit religious commitment. As he would write a decade later, "Mr. Wurts was ever good to the poor=during the three years I lived with him=I never knew him to turn the poor from his door; without something except their action condemn them to be impostures His rules were Christian-like="[7] For both Wurts and Webber, the imperative to accept personal responsibility for one's innate sinfulness, and to act accordingly, formed the bedrock of their moral vision. It also provided the foundation for their public engagement with such social issues as poverty, slavery, and temperance. Charles Wurts did not provide the younger man with these values—the congregants of the Bethlehem Colored Methodist Church had largely seen to that—but, in their three years of close interaction, Wurts clearly influenced Webber, reinforcing basic values and exposing his Negro servant to the cultural practices of a portion of the elite white world. In time, Amos Webber would apply these values to America's social and political problems in a manner sharply different from, yet not inconsistent with, his employer.

DESPITE THE DEMANDS of his employment in the Wurts household, Amos Webber developed relationships with other Philadelphians, particularly other blacks. One person especially attracted his attention in the early 1850s, a light-skinned mulatto woman from New Jersey named Lizzie Sterling Douglass.

Born in Burlington County in 1829, Lizzie Douglass migrated to nearby Philadelphia in her late teens. Susan Beulah, a childhood friend, came to the city as well, and together with Sarah Frances Middleton the three women formed a deep friendship that endured for more than half a century. Each of the women professed a strong religious faith, and Webber may have first met and courted Douglass at church functions. The relationship proceeded and on March 24, 1852, the young couple married. The ceremony was rather simple. Amos and Lizzie gathered at Sarah Middleton's home on Quince Street, between Lombard and Walnut, above Thirteenth Street, a few blocks east of the Wurts estate; Middleton or Susan Beulah stood witness for Lizzie; and someone (perhaps his brother, Samuel) stood for Amos. The Reverend Benjamin Templeton, pastor of the Second African Presbyterian Church, blessed the union, offered a few words of guidance, and then joined the small group in a refreshment. It was a wedding not unlike many others performed that month throughout the city. As the Webbers were not listed in the city directories for another four years, precisely where they lived in the city is unclear.[8]

That Reverend Templeton officiated at their wedding suggests something of the Webbers' social and religious involvements. Born a free black in Cincinnati in 1818, Templeton received his education in the schools of Athens, Ohio, and arrived in Philadelphia in 1845 an ordained Presbyterian minister. The Second African Presbyterian Church called him to the pulpit soon after.[9]

Reverend Templeton assumed the pulpit at a critical time. The church was burned to the ground during the vicious 1842 race riot, and the congregation and its then pastor, Reverend Stephen Gloucester, suffered severe internal dissension in the years immediately following as they rebuilt it. Gloucester, a son of the early leader of black Presbyterianism in Philadelphia,[10] was an active black abolitionist who, in 1840, with seven other black ministers, broke ranks with William Lloyd Garrison, Frederick Douglass, and other leading abolitionists in demanding political rights for black men. At that time Garrison and Douglass scorned as corrupt political action in a system that legitimized slavery, and instead emphasized a fierce moral agitation to alter individual American minds. The intensity of the white rage in 1842 stunned

Gloucester, however, and in its aftermath he sought to downplay, if not deny, some of his past commitments. This attempt in turn sparked an intense debate within the congregation over Gloucester's pastorship. In 1844, despite a majority vote of the congregation to retain Gloucester in his position, the church elders, who together with the pastor constituted the session (the governing body for a Presbyterian church), refused to endorse the minister. Gloucester then led "a considerable number of persons" out of Second African to form a new congregation, the Lombard Street Central Presbyterian Church. William Laws, Webber's fellow servant in the Wurts home, was one of the six signatories to a petition requesting Presbyterian officials to approve the new church.

Reverend Templeton thus assumed leadership of the Second African congregation in the midst of an intense political debate whose echoes reverberated for some years. In 1847, five years after the riot and three years after the schism, Frederick Douglass excoriated Gloucester as "the recreant priest" who now held that the cause of antislavery "had nothing to do with religion." To deny the connection between the black church and black social activism was anathema to Douglass.[11]

What Amos and Lizzie Webber made of this issue is not clear. Unlike his brother, Samuel, and sister-in-law, Leanah (who joined the Lombard Street congregation in 1853), neither Amos's nor Lizzie's name appeared on the list of those who had "a satisfactory examination" before the session as a condition of admittance; thus there is no record of their thinking on this dissension. Political differences that had so incensed Frederick Douglass may have had little meaning for them. Personal relations with Reverend Templeton may also have been a factor since, in 1856, the Webbers lived on Ivy Street, almost directly across from Templeton, his southern-born wife, and their young, school-age child. If Amos and Lizzie Webber had been members of Templeton's Second African congregation after their 1852 marriage, and if they later entered the Lombard Street church together with Templeton, then there would have been no record of the "satisfactory examination." Those entering the congregation as part of a dissenting group were accepted and invested *en masse*.

Then too the Webbers' family life grew busier after Lizzie gave birth to a son, Harry J., in January 1853. Caring for her son and husband, maintaining some involvement as a shirt- and dressmaker working out of her home, and making frequent visits to her mother in Smithfield, north of Bucks County—all this activity and more left Lizzie Webber little time to consider political issues.[12]

Twenty-seven in 1853, married, and a father, Webber exuded a maturity and sense of purpose that defined his place in the world. It was with that inner confidence that he began a new job that summer.[13]

HART, MONTGOMERY AND COMPANY was one of a handful of wallpaper manufacturers and retailers in the city of Philadelphia. Its offices and retail store were on Chestnut Street, above Third, in the heart of the business district just three blocks from the waterfront. The firm occupied a four-story building, allowing for ample showroom displays, and shared the block with an express company, printers, jewelers, perfume importers and manufacturers, and a publishing firm. Hart, Montgomery's manufacturing plant was a few miles to the north. Although not a large employer, the firm was quite competitive during the mid-1850s. Deemed "in gd. cr. for any reasnbl amt" by the R. G. Dun credit assessor in 1852, the firm was judged "well of" and in "gd standing" five years later. Although William Hart and Alexander J. Montgomery were the public partners, the actual owner was Isaac Pugh. A wealthy Philadelphian adjudged "A. 1. rich," Pugh was, a Dun rater noted in 1852, "the Co. in 'Hart, Montgomery & Co.' "[14]

Webber may have gained employment at the firm through the recommendation of Charles Wurts or Reverend Benjamin Templeton, who had some access to white elites through Presbyterian circles. It was also possible that some of the Attleborough abolitionists, black or white, who knew him as a youth, interceded, for the firm had close links with the abolition movement. Isaac Pugh's sister Sarah was an active abolitionist, longtime president of the integrated Philadelphia Female Anti-Slavery Society, and a close friend and political collaborator of Lucretia Mott, an activist in abolition and other reform movements. While Sarah Pugh had no formal role in the firm, the politics of the Pugh family may have led to Webber's hiring; those commitments certainly made his years there agreeable.[15]

Although the moral strictures at Hart, Montgomery encompassed a greater latitude than in the Wurts home, one pattern remained constant for Webber. In both positions his own sense of moral order and personal rectitude proved attractive to the white elites who were his employers. His work at the firm varied and, within broad limits, he could set the pace for managing his daily tasks. He washed windows in both the office and the store, swept the floors, made fires when the weather turned cold, and had partial responsibility for shipping orders to the firm's customers. He also unloaded and stored deliveries, ran errands throughout the city, readied the pattern books for certain accounts in preparation for the final cutting, and assisted in the yearly inventory of stock. Literate and possessed of at least rudimentary mathematical skills, Webber proved a valuable employee who worked well on a daily basis with others in the firm. Although Webber was acquainted with working people in surrounding businesses, such as John Walls, a teamster, far and away his most sustained exchanges at work occurred with the white-collar clerks, buyers and sellers, and the partners associated with Hart, Montgomery and Company.[16]

In contrast with his years in Charles Wurts's home, Webber's employment at Hart, Montgomery immersed him in the diverse secular and cosmopolitan atmosphere that permeated daily life in urban Philadelphia. That influence did not undermine Webber's sense of purpose, but it did propel him to experiment with a new form to understand himself in the world. After sixteen months at the firm, he began keeping what he called the "Amos Webber Thermometer Book." Now twenty-eight years old, Webber used his chronicle to record, order, and understand the world he inhabited. His employers may have known, or even encouraged, his writing. It quickly became evident, however, that a more mature and reflective Webber kept the chronicle for himself.

On the front cover of his chronicle Amos Webber wrote:

Resident 1213 Anita
above Federal

Amos Webber
Thermometer Book
From Dec. 8th 1854
To = Oct 1860

Upon opening the book, however, the inscriptions on the inside of that front cover made more complex that rather simple representation:

This Book Was Made August 1ˢᵗ 1858
× *Back=*

Amos Webber Book
From December 8ᵗʰ 1854
To = *Oct.   1   1860*

This juxtaposition between when the book "was made" and the year of the first entries becomes sharper when one compares entries dated before and after August 1858. The entry for December 1854 was precisely that, an entry for the month, written retrospectively, possibly at the end of the month, possibly later:

Local Page =
December 1854=
Their was two very Large fires this month = on monday= night=11ⁱⁿˢᵗ Cornelius & Baker Lamp factory in cherryˢᵗ burnt= down = The 2ⁿᵈ fire was at the N.=W. coner of 5ᵗʰ & chestnut ˢᵗ=4 or 5 stores was burn-down= It happened on the night of the= 14ⁱⁿˢᵗ {Thursday}= They ceased to play on the atnoon on the 16ⁱⁿˢᵗ when they got it all out = The loss was very heavy= The coldest xᵈᵃʸ this xᵐᵒⁿᵗʰ was on the 20ⁱⁿˢᵗ Thermometer stood 10ᵈᵉᵍ The wind N.W= all day= Clear & Cold= A.W.[17]

Contrast this with an entry three and one-half years later:

June 25 1859 = Between 10 & 11 O'clock this morning a fire broke out in the roof of a large building Nº 837 marketˢᵗfirst floor was occupied by Henry S. Adams Dealer in country produce= Upper stories by W.J. Warren = dealer in furniture = The accident happened from the shavings in the work shop = The following houses were burnt & damaged No 835 - 839 - Marketˢᵗ Nº 235 - 237 - 239 Ninthˢᵗ Nº 837 Marketˢᵗ The Loss is about $2000 all covered by insurance Nº 835 is owned by W.B.T.Curtis Nº 837 by Gideon *Cox = Nº 839 the Norris estate & A.W.*[18]

This 1859 entry possessed the immediacy of either an eyewitness or one who recorded the news the same day. The style of these later entries would also allow the chronicler to develop over time a more spontaneous and self-confident commentary on the events he recorded.

Those retrospective, earlier entries were probably not written after August 1858. In late 1858, it was unlikely that Webber could recall, or would feel compelled to record, his September 1855 notation: "Several accidents this month = The 6^{inst} their was a woman shot in Broadst The name is not given=" Similarly, his specific daily comments on the weather ("drizling, misty, bad walking," "clearing off, mild," in January 1855, for example) could likely not be recalled at such a distance.[19] Rather, it is probable that this 1858 volume "was made" from another volume, necessitated perhaps by the fact that Webber's observations physically outgrew the original book. If so, Webber's selection of the new volume guaranteed ample space for his entries. Bound in leather and cardboard, the book measured 20 inches long by 14 inches wide, and contained more than 200 pages, which Webber divided into two sections. In the "Local Pages" he wrote on a variety of topics, briefly or at length. Any given date could contain multiple entries, or weeks might pass between recordings. The other section he referred to as "Thermometer." There, he lined the page with vertical columns and twice a day entered the temperature, the wind direction, and often a note on climatic conditions. With the exception only of the Sabbath, Webber maintained this meteorological record every day between December 8, 1854, and October 1, 1860, whether or not he penned an entry in the "Local Pages" section.

Webber probably outgrew the original volume in another way as well. His later commentaries reflect a growing confidence and maturity as a chronicler. After August 1858, Webber addressed a broader range of issues, at greater length, and with a more focused perspective. His was never a confessional diary, and one will look in vain for an introspective analysis of his emotions and motives. Yet his self-confidence with his chosen form evolved over time. Less a diarist than a recorder, a chronicler, a commentator on his world, Amos Webber grew into his task over the course of the first volume, expanding his understanding of the uses he might make of the chronicle. Though Webber never stated precisely where he physically kept his book, he most likely did so at work. This may explain why, in the almost six years of daily entries, he never once recorded the temperature on Sunday: because that was his regularly scheduled day of rest, the thermometer he used to make his notations was probably at work.

At first Webber's chronicle simply reflected the world he observed. He kept a close eye on many of his bosses and co-workers, recording their business trips, marriages, and vacations with some regularity. Something as common as "Mr. Hart dined in the City" caught his attention in February 1855; a few days later the more unusual activity of Alexander Montgomery, who "amused himself on the 11th by walking across the Delaware on the ice. to see the Jersey fashions=" drew Webber's notice as well. With some concern, Webber noted Isaac Pugh's prolonged illness in the fall of 1858 and itemized the unexplained absences, vacations and business trips, and the 1857 marriage of John Largy, a prominent co-worker, without ever explaining the nature of their relationship. Similar entries followed the hiring of William H. Kimber as a bookkeeper in 1856, although Webber and Kimber may have developed a certain work-related friendship. In fact, Kimber was the only other person Webber ever allowed an entry in his chronicle: "It was so cold last night," the signed entry by Kimber on September 6, 1859, read, "that they had to make a fire at Chelten Hill, to keep warm."[20]

Although terse and circumscribed at first, Amos Webber's entries grew as his confidence as a chronicler deepened. The greater variety of topics reflected his innate curiosity, and his more assertive commentary testified to the fundamental strength of his character. The pace of his daily work allowed him the time to follow the fire engines, parades, or the police; to read newspapers such as the Philadelphia *Public Ledger*; and to maintain a network of friends, co-workers, and informants, both black and white. His work rhythms also provided the opportunity to enter his thoughts in his book.

Technology's effect on public and private life, and the meaning of technological change for moral and religious values, fascinated and intrigued Webber. He frequently noted the spread of the urban railroad and advances in the speed of transportation on both land and sea. When a steam-driven fire engine arrived in Philadelphia in the summer of 1859, Webber was an eyewitness to its first run. He explained its workings (by switching valves the firemen could direct the steam power to propel the water through the hoses and, when finished, to drive the engine back to the firehouse) and thought it "[q]uite a museing" how Philadelphians reacted to the engine's first trip through city streets:

[A]ll the people run out and declare that it was a Locomotive run off the track at Willow and Broad. It was sometime before they could get it in their brain that it was a fire Engine moveing along with steam[;] upon the whole it tis quite a curiousity.=what is to become of america=

As if to answer his own question, a few months later he observed that this same steam engine ran over the city's oldest fireman, killing him instantly. The new technology could introduce both progress and pain.[21]

Like that of many other Americans, Webber's interest in technology and in disasters, both natural and man-made, lay rooted in a broader involvement with scientific thought.[22] This fascination was characteristic of elites and of nonelites as well. Technology, for example, transformed the experience of work and the infrastructures of the cities and towns in which that work occurred; natural phenomena regularly undid the work of man on the farm as well as on the city street.[23] The drive to know transcended economic status, as the diverse social backgrounds of American tinkerers and inventors suggest. Rarely, then, was a town too small to host a scientific lecture by a luminary such as James Pollard Espy, a leading meteorologist who would soon head the Navy Department's scientific efforts, or by lesser-known figures. Mark Twain's wry observations about the incredulity of Americans notwithstanding,[24] this broad interest revealed a cultural pattern similar to the contemporaneous revivals of religion. All could aspire to scientific knowledge, and the attainment of extensive education did not necessarily add one whit of credibility to a speaker's reception. Budding amateur scientists flooded the nation's news-papers with articles and letters on scientific matters; and these same newspapers frequently reprinted articles from more technical journals. This interchange between popular and professional science promoted an egalitarian ethos even as it also conveyed the desire of many to distinguish their community from those thought more provincial. In 1842, when Espy requested Americans to keep weather journals and to send them to him monthly at the Navy Department, popular involvement in scientific matters grew again. Even those without such instruments as barometers, thermometers, and rain gauges, Espy stated, "can be useful in the advancement of science." Espy asked of these nonprofessionals that they record the start and finish of storms and snowfalls, the direction and estimated force of the wind, and the time of important changes in the wind's characteristics during a storm. The accumulation of these reports, Espy explained, "will do much that is particularly wanted."[25]

The popular interest in meteorology—the study of the atmosphere, weather patterns, and the causes of storms—was widespread and not new to American culture. Driven in part by the utilitarian premise that knowledge of the patterns might enable mankind to control for their effects—thereby blessing economic activity such as agriculture and commerce—many Americans, including George Washington and Thomas Jefferson, both of whom maintained extensive meteorological journals, became interested in meteorology.[26] In 1814 U.S. Army surgeons at military posts throughout the United States were ordered to keep meteorological journals, a practice continued throughout the nineteenth century. By the 1830s, a series of civilian observers in New York, Massachusetts, Pennsylvania, and other states, organized by leading scientific investigators such as Joseph Henry and James Espy, augmented their military colleagues' efforts. Dramatic natural events also spurred scientific inquiry. The meteor shower of 1833 so impressed Elias Loomis that he ceased teaching classical languages at Yale College to devote himself to scientific experiments. By the early 1840s these pressures toward a more professional approach to scientific inquiry coalesced. Espy moved to Washington in 1842, became attached to the Navy Department, and was then in essence the nation's first official meteorologist. It was from this perch that he orchestrated the

voluntary national effort to collect information on weather patterns and other climatic data. Four years later Henry became secretary to the newly founded Smithsonian Institution. By 1858,
with the help of the new telegraph system, the Smithsonian instituted a daily national weather map, drawn each morning at the
Washington, D.C., headquarters.[27]

Amos Webber, of course, had little formal education and he
never participated in the more professional aspects of scientific
study. Yet in beginning his meteorological journal—which he
would diligently maintain for more than forty years—Webber underscored both the broad range of popular interest in scientific
matters and, in his own meticulous record keeping, the depth of
his own involvement with this aspect of popular American culture. By recording precisely what Espy requested, Webber participated in a cultural phenomenon broader than both his own
individual traits and the social role allowed blacks by most whites.
As did many other Americans, Webber joined in this experience
even though he did not send his notations to Washington.[28] His involvement revealed another dimension of his character as well. As
aware as he was of widespread white attitudes that denied blacks
any essential humanity, Amos Webber would not allow white
racism to limit the range of his mind or dominate the essence of
his identity.

In a culture that had yet to feel the stunning impact on religious
belief of Darwin's ideas, science did not preclude a profession of
religion. As early as the era of the American Revolution, Benjamin
Rush, the Philadelphia scientist, medical doctor, and reformer,
could both embrace scientific inquiry and maintain his lifelong
belief as a evangelical Christian in man's sinfulness.[29] Three generations later Edward Hitchcock, president of Amherst College,
argued in his book *Religion of Geology* that scientific study coex-
isted easily with religion. There was nothing "in the constitution
of Nature so far revealed to us by the discoveries," the scientist
George I. Chace, wrote in 1854, that conflicts with a belief in "divine intervention in the regular order to provide some special
meaning for human history."[30]

Webber was in and of this culture, and the world reverberated
for him with a divine presence. He marveled at the aurora borealis
of 1859, and felt compelled to enter from contemporary news-

paper features discussions of earlier appearances of the northern lights to provide some sense of the observable pattern:

> On the 28^{inst} Sunday about 9 o'clock P M. The skies Northern part was light up gloriousty it Look as if the heavns was on fire= the st[r]eaks of rays would shoot=up, as if from the flames; some of the people began to get frighten= the fire bells began to ring= great Light=

> February 16 1750. A bright aurora borealis or Northern Light was at that time; is represented much like this light= May 7th 1737 the same light is observed *though we generally* look for them *in the fall=A.W.*[31]

That the world was charged with God's meaning was a common nineteenth-century popular belief. In 1833 a young Frederick Douglass witnessed the same meteor shower that impressed Elias Loomis and "was awestruck. The air seemed filled with bright, descending messengers from the sky." At that moment, Douglass later recalled, he thought that the spectacular display might be a sign, "the harbinger of the coming of the Son of Man."[32]

WEBBER'S BOOK SERVED multiple purposes. It was a weather journal, a commentary on nature's patterns, and a vehicle to record his observations of the world about him. It also afforded him an opportunity to express the moral sensibility that flowed from his understanding of the divine purpose that permeated even the physical world. The explosion of a fireworks factory on Sunday, July 3, 1859, as workers feverishly prepared firecrackers for the next day's Independence Day celebration, emphasized what was for Amos Webber a violation of a fundamental moral rule: "It should be a warning for Mr. Jackson [the owner] for working on the Sabbath day= Just that day one year=he was burnt out=A. Webber."[33]

But Webber also used his chronicle to mark events in his personal life. On January 24, 1857, for example, he noted: "=Bought house." In February he paid a contractor to lay pipe into the street and he obtained a water permit. Over the following year, as the house was readied, the Webbers rented rooms on Miles Alley, a few blocks from Sarah Middleton's Quince Street home and only a nine-block walk to Hart, Montgomery. Then in January 1858, in the middle of a serious economic depression, "A.W. moved to Anitast N° 1213."[34]

It was a brief note for such a momentous move. The house—in the Moyamensing district about a mile south of their Miles Alley home—was a modest one, as befitted a family reported in the 1860 census as possessing only $400 in real property. A small wooden house with a fireplace and a yard, the Webber home occupied a small lot on a residential street just north of Federal Street's stores and traffic. That proximity to a larger thoroughfare may have allowed Anita Street residents such as the Webbers to have the gas lines for interior lighting laid sooner than home owners in other neighborhoods.[35] However modest the house appeared—and it certainly was in comparison to Charles Wurts's estate about a mile to the northwest—the very owning of any residential property distinguished Amos and Lizzie Webber from most of their new neighbors, white and black, the overwhelming majority of whom reported neither real nor personal property. The move carried additional significance: the Webbers, who had rented on Miles Alley in the Seventh Ward, where 12 percent of the population was black, now owned a home in the First Ward, nearly a mile due south—where just 2 percent of the residents were black. Further, while the Webbers were not wealthy, the value of their house, combined with the $550 in personal property they reported to the census enumerator, elevated them into the ranks of middle-income black Philadelphia. Webber may have been a janitor and a messenger, but steady work at livable wages at Hart, Montgomery allowed him to buy a house even in the middle of a depression. Coupled with the sharp compression of wealth in black Philadelphia, the resources of this unskilled worker resulted in a dual economic status: where his assets might only place him in the middle third of white Philadelphia's working class, in the impoverished black sections of that city those same assets made him part of an emerging middle class. This complex interaction of racial and class attributes was further compounded by the fact that white prejudice prevented Amos Webber from acting in concert with most of middle-class white Philadelphia.[36]

If the structure of their world nonetheless seemed secure following their move to Anita Street, only four months later, two
months past their sixth wedding anniversary, the Webbers' family
life changed forever. A controlled Amos Webber struggled with
his pain: "Harry J. Webber died last night. 10 mins before 12
O'clock midnight inflamation on the brain aged 5 years. 4 mo. 18
day." This clinical precision could not suppress the father's sorrow. For a week following the death there were no entries in the
chronicle, no mention of the funeral conducted at the Anita Street
residence on Saturday, May 29, or of the subsequent burial at
Lebanon Cemetery, a short walk north from his home. Never
again would Amos Webber mention his son in his chronicle, although he could pass the grave site twice daily on his walks between home and his job on Chestnut Street, more than a mile to
the north and east.[37]

Some thirteen years later the depth of his sorrow did burst forth
in indirect fashion. In April 1871 Webber recorded the death of a
ten-year-old boy whose legs had been severed in a railroad accident. The lad lingered for an hour and one half, he explained, long
enough for his parents to be called. "Good-bye was the last words
he spoke. Ah; how sad, this is, no one can feel with them. Only
those that has felt the same. The affliction is great."[38]

The circumscribed expression of sorrow that Webber allowed
himself was not unique in his experience. When the Reverend
Benjamin Templeton died the February before young Harry, he
received but the sparsest of entries. A year later Amos reacted in
similar fashion to his brother's death. "Sam[1] Webber died this
morning about 2 Oclock," he wrote on December 23, 1859. Two
days later: "Christmas Day Sam[1] Webber buried this afternoon—
3 Oclock". Webber's reserve was certainly a reflection of a central
personality trait: he was not given to emotional outbursts; he
was careful, even in private, to control turbulent feelings; and he
valued order and structure, perhaps especially in times of great
adversity. In this attitude one can also find echoes of mid-
nineteenth-century cultural norms for men, especially those with
middle-class standing or aspirations. But Webber's terseness was
no simple suppression of feeling. For many, even in the presumed
privacy of a diary, to write of those one loved deepest after
their passing proved almost impossible. The Reverend Amos G.
Beman, for example, the black New Haven minister who had

"Amos Webber Thermometer Record and Diary," Volume I, May 1858, no page. Note especially Webber's controlled entry recording the death of his son in the lower right column. *Courtesy of the Baker Library, Harvard University Graduate School of Business Administration, Boston* twice been solicited as minister by black Presbyterians in Philadelphia, lost his wife, his oldest son, and one daughter in a typhoid epidemic during 1856–1857. In his diary he entered only the stark cry of despair "I am alone." For Amos Webber, Amos Beman, and many other nineteenth-century Americans, such compact sentences on the death of loved ones revealed in their fashion the depth of the pain felt.[39]

As Amos Webber grieved, largely in solitude, his feeling of loss eased, perhaps, by an occasional moment of shared anguish with Lizzie, he sought to regain his composure. In this effort his temperature recordings proved helpful, because they allowed him to focus on an observable world and its rational and understandable patterns and purposes. As time passed, and his immediate pain ebbed somewhat, he turned again to a broader social commentary. In June 1859, it was his employers, their families and friends, who captured his attention.

In the capacity of waiter, Amos attended the wedding of his employer's daughter, Lizzie E. Montgomery, to Henry Neall, in 1859. Along with two other black men, A. Williams and John Bond, Webber prepared the reception and then served the guests. In his chronicle of the day's events, Webber re-created his role with an almost geometric precision that suggests both his orderly personality and an assertion of a common equality. Webber carefully re-created the interior of the Montgomery home, where the evening ceremony took place on June 1, and placed himself precisely within this tableau. "Enter the Dining room," he wrote. "At the S.E. corner of the room the bride & groom stood= at the South end of the table, stood A.J. Montgomery . . . John Bond {waiter} in the N.E. corner A Webber {waiter} in the entry=A Williams {waiter} at the front door". As the guests ate sherbet, fruit, and cake from a table "bestrewed With roses & flowers of different kinds," Webber's attention turned to the second floor of the house, where he assisted in another form of celebration: "yes. in the 2nd story back room their was some Segars= and some eye opener, kind of a drink that is use for gentlemen= So ends the wedding= N.B. Mr. Thackrad Mr. Montgomery Mr. Neall was the only gentlemen that kept the fun up=for the Evening=" With the exception of one honorific notice of the bride, who he thought looked as "pleasant &

smiling like the rose that comes from bud," no women graced his account of the festivities.[40]

That Amos Webber focused his attention on the men attending the wedding was not in itself unusual for mid-nineteenth-century American males, white or black. Women were relegated to largely private, almost invisible roles in the male imagination, and Webber's report of the wedding, written by the man who rarely mentioned his wife throughout his chronicles, simply followed form in this regard. More surprising was his easy accommodation to the drinking. Temperance was an issue for black religious and political activists in both Attleborough and Philadelphia, and throughout his notebooks Webber wove moral tales that depicted the devastation liquor wreaked upon individuals and families alike. Webber's comfortableness with these men, their social standing, and the occasion itself may have allowed him to ease his intense moral imperatives.[41]

Yet in other ways Webber's moral perspective was quite evident. Pleased at the match (he thought the groom seemed "steadfast . . . intelligent. and understood what he was about"[42]), Webber also recognized a level of solemnity as well. He began his description of the ceremony: "The hour {8 o'clock} arrived when the Hymeneal & Conjugal Knot had to be tied.=which they could not untie the next day=". The minister, Reverend G. D. Carrow, gave a stern sermon on the responsibilities of marriage, for Webber noted approvingly that "[t]he bride & groom, gets hungry after hearing a Lesson which they never Learned at school———" Webber's somber eye passed over the guests as well. Piecing together snippets of conversation as he worked the room, Webber fancied that the youth of the newlyweds led some guests to wistfully recall their own youth and their weddings. "[B]ut they all woke up again, and found themselfs mistaken" was his rather melancholy conclusion.[43]

Webber followed the fortunes of the newlyweds and, ten months later, happily reported another "great time" in the life of the Montgomery family. Referring the reader back to the wedding itself—"It will be remembered (see page 8)," he began—he announced that "a son was born" to the Nealls early on the morning of April 7, 1860.[44] This proved to be the last entry made concerning the Montgomery family, however, for Webber's close associa-

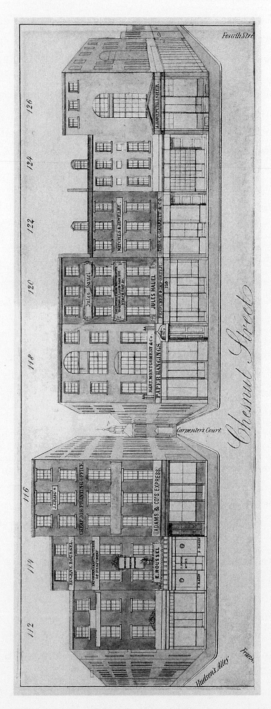

The north side of Chestnut Street, 1851. After the reorganization of Philadelphia in 1854, Hart, Montgomery's address became 322 Chestnut. *Courtesy of the Library Company of Philadelphia*

tion with both the family and the firm was soon to cease. Hart, Montgomery had teetered on the edge of bankruptcy the spring that the Neall heir was born, and it closed its doors permanently five months later.[45] Before that finale, however, Webber and his co-workers experienced a rather spectacular attempt to salvage the firm's fortunes with Japanese customers.

During the spring of 1860, Hart, Montgomery and Company sought to interest the Japanese Embassy in Washington in its fancy wallpaper. In the aftermath of Commodore Matthew Perry's visit to Japan six years earlier, a large delegation of Japanese diplomats and their staff were in Washington to negotiate a treaty. In March and twice again in May, William Hart visited "[t]he Japanese Embassy at Washington." That June a party of seventy-six Japanese men arrived in Philadelphia and, Webber thought, they set the city "astir from centre to Circumferences to get a sight, at the stranges." But he also thought their reception fell short of what the Japanese expected. The American soldiers participating in the Philadelphia welcome were "a mere handful, compared to the reception of Commodeer Perry in Japan with 80,000 soldiers=; (1854) or (1852)." Webber interacted with the Japanese directly when they visited Hart, Montgomery and Company during their four-day visit:

Likewise they visited Hart, Montgomery & Co paper hanging store N° 322 Chestnut, While looking at some of their fancy papers. they desired to see some views with battles, printed of them; So as to make their wants Known one of them Sung out "burn, burn," So we understood well what they wished.

Whether language difficulties proved formidable or the delegation felt slighted by the city's reception is not known, but any purchase the Japanese delegation placed with the firm did not prevent its closing three months later.

Webber took particular enjoyment in the jocular conduct of one of the Japanese visitors, a man whom "the [American] Ladies call Tommy. (A favorite, Jolly Soul)", Webber observed with amusement as Tommy expressed confusion at "how it was that the Ladies was so Large (hoops)". While the American women "were taking their fun with Tommy," professing that their image reflected their actual size and not the wire hoops and crinoline skirts underneath their dresses, Webber discovered Tommy making his own observations. Watching the women as they walked through the store, he "found out, they haile[d] under false colors, puff out with hoops;". Continuing, Amos wondered: "I do not (Know) no wether Tommy tried the fashion or not *perhaps he will try it when he arrives at home.*" Webber's vignette, with its playful humor and innuendo, revealed another side of his personality that was, perhaps, not as evident when he lived in the Wurts household.[46]

——————— ———————

WEBBER BENEFITED CONSIDERABLY from his rather close association with white elites. He found steady employment at livable wages, a condition not shared by a majority of the city's black population. He also had the opportunity to observe at close quarters a wide swath of white society, from draymen and clerks to salesmen and partners, and from a variety of perspectives: Webber was, in turn, servant, co-worker, moralist, chronicler, and perhaps, at times, friend. This familiarity with the white world and his ability to maneuver diplomatically through the racial currents of sympathetic and not so sympathetic whites would prove invaluable. His work experience also broadened him in ways shared by few whites or blacks outside the elite. Webber's encounter with the Japanese delegation was an exceptional individual experience, but not unrepresentative of a type that occurred throughout his seven years' employment at Hart, Montgomery. The firm's salesmen and buyers regularly returned from a potpourri of American and European cities, bringing with them news, stories, and newspapers. These Webber absorbed and pondered and through them learned about that broader world.

Yet even as he grew in confidence as a chronicler, Amos Webber remained intensely circumspect about his personal life. The death of his son, the pleasure of Lizzie's company, the proximity of his brother, Samuel—these experiences received at most a fleeting acknowledgment. Vast emotional silences surrounded Webber's life in his chronicle. Even what he chose to record was tinged with this quality. Webber never explicitly acknowledged an audience for his chronicle beyond himself and his entries have the feel of a conversation with himself, with his questions often rhetorical. And indeed it was his book, as he made it, as it grew under his care, and as he claimed it from the debris of Hart, Montgomery and Company. For a man who actively grappled with his world and its problems, yet who possessed throughout his life a solitary inner core, he may have thought that was sufficient. But despite his chronicle's terseness, Amos Webber did not live in isolation.

CHAPTER THREE

A SENSE OF WORTH

RAISED IN THE BETHLEHEM COLORED METHODIST CHURCH, Amos Webber moved into the heart of the northern black Methodist world when he arrived in Philadelphia. Bethel Church, the mother church of the denomination founded by Richard Allen, the A.M.E.'s founder, had the largest congregation in the city, and claimed fully a quarter of the approximately 4,500 black churchgoers.[1] Yet Webber did not affiliate with the Methodists in Philadelphia. The influence of his wife, Lizzie, his brother, Samuel, and possibly William Laws as well may have drawn Webber toward the black Presbyterian faith, but the structure of the Presbyterian ritual also appealed to Webber. Where Methodism was an evangelical religion, centered on achieving individual emotional conversion, black Presbyterian services focused more on "a carefully prepared sermon" that stressed "order and predictability." This more cerebral approach also contained a stern moral code of conduct that, in the words of one black Presbyterian minister, required potential members "to be broken into the rule and order of the church."[2] Black Presbyterianism was a faith fitted to Amos Webber's personality.

Popular perceptions of black Presbyterianism were sharply divergent. The fact that these black Christians never formed their own denomination but—in contrast with black Methodists—remained in communion with and therefore subject to the white synod was widely noted. The pervasive poverty among the black Presbyterian churches, which resulted in persistent pleas throughout the antebellum years for aid from the synod, underscored the perception of dependency. The Presbyterian position on slavery also proved contentious. While there were some white Presbyterian abolitionists, few were found among the national officials or in the Philadelphia Presbytery, because both groups refused to bar slaveholders from communion. By the late 1840s the Reverend Henry Highland Garnet, a leading black Presbyterian minister in New York, had resigned his pulpit (even as he affirmed his profession of faith) to become an itinerant minister among blacks in upstate New York, so disgusted was he with the Presbyterian accommodation to slavery.[3]

But Amos Webber's involvement with Presbyterianism did not necessarily distance him from others within black Philadelphia. He was not a member of the First African Presbyterian Church, which claimed many of the city's leading black families.[4] And Webber himself maintained interest in a broad variety of religious experiences, and often remarked upon them in his writings. When the Bethel Church baptized fifty converts on one afternoon, Webber proudly entered that fact in his chronicle. A year later he observed that the picnic of Bethel's Sunday school, "the largest school of Colored in the city," had been enjoyable. Reflecting on the city's racist atmosphere, where large public groupings of blacks had stirred whites to violence before, he reported with relief that "everything passed off quietly."[5]

Webber also took great interest in the numerous religious revivals that swept Philadelphia in the late 1850s. "Great Excitement in all the church in N.York Phil^a and in all the world," Webber exclaimed on March 12, 1858. "Never such a time Know before among the people=both White & Colord," he continued, as he explained matter-of-factly the integrated nature of the revival's converts. Webber shared the excitement of these revivals, whose audiences could approach 5,000 enthusiasts, but it was not clear that he himself was a revival convert. In fact, it was a skeptical Webber who reevaluated the 1858 revivals, after the first rush of enthusiasm settled: "It appears that the community has just found out, that their is a living God, to worship,=instead of going to church for fashion, To see, and be seen. as general custom. & &".[6]

Webber's commentary suggests an individual whose religious commitments and principles were well formed by 1858. Suspicious of the staying power of emotional enthusiasm and critical of some church members for their superficial motivations, Webber, according to his own religious beliefs, emphasized his duty to the "living God, to worship," and the attendant requirements for personal and public conduct that entailed. The precise relationship between these religious beliefs and his scientific rationalism remains murky; it is possible, however, that his skepticism toward organized religion, based on an uncompromising faith, caused him to hesitate before submitting to any ecclesiastical authority.

However skeptical Webber was of the religious practices of black and white Philadelphia, he could not comprehend a personal or social morality divorced from at least some formal profession of religious faith. That belief, which he shared with many of his contemporaries, ensured his involvement with the Lombard Street church in numerous ways after 1856.

The last of the three antebellum African Presbyterian churches established in the city, the Lombard Street Central Presbyterian Church occupied a large stone building on Lombard Street, just east of Ninth Street. From his home on either Miles Alley or Anita Street, Webber regularly passed the church on his way to work. Although not an ornate structure, the large sanctuary housed an organ and pews for a reported membership that was larger than those of the other two black Presbyterian churches combined. The Lombard Street building also had classrooms big enough to enroll the largest number of Sabbath school pupils among the three congregations. Although he was a controversial minister, Stephen Gloucester had provided a sound foundation before his death in 1850, and membership grew consistently, encouraged by the prayer meetings and evangelical techniques he advocated. While the congregation remained financially dependent on the synod, Gloucester's leadership maintained traditional patterns of authority within the church. The congregation could make its collective voice heard on an issue, but the church's effective ruling body remained the session, composed of a small group of church elders, trustees, and the minister.[7]

Two issues dominated the institutional life of the church throughout the 1850s. Gloucester had raised an impressive church structure, but the congregation's pervasive poverty made it difficult to attract a permanent minister following his death. Occasional ministers appeared—one of whom, William Jermon, was white—but none stayed long enough to establish a firm presence.

In 1854 the church called the Reverend Ennals Adams, an A.M.E. minister, to this Presbyterian pulpit, and he remained there for two years until the congregation's inability to meet his $400 per year salary led to his resignation. In September 1856, Benjamin Templeton accepted the pulpit, but his death, a short seventeen months later, created yet another vacuum in church leadership. The Lombard Street ministry remained empty for three more years, temporarily filled by visiting ministers until June 1861, when the Reverend John B. Reeve accepted the call. He would provide the ministerial leadership for the next fifty years.[8]

The second difficulty during the 1850s, which stemmed from the first, was a lack of religious discipline. The brief ministry of Jermon, the white Methodist, who later proved not to be licensed, in 1851–1852 exemplified these problems. Jermon was so popular that extra chairs and benches were added when he preached. He largely rejected the formal sermon in favor of revivalistic techniques; ignored the church elders; and used a small, private bible class, taught in people's homes, as a primary organizing strategy. It was not long, however, before rumors spread throughout the congregation of sexual license and other irregularities at these classes. Under the leadership of Robert Jones, a founding elder, the session removed Jermon and later warned another black church in the city not to call him to its pulpit. This experience, Jones thought, indicated that the church contained far too many "derelict and unruly members." Two years later, with the Reverend Adams in the pulpit, the pastor and the elder undertook an examination of the entire membership "whereupon many were found to be unworthy or not proper members of the church and therefore dropped, excommunicated, and others delinquent in church duties to be visited by Ministers and Elders."[9]

The Amos Webber who applauded Charles Wurts's moral code and who criticized halfhearted, lackadaisical Christians welcomed this restoration of discipline. On Wednesday evening, April 29, 1857, Webber took the opportunity to act on these beliefs in the trial to determine whether Guy M. Burton, a member of the Lombard Street church, should be excommunicated. Burton stood charged before the session of "[t]aking goods the property of Granville Stokes—and disposing of them, or appropriating them to his own use." The accused pleaded not guilty and the session, under the direction of Reverend Templeton and Elder Jones, presented the case against Burton. They submitted the testimony of the police officer "who made the arrest *and took the goods from his* [Burton's] *House*," as well as a copy of the indictment Granville Stokes had filed before a city alderman. In addition, Stokes, Henry Penington, and Amos Webber appeared, and declared their willingness to testify against Burton in the actual trial scheduled a few days later. Burton maintained his innocence but two days later he reappeared before the session to confess some guilt. "He admitted," the clerk recorded, "that though he did not exactly steal the Goods, yet he did not come by them as he ought, and admits he has committed a sin, and brought disgrace on himself and the Church—" The session accepted the changed plea but suspended Burton from membership for seven months. Parallel with these actions, Stokes withdrew his criminal charges.[10]

No record exists of Webber's involvement in other church trials, although his own moral standards certainly would have allowed further participation. The Burton case, moreover, was anything but unique for the Lombard Street church. In their collective search for moral order and institutional stability, the congregation and its session prosecuted three broad categories of cases. The first involved violations of church law, especially of the duties expected of church members. In 1851, for example, John N. P. Gloucester, Stephen Gloucester's son, faced charges of nonattendance and not paying his pew rent, the major source of regular income for the church. Pleading poverty, Gloucester satisfied the session and charges were dropped.[11] A second category also concerned church law, but particularly violations of a sexual nature. In 1852, for example, the same John N. P. Gloucester charged Mary Jane Elizabeth Norman with slandering his character by spreading rumors that the married Gloucester planned to elope to Canada with another woman; that he "was guilty of ruining the character" of this woman already; and that he was also "guilty of dark deeds with said Miss Norman." After deliberation the session decided against a trial and prevailed upon Gloucester to withdraw his charges in exchange for an acknowledgment that the rumors were false. Nine months later, however, when it was discovered that the unmarried Norman was "unlawfully pregnant,"

Lombard Street Central Presbyterian Church, ca. 1870, the Philadelphia building where Amos Webber worshiped and played the organ.
Courtesy of the Library Company of Philadelphia

the session immediately resolved that she "be cut off from the Communion of this Church."[12]

Finally, members were disciplined who would not withdraw legal charges despite the intervention of the session. Antebellum Philadelphia's system of primary justice consisted largely of private prosecution of alleged wrongdoers before neighborhood-elected aldermen who essentially acted as third-party mediators. This system did not necessarily meet with church approval, as an examination of the two trials of Guy M. Burton suggests. Central to the resolution of the 1857 case (in which Webber testified) was not only Burton's admission of guilt but also the plaintiff Stokes's willingness to drop criminal charges in deference to the church tribunal. A year earlier, when Mrs. Eliza Howe brought unspecified charges against Burton and refused to drop her civil suit at the request of the session, she experienced a far different fate. Unable to "prevail upon her to withdraw the suit," the session ruled that she "was debarred from the Communion until further process" for "going to law contrary to the rules of the church." For Elder Jones and the Lombard Street session, a congregant's primary responsibility was to the religious community.[13]

That many of those brought before such sessions either pleaded guilty or sought readmission after a suspension testified to the authority and legitimacy of these tribunals, as did the church's continued growth. In part, this call to moral order involved intensely individual concerns, as codes of conduct and patterns of behavior might directly reflect a member's interior religious life and prospects for final redemption. Yet this moral vision did not exist in a social or political vacuum. A dissolute people, at odds with God's will, could not maintain strong family bonds, nor could they take effective action for emancipation or to improve the status of free blacks. This moral perspective, which held one's individual actions accountable to a higher authority, also provided many, including Amos Webber, with the foundation for a sense of social justice.[14] Temperance, school reform, and a concern for the destitute were but some of the issues that demanded their attention. The question of racism was also central to these activists, and the attitudes of white churchgoers toward blacks may have fueled a certain skepticism about religion in general, a skepticism evident in the writings of Webber and other black Philadelphians.

Nancy Lester had recently moved from the city when she reflected on the revivals in 1858: "If it is genuine I hope soon to hear of many among the converts laboring with whole souled vehemence to undo the heavy burden and let the oppressed go free. Then my faith will be strengthened, and I shall believe the hand of the Lord is in it."[15]

But in their own church the members of this voluntary organization possessed a unique area of cultural freedom within a largely antagonistic white city. Through the collective strength of their congregation, members could alleviate some of the consequences of racism in their individual lives, and as a result, they defended the authority of the church, and specifically of the session, from internal and external attack. That was part of the reason Mrs. Eliza Howe had received the severest penalty the session could administer. In refusing to drop her civil charges she was challenging the special role the church occupied in members' lives. This same vigilance made the congregation sensitive to incursions on their judgments by outsiders. When an oversight committee of the governing white Presbytery ruled that the session had been too harsh in its punishment of Charles Beulah for dancing in public in 1857, the Lombard Street Presbyterians reacted swiftly. The session, with the congregation's support, rejected the Presbytery's ruling, retried Beulah, and increased the punishment from censure to suspension. As Elder Jones later explained, "the session was determined, if possible, to suppress insubordination and conduct that leads to immorality."[16]

In one area, however, the social customs of the church differed minimally from those practiced in white congregations. Male church leaders, both black and white, frequently perceived women, often the most active church members, as a threat to the authority of the session. When Stephen Gloucester and the elders approved the establishment of "the First Colored female Prayer meeting" under the direction of Belinda Davis and Eliza Edwards (who would later marry Guy M. Burton in the first wedding service in the church), both women agreed to be "subject to the control of the session." That compact soon collapsed and the session withdrew its approval. Some years later the session declared that another largely female Friday evening prayer meeting was "not and has not at any time been under the direction of this session";

while in 1852 they admonished Mrs. Caroline Freeman and her daughter, who had come under the influence of William Jermon, for hosting bible classes "on a meeting evening of the Church, and also using an influence detrimental to the interest of the Church." Similar problems with predominantly female evening prayer meetings continued through the decade.[17]

The case of Mrs. Mary Harman sharply etched the secondary status of women within the congregation. In 1856, Mrs. Harman accused church elder George Potter of being a liar and a gambler. Potter immediately pressed charges of slander against her before the session of which he was a member. In a preliminary meeting, when asked about her accusations against Potter, Harman readily acknowledged the charge and defiantly claimed "that she could prove it." But no action was taken. At a subsequent meeting held in her absence, the session heard Potter's slander charges, found her guilty, and immediately suspended her from communion. Some months later the oversight committee of the Presbytery reviewed the session minutes and singled out the Harman case as one they could not approve. "A person was suspended," the white Presbyterians wrote, "without proof or record of guilt,-as she said she could prove the truth of what she said." An infuriated Robert Jones responded for the session:

There was proof of the assertion being made, the want of record is a neglect of the Clerk- The Complainant [George Potter] is a member of Sessions, and the defense was conducted by a member of Session. The decission was made by the remaining Members & the Moderator- The fact of *insubordination, declared* to Session having weight in making the kind of decission that was made—

With that the session refused to reverse its decision or to rehear the case in a more equitable manner.[18]

The available evidence suggests that tension between male church authority and independent female members occurred with some regularity in this congregation: from Mary Harman's "insubordination" and Eliza Howe's refusal to drop her civil charges (possibly a reflection of her suspicion of the men who would hear her case) to Mary Jane Elizabeth Norman's expulsion, the assertion of male authority persisted despite a female majority in the congregation. Mary Still, a black Methodist woman who later joined Philadelphia's First African Presbyterian Church, wrote that "[w]e are sometimes told that females should have nothing to do with the business of the Church." Those who would exclude women, she continued, "have yet to learn that when female labor is withdrawn the Church must cease to exist."[19]

But for Amos Webber the church—for all his skepticism—remained a welcoming place. Besides his involvement in its trials, he became the church's organist in 1860.[20] Webber, who was musically proficient on the violin and piano as well as the organ, thus increased his ties—both formal and informal—to the church. But the Lombard Street Central Presbyterian Church was not the only communal institution in black Philadelphia that laid claim to Amos Webber's commitment.

———

IN A CHARACTERISTICALLY cryptic entry in his chronicle, Webber wrote on Sunday, May 13, 1855: "G.U.O. of O.F. = Sermon." Mysterious to the uninitiated, his meaning was nonetheless clear. On that Sunday morning, as on occasional other Sundays throughout the year, Webber, wearing the regalia of the Grand United Order of Odd Fellows (consisting of variously colored aprons and collars, as well as jewelry, badges, and insignias), walked to the meeting room of Carthagenian Lodge No. 901, a few blocks from his church. The lodge then paraded in public procession to one of the city's black churches, where they occupied a group of pews. By design, the pastor's sermon lauded the Order and explored some aspects of the Odd Fellows' moral value to the community for the benefit of the other congregants. Webber's participation in this ritual placed him at the center of organized collective life in black Philadelphia, at the confluence where church and fraternal lodge mingled in their effort to uphold a moral vision, provide for mutual assistance, and develop a network of activists ready to respond to a variety of crises.[21]

The Grand United Order of Odd Fellows had been founded only twelve years before in New York City. Patrick H. Reasons and other members of the Philomathean Institute, a black literary club, desiring a benevolent society for their mutual assistance, approached the whites-only Independent Order of Odd Fellows. Rebuffed "with contempt" in their effort to affiliate, they responded favorably when Peter Ogden, a black seaman and British Odd Fellow who shipped out between New York and Liverpool, England, suggested that his more tolerant Liverpool lodge would sponsor a black New York affiliate. The British officials did so and, in 1843, the Philomathean Lodge No. 646 received its charter. A year later, Unity Lodge No. 711, the first Philadelphia lodge, formed; it claimed 57 members by December 1844. By 1851 the Order had grown considerably. Active organizing among free blacks throughout the Northeast and, increasingly, the Midwest had led to the establishment of twenty-five lodges, with just under 1,500 members, with an assistance program for members and their families in need due to financial distress, sickness, or death.[22]

From its inception the Order committed itself to a code of proper moral conduct. In 1844, the governing committee of the national order declared ineligible for membership any candidate "who is know[n] to be (directly or indirectly) a gambler in Lotteries or policy playing." Men already members faced a fine and a reprimand for their first offense and expulsion "from the Order, as a gambler, and his name published in the circulars of the Order" for a subsequent incident. Individual lodges possessed the power to discipline members for other infractions as well, such as adultery and a persistent refusal to pay one's dues.[23] Odd Fellows were also encouraged to exercise care in sponsoring new lodges. In 1846, Philadelphia's Unity Lodge sent James McCrummell to Washington, D.C., to examine a prospective new lodge. In his favorable report McCrummell stressed that Harmony Lodge contained only "one or two members . . . but owns the property in which they live, and all but one are close members of churches."[24]

This world of regalia, ritual, parades, and sermons provided those such as Webber who were skeptical of organized religion with a parallel but more secular vision to that of the church. In championing the scientific pursuit of knowledge, the study of the universe, and the worldwide struggle for democratic rights, black fraternalism reflected the rationalist influence of the American Enlightenment while preserving intact a basic commitment to fundamental Christian principles. This too may have attracted Webber to the lodge.

McCrummell's emphasis on the degree of home ownership and church participation, while possibly exaggerated, nonetheless revealed the Order's essential self-image. It sought ambitious younger men, possessed of strong moral fiber, who were willing to join together for fellowship and mutual aid. These qualities described Amos Webber precisely. But McCrummell's report also identified a key obstacle to the Order's growth. Harmony Lodge was "prospering as fast as can be expected," he wrote, "taking into consideration the opposition of the masonics, for they have opposed them tooth and nail." In the eyes of the Prince Hall Masons, a national black Masonic organization founded in 1784 in Boston, the Order was indeed a competitor, even though numerous black men held membership in both organizations. Unlike the Odd Fellows, Masons did not immediately establish mutual insurance programs, since they were convinced their members were the elite of the black world and thus more economically secure than those in the Order. Yet membership in either fraternal organization conveyed a standing that distinguished these men from others within black Philadelphia.[25]

Odd Fellows were of a more secure economic standing than most blacks. Where, for example, only one in twenty adult black males in the city owned real property, the ratio was one in five for members of fraternal, religious, and literary organizations. Members of these voluntary associations—including, in addition to the fraternal lodges, the Library Company for Colored Persons, the Banneker Institute, and the Institute for Colored Youth—were seven times more likely to be professionals than black men in general; were six times more likely to work as small entrepreneurs or in white-collar positions; and were three times more likely to be skilled craftsmen. Still, while these ratios were relatively high, most members were unpropertied and at least one third worked at unskilled jobs. The peculiar nature of black economic life—the crowding of all but a handful of employed blacks into the lowest occupational categories—resulted in a society that lacked the complex economic layers usually associated with urban industrial communities. Thus membership in these organizations, by a janitor and handyman at Hart, Montgomery, for example, suggested a standing within the community that direct economic criteria might never reveal.[26]

As a leading voluntary organization (one observer referred to it as "the strongest of the major and minor fraternal groups" among black Pennsylvanians[27]), the Grand United Order of Odd Fellows signaled a professed moral stature, attentiveness to familial and communal responsibilities, and ambition to improve both one's own personal prospects and the collective standing of black Philadelphia. In keeping with their self-image of men aggressively on the rise, Odd Fellows also recruited from among the younger members in the community. The national organization actually penalized lodges for enrolling older men by requiring an additional initiation fee of a dollar for every year a prospective member was over forty.[28]

Good Samaritan Lodge No. 895 and Carthagenian Lodge No. 901, the lodge that Webber would join a few years later, were founded in 1847 and 1848, respectively. During the lodges' early years the weekly meetings were held in a series of rented rooms; in September 1857, with Odd Fellows from throughout the Northeast in attendance, the Philadelphia Order laid the cornerstone for its own building on Lombard Street near Seventh, less than two blocks from Webber's church. But in either case the interior of the meeting room invariably conformed to the Odd Fellows' ritual: the officers of the lodge sat by rank according to the four major compass headings (the master of the lodge occupying the east), each facing the altar in the center of the room. Lodge brothers, after gaining admission to this sacred space by means of a password, sat in back of the officers, who regularly gave instruction on the purpose and ritual observances of the Order. Some lodges used a piano, a few even an organ, and prepared skits, lectures, and debates frequently followed the official business meeting.

Of the sixty-three founding members of Good Samaritan and Carthagenian lodges, we know the occupations of twenty-nine. Of these, 86 percent reported working-class jobs, almost evenly divided between unskilled and skilled positions. Among the thirteen unskilled men were laborers, porters, and skilled men unable to practice their trade; the twelve skilled workers consisted of barbers (whose status frequently fluctuated between that of a small entrepreneur and an employee), carpenters, and one oysterman. There were four professionals: a minister (who, given the poverty of black congregations, quite possibly worked another job for his livelihood), a lumber merchant, a doctor, and a dentist. Although the sample is small, the percentage of skilled men who could obtain work at their craft was considerably higher than throughout black Philadelphia. Sixty-five percent of the adults in the household units of these members, as recorded in the 1856 Quaker census, reported themselves at least literate, and many claimed basic mathematical skills as well. These latter figures were significantly above the citywide rates for all blacks. The ages of the members of Good Samaritan Lodge, the only available, reveal the emphasis on youth in accordance with the directives of the national officers. Sixty-two percent of the twenty-nine members listed were twenty-nine or younger in 1847, with the majority of them aged twenty-five or below. Another 27 percent were in their thirties, with half of these younger than thirty-four. Interestingly, four of the five delegates elected to represent the lodge in the citywide meetings of the Order were in their twenties, two of them but twenty-one years old.[29]

Amos Webber, in keeping with this trend, was not yet thirty when he joined the Odd Fellows. Although Carthagenian Lodge would mushroom to more than 130 members by the mid-1850s, there is no reason to suspect that the broad social characteristics of the members altered dramatically. Webber's membership in Carthagenian Lodge did not catapult him into Philadelphia's black elite, but it did provide him with important access to that world. Admittance to the lodge brought with it the opportunity to mingle as a brother with those who might be helpful in obtaining a more secure economic foundation. One of the founding members of his lodge was Dr. J. J. G. Bias, a former slave, Methodist preacher, physician, dentist, and Mason who was active in political and educational affairs. Similarly it was through Odd Fellowship that Webber met Stephen Smith, a founding member of Good Samaritan Lodge and a former slave who made a fortune in the lumber business. On Smith's death in 1873, Webber remembered him in some detail and concluded approvingly that Smith had used his money to "always look after the interest of the Colored race."

Fraternal associations also provided Webber with additional access to Jacob C. White, Jr., the son of one of Philadelphia's leading black families. White, an educator, active abolitionist, and acknowledged leader of the younger congregants in the First African Presbyterian Church, had a very personal connection to Amos and Lizzie Webber as well. The basis of White's family estate was a controlling interest in Lebanon Cemetery, where young Harry J. Webber was interred. For years the two men communicated about fees for the upkeep of the plot and used the occasion to exchange family news and express cordial regards. Finally, it was through the Order that Webber met David Bustill Bowser, an artist, a longtime national officer of the Odd Fellows, an abolitionist, and a civil rights activist. These two men remained friends for more than thirty years.[30]

Fraternal membership also provided access to a wide range of educational, social, and political organizations. Members of the Order were active in such centrally important black institutions as the Banneker Institute, the literary and debating society; the Library Company for Colored Persons, with its books and reading rooms open to blacks; the independent school, the Institute for Colored Youth; and a host of other associations that stressed temperance, self-improvement, education, and cultural development. The Order connected members to political leaders within the community. In the twenty years following the disfranchisement of black voters throughout the state in 1838, Odd Fellow leaders David B. Bowser, Stephen Smith, and J. J. G. Bias, among others, drafted petitions that demanded restoration of the ballot and protested Philadelphia's segregationist practices on its streetcars. They were also elected delegates to a variety of state and national black conventions.[31]

When the national officers of the Order acknowledged in 1845—one year after its founding—that Unity Lodge in Philadelphia had, like all lodges, the right to "try their own members" for immoral conduct, they affirmed the complex role that the Order would play within the black community. The Odd Fellow emphasis on moral conduct was not substantially different from that found in the Lombard Street church—indeed, church elder Robert Jones was also a leading member of the Order—and the discipline within the Order served similar functions. The threat of expulsion could and did channel behavior along certain paths and, as with church trials, possibly kept some issues away from more official, and potentially hostile, white forums.[32]

Many northern black advocates of self-improvement felt that, by the very nature of their freedom relative to the slave, they bore a very particular responsibility. Philadelphia's African Temperance Society, among many other black associations, made this point repeatedly. So too did Frederick Douglass express the sentiment concisely: "I am a temperance man because I am an anti-slavery man."[33] This sense of personal responsibility was also held as the goal each member of the Odd Fellows strove to attain.

But this fraternal moral conduct also served an essential function within the black community. As people tried to make sense out of the pattern of insults and racial violence that was the latticework of daily life, such moral exhortations offered some black Americans a possible response to the chaos about them. While economic exclusion from all but the most menial jobs played havoc with family life, drinking, gambling, and loose sexual conduct—all within one's power to choose—could only further the corrosive pressures. In upholding a stern moral code, black churches and fraternal associations encouraged members to positively direct those aspects of their individual and collective lives over which they did possess some discretion. These exhortations to morality actually spoke to a deep sense of individual and collective identity and pride, and these men and women used this moral vision to assert a very real control over their lives. That they were unable to persuade the majority of whites of their common humanity in no way diminished the central meaning of their efforts. In building viable social and cultural organizations that reflected these needs, these proud activists—the famous as well as the unknown—also erected the institutional framework for the expression of a distinctive black culture in the North, a culture whose synergism and diversity reflected the labyrinthine circumstances of being black, Christian, and American in an environment largely hostile to their very presence.[34]

When Amos Webber donned his regalia to attend a Sunday sermon or the funeral of a brother, or celebrate the anniversary of his lodge, it was never a private affair. Webber's march through Philadelphia's streets with his fraternal brothers asserted a proud collective identity to whites and blacks alike.[35] Given the potential for hostile white reactions, this ordered black public presence assumed a sharp political meaning even for some white sympathizers. Thomas Cope, a merchant and abolitionist, worried, in light of Philadelphia's history of antiblack riots, "[h]ow far it is prudent in them" to march in public "while so much prejudice exists against them." But these black activists persisted, and during the 1850s city authorities on occasion even provided police escorts to assure that "the utmost good order prevailed." In marching from lodge to church on Sunday mornings, Amos Webber asserted and claimed his rights as a citizen and, in consort with his fellows, self-consciously presented himself in public as a member of a community of moral activists. In the process he and they reinforced the idea that moral conduct and industrious habits, even if ignored by whites, were critical for individual dignity and group identity within black Philadelphia.[36]

This fraternal world was preeminently a male world and the lodge offered a distinctly male sphere within which members might control and, in the process, explore the meaning of that elusive term "manhood." But, by the 1850s, while never relinquishing its primary male focus, the Order sought to involve women more actively in its affairs. To this end Patrick Reasons, one of the Order's founders, created a female auxiliary, the Household of Ruth, in 1857, two years after Webber had joined. In Philadelphia one of the first of the women to join the auxiliary was Lizzie Webber. For Amos Webber and other Odd Fellows, this inclusion of women provided the lodge with even deeper roots within black Philadelphia and altered, agreeably it would seem, aspects of the Order's social life. Webber, at least, thoroughly enjoyed the eleventh-anniversary celebration of Carthagenian Lodge on June 2, 1859:

> on which occasion Mrs Bacon. Mrs N.G. Bacon Miss ester armstrong & sister M^{s} Matthews Miss Cooper = Miss Jackson Miss Oliver presented to the said lodge a melodeon = Likewise Mrs A. Webber made & presented a handsome Grecian cover = for to cover the melodeon - also Mrs Freeman presented a handsome Stool A piece of poetry composed by A. Webber especially for the Ladies = was sung; accompanied by the composer . . . on the melodeon.

After speeches by lodge leaders Nathaniel G. Bacon, J. B. Matthews, and Elijah J. Davis, and by the Order's grand master,

David B. Bowser, the company joined in a "Closing ode by the order accompanied by their new presents —adjourned."[37]

That a select group of men such as Bowser, Davis, and Bacon led the lodge, represented it in public, and ran its meetings did not mean that less prominent activists, male and female, were therefore discounted. Members such as Amos and Lizzie Webber created the social framework of the lodge, took pleasure in their activity, and found meaning in the Order's larger purposes. The addition of women in their auxiliary did not question male prerogatives but it did broaden the social foundation of the Order.

Black Americans counted, the fraternal lodge's public presence announced time and again, regardless of white attitudes. In assisting one another morally and materially, and in nurturing an organization whose members were active politically as well, the Grand United Order of Odd Fellows was one among a number of black organizations that recognized that truth. This sense of worth, personal as well as for the race, was perhaps black fraternalism's most important contribution.

<hr/>

THE SEVERITY OF his expectations for himself and others concerning personal conduct and social responsibilities did not therefore prevent Amos Webber from participating in the day-to-day life and culture of the streets in antebellum Philadelphia. Fires, building collapses, street parades, and assorted other public gatherings all captured his attention. He attended fairs, observed a "fox chase," or hunt, one Sunday in 1856, and interacted regularly with street vendors, working people, and others he encountered during his workday.[38] While his work had its demands, it was flexible enough that he could leave the firm to witness a colorful parade or a dramatic catastrophe. At times his interest in science and his involvement in this culture merged in revealing ways. During a major storm in September 1859, Webber walked through the city streets in the vicinity of Hart, Montgomery, marveling at the force of nature. Fallen trees and toppled chimneys cluttered the walkways. "[A]n amuseing seen at third & chestnut" particularly attracted Webber's attention. As pedestrians crossed the street, the fierce wind turned "all umbrellas inside out: the woman suffered the most= for the wind would turn their skirts inside out: quite a crowd congregated at the corner to see the fun=”[39] Neither moral scruples nor nature's power turned Webber from his dalliance with that integrated male crowd.

It was perhaps Webber's deep involvement with music that revealed most clearly the complexity of the cultural forces that influenced him. A church organist who also played the melodeon, piano, and violin, Webber possessed wide-ranging musical tastes. As with many antebellum Americans, he did not perceive a sharp divide between popular and elite cultural expressions; he certainly listened to a great variety of musical styles. In both 1857 and 1858, for example, he attended sessions of the annual German music festival. Protracted affairs lasting four or five days, drawing more than fifty bands from across the Northeast and Midwest, the festivals culminated in a public extravaganza as more than 1,500 band members played as they marched the length of Chestnut Street.[40]

Less dramatic for its greater regularity was the popular music of the streets. Work songs—especially by black longshoremen, casual laborers, and street vendors—surrounded Webber as he walked the city; on occasion he encountered groups of blacks who, in the words of John F. Watson, a white Philadelphian, sang “short scraps of disjointed affirmations, pledges, or prayers lengthened out with long repetitious *choruses*.” Accompanying every word, Watson wrote, was “a sinking of one of the other leg of the body alternately, producing an audible sound of the feet at every step.”[41] The varied music of the street formed a constant background to Webber's urban travels. But it was not just festivals and street performances that attracted Amos, and an entry in his chronicle on November 30, 1856, underscores the intricacies of his musical tastes: “At Chilo Church last night, Miss Greenfield.”[42]

Elizabeth Taylor Greenfield was born a slave in Natchez, Mississippi, in 1809. The next year her white mistress moved to Philadelphia, taking the young, now emancipated slave with her. There Greenfield received an education, took music and voice lessons, and won recognition as a talented singer. Inheriting her former mistress's estate in 1844, Greenfield lived comfortably in Philadelphia, teaching voice to others, as she prepared for her public debut as a concert singer. In Buffalo in 1851 she began a tour that took her across the northern tier of New York State and into

Massachusetts—an itinerary selected to diminish possible racial incidents. The reviews were overwhelmingly positive. The Buffalo *Express* compared her favorably to Jenny Lind, a great favorite with Americans; while papers in Rochester and Albany, New York, and Worcester and Boston, Massachusetts, applauded heartily. Harriet Beecher Stowe thought Greenfield possessed "a most astonishing voice. . . . [It] runs through a compass of three octaves and a fourth." Greenfield's concerts explored an enormous expanse of musical expression: from slave spirituals to Rossini and Beethoven, from Verdi and Handel to such popular songs as "Home Sweet Home." Following this triumphal tour, Greenfield, already known by the sobriquet "the Black Swan," took Europe by storm during a fourteen-month engagement.[43] Her success there and in America expanded the number of cities in which she could perform, and when she gave concerts in Philadelphia, Amos Webber was in the audience not once, but twice.

Out of the urban taverns, bawdy houses, and dance halls frequented by both whites and blacks emerged yet another musical possibility, one that Webber never acknowledged. There, small groups of black musicians produced, in the words of one unsympathetic white observer in the 1840s in New York, a trumpet sound like "red-hot knitting-needles" while the "bass-drummer . . . sweats and deals his blows on every side, in all violation of the laws of rhythm, like a man beating a baulky mule."[44] Webber's silence about this music was not accidental. He did not frequent the bars and the brothels. His cultural activities were indeed eclectic, traversing aspects of white and black Philadelphia and spanning the distance between a raucous male "blood" sport such as the fox chase and the more sedate melodeon performance at a lodge meeting. But the subculture of young men who flocked into the saloons and clubs of the city never enticed Webber. He was not an elitist— his activism had already made him an organizer of other black people into the institutions he found valuable. Rather, Webber feared the personal and social consequences of the pattern of dissolute action associated with that subculture.[45]

Despite these different musical traditions, the strongest institutional influence upon black musical development in Philadelphia during these years remained the black church and the schools associated with it. As the church tradition expanded from its base in sa-

Elizabeth Taylor Greenfield (1809–1876), "the Black Swan." *Courtesy of the Library Company of Philadelphia*

cred music to encompass classical secular music, a significant portion of black Philadelphia was exposed to these new sounds and melodies. This expansion was not always easy: as a young preacher in 1850, future Bishop Daniel Alexander Payne found that one A.M.E. congregation rejected him as pastor in part because he had "endeavored to modify some of the extravagances in worship in Bethel Church." Specifically, Bishop Payne "would not let them sing their 'spiritual songs' . . . know as 'Corn-field Ditties.' " Even within the confines of the rather staid First African Presbyterian Church of Philadelphia similar tensions emerged. A group of younger members, including Jacob C. White, Jr., Ellen Black, and Elijah J. Davis, the Odd Fellow leader, formed the Singing School Association to thoroughly revise "the manner in which the singing is performed in the devotional exercises of the Sabbath day." Petitioning the session in 1859, the association asked for protection "from those whose age is an invulnerable shield behind which they place themselves with the most perfect security and heap upon us scurrility, abuse, and insult with the utmost impunity."[46]

Francis Johnson, Philadelphia's preeminent black composer and orchestra leader, had greatly influenced the evolution of church music. In 1837 he returned from a triumphant tour of England, where he offered in one program selections from Bellini, Rossini, Mozart, popular comic songs, and patriotic airs of both England and America, to introduce the current continental rage "Concerts à la Musard" to Philadelphia. Named after Phillippe Musard, the Parisian who created them, these concerts combined light classical music with a promenade. They proved wildly popular among white Philadelphians (segregation kept black audiences away); and Johnson capitalized on this popularity to integrate his teams of vocalists during the 1843–1844 season.

But Johnson also exerted an important influence directly on black Philadelphia. The frequency of his concerts for blacks grew after 1841, when the Library Company, the philanthropic institution committed to black education, sponsored an orchestra under his direction. His compositions celebrating Haitian independence and foreshadowing the end of American slavery achieved broad popularity. The exposure of many black Philadelphians to these new musical energies expanded and invigorated black musical sensibilities.[47]

In this fashion the vibrancy and complexity of Philadelphia's urban culture exposed Webber to a great variety of musical expressions. Webber chose among them, to be sure, but his choices themselves reflected diverse influences. Webber drew on both Euro- and Afro-American music, and found no sharp line between elite and popular musical offerings. Whether at a concert by Elizabeth Greenfield, by his friend Odd Fellow David Bowser, or by one of the numerous ethnic associations in the city, Webber absorbed a mixture of religious, classical, and popular music, some of which influenced him more than others.

Yet some social distinctions remained. When Webber and other black Philadelphians attended a concert by Elizabeth Greenfield, they occupied a social space different from that of the saloon. In both cases blacks and whites intermingled, and in both settings black Philadelphians used their limited discretionary income for entertainment. The cheapest tickets to a Greenfield concert cost twenty-five cents, an amount equal to a night at a club or saloon. What was different, of course, was the sense of order and purpose that structured the leisure-time entertainment of men like Amos Webber. Their economic standing was not all that different from that of many of the habitués of the saloon; and as the church and lodge trials suggest, there were numerous examples of church members slipping into the places Webber so diligently avoided.[48]

Differences in dress underscored this distinction. Whereas the saloon imposed no formal dress code, black concertgoers, performers as well as the audience, were expected to meet a different standard. Following a concert in Utica, New York, in 1853, Elizabeth Smith Miller, the daughter of the abolitionist Gerrit Smith, complimented Elizabeth Greenfield on her dress but urged her to consider a looser gown, one with "no whale bones [to obscure one's bust] (but perhaps you are not prepared for that reform)." Miller acknowledged why this issue was so important. "I rejoice in the dignity of your deportment," she continued,

> and in the good hours you keep. I have said this much in relation to your dress, because I know how important it is that, in the midst of all the prejudice against those of your colour, that your appearance should be *strikingly genteel*.[49]

Some black Philadelphians rejected this social context and the music itself, perceiving in it a certain truckling to white opinion. Contemporary enthusiasts of "the Black Swan" understood this quite clearly. "I am sorry to hear that the colored people persecute Miss Greenfield," one black fan observed, "but as it was with the Prophet so it is with her, 'not without honor' save in her own country and among her own people."[50] Undoubtedly Webber, a Greenfield supporter, knew of this tension, but it did not deter him. He maintained his diverse cultural engagements, guided by a moral compass whose bearings reflected his commitments to church and lodge. A home owner with steady work, given by disposition as well as by faith to order and morality, Webber framed his personal sense of worth through the force of these imperatives. His activism within this moral community brought him beyond himself, moreover, to a broader collective impulse. It was at that juncture that Webber joined with other black Philadelphians to directly combat the forces of racism that oppressed him and his people in the city and throughout the nation.

CHAPTER FOUR

In the Cause of Liberty

On a warm July day in 1855 a young black boy delivered a note to William Still, the black leader of Philadelphia's Vigilant Committee. The note requested Still to come to a local hotel, where three fugitive slaves needed his help. Still responded immediately, although he did not know the boy and the note was unsigned. Similar notes from black Philadelphians had enabled the committee to assist 121 fugitives in 1854; in 1855, the number of cases would increase by a third. As he rushed from his office, Still alerted Passmore Williamson, one of the committee's white lawyers.

At Bloodgood's Hotel, near the wharf where Spruce Street met the Delaware River, a group of five black porters, all unknown to Still, told him that Jane Johnson, a slave, and her two children were in transit through the city in the company of their owner, Colonel John H. Wheeler, the United States minister to Nicaragua. As Still's group conferred, Wheeler herded his slaves aboard a New York–bound ship from where he intended to sail to Nicaragua. Running from the hotel to the dock a few blocks away at Walnut Street, Still, the porters, and Williamson, who had just arrived, boarded the ship. Still informed Jane Johnson that Pennsylvania's 1847 personal liberty law denied slave owners right of transit through the state for their slaves, and that she and her children had been freed the moment they entered Pennsylvania. While Williamson engaged the colonel in legal debate, Still and his five companions led the slaves off the boat to a series of safe houses and, ultimately, to New York. The United States marshal arrested all seven men; in addition, Passmore Williamson was charged with contempt of court.[1]

The Rescue of Jane Johnson and Her Children at the Camden and Amboy R.R. Wharf in Philadelphia. Passmore Williamson engages John H. Wheeler while William Still leads the Johnson family to freedom and unidentified blacks vigilantly watch from the deck of the steamer and from the dock. *Courtesy of the Library Company of Philadelphia*

First held on $7,000 bail each, the black porters—William Cur-
tis, James P. Braddock, John Ballard, James Martin, and Isaiah
Moore—had bail reduced to a still prohibitive $1,000 on July 28.
Eleven days later, on August 8, the grand jury returned indict-
ments for riot and assault and battery against these men, Still, and
Williamson. The next day, these men were arraigned before Judge
William D. Kelley, Isaac Pugh's son-in-law, who rejected the prosecution's demand for an immediate trial. In the courtroom,
among the crowd, was Amos Webber.[2] In order to attend the trial
he had not gone into work, and he was joined in the courtroom
that day by numerous black Philadelphians as well as by Lucretia
Mott, Sarah Pugh, and other members of the Philadelphia Female Anti-Slavery Society. At the trial some weeks later, all the
defendants were cleared of criminal charges, helped immeasurably by the dramatic testimony of Jane Johnson, who returned
from safety to testify for the defense. Williamson, however, served
one hundred days in jail on the contempt charge and Webber
recorded his November 3 release in his chronicle.[3]

Local reaction to the case was intense. Anti-abolitionists redoubled their efforts to limit the effects of the personal liberty law and
to apprehend fugitive slaves. Antislavery whites, a distinct minority, renewed their dedication to the cause and, amid the joy in Jane
Johnson's escape, expressed a sadness over the future of the country. "The land I so love," one wrote, "has become a reproach and
a shame to me." As indicated by the hatred against blacks stirred
by this case, America had rejected the opportunity "to achieve a
truer greatness than any nation has known."[4]

This case also revealed more clearly the dual nature of political
activism within black Philadelphia. In 1839 the Vigilant Committee had undergone a profound transformation as black activists
largely supplanted white abolitionists in the leadership positions.
This new leadership felt that too many white sympathizers offered little more than words, when the rescue of fugitives demanded deeds; that most white allies proved unwilling to risk
themselves to assist free blacks threatened with kidnapping or the
daily racial violence of Philadelphia's streets; and, finally, that
even antislavery whites revealed a profound ambivalence toward
black political and civil equality. The knowledge that many white
abolitionists refused to eat at the same table with blacks and re-

fused to denounce their disfranchisement rankled deep within black Philadelphia.[5]

The rescue of Jane Johnson and her children also revealed the extent of activism among the black residents of the city. Many of the black elite, themselves officers in religious and fraternal organizations, did assume primary roles in assisting fugitives, but the committee's directors also included men like Peter Lester, a shoemaker, and other working-class blacks. Furthermore, the directors did not represent the whole of the committee, and there was a real sense that its inner strength and effectiveness were the product of a broader segment of black Philadelphia. William Still, for example, knew neither the young messenger nor the five working-class black men at the hotel. Yet he responded immediately to the note, with an implicit trust at the moment of crisis. Nor was this the first time that committee leaders had been approached by unknown members of the community. In 1838, a black man identified only as Simpson met the fugitive James L. Smith on the street, interrogated him, and, only when satisfied with his story, passed him on to the committee for eventual transfer to New York.

William Still (1821–1902) of Philadelphia. Fraternalist, Presbyterian, abolitionist, and advocate of independent black political action. *Courtesy of the Library Company of Philadelphia*

In fact, the records of the Vigilant Committee reveal numerous other instances when black Philadelphians, at considerable remove from the social circles of the black elite, acted independently of, but in concert with, the committee's formal structure.[6]

When Webber was "at Court," then, that August morning, he was not simply an interested onlooker. Like the majority of Jane Johnson's rescuers, Webber was an unheralded man whose working conditions allowed him regular access to city streets, where he might convey important messages or join a public demonstration. For him personally, involvement in this case, given the presence of William Kelley and Sarah Pugh, revealed again how the worlds of white elites and black activists touched in his experience.

As they had before and would again, these men and women crowded the courtrooms in fugitive slave cases, bearing witness and prepared for action against the authorities in the event of a guilty verdict. In part this was an extension of black Philadelphia's attempt to correct the racial bias many thought infused the city's system of justice. Blacks frequently filled courtrooms in criminal cases in an effort to direct the outcome, and with equal commitment sought to prevent criminal arrests they considered unjust or prejudiced. When the police came to arrest a young black boy for larceny in 1839, the *Public Ledger* reported, the boy's father "gathered together a mob of neighbors to prevent the arrest. The officers complained that whenever anyone attempted to make an arrest in the black areas of Moyamensing they were similarly mobbed."[7]

Amos Webber's political activism grew from a sense of justice nurtured in the black organizations he joined. These religious and fraternal associations acquainted Webber with some of the black leadership; abolitionist sentiments in Isaac Pugh's family may have eased potential tensions at Hart, Montgomery. But the core of Webber's involvements lay less with elites, white or black, than it did with the other black workingmen and -women who could be counted on in a crisis to respond with simple everyday courage. Like many of them, Webber's religious beliefs, grounded in a biblical tradition, abetted his activism. In the God who ruled history, black Presbyterians, Methodists, and Baptists preached, lay ultimate assurance of religious and secular liberation. Human effort, girded by this faith, molded both the vision of a moral life and the forceful assertion of the rights and privileges due black Christian

Americans. As one black Presbyterian minister asserted, "We will *preach* the Declaration of Independence till it begins to be put into PRACTICE." Some went even further, claiming that blacks and those few whites who embraced the living religion of personal salvation and national redemption through the abolition of slavery were actually America's elect, the chosen people prophesied in sermon and political text since the seventeenth century. This complex, potent faith, enhanced for Webber as for countless other blacks by the public orations of Frederick Douglass,[8] offered powerful, positive understandings of private identities and public responsibilities.[9]

ON AUGUST 1, 1860, Webber acknowledged, as he had in past years as well, one of the central political events in the collective life of northern free blacks: "celebration of the indies." August 1 was the anniversary of the abolition of the slave trade in the British West Indies in 1834, and speeches and parades accompanied these celebrations throughout the free states.[10] These freedom celebrations defined a unique aspect of antebellum black life. With blacks denied electoral participation (Webber could protest the election of Mayor Richard Vaux only by private sarcasm in his chronicle: "put in by the Democrats=or *Demo*goges=),[11] these ceremonies encouraged another approach to political activity. Rooted in the churches, these festivals included community choirs and prayers, sacred music as well as freedom songs, and sermons that evolved, in the very act of delivery, into orations of topical political significance. For those northern blacks who participated—and the crowds were often quite large—these occasions served many needs. They commemorated a signal day in the history of the world's struggle against slavery and simultaneously recalled the pain of those still enslaved in the American South. In the speeches that were central to these celebrations, moreover, orators black and white utilized the moment to remind Americans of the hypocrisy that festered in the core of the national declaration of freedom and democracy.

Such festivals also acquired a broader social purpose. In coming together, often in largely black crowds, free blacks asserted a sense of collective identity and purpose that stood in sharp contrast to the images most whites held of them. Such festivals allowed northern blacks to define themselves to themselves as a self-conscious community committed to a set of beliefs and ensuing actions. When blacks in New York State celebrated the 1827 abolition of slavery in that state, for example, they often chose not the day it formally ended, July 4, but rather the following day, July 5. They had no wish to confuse their freedom festivals with the white national celebrations held amid a still expanding slave system. Frederick Douglass made the point clearly in Poughkeepsie, New York, in 1858, in his address commemorating West Indian emancipation. "This celebration comes opportunely," Douglass told his racially mixed audience, "just after your National Anniversary." Douglass sharply distanced himself from the bombastic July 4th rhetoric and excoriated the majority of white Americans who could applaud both their democratic rights and their slave system. But the source of his critique of American society remained grounded in a vision of the possibilities of that same society. The celebration of August 1, Douglass continued to his Poughkeepsie audience, "takes up the principles of the American Revolution, where you drop them. . . . American Slavery . . . has seduced and bribed American orators into the most shameless contraction, mutilation and falsification of the Revolutionary principles of American Freedom and Independence. . . . [in limiting their application] to one race, to one complexion, to one type of features, to one variety of men." These beliefs, "these cardinal rights," Douglass stressed, must be secured "to the weakest and humblest of the American people.[12]

Freedom festivals thus transmitted a dual vision, of being both black and American, and did so across generations. From the earliest celebrations in the 1830s, which reflected the themes of the black convention movement, to the August 1 celebrations of the 1850s and 1860s, the specific agenda evolved to meet changed circumstances. Yet certain elements endured. The religious foundation of black political activity persisted; the commitment to moral and temperate behavior continued; and the movement remained largely, but not solely, led by men. Most important, these occasions always reaffirmed the conviction that slavery would end and foretold a time when all black people would enjoy their full rights. The very act of organizing to proclaim these rights made visible to

other blacks the network of moral and political activists that crisscrossed Philadelphia and other black urban centers during these
years.[13]

The results of this activism were evident throughout the antebellum years. After they were formally denied the right to vote
after 1838, blacks in Philadelphia and throughout the state sent
numerous protest memorials to the legislature. Although they
were ignored by white officials, the very act of organizing the petition meetings encouraged the growth of that network of activists.[14] A similar process marked black demands for equal
education. Despite early attainment of free public education for
whites, Philadelphia's black children were either denied access to
public schools or shunted off into underfunded segregated
schools.[15] Rebuffed in their demands for equal treatment but intent on educating their children, these politically active black
adults created private, usually church-related, schools. Although
enrollments remained small (numbering only 330 in 1854), students were able to study in a sympathetic atmosphere in which the
principals and the teachers were also black. The establishment of
these schools did not prevent students from demanding their civil
right to an equal education at public expense. When Governor
James Pollack paid a ceremonial visit to the Institute for Colored
Youth in May 1855, the young Jacob C. White, Jr., welcomed the
governor and reminded him that "though not recognized in the
political arrangements of the commonwealth we are nevertheless
preparing ourselves usefully for a future day when citizenship in
our country will be based on manhood and not on color."[16]

The question of placing black teachers within the public school
system proved controversial within black Philadelphia. Some
leading blacks opposed the demand for race-based teacher ap-
pointments in the city's segregated public schools. This angered
David B. Bowser, among others, who thought that since entrenched segregationist attitudes among whites would guarantee
inferior separate schools for black youth well into the future, such
a position was "disgraceful."[17] Webber never commented on this
dispute. Perhaps the death of his son, as he approached school
age, made the issue too painful for him to consider. Nor did Webber comment on the policy of segregation on the city's new streetcar system in the late 1850s, although he frequently noted the

inception of a new run.[18] In 1859, however, Webber did directly address the denial of black civil rights in an area that, as an Odd Fellow who regularly used the city streets in full regalia with his fellows, particularly affected his world.

On August 16 the Johnson Guards, a paramilitary organization named after the black orchestra leader who had introduced "Concerts à la Musand" to Philadelphia, paraded through the streets in celebration of their founding. Numbering more than fifty men, the guards turned out in full military style, each dressed in a blue frock coat with "shoulder knots," white pants, a cap with a pompom, and bedecked with infantry ornaments, various belts, and cartridge boxes. To the accompaniment of resounding martial music, each man carried over his shoulder, as the parade wound its way through the downtown section of the city, a United States Army musket. Webber applauded the guards and thought the procession "a grand parade. . . . It was witness by several hundred person includeing 2 or 300 white=" He followed the march to Masonic Hall, where he pronounced the speeches "very interesting." The next day's *Public Ledger* agreed that a large crowd of black men and women had gathered at the hall, and that many whites watched as well, "curious" at the sight of armed black men in public assembly. Beyond this, the reactions of the paper and the porter widely diverged.

The *Public Ledger,* while praising the military demeanor of the Johnson Guards and their leader, Captain Henry Grepper, nonetheless reminded Philadelphians that state law required that none but "able-bodied white male citizens shall be liable to do military duty" and asked: "Under what law do our colored military friends organize themselves into a military company? Where do they procure their arms, and who commissions the officers?" Webber's anger was palpable. The paper, he wrote, "says= *The state Law says that white men shall have military companies and carry the United States muskets: & care for the implements of war=* We might know that somebody would have something to say= or find a Law aginst the colered mans progress="[19] To assert the right to march in public procession—bearing on one's shoulders the preeminent symbol of manliness recognized—and then to face criticism for conduct unbecoming mere colored men, infuriated this proud man, who regularly used the city's streets in uniformed, collective fashion with other black men.

These attitudes, coupled with the denial of civil rights and the persistent, individual acts of racial violence that still peppered their daily lives, led some black Philadelphians to explore emigration to Haiti. Jacob C. White, Jr., the Philadelphia agent for the *Anglo-African,* a magazine supportive of immigration, discussed this with friends. Never intended to be a popular movement, this migration, as William Parkham, a friend and former Philadelphian, wrote White in 1861, was envisioned as an "individual emigration. Emigration of men of mind, of men of means." Very few black Philadelphians considered this possibility. Practical financial difficulties proved insurmountable for many, and negotiations with the Haitian government over inducements for the potential emigrants faltered. For many black Americans, emigration sentiment peaked when racial antagonism was most intense. In contrast, when hope, however fragile, budded, the expectation that whites might yet acknowledge that one could be both black and American reemerged.[20]

Emigration to Haiti did not interest Amos Webber. The burden of his commitments rooted him profoundly in an American cultural context that made emigration unattractive no matter how severe the racism. In the language of the freedom festivals, a language of injustice recognized, democratic rights proclaimed, and God's blessing acknowledged, Webber found the words that enabled him to envision an America that could recognize and accept his presence as a man and a citizen. His continued activism during 1859 and 1860 would test and reveal the depth of his commitment to racial justice on his own native soil.

ON APRIL 2, 1859, agents for a Virginia slave owner procured federal warrants under the Fugitive Slave Act for the arrest of Daniel Dangerfield, also known as Daniel Webster, then residing in Harrisburg. They arrested Dangerfield and, as the following day was a Sunday, scheduled Dangerfield's arraignment for Monday, April 4, in Philadelphia. A large crowd filled the courtroom, the Philadelphia *Public Ledger* reported, including "prominent members of the Abolition Society, male and female." An even larger crowd swelled the streets in front of the courthouse, publicly debating "the fugitive slave law, the propriety of the officers making the arrest, and the probable result of the case." Inside the courtroom, into which were crammed more than 300 people each day during the three-day trial, three black men testified that Dangerfield could not be a runaway because they had known him as a free man in both Harrisburg and Baltimore. When the charges were dismissed on April 6, the crowd, "composed mainly of colored persons," jubilantly surrounded Dangerfield, placed him in a carriage, and drove him through the downtown area. At one point the celebrants removed the horses from the carriage, "and a long rope being procured, as many as could get hold of it did so, and Dangerfield, in company of several other colored men in the carriage was drawn along . . . past the Court-house, followed by a great crowd of colored people." This was the event, as recorded in some detail, by one of the city's leading newspapers.[21]

Amos Webber also commented on these events in his chronicle. "[S]ome slave hunters from Virginia . . . on the hunt for one Daniel darefield= or Webster," he acknowledged, instigated the "great excitement in the city" on April 2. After obtaining the warrant from the United States marshal, they left for Harrisburg, where "they found Daniel attending market" and arrested him on the false charge that "he had been Robbing." "The news soon flew to philadelphia Long enough=before they got there;=" Mrs. Lucretia Mott "and many other friends" secured legal counsel and,

> while the trial was going on the inside = hundreds of person was on the outside. discussing the merits of the fugitive slave Law = and if they expressed their opinion to Loud. they where arrested by one of the 300 police put their for that purpose. A man named J. Purnell {Colord} took 12 policemen to put that man in the prison vault 5*th* & Chestnut *st* when the trial of Purnell. heard. the policemen where all in fault = The multitude of people that was standing about the Court house was doing nobody any harm But however on the 6*inst* Daniel was discharged *and shipped in the under ground R. Road to Canada.*

But before Dangerfield left for Canada, the crowd joyously celebrated his release from custody at "5½ O'clock" on April 6. As Webber remembered:

Great rejoicing with the people. = gets Daniel in carriage= = =
takes out the horses=attaches a rope=and 200 or 300 person=
of all colors = pulls Daniel over the city the crowd in rejoice-
ing=torn the clothes of him = each takeing a piece of his garment
= then bought him a new suit. then sent him to Canada.[22]

Webber's account differed from the *Public Ledger*'s in signifi-
cant ways. First, he emphasized the persistent problems con-
fronting free blacks in Philadelphia. Dangerfield's removal to
Philadelphia, intended to strip away the support of friends in
Harrisburg, recalled the kidnappings that had long plagued
Pennsylvania blacks. Tensions remained high in Philadelphia, as
Webber suggested: Dangerfield did not simply return home following his release, as implied in the newspaper account; rather,
Webber twice stated that Dangerfield's ultimate destination was
the haven of Canada. Second, Webber's description of the dem-
onstrators differed from that published in the *Public Ledger*.
Where the newspaper noted white supporters present in the
courtroom but conspicuously absent from the rowdier street
demonstrations during and following the trial (an account that
conforms to the official abolitionist history as well[23]), Webber
emphasized that there were people "of all colors" in the throng
that day. His own close involvement with whites at work made
him sensitive to the numerous racial currents within the white
community, and he may have understood this involvement,
minor as it was, relative to the entire white population, as welcome support and a hopeful omen.

Most important, Webber's version recognized the critical importance of the Underground Railroad for northern urban
blacks. "The news soon flew" from Harrisburg on April 2 and
mobilized activists such as himself; that same network immediately spirited Dangerfield to safety upon his release. Black men
and women crowded the Philadelphia courtroom for Dangerfield, and probably for Purnell as well, and they commanded the
streets in a joyous celebration that also achieved a more serious
purpose. Although Webber did not give the specifics, other accounts suggest that following the celebration in the streets John
Lewton, a black chimney sweep living in Paschall's Alley, nearly
a mile north of Chestnut Street, sheltered Dangerfield. The next

Harper's Weekly, March 31, 1877. Black "street politicans" in Philadelphia, who, the original caption suggested, "find their counterpart in
every large city." As black workingmen "are generally readers of newspapers, their views are often intelligent, and their arguments right to
the point." *Courtesy of the Library Company of Philadelphia*

day the family of Norwood P. Hallowell, soon to be a white officer of the black 55th Massachusetts Infantry in the Civil War, took Dangerfield from their country residence north of the city to the next station on the road to Canada. To recognize this intricate structure of the Underground Railroad within black and, to a lesser degree, white Philadelphia was to acknowledge the political organization of a significant segment of that community of which Webber was a part. It was a pattern that the *Public Ledger* failed to see or refused to acknowledge.[24]

The defense and rescue of Jane Johnson, Daniel Dangerfield, or Moses Horner in March 1860—when a large group of black Philadelphians attacked the police escorting Horner to jail following his conviction as a fugitive and spirited him out of the city—transformed the self-perceptions of the men and women who participated. The porter James Martin, for example, followed his role in the rescue of Jane Johnson and her children the next year by bringing suit against the local white alderman for "corruptly and maliciously demanding of him excessive bail" and for conspiring to oppress and mistreat him. Martin lost his suit, but he did not lose his dignity.[25] For men such as James Martin or Amos Webber, this evolving definition of themselves as public activists occurred within a collective context. In the crowds in the courtrooms they discovered like-minded individuals, many of whom they recognized from other voluntary organizations—religious, fraternal, literary—in black Philadelphia. This complex social structure provided many such as Webber with the foundation needed to engage the critical political issues of their world.[26]

———

SOME MONTHS FOLLOWING THE DANGERFIELD TRIAL, Webber left Hart, Montgomery without a detailed explanation. On Saturday, October 1, 1859, he wrote in his veiled style: "A.W. = started for Canada". Eleven days later, in an equally circumspect entry, "A.W. arrived from Canada Last night". There is no evidence that he ever went to Canada on either Hart, Montgomery or Odd Fellows business; his position in either organization would not make that possibility likely. Given his activism, there was only one context that would explain this trip: Amos Webber either escorted fugitives to Canada or he traveled there on some

mission for the Vigilant Committee, perhaps carrying information to Canada's black abolitionists. Webber left no itinerary of
his trip, nor did he discuss his Canadian stopovers. It is likely,
however, that he visited what was then known as Canada West,
that segment of Ontario near the American border and home to
Canada's growing population of American former slaves. From
Philadelphia, Webber's route may have veered westerly, through
Rochester to Buffalo, New York, or Detroit, Michigan. More
likely he traveled northeast, to New York City, and from there
to Canada by way of Massachusetts and Vermont, either by train
north through the Connecticut River valley or by boat to Boston,
and then west by train through Worcester, Massachusetts, and
north to Vermont. Webber thought the trip important enough to
record, though his elusiveness in this case is quite understandable—his activity was a sensitive one and his chronicle was probably kept in a semipublic space at work. It was not surprising
that, in this instance particularly, Webber remained an observer
keenly aware of the possibility of being observed himself.[27]

Although Webber was by no means as well known even among
blacks as William Still, David B. Bowser, or J. J. G. Bias, his trip
and the antislavery activities that preceded it placed him at the
center of the black abolitionist movement in Philadelphia. His fellow activists provided the context in which Amos Webber redis-
covered as an adult that quality of singular yet typical courage he
first witnessed as a youth in Attleborough.

Five days following his return from Canada, the most dramatic
antislavery act since Nat Turner's 1831 rebellion threatened to
overthrow slavery in Southampton County, Virginia, electrified
Amos Webber and, indeed, the entire country, North and South,
white and black. "It appears on the Evening of the 16th (October
1859)," he began the following day under the title "Harper Ferry
insurrection," that "John Brown and his associates, Viz. Green,
Copeland, Coppie & Cook = making the number about 19, John
Brown being Leader, = For the purpose of raising an insurrection, so as to free the Slaves:". A page-long account followed,
much of it written following the trials and convictions of Brown
and his men that November. Webber thought that Brown, whose
plan to arm rebellious slaves with weapons taken from the federal armory at Harpers Ferry was defeated by United States

troops under the command of Robert E. Lee, had prepared well but lacked the numbers needed to succeed. Sadly recording the execution dates, Webber briefly discussed the "great excitement in Virginia" over this event, as "Governor Wise had his nerves, put upto Blood heat, by false reports" of further insurrections.[28]

Webber was by no means unique in underscoring the significance of the actions of John Brown and his men. From Richmond, Governor Henry Wise decried the northern sympathy for Brown as "so general, so fanatical, so regardless of social safety, & so irreverent of the reign of law" that the very existence of these sentiments "demands his execution, if sentenced by the Courts." Throughout the North, blacks held prayer meetings during November to simultaneously pray for, and protest the sentence of, John Brown. A week before the December 2 execution, a group of black women in New York City wrote John Brown's wife, Mary, of their intention "by God's help—to organize in every Free State, and in every colored church, a band of sisters, to collect our weekly pence, and pour it lovingly into your lap." On the night of December 2, sorrowful protest meetings were held throughout the North. The Anti-Slavery and Temperance Society of Colored Citizens in Worcester, Massachusetts, passed resolutions asserting that in Brown's execution black people suffered a blow to their freedom and specifically recorded their sympathy for the families "of those colored patriots who so nobly sacrificed their lives on the altar of Freedom."[29]

Philadelphia held two meetings on December 2, both beginning about 11:00 A.M. so as to coincide with Brown's scheduled execution. One, held at National Hall, on Market and Twelfth Streets, was addressed by a number of prominent abolitionists, including Lucretia Mott, Robert Purvis, and Theodore Tilton. It was repeatedly interrupted by a large group of anti-Brown, if not pro-southern, Philadelphians, who consistently cheered Governor Wise, the state of Virginia, and the United States government as it then was constituted. The other meeting was quite different.

At the black Shiloh Baptist Church, adjacent to Lebanon Cemetery, more than 400 John Brown supporters, estimated by one reporter as perhaps two-thirds women with fewer than 20 who were white, gathered. Following an opening prayer by a white minister, who read from the 58th chapter of the prophet Isaiah, with its imperative for the chosen people "to loose the bonds of wickedness, to cut off the bands of treachery, to let the oppressed go free, and to break every yoke," a series of local black ministers addressed the meeting. The Reverend Jonathan C. Gibbs prayed for John Brown and then delivered a stirring protest against the treatment of blacks, North and South, in America. The Reverend Jesse F. Boulden prayed for John Brown and then excoriated the "legislative, the executive, and the judicial power of government" for their systematic discrimination. The Reverend Jeremiah Asher prayed for John Brown and then sharply criticized the officers of the Bethel A.M.E. Church, who had refused their building for this meeting, concerned over the possible white retaliation against their ministers in the South. Reverend Asher also attacked a tendency he thought prevalent, especially among the local black clergy, of truckling to whites, and his comments generated shouts of support and enthusiasm.

The participants then debated whether only blacks in attendance should contribute to the collection for Brown's family. After some discussion, the meeting decided to allow all present, white or black, to donate. Later that evening, the church filled again with another prayer and protest meeting. Two days later, "M' Browns body pass=" through Philadelphia. Webber, along with a large number of black supporters, crowded the train depot to pay homage to this martyr for freedom.[30]

Black Philadelphians did not forget their obligations to the Brown family the following year. Some sixty black men and women, leaders and activists in a host of religious, fraternal, and cultural associations, sponsored a "Complimentary Concert" for Mary L. Brown. Elizabeth Greenfield led the evening's entertainment. The concert both aided the Brown family and publicly reaffirmed the importance of John Brown's act in the collective memory of black Philadelphia.[31]

For Webber, these events excited thoughts that demanded further attention. Brown was "the great man [who] was to swing, to pay the penalty of the Law, of Virginia". In consequence of Brown's stature, Webber sharply noted, the whole state "was astir from center to circumperance"; and the military escort ordered by the governor further belied the charge that Brown was but a criminal. "The soilders fife was heard, to play the mournful sound the drum with its solmn taps, gave Virginia to understand that it took

3000 soilders to execute one man; Governor Wise, stood appalld, to think that he had honored Mr. Brown, with an escort of so many soilders= forgetting the several thousand dollars worth of expenses to the state." Once Brown's "firm step & undaunted heart" led him atop the scaffold, Webber envisioned Brown "looking around: . . . He saw nothing but soilders (3000) no citizens stood near him; He had nothing to say; at 11¼ O'clock he paid the penalty of Virginia".

The juxtaposition of Brown as the "great man" and the "appalld" governor whose fears betrayed him into honoring one whom he wanted to brand a common criminal pleased Webber. In repeating that Brown paid the penalty of Virginia, Webber implied the existence of higher moral laws, whose application would have placed a different defendant on trial.

More directly, Webber discussed the political meaning for the nation of Brown's execution. The mass meetings throughout the North, especially in the black community, profoundly disturbed the South, he argued, and led to widespread southern cries for the "Dissolution of the Union." This, in turn, elicited a northern effort to soothe the South. Here Webber entered into an elaborate familial analogy, with the South depicted as a crying baby and northern sympathizers as the nurse. When the baby cries, it does so knowing that the nurse has "sugar candies for it"; but if the candies were all gone, if the decades of compromise had proved inadequate, only two alternatives remained: either the North "must do something to reconcile the south, or the Union will be split into (splinters:)". Webber thought northern whites favored even further compromise: "we," he wrote, assuming a white persona, "must give the baby to the mother So the child can have some titty; i.e.: their must be Union meetings call to show to the south, that their where no sympathsirs for Brow. But only for the south &&& That is about the synopsis of the matter, but the baby still cries; Secede from the Union."[32] White Americans, he thought, used blacks as a scapegoat for national problems: "Still they cry the Negro race is the cause of the irresistible conflicts; the color may be so, but the man, himself is not the cause, but politicans is the cause Viz; the administration democrats wishes to extend Slavery. . . . Likewise the american does not wish slavery extended, This is the conflict."

In this shorthand summary of a decade of heated political debate and even armed conflict in Kansas and elsewhere, Webber
left much unclear, but his central theme was unambiguous. Slavery and race—and therefore he and his fellow black Americans—
were at the center of this national conflict. Appeals to the mother
lode of national union, however nourishing in other contexts,
would not be successful here unless white Americans redefined
their very conception of the national family. With that in mind,
Webber concluded his discussion of John Brown with a wry comment on the relatively few whites who sought precisely that redef-
inition: "The abolishist," he noted, "are creating a sensation in the
family."[33]

AMOS WEBBER, like Frederick Douglass and many other black
abolitionists, embraced the language of democracy even as he
worked to transform his experience of it. These activists were not
socially homogeneous. The group included such well-known
elites as Robert Purvis, Jacob White, father and son, and James
Forten, men whose economic standing placed them in the very top
echelon of black society. Others were less well off, but neither
racial prejudice nor their soporific poverty paralyzed them in the
face of calls for action.

Webber, however, belonged to yet another critical sector of black
Philadelphia. Counted neither among the elite nor among the majority who were desperately poor, he represented a segment of
black Philadelphia that, as workingmen and -women, often with
relatively secure, if low-paying jobs, provided the bulk of the
membership and some of the minor leaders for the religious, fraternal, and political networks. Although working-class by every
economic criteria, they were functionally more akin to the emerging white middle class in their concern for social order and personal rectitude. But their passion for racial justice transcended the
narrow individualism often associated with middle-class values,
since for these men and women, public and private life were not
isolated and separated.

The diverse social composition of these networks had certain
consequences for a man like Amos Webber. Among the more

than 20,000 black Philadelphians in 1860 there were more than enough men from elite families to assume the dominant leadership positions in most of the city's numerous black organizations. Webber, and others in his circumstances, had neither the financial security nor the familial connections to assume such positions. A few fugitive slaves who arrived before 1840, such as Stephen Smith and J. J. G. Bias, were able to enter this elite cohort, but they were clearly exceptions. The presence of this small but powerful leadership group meant that in Philadelphia there were distinct limits to the public stature a man like Webber might attain.

In other ways as well, Webber's role was circumscribed. As a relatively young man from a family lacking in social standing, Webber may not even have thought of himself as a potential leader. There is no evidence that he was ever a lodge officer or a church deacon during the 1850s. His role of church organist, while important, turned out to be short-lived and in no real way involved his directing group policy. Webber may have been an activist—indeed, an important one—but he was not yet a leader. Aspects of his personality still remained submerged, blocked by the presence of a well-established black elite and, perhaps, underdeveloped in the absence of a major personal and public challenge that might draw them forth.

That challenge would not be long in coming. Within a year after the close of Hart, Montgomery in September 1860, the Webbers moved to Worcester, Massachusetts. There they found a small black community, constituting slightly more than 1 percent of Philadelphia's total black population. A small elite did exist, but its members could be counted on one hand and its presence could not forestall the rise of other talented men into leadership positions. In Worcester, and with the coming of the Civil War, Amos Webber would discover within himself previously unfathomed leadership abilities, and he developed from one activist among many in the crowd into a leader within his northern black world.

PART TWO

THE WAR FOR FREEDOM: 1861–1876

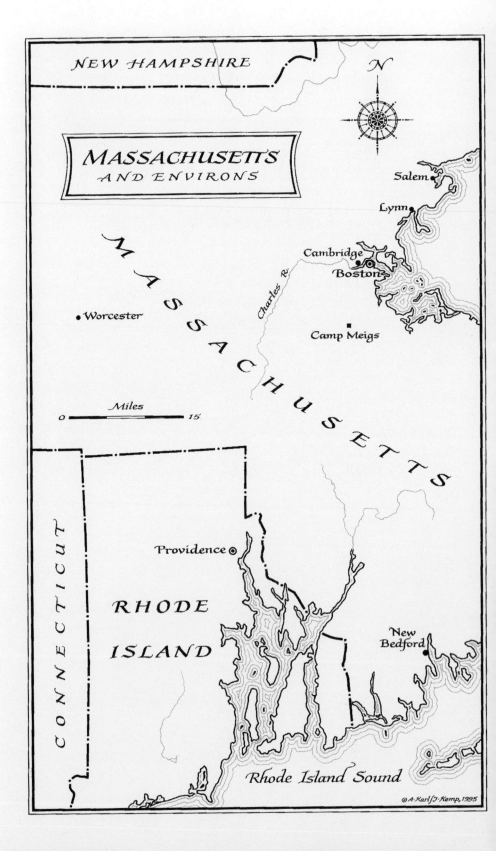

NEW HAMPSHIRE

MASSACHUSETTS
AND ENVIRONS

N

Salem

Lynn

Cambridge

Boston

Charles R.

Worcester

Camp Meigs

MASSACHUSETTS

Miles

0   15

Providence

RHODE

ISLAND

CONNECTICUT

New
Bedford

Rhode Island Sound

© A·Karl/J·Kemp, 1995

CHAPTER FIVE

THE SPARK OF MANHOOD

AMOS WEBBER NEVER recorded his reasons for leaving Philadelphia. The bankruptcy of Hart, Montgomery and Company was undoubtedly a catalyst, but by itself was not enough to pry him away. Perhaps Webber's Canadian trip in 1859, during which he most likely visited Worcester or met Worcester abolitionists, inspired the move. Furthermore, in the aftermath of their son's death in 1858, the Webbers may have welcomed such a move to avoid constant reminders of their loss. Since Webber kept no chronicle between the conclusion of the first volume in October 1860 and the start of a second volume a decade later, however, his motivation forever remains a puzzle.

IN CONTRAST TO PHILADELPHIA, a commercial and manufacturing metropolis with more than 565,000 residents in 1860, Worcester, with fewer than 25,000 inhabitants, represented a dramatic change for the Webbers. The central Massachusetts community was neither a port city nor a commercial center, and in many ways it remained a satellite of Boston, the capital of the state and the commercial heart of the New England region. In the 1860s Boston and the communities within a twenty-five-mile radius contained more than half the state's population and almost 70 percent of its real and personal property. Yet Worcester, another fifteen miles beyond that radius, which grew with less intensity and at a slower pace than either Boston or Philadelphia, was by no means a backwater. During the 1850s, as manufacturing replaced agriculture as the dominant occupation of the residents, the city reported growing concentrations in textiles, wire production, machine shops, and boot and shoe manufacturing. By 1865 a quarter of the city's residents were immigrants, the majority of whom filled the new jobs created by an expanding industrial economy. Although Worcester never quite matched its boosters' expectations that the city would become "the heart of the Commonwealth," it possessed a vibrant, expanding economy that created wealth and jobs throughout the last third of the nineteenth century.[1]

Worcester's nonwhite population increased by 80 percent between 1840 and 1860, while the white population grew by more than 230 percent, making Worcester's 272 black residents only 1 percent of the city's population in 1860. This overwhelming minority status reflected conditions throughout Worcester County and the entire state. Only once during the nineteenth century did blacks constitute as much as 1.5 percent of the state's population, and that was in 1800, prior to the transformation of the agricultural Commonwealth. Industrial, immigrant Massachusetts, before and after the Civil War, remained largely white.[2]

The Webbers arrived in Worcester too late to be included in the 1861 edition of the city directory, but the 1862 directory listed Amos Webber as employed at the Grove Street wire mill of Ichabod Washburn and Company, one of Worcester's many energetic and expanding industrial firms. The directory also noted that the Webbers rented rooms at 7 Liberty Street, a small artery in northeast Worcester which ran one and one-half city blocks between Belmont and Arch Streets in the city's Second Ward. The Webbers' initial choices proved to have lasting importance for their life in Worcester. With the exception of two years in the mid-1860s, Amos Webber remained employed at the wire mill until his retirement more than thirty years later. Similarly, with the same exception, the Webbers resided in the same immediate neighborhood, on the same short block, at but three different addresses from the one they first occupied in 1862, over the next forty-two years. By disposition, Amos and Lizzie Webber favored a life with established structures and strictures. In ways quite different from their experience, the Webbers were able to root themselves, quickly and deeply, in their new environment.[3]

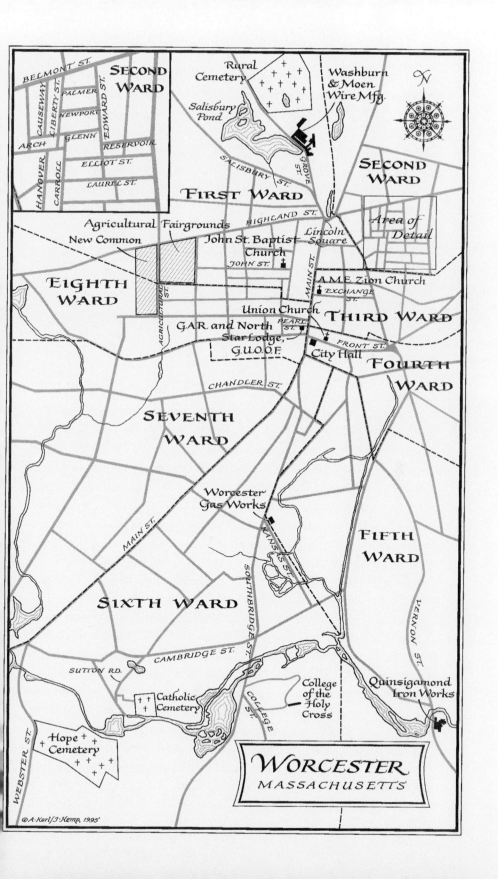

SECOND WARD

BELMONT ST.
CAUSEWAY
LIBERTY ST.
PALMER
NEWPORT
EDWARD ST.
ARCH
HANOVER ST.
GLENN
CARROLL
RESERVOIR.
ELLIOT ST.
LAUREL ST.

Rural Cemetery

Washburn & Moen Wire Mfg.

Salisbury Pond

N

SALISBURY ST.

GROVE ST.

SECOND WARD

FIRST WARD

HIGHLAND ST.

Area of Detail

Agricultural Fairgrounds
New Common

John St. Baptist Church

JOHN ST.

Lincoln Square

MAIN ST.

EIGHTH WARD

AGRICULTURAL ST.

A.M.E. Zion Church

EXCHANGE ST.

Union Church

THIRD WARD

G.A.R. and North Star Lodge, G.U.O.F.

PEARL ST.

FRONT ST.

City Hall

FOURTH WARD

CHANDLER ST.

SEVENTH WARD

MAIN ST.

Worcester Gas Works

KANSAS ST.

FIFTH WARD

SIXTH WARD

SOUTHBRIDGE ST.

CAMBRIDGE ST.

SUTTON RD.

VERNON ST.

Catholic Cemetery

COLLEGE ST.

College of the Holy Cross

Quinsigamond Iron Works

WEBSTER ST.

Hope Cemetery

WORCESTER
MASSACHUSETTS

© A. Karl / J. Kemp, 1995

The density of Worcester's black residents did not differ significantly from their numbers in other small northern cities in 1860. Chicago had 955 Negroes, in a population of almost 110,000; fewer than 800 resided in Cleveland, while Albany and Hartford had even fewer. Within Massachusetts a similar pattern prevailed. Boston contained 2,261 blacks, slightly over 1 percent of the city's 177,840 people. Among communities more comparable in size to Worcester in 1860, Salem had 378 blacks; Cambridge, 354; Lynn, 226; Roxbury, 60; and Lowell, but 41. Only New Bedford, a seaport town and a haven for escaped slaves throughout the period, sharply broke this pattern, with 1,515 blacks in a total population smaller than Worcester's. In part, these numbers reflected slavery's power to prevent all but a trickle of southern blacks from migrating northward. The intense racial violence of the two previous decades in the North had also had an effect, as some northern blacks migrated to rural areas or to Canada to escape such conditions.

There was an internal factor that influenced the size of the northern black community. Between 1850 and 1870 the fertility rate for all black women in the United States, slave and free, declined. For Worcester the evidence is somewhat limited but indicates that between 1860 and 1865 the birthrate in the city's black community was a third below the already declining national figure. The Webbers themselves reflected this trend. Following the birth of her son in 1853, Lizzie Webber, then aged twenty-four, never had another child. Although Worcester's black population grew by 8 percent between 1860 and 1865, to 295 people, it continued to shrink relative to the number of white residents, which grew by 20 percent, largely because of immigration.[4]

Black Worcester thus lacked the necessary numbers to influence the city's restructured political coalitions, yet the black community was not simply dependent upon or necessarily subservient to white patronage. When the white majority suggested, at an interchurch revival meeting in August 1861, that a prayer for Jefferson Davis, the president of the Confederacy, was in order, one black Worcesterite took heated exception, expressing "astonishment that the name should be mentioned in such a connection, adding that, for his part, he should pray *for all the devils in torment* before he remembered Jeff Davis."[5] Thus, when Amos Webber arrived

THE SPARK OF MANHOOD

in Worcester, he discovered a black presence that, despite its size, was quite self-conscious of its goals and traditions.

In contrast with Philadelphia's rich, competitive profusion of organizations and community institutions, black collective life in Worcester appeared rather thin. In 1860 there was only one black church, the A.M.E. Zion congregation, which had been organized in 1846 and met at the church building on Exchange Street, near the downtown business district. That church, in turn, sponsored the only black political group, the Anti-Slavery and Temperance Society of Colored Citizens. Worcester contained no black fraternal lodges or literary organizations, and a vibrant, black public culture such as Philadelphia's did not exist.[6]

Worcester also differed politically from Philadelphia. By the time the Webbers had established their residence in the Massachusetts community, Republican Party stalwarts, some of whom were staunch abolitionists, dominated both city and state politics. Abraham Lincoln and John Albion Andrew, the abolitionist Republican candidate for governor, both carried Worcester by decisive margins in 1860. Andrew repeated the feat in 1862, and many of the city's mayors between 1859 and 1870 were also Republican. In addition, industrial leaders such as Philip L. Moen and William E. Rice were abolitionist sympathizers and local Republican Party activists. Moen, the son-in-law of Ichabod Washburn and an officer in the wire mill, was a successful Republican Party candidate for Common Council from the city's Second Ward in 1862. Most important, in Worcester as throughout the Commonwealth, black men such as Amos Webber could vote, although all voters had to pay a poll tax. In fact, Amos Webber's first vote may have been for Moen, a fellow abolitionist who was also his employer. At first glance, then, the city seemed free of the dominating influence of Philadelphia's *dem*agogues, whom Webber had satirized some years earlier.[7]

For all these differences, however, aspects of Webber's life in Worcester appeared quite familiar. He was once again one of a handful of black employees in a largely white firm. Philip L. Moen, moreover, was not unlike elite whites Webber had encountered in Philadelphia, especially Charles Wurts. The son of upstate New York farmers and a clerk in a hardware store before his marriage to Eliza Washburn, whose father, Ichabod, made him a

partner in 1850, Moen practiced stern personal and public morality. Described as an "orthodox" Congregationalist, Moen rooted
his moral vision in a stark individualism with its origins in Calvinism's perpetual penitent prostrate before an all-powerful deity.
Yet Moen gloried in the success of individuals since—paradoxi-
cally, given the individual's essential powerlessness before his
God—temporal achievement in itself suggested a divine benedic-
tion. The unavoidable corollary, which Charles Wurts would have
agreed with, was that failure reflected a moral inadequacy in the
individual that could not be remedied by lavish public or private
charity. Moen never commented on the spiritual significance of
his own well-placed marriage. His abolitionist principles flowed
from this same moral vision. Slavery was both a moral stain on the
nation's soul and an artificial barrier blocking black achievement
and the development of the moral qualities associated with success.[8]

Although the attitudes of his new employers were familiar to
Webber, the industrial plant they dominated was less so. Ichabod
Washburn established his firm, which manufactured metal rods,
screws, and wire for hoop skirts and pianos, in 1831 with 13 employees. By 1860 the firm employed 120 workers, who produced
more than three tons of wire and as much as six tons of other
metal products daily.[9] Webber's work in this industrial setting
differed sharply from his duties at Hart, Montgomery. In that
smaller commercial firm, Webber had interacted with a largely
native-born, white-collar workforce, and the firm's partners occupied offices adjacent to his work area. At Washburn and Moen, a
far more hierarchical industrial organization sharply delineated
the social boundaries separating front-office executives, the growing sales force, and the complex governance of production work
itself.

The production force consisted of a polyglot mix of working
people. Native-born and Irish immigrant workers predominated
in 1862, with Swedes and especially French-Canadian workers
growing in numbers over the decade. Together they streamed into
the plant each morning, to work cheek by jowl for eleven hours or
more; and they brought with them distinct perceptions of one another's ethnic and racial identities. Yet little evidence remains of
overt racial conflict at the firm for these years. Each of the firm's

three plants in the city had its own supervisor, who in turn had assistants overseeing different divisions within the plant. Under
them, and in closest contact with the workforce, foremen ran the
various departments where production actually occurred. It was
in Henry C. Willson's noisy, hot, and at times dangerous tempering room that Webber was employed as a janitor. Philip Moen was
at some remove.[10]

Worcester itself did not run so cleanly. Racial violence and discrimination regularly intruded on the lives of the city's black residents. The local division of the Sons of Temperance, a national
organization, denied admittance to Julian B. McCrea, a black city
resident, because it would "make trouble in the division to bring a
nigger in." At times during these years whites randomly assaulted
blacks on city streets and in public spaces such as taverns and theaters. Still, Worcester was not antebellum Philadelphia or New
York. Although a quarter of Worcester's residents were foreign-
born—75 percent of them Irish—Worcester actually had a lower
percentage of immigrants in 1865 than many other Massachusetts
communities. This, in the context of an expanding economy and a
small, and therefore nonthreatening, black population, may have
muted racial hostility. In addition, Worcester's abolitionist sentiment remained strong enough to prevent overt racial animosity
from dominating public discussion, and, while small in number,
Worcester's black residents themselves played an important role
in establishing the nature of the public discussion that did occur.[11]

At the time the Webbers arrived in the city, there existed a rec-
ognizable black leadership group, which included Francis A.
Clough, Isaac Mason, Gilbert Walker, Alexander F. Hemenway,
and William Brown. Clough, Walker, and Hemenway were barbers, each with a significant white clientele; Mason was a janitor,
and Brown ran a carpet-making and upholstery business. Only
Brown was an economic success, his business prospering as a result of the patronage of elite white families. Walker, at the other
extreme, lost what economic standing he had with a series of ill-
fated horse-breeding investments. Mason and Walker had been
born slaves in Maryland; Brown and Clough were Massachusetts-
born; while Hemenway was a fourth-generation Worcester native.
In 1861, all had been in the city at least a decade, and ranged in age
from the young Hemenway (twenty-seven) to the more mature

Walker (forty-three) and Clough (forty-five), with Brown and Mason, at thirty-eight and thirty-nine, respectively, quite close in age to the thirty-five-year-old Webber. Each in his way had been quite active in the political issues of the 1850s. All were involved to some degree in the work of the Anti-Slavery and Temperance Society, raising money, attending meetings and demonstrations in both Worcester and Boston, and ferrying fugitives farther north to Canada. William Brown had chaired black Worcester's memorial meeting for John Brown in December 1859. Clough was the first black to serve on a jury in the state, and Brown's family had been Free-Soil Party activists in Salem a decade earlier.

Perhaps most dramatic were the activities of Isaac Mason, who had fled his Maryland owner in 1846. In Philadelphia in 1850, Mason recognized his former master's son, bearing warrants for his arrest, as he passed the construction site where Mason worked carrying bricks. Mason "at once notified some of the leading colored men, in whom [he] had confidence," and they immediately sent him to Boston, armed only with a letter of introduction to Lewis Hayden, the black abolitionist. Mason stayed at Hayden's house for some three weeks and, when it proved difficult for him to secure employment, was sent to Worcester with an introduction to William Brown. Brown helped Mason find work and permanent lodging with Ebenezer Hemenway, Alexander's father. When slave catchers arrived in Worcester in 1851, Mason fled to Canada.

He returned to Worcester some years later and became active in the antislavery movement, but the prospect of black Americans' colonizing Haiti intrigued him. Attracted by "the possibility of soon becoming well-to-do there" and by the desire to discover "if there was anything in it or not for the good of the race," Mason paid his own expenses to Haiti in 1859. What he found there appalled him. The Haitian government had no money to aid immigration; the promised land was nonexistent; and sickness and poverty abounded. Returning to Worcester in August 1859, Mason publicly denounced emigration as "a premature graveyard for the race." Like other would-be exiles, he discovered in himself a sense of patriotism that he had not known existed before. A chance viewing of the American flag while he was in Haiti, after his experiences had deflated his expectations, led Mason to ac-

William Brown (1823–1892). A businessman and political and social activist, Brown worked closely with Webber for decades. Undated photograph, probably ca. 1880s. *Courtesy of American Antiquarian Society*

knowledge a new, powerful emotion: "Its grander was such that I felt a spirit of national pride for it, that I had never felt before." Amos Webber, if he traveled through Worcester when making his Canadian trip in 1859, undoubtedly met Isaac Mason, and a friendship, based in part on a mutual recognition of this dual American identity, began as soon as Webber settled in Worcester.[12]

Although less renowned than Worcester's leading white abolitionists, Abby Kelley Foster and Thomas Wentworth Higginson,

Isaac Mason (1822–1898). Born a slave in Maryland, Mason was Amos Webber's friend and fellow activist in Worcester for more than thirty years. *Courtesy of Division of Rare and Manuscript Collections, Carl A. Kroch Library, Cornell University*

or their black Boston contemporaries, Lewis Hayden and William C. Nell, Worcester's blacks were nonetheless quite politically active during the 1850s. When the State Supreme Court upheld the Boston School Committee's decision to create separate but equal schools in 1849, blacks in Worcester responded by joining with white abolitionists to abolish the African school, considered by many the last vestige of a segregated system, and integrating the relatively small number of black students into the public system. They also participated in a statewide petition drive, orchestrated by Boston's black leaders, to demand a legislative reversal of the court's opinion. When that reversal was achieved in 1855, Nell praised the efforts of black and white abolitionists but very particularly applauded the black women and children of the Commonwealth who had obtained the majority of the signatures.[13]

Such political commitment generated additional activity. One of the more dramatic occurred in October 1854, when a deputy United States marshal, Asa O. Butman, arrived in Worcester intent on apprehending fugitives. Well known to Worcester's activists, Butman had played a leading role in two famous fugitive cases in Boston, involving Anthony Burns and Thomas Sims. Now he came for William H. Jankins, a local barber who had escaped his Virginia master in 1842. Soon an angry crowd of blacks and whites gathered to confront the marshal, who made the mistake of appearing before the crowd brandishing his government-issue pistol—for which he was immediately arrested on charges of carrying a dangerous weapon! While Butman remained in custody, three black men, backed by an even larger crowd of blacks and whites, broke into the jail and proceeded to beat the marshal about the face and body. "The colored men especially," one account suggested, "were almost beside themselves in their desire to convince him that it was a dangerous mission upon which he had come to the city." Recognizing the seriousness of the crowd's anger, Thomas Wentworth Higginson, the abolitionist and future Civil War officer, and George Frisbie Hoar, a local judge and future United States senator, spirited Butman out of Worcester and on to Boston after extracting his promise never to return to the city.

In Worcester, the three black men who attacked the marshal— Alexander Hemenway, Solomon Dutton, and John Angier, Jr.— were widely acclaimed by blacks and some whites. William Jankins, who had actually been out of town at the time of the incident, returned to discover his vulnerability to other slave catchers. Shortly thereafter he purchased his freedom because, it was said, he "had too many [business] interests here and too much at stake" not to do so.[14]

What made this type of political involvement particularly noteworthy was that it occurred despite the absence of the complex web of institutional affiliations that, in black Philadelphia and Boston, provided an interlocking leadership cohort. This small urban community in 1860 consisted of fewer than fifty men and

Martha Brown (1821–1889). Churchwoman and social activist within Worcester's black community, she was married to William Brown. Undated photograph, probably ca. 1880s. *Courtesy of American Antiquarian Society*

about sixty women between the ages of twenty and fifty. Moreover, not all of these men and women were affiliated with the A.M.E. Zion Church, the one established black institution in the city. The Rhode Island–born Martha Brown worshiped with her husband, William, at the First Unitarian Church, where she was the only nonwhite member of the Ladies Benevolent Society. Bethany Veney, a former slave, joined the Park Street Methodist Church when she came to Worcester in 1858 and stayed a member, she later recalled, because she "was treated with such kind consideration by the brothers and sisters there that I was at home with them." In contrast with Boston, where the black Masonic lodges and diverse church congregations provided many of the leaders in the school desegregation case and for the local Committee of Vigilance, Worcester blacks developed leaders in a less structured fashion that allowed considerable opportunity for ambitious, self-confident newcomers.[15]

Worcester's representative to the New England Colored Citizens' Convention in Boston on August 1, 1859, suggested as much. Black representatives from towns throughout the region passed resolutions endorsing temperance and agricultural life for black urbanites and rejecting migration to Africa, while condemning that "deep-seated hostility [which] exists against our complexion." The leading delegates included such well-known northern blacks as the Reverends Amos G. Beman and John N. Gloucester, Lewis Hayden, William C. Nell, William Still, and William Wells Brown. But Worcester's delegate was J. J. Mobray, a bootmaker unknown beyond his own community.[16]

In their residential patterns Worcester's black residents also exhibited a considerable collective sense of self. Worcester contained no black neighborhood, but blacks were not therefore scattered randomly throughout the city. In the fifteen years following the Webbers' move to Worcester, black residential clusters became evident, a conscious response, it would seem, to the influx of foreign (especially Irish) immigrants to the city. Blacks were a distinct minority in all of Worcester's eight wards, but in 1860 the four wards with the lowest percentage of foreign-born (the First, Second, Seventh, and Eighth) accounted for 54 percent of all black residents. Five years later, that concentration increased to 59 percent; a decade later, with the greatly increased foreign-born population crowded into Wards Three through Six, 71 percent of Worcester's black community resided in the other four wards. Over these years Wards One and Two accounted for the overwhelming majority of the city's black residents. Yet the Second Ward's residents remained predominantly white and native-born, Protestant in their religion and Republican in their politics. Philip Moen was but one of numerous leading citizens with homes in the ward. When the Webbers rented their rooms at 7 Liberty Street in 1861, then in the middle of the Second Ward, they entered a predominantly white area even as they simultaneously moved into the heart of the city's black community. Isaac and Annie Mason, William Bostic and his family, and Gilbert Walker and his wife were among the black neighbors on Liberty Street who introduced them to the tangled worlds of blacks and whites in the city.[17]

Resilient and resourceful, Worcester's black community viewed the approaching civil war with a certain expectation. Their experiences in the previous decade had fostered a more self-conscious group identity and convinced many that, however painful the

coming cataclysm might be, it was the cleansing necessary to elim-
inate "the prejudice against our color" that was "the barrier to our
elevation" and the "crushing and blighting influence upon the
hopes and happiness of the rising generation."[18] In the process
new challenges and new leaders would emerge.

ON APRIL 12, 1861, at 4:30 A.M., Confederate forces under
Pierre Gustave T. Beauregard began their bombardment of the
Union garrison at Fort Sumter in Charleston harbor. The political maneuvering of the previous decades had finally run its
course, never able to circumvent the consequences of the South's
intractable demand to protect its "peculiar institution." Two days
later Federal forces under the command of Major Robert Anderson, a Kentuckian and former slave owner, surrendered, and the
Confederate stars and bars fluttered over captured Union terri-
tory for the first time. South Carolina, the first state to secede,
sparked a conflagration that would ultimately engulf the secessionists and their institution.

At first, there was little thought by either side of the blood that
would flow. The fall of Fort Sumter propelled those slave states
still in the Union to dissolve their ties within days. Joyous celebrations filled southern communities; in Virginia, in a move
fraught with symbolic meaning for a buoyant South, former Governor Henry Wise engineered the capture of the Harpers Ferry
armory, with its critical rifle-producing capability. Expectations
colored perceptions in the North as well, and many thought that
the Union would quickly vanquish its foe. Massive demonstrations occurred in many northern cities while volunteers filled up
regiments with lightning speed.[19]

In Worcester the fall of Sumter "caused a general and intense
excitement, in our generally quiet city," one anonymous diarist
wrote. "Nobody remembers such a time ever before." Newspapers could not print enough editions, so strong was the hunger for
the latest news from the South and for instructions on enlistments. Throughout Worcester, a diary entry for April 15 read, it
was "difficult to distinguish between the *republicans* and *democrats,*
so earnest were all in declaring that the authority of the federal

government must be preserved and maintained." This pitched excitement caused a group of doctors to offer free treatment to "the
families of those who have gone or may go"; while the normally
prudent directors of the City Bank of Worcester voted to guarantee a teller "his situation . . . till his return and to continue his
salary while absent." William H. Jankins and Gilbert Walker, two
of the city's black barbers, encouraged departing soldiers "to call
at their hairdressing saloons and get trimmed up, without charge,
before leaving." Philip L. Moen underscored this sense of mass
enthusiasm by publicly explaining that the patriotic demonstrations at the wire mill were the spontaneous expressions of the
workingmen, and not company-sponsored.

Even a year later, when returning casualties and battlefield re-
versals suggested a more bitter and protracted campaign, emotions in the city remained high. In July 1862, a number of
Worcester businesses, including Washburn and Moen (as Ichabod
Washburn and Company had been renamed), offered an additional bounty of $11—the city already offered $100—to all
enlistees and guaranteed them positions upon return. Charlotte
Forten, the granddaughter of Philadelphia's James Forten, who
spent almost two months in the city, witnessed the excitement and
interest "when day after day, in the streets of W.[orcester] we used
to see the indefatigable *Capt*. H.[igginson] drilling his white company." This ardor extended to women workers as well. Helen
Wheeler Smith, a vestmaker, left for South Carolina with the
United States Sanitation Commission to nurse the Union
wounded and aid the freed men and women. Her Worcester employer felt compelled to hire "a girl immediately," but promised
that Smith "should have a place in the shop when you come
back."[20]

This enthusiasm obscured profound differences among white
Americans over northern military policy and political goals.
Within a month after the fall of Fort Sumter, for example, the
Massachusetts legislature rejected petitions from black citizens
requesting the removal of the word "white" from the militia laws
and the creation of a black Home Guard. For some legislators the
desire to limit black participation in public life determined their
vote; but many who voted no were more pragmatic in their thinking. Alexander H. Bullock, the Republican representative from

Worcester and future governor of the state, stressed his support for black rights but insisted that the "firebrands" who urged passage would undermine the delicate negotiations even then under way to retain the border states within the Union.[21]

Similar strains appeared nationally as well. Early in the war, Ulysses S. Grant, then an unknown officer who had just reenlisted in the military following a depressing, alcohol-filled tour of duty in the 1850s, wrote his father of his intention "to whip the rebellion into submission" while "preserving all constitutional rights." Grant thought that "a war against slavery" might be necessary but condemned those who would incorporate abolition as a central war goal from the beginning "as great enemies to their country as if they were opened and avowed secessionists." A year later, writing from his campaign tent, Grant raised the central issue the Civil War placed before the nation. "I have no hobby of my own with regard to the Negro either to effect his freedom or to continue his bondage," he explained. Grant acknowledged that he used the fugitives then flooding the Union's lines as laborers, "thus saving soldiers to carry the musket"; but he remained doubtful of the role of freed blacks in the nation: "I don't know what's to become of these poor people in the end, but it weakens the enemy to take them from them."[22]

The tension inherent in these attitudes at times spilled over into racial violence, as some of Webber's Pennsylvania friends discovered. Union soldiers in Harrisburg, a friend wrote Jacob C. White, Jr., in 1862, "are at large in the city and their prejudice against '*the peculiar people*' is evidenced by the kicks and cuffs they administer to our poor sable brethren. It is dangerous for colored people to walk the street after night." Soon after receiving this letter, White described the atmosphere in Philadelphia to his friend Joseph C. Bustill: "Rumors of the *making up of the proscribed* in various parts of our city are prevalent and I have concluded that it is wise policy for Jacob to move around cautiously & go home early." While hostility toward blacks dominated the attitudes of many white residents, "the Irish women," White thought, became "incensed when they think that they are to be deprived of the companionship of their husbands while no such sad catastrophe is liable to befall the *Nagur* women. Times are indeed getting troublesome," White concluded, and he wondered whether this racial violence would finally compel him and other blacks "to seek refuge among the palms of Hayti."[23]

As happened throughout the North, Worcester's black residents kept themselves well informed on these issues. The local newspapers reported in detail the political and military news of the day, and carried numerous stories exploring the conditions of Negroes elsewhere. During the first years of the war, the Worcester *Daily Spy* reported on the violence against blacks in Brooklyn, Detroit, and Cincinnati. The same paper also reprinted at great length the resolutions of Queens, New York, blacks who met in the summer of 1862 to reject Lincoln's suggestion that freed men and women colonize Central America. Echoing Isaac Mason, they affirmed that they "love this land, and have contributed our share towards its prosperity and wealth," and they rejected Lincoln's proposal by affirming *their* national identity: "Nor can we fail to feel a strong attachment to the whites with whom our blood has been commingling from the earliest days of our country. Neither can we forget and disown our white kindred. This is the country of our choice being our father's country."

Black periodicals as well, perhaps especially Frederick Douglass's *North Star* and Thomas Hamilton's *Anglo-African,* played a role in forming black Worcester's attitudes, as did the occasional visits of such prominent blacks as Harriet Tubman and Douglass. The less famous spoke as well. William Davis, a recent fugitive who escaped during battle from his master, addressed the question of policy toward "contrabands," those former slaves now behind Union lines; while J. J. Mobray discussed "his views on national matters" in a public lecture in January 1862.[24]

Celebrations in Worcester also focused on issues raised by the war. Two other local barbers, Allen Walker and Edward Gimby, organized a freedom festival on August 1, 1862, to celebrate both West Indian and hoped-for American emancipation. Speakers included the Reverend Joseph G. Smith, pastor of the A.M.E. Zion Church, Reverend Lunsford Lane, a former fugitive then living in the Worcester area, and several white ministers as well. For thirty-eight cents the celebrants received transportation by omnibus to Davis Grove, a local park, a fish chowder dinner, and the opportunity to join in songs of freedom interspersed among the speeches and discussions. They returned home, the local paper reported, "cheered by the hope that they might soon enjoy another day in a similar manner, in commemoration of the greater emancipation which must take place in our own country." Following Lincoln's Emancipation Proclamation in January 1863, additional festivals took place on January 1 during the remaining war years. But as the proclamation did not grant freedom to slaves in those states under Federal control (such as Kentucky or Tennessee), yet more public celebrations were held when individual border states abolished slavery. Frances E. W. Harper, the black poetess and novelist, addressed one such gathering at A.M.E. Zion Church, and a gala festival, which lasted "into the small hours of the next morning," followed.[25]

The war also created avenues for more direct support of the Union cause. As a few contrabands arrived from the South, black Worcester assisted them in finding work and surviving the often painful transition between cultures that migration necessitated. Others volunteered as nurses and hospital stewards to aid the returning wounded soldiers. As the desperate need of the southern freed men and women for clothing and supplies became widely known, Worcester's black women formed the Colored Freedmen's Aid Society of Worcester to assist former slaves. This group of black women organized separately from the white Ladies Aid Society presided over by Mrs. Ichabod Washburn. In the A.M.E. Zion Church, and in the two societies affiliated with that church, black Worcesterites proclaimed their commitment to their southern brethren's liberation and, not insignificantly, asserted an expanded role for themselves in Worcester's public life.[26] In the process, Amos Webber began to imagine a quite different public role for himself than he had experienced in Philadelphia.

Yet, for all this, blacks in Worcester, as throughout the North, were denied the right to participate in this struggle in the manner most visible—namely, as armed soldiers in battle against slavery. Both whites and blacks understood the profound stakes at the core of this controversy. Governor John A. Andrew, a staunch supporter of enlisting black soldiers, worried privately that were black men allowed no part in the war, even the successful destruction of the slave system would have a baleful effect, for "the result would leave the colored man a mere helot; [and] the freedmen a poor, despised, subordinate body of human beings, neither strangers nor citizens, but 'contrabands,' who had lost their masters, but not

found a country." The possibility of an expansive national identity—that same year Andrew urged General Joseph Hooker to
"[t]ell the boys that *all* have a country; *all* will hereafter have a history" as a consequence of their military service—propelled many
in their efforts. "The day that made the colored man a soldier of
the Union," Andrew wrote his black advisor, Lewis Hayden,
"made him a power in the land. . . . No one can ever deny the
rights of citizenship in a country to those who have helped to create it or *save it*."[27]

Nor were these attitudes simply the provenance of sympathetic
white politicians. "I believe as you do," G. E. Hystuns, a black future sergeant of the famous 54th Massachusetts Infantry, wrote to
William Still from Morris Island, South Carolina, "that the arming of every able co^{ld} man North & South [is the best] method
which cold [could] be devised to eradicate that semblance of infe-
riority of our race, which cruel Slavery has created[.] [I]f there is
one spark of manhood running in the blood of the Race that has
resisted the . . . waves of oppression, the school of the soldier will
fan it to a glowing flame and it is the means—only means—by
which the collective power of the Negro race can be brought to
bear on the civil and political affairs of the country."[28]

It was this promise that the northern black community embraced. In a contemporary memoir the Reverend Jeremiah Asher
recalled how, as a child in North Branford, Connecticut, he had
listened to stories told by black veterans of the American Revolution, stories of "the terrible and never-to-be-forgotten battle for
American liberty." So embedded in his person were the stories
and the cadences of the proud old men that the young Asher "almost fancied to myself that I had more rights than any white man
in the town. . . . Thus, my first ideas of the right of the colored
man to life, liberty and the pursuit of happiness were received
from those old veterans and champions for liberty."[29] Clearly a
northern black tradition of considerable standing understood the
relationship between military service in time of crisis and the
promise of a more public recognition of a common civic identity;
even in the face of the white community's prior lack of faith in that
promise, black citizens responded yet again, motivated by an optimism profoundly American in its conviction that this time all obstacles might fall before it.

Precisely because military service carried such intense personal and civic meaning, white antipathy to black military service ran deep both in the popular culture and in governmental councils, and even among black Americans there were doubts. "I claim that the raising of black regiments for the war would be highly impolitic and uncalled for under the present state of affairs," wrote a correspondent in the *Anglo-African Magazine* in September 1861, "knowing as we do, the policy of the Government in relation to colored men." To support black enlistments when the northern war aim was solely to preserve the Union as then constituted would but show "our incompetency to comprehend the nature of the differences existing between the two sections now at variance."[30]

In Worcester caution also dominated at first. When news came in August 1862 that Rhode Island's militia would enroll black men, Worcester's blacks met to discuss the issue. Recognizing that Rhode Island's initiative "has met with no favor at the hands of the general government, but has tended rather to create dissension in both the government and the army," the unsigned resolutions passed at the meeting deemed it "the duty of the colored people to engage in no move" that might "disturb the harmonious and vigorous action of the government in its aim to suppress the rebellion and restore the nation to its former prosperity." But, they added, should the government "need the aid of the colored man as a military element to be employed in this stupendous struggle, we shall ever be found ready, with patriotic and willing hearts, to promptly respond to the call of the government." Sensitive to white attitudes and only too aware of the limited war aims then espoused by Lincoln, these Worcester activists thought it impolitic for the larger New England black community to take the lead on this issue.[31]

Yet shortly after this meeting, the Attorney General of Massachusetts, following intense negotiations with federal officials, announced that the state's military assessors could now include black men on their rolls. Because there was not yet a black Massachusetts regiment—and not even Governor Andrew suggested an integrated unit—attention turned again toward the Rhode Island proposal. Taking the Attorney General's opinion as a sign of a new governmental attitude, Worcester blacks held a second public meeting on September 10. Black activists from Providence successfully urged the meeting to reconsider its earlier position and to endorse the Rhode Island initiative. Five days later at a "war meeting" held at Mechanics Hall, on Main Street in downtown Worcester, to raise volunteers, black Worcester was noticeably present. Within days Gilbert Walker, Webber's neighbor, announced that he had already enrolled seventeen black men and that others should see him at his "hair dressing rooms" in the city's business district. Ultimately the War Department rejected the initiative once again, but not before blacks in Worcester and throughout the North gave further evidence of their willingness to serve.[32]

As continued Federal casualties and defeats deflated northern expectations for a rapid victory, white public opinion shifted on the issue of black troops. The drain on northern manpower, and the prospect of yet further demands with the implementation of a military draft in 1863, led industrialists such as Boston's John Murray Forbes to aggressively (though demeaningly) support black enlistments as "it is better than draining our artisans and free laborers." The political climate had changed as well. The Militia Act of July 17, 1862, gave President Abraham Lincoln discretionary power to enroll black troops, and the Emancipation Proclamation, declaring all slaves in the rebellious states free, took effect on January 1, 1863. When Governor Andrew again requested permission to raise a black regiment in January 1863, Secretary of War Edwin Stanton—marking a dramatic transformation in northern public opinion concerning the use of black troops—agreed, although with certain reservations: he explicitly prohibited enrolling black commissioned officers and set the pay for black noncommissioned officers at less than half that paid white privates.[33]

Despite these slights, Andrew and his advisors enthusiastically grasped the opportunity. The governor appointed an organizing committee that, in turn, chose such well-known blacks as Lewis Hayden, William Wells Brown, Martin Delany, and Henry Highland Garnet to recruit throughout northern black communities. These national organizers relied on local black leaders such as Gilbert Walker and William Brown, who became, in Worcester, important recruiters of black troops. White insults and slights notwithstanding, more than 2,000 black men from throughout the nation filled the 54th Massachusetts (Colored) Infantry by May and they shortly subscribed a second regiment as well, the 55th Massachusetts (Colored) Infantry. In January of the following year, a third unit, the Fifth Massachusetts (Colored) Cavalry, was mustered into the army.[34]

The reaction to these new opportunities in Worcester was immediate and enthusiastic. At an integrated mass meeting at City Hall on March 12, 1863, Reverend Merrill Richardson, who was white, and William Brown sought recruits for the 54th Infantry and donations to assist the families of black enlisted men. Unlike their white counterparts, black recruits were still denied federal bounties for enlisting. Four wealthy whites stepped forward to pledge, for each black recruit, five dollars to the fund; four other donors, including William H. Jankins, the former fugitive from slavery, pledged one dollar. Within a week of that meeting, eleven of Worcester's black men enlisted, including Amos Webber.[35]

THROUGHOUT THAT SPRING blacks recruited from across the North passed through Worcester on their way toward a military training camp at Readville, Massachusetts, outside Boston. By the end of May, after basic training in infantry tactics, the 54th left for the front, while the 55th approached its full complement.

On July 18, 1863, on Morris Island, South Carolina, the 54th Massachusetts Infantry, under the command of a white Bostonian, Robert Gould Shaw, led the Union assault on Fort Wagner, a Confederate stronghold. Passing through a narrow defile that allowed Confederate gunners to decimate its ranks, the 54th fought valiantly. To the astonishment of many whites, both military and civilian, the 54th held its ranks, persisted in its assault, and, although the attack failed, provided an example of courage under fire that soon impressed the nation. Sergeant William H. Carney, of Company C, who carried the colors when the original standard-bearer fell, received a congressional Medal of Honor for his action that day.[36]

For Alexander Hemenway, a sergeant in Company F, participation in the 54th Infantry's assault on Fort Wagner formed the core of his public identity in the years to come. When he returned to Worcester on leave in November 1863,[37] his pride in his unit's achievements inevitably infused his war stories. For Amos Webber, this may have produced mixed feelings since, although they had enlisted together, Webber had not charged Fort Wagner with Hemenway. Sometime before the 54th Infantry left Readville, Webber withdrew, whether due to illness or another acceptable military reason is unclear—the army filed no charges against him then or later. During that explosive week in July 1863, while the men of the 54th by their valor laid claim once again to a new standing for themselves and for all black Americans, Webber was back on Liberty Street, walking the half mile each day to the wire works.

Another event that same week honed Amos Webber's discomfort in remaining in Worcester. Just a few days before the Worcester newspapers bore the news of the 54th's assault, the same papers carried the reports of New York's horrific draft riots. Mobs of largely Irish working-class men and women, angered at the ability of the wealthy to buy an exemption from the draft and incensed at the thought of fighting for abolition with black troops, rampaged that city's black neighborhoods. The virulent racism that propelled the rioters was openly discussed in Worcester newspapers. In a strongly worded editorial, the *Daily Spy* rejected the argument that the Irish working people who held black New York hostage for five murderous days were simply asserting their rights to a livelihood in a period of economic inflation. "Now if that were so," the paper insisted, the rioters' "violence would have shown itself against those who had power" and not against "the poorest of the poor—a class utterly defenseless—a body of people beside whom the rioters were rich."[38]

Although removed from either theater of violence, Webber understood their painful juxtaposition. Nearly a decade later he recalled with anger and horror the spectacle of "the Bullies of 1863, hanging Loyal Colored men to the Lamp Post etc." But for the moment he remained home, in Worcester, in the familiar, if now perhaps chafing, role of the observer.[39]

As Webber watched, circumstances shifted yet again. That summer's battle at Gettysburg marked a decisive victory for the Union forces. Black troops saw action in many military theaters, engaging Confederate soldiers and liberating former slaves in numerous southern states. Grant now told Lincoln that "by arming the negro we have added a powerful ally. . . . [t]hey will make good soldiers, and taking them from the enemy weakens him in the same proportion they strengthen us." Lincoln in turn used this information in a public letter addressed to the Democratic Party in August 1863. "You are dissatisfied with me about the negro," he wrote his bitterest political opponents, but some of the most successful Union commanders "believe the emancipation policy, and the use of colored troops, constitute the heaviest blow yet dealt to the rebellion." The president, who but a year earlier had publicly endorsed colonization as the only suitable proposal for slaves freed by the war, now told his Democratic adversaries that with the coming Union victory "there will be some black men who can remember that, with silent tongue, and clenched teeth, and steady eye, and well-poised bayonet, they have helped mankind on to this great consummation; while, I fear, there will be some white ones, unable to forget that, with malignant heart, and deceitful speech, they have strove to hinder it."[40]

Military officers arrived in Worcester in July 1863 to administer a new draft law. There was no violence, but neither was there enthusiastic compliance with the spirit of the law. Of the 700 men called in the July draft in the city, only 182 actually reported. Some were found to be unfit for service, while fully a third of those called received either "special exemptions" or were able to pay between $650 and $800 each (more than a year's salary for all but a few workers) to purchase a substitute. Of those who did report, moreover, nearly two thirds were residents of Wards One, Two, Seven, and Eight—wards with the smallest percentage of Irish-born residents. Despite the reputation of New York's Irish Brigade as fierce fighters for the Union, the Irish remained the most underrepresented immigrant group in proportion to population in the army. In Worcester, Provost Marshal Samuel Stone discovered one cause for that low figure. Many of the city's Irish immigrants possessed forged certificates of alienage, all sworn to by one parish priest in Ireland, that made them too old to serve.[41]

Through all this, Amos Webber continued to work and to watch. He was not drafted in July, nor did he respond in October when the army set a new quota of 347 enlistments for the city. Despite

the continued difficulties Lewis Hayden and other black recruiters encountered (black volunteers were regularly attacked in
Jersey City and New York on their way to Massachusetts, and
Hayden referred to some of his recruits as kidnapped),[42] a stream
of black men passed through Worcester that fall on their way to
Readville. Webber maintained his public silence through these
months.

But that silence was not to last. On the final day of 1863, amid
the revival-like atmosphere of mass meetings striving to fill the
most recent draft quotas, Amos Webber, four months shy of his
thirty-eighth birthday, stepped forth and enlisted in the Fifth
Massachusetts (Colored) Cavalry.

CHAPTER SIX

TEMPERED IN STRUGGLE

ON JANUARY 28, 1864, Amos Webber reported to Camp Meigs, at Readville, Massachusetts. A self-described laborer, this new recruit, one of slightly more than 100 in Company D, Fifth Massachusetts Cavalry, quickly impressed his white officers with his potential leadership qualities. After only three days, Major Horace N. Weld detached Webber and another private "for daily duty at Regt' Hospital." Private Webber became Corporal Webber by the end of February, assigned to the company commander's office. His work there must have pleased Captain Charles C. Parsons, an 1860 graduate of Harvard College and the commander of Company D, for on April 28, three months after reporting, Amos Webber was again promoted, this time to sergeant.

The rapidity of these promotions reflected both Webber's personal qualities and the wartime demands made upon the army's usually cumbersome promotion system. Webber was literate and circumspect, and, perhaps most important in the eyes of the white officers, knew how to interact with white superiors. His experience with elite whites since his years in Charles Wurts's house undoubtedly propelled his rapid rise. These particular characteristics appealed to white officers precisely because many considered the men of the Fifth largely unfit for leadership positions. Charles P. Bowditch, the white captain of Company F, thought these black soldiers compared poorly to those in Massachusetts' two other black regiments (Bowditch also had a low opinion of the white officers in the Fifth); and Webber's company commander thought that, in black regiments, "men fit for non commissioned are much more scarce than in a white regiment." Against these perceptions Amos Webber's working familiarity with white superiors distinguished him in their eyes from other black enlisted men.

The demands of war also contributed to Webber's rapid elevation from private to sergeant. The white officers who evaluated Webber and his comrades were themselves the recipients of similar dramatic promotions. Charles Parsons, on transferring from the white First Massachusetts Cavalry to the Negro Fifth, jumped from lieutenant to captain; Horace Weld, transferring between the same regiments, rose from captain to major. For others promotions came at a furious rate after reporting to Readville. In less than a month Jacob B. Cook went from second to first lieutenant of Company D; while it took Cyrus C. Emory but five days to gain promotion from first lieutenant to captain of Company B. Whatever racial perceptions structured the opinions of some white officers, the rapid promotions Webber and a few other black soldiers received paralleled the experience of many white soldiers as well.[1]

As a sergeant attached to the company command, Webber worked closely with Captain Parsons and Lieutenant Cook. Both officers were young men (twenty-three and twenty-one, respectively) and both were from the Boston area. While Parsons was a veteran, with eighteen months' service before transferring to the Fifth, Cook entered the military in December 1863 and simultaneously received his commission as a second lieutenant. Like most northern white Americans at the time, neither officer had had extensive contact with black Americans, slave or free, before reporting to Readville. This, coupled with the juxtaposition of younger white officers commanding older black soldiers, complicated the life of black noncommissioned officers. Men such as Amos Webber, William D. Curtis, Gustavus Booth, Andrew Lepo, Samuel E. Wright, and the other black sergeants and corporals of Company D had to assume, along with their other duties, the role of intermediary between white officers and the body of black soldiers.

Further exacerbating the problems confronting black noncommissioned officers was the racism prevalent in some of the white officers, and in society at large. Whether on or off the military post, the Federal uniform did not protect black soldiers from racial attacks. Even as the Fifth Cavalry trained in Readville, two white men assaulted and beat a black recruit as he walked along a railroad track.[2]

Amos Webber and the other fifteen black noncommissioned officers of Company D who lived in this tense environment were a varied group of men. Six of the seven sergeants were residents of northern states at the time of their enlistments—five of them from Massachusetts. Three of the eight corporals and the one hospital steward were also northern-born. More men listed their premilitary occupations as unskilled (four) than skilled (two); three were service workers, including two barbers, whereas George Whitsel (who, along with Webber, had been assigned to the regimental hospital in January 1864) was the lone professional, a teacher from Ohio. Six described themselves as farmers, including four who had recently arrived from the South. Ten were thirty years or younger, but a majority of the sergeants were older men, between thirty-one and forty. The two men who would rise to the top positions among the company's black soldiers, William D. Curtis and Amos Webber, were thirty-six and thirty-seven, respectively, when they enlisted. Curtis, like Webber, was northern-born and a Massachusetts resident and, as a barber, had probably had sustained contact with whites as well prior to his service.

Collectively the black leaders of Company D stood in contrast with the more than 100 men who filled out the ranks of the company. Over half (53 percent) of the privates were born in slave states or in the District of Columbia, and more than 30 percent listed a slave state as their last address. Seventy-nine percent of these men were thirty years of age or younger; as for their premilitary occupations, unskilled workers constituted almost 40 percent and farmers another 27 percent. Given this broad mix of backgrounds, skills, and experiences, the potential for tension within the ranks, and between those ranks and their black and white superiors, was high.[3]

Webber's three months at Readville were intense and full. Like all enlistees, he slept in tents with other recruits, ate army food, and had his day ruled by bugle calls and the barked orders of military superiors. To achieve battle-ready status Webber and his comrades, like other civilians, required instruction in military discipline and procedures, training in weaponry, and experience in moving swiftly in group formations as small as a squadron or as large as a regiment. As cavalry, of course, they also received extensive instruction in tactics specifically suited to mounted soldiers. Six weeks into training the clerk of Company A deemed morale high and the troops quick learners. "This company," he boasted, "at this date is decidedly the best instructed and the best disciplined of any of the commonwealth."[4] Yet any in the Fifth who had preserved romantic images of war this far into training camp soon had cause to reconsider.

On April 12, 1864, Confederate troops under General Nathan Bedford Forrest overran the Federal garrison at Fort Pillow, Kentucky. As the nearly 600 Union troops, including 270 black soldiers, sought to surrender, the Confederate forces continued their attack. Incensed that black men and former slaves fought them, the southern soldiers entering the fort refused to accept the surrender. Union men, black and white, were shot as they lay down their arms, and there were reports that Forrest's men buried alive wounded black soldiers and maimed the white officers. While some contemporary accounts exaggerated the carnage, it was widely accepted that "an indiscriminate butchery of white and black soldiers" had in fact occurred. As the men of the Fifth absorbed this somber news, they prepared themselves to depart for the southern battlefields.

Three weeks later the First Battalion of the Fifth Cavalry, consisting of Companies A, B, C, and D, left Massachusetts for Camp Casey, Virginia, just outside Washington. In camp since January, they were the best trained of the regiment's three battalions. The other two battalions, some of whose companies had less than a month of training, arrived at Camp Casey by May 12. There the Fifth Cavalry, under the command of Colonel Samuel Chamberlain and Major Horace N. Weld, awaited orders.[5]

THE FIFTH CAVALRY arrived in Virginia at the beginning of a decisive campaign that would transform the course of the war. Newly appointed as commander of all Union troops, Ulysses S. Grant proved to be a daring, pugnacious general who simply did not consider retreat a normal part of military strategy. In the battles of the Wilderness, Spotsylvania, Cold Harbor, and before

Richmond and Petersburg, Grant's brilliant movements in Virginia throughout May and June 1864 gave notice that this Union commander played by different—and successful—rules. His maneuvers forced Confederate general Robert E. Lee to commit his troops to a defense of the twenty-three-mile-long axis between Richmond and Petersburg, thereby removing the Confederacy's most successful army from offensive sorties for the remainder of the war. Grant fully grasped the grim consequences of his operations. In the six weeks between May 4 and June 18, 1864, his troops absorbed between 60,000 and 70,000 casualties in a war of attrition that fell short of outright victory. But Grant thought the alternative was worse: a lack of decisiveness that, in postponing the war's end, would actually cost far more lives. It was into this maelstrom that the Fifth Cavalry arrived on May 16 at City Point, Virginia, assigned to the Third Division, 18th Army Corps, under the command of General Edwin W. Hinks.[6]

Located at the junction of the James and Appomattox Rivers, some eight miles northeast of Petersburg, City Point's port facilities and location made it a supply depot and transfer point for Federal troops engaged with either Lee's armies at Richmond or with General Beauregard's forces at Petersburg. Less than a week before the Fifth arrived, 1,700 black cavalry troops attached to Benjamin Butler's Army of the James assembled at City Point before attacking Confederate troops across the northern bank of the James River. Slicing elements of Beauregard's troops in half, Butler's black soldiers forced Lee to divert Richmond's needed reinforcements to his beleaguered subordinate's defense. As Samuel A. Duncan, a white colonel of those black cavalrymen, told his fiancée, his men's efforts throughout the campaign were superlative: "The white brigade doesn't exist that would have done it."[7]

In the middle of this complex, shifting battlefield, the Fifth Cavalry disembarked at City Point. "An almost constant roar of cannon and rattle of Musketry" greeted these untested troops; so dense was the barrage that one veteran of a neighboring Connecticut regiment wrote his wife that "it is astonishing to me how a man escapes alive." Scheduled for guard duty, perimeter defense, and for expeditions against the enemy as needed, men of the Fifth anticipated their baptism by fire. They were, however, saddled with a serious disability. Prior to leaving Camp Casey, the

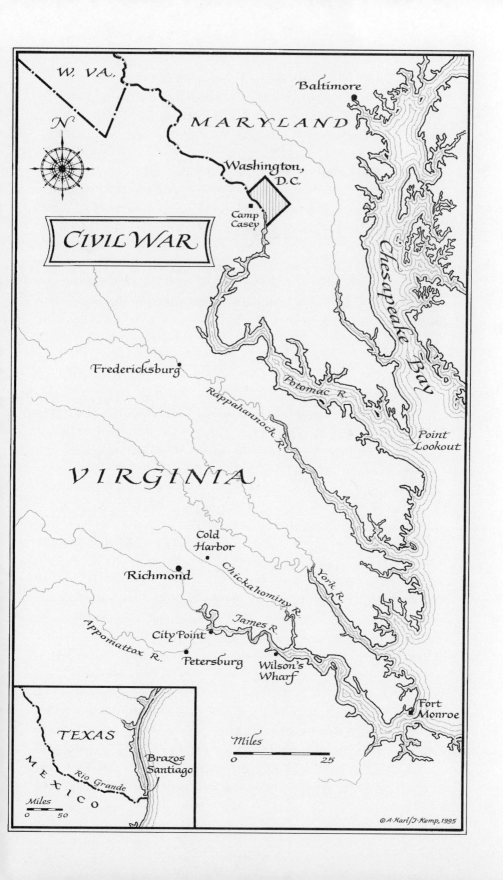

CIVIL WAR

W. VA.

N

MARYLAND

Baltimore

Washington, D.C.

Camp Casey

Chesapeake Bay

Fredericksburg

Rappahannock R.

Potomac R.

Point Lookout

VIRGINIA

Cold Harbor

Richmond

Chickahominy R.

York R.

James R.

City Point

Appomattox R.

Petersburg

Wilson's Wharf

Fort Monroe

Miles

0   25

TEXAS

MEXICO

Rio Grande

Brazos Santiago

Miles

0   50

© A. Karl/J. Kemp, 1995

army "dismounted" the Fifth Cavalry—turning them instantly into infantry—and ordered them "to take the field without delay." With no time for retraining and with their earlier drilling almost useless, the Fifth dug in around City Point at a greater disadvantage than most raw troops.[8]

In the first month at the front the Fifth Cavalry guarded the vital depot at City Point, and could only watch other troops engage the enemy. Beauregard's forces attacked Wilson's Wharf, some twenty miles below City Point, a week after the Fifth's arrival, announcing in advance that they would take no responsibility for the fate of captured black troops or their officers. As other black soldiers repulsed the Confederates, Webber and his comrades were held in reserve. Some ten days later, in a massive Union assault against entrenched Confederate troops at Cold Harbor, Grant's forces suffered some 7,000 casualties in one day, yet failed to dislodge Lee's men. Again the Fifth waited. The closest it came to action during that first month occurred when four of the regiment's companies sailed up the Appomattox River. In place and ready to cross a pontoon bridge to engage the enemy, orders came to cease the operation and to return to City Point. It was a disappointing retreat, and it became more difficult for the noncommissioned officers to maintain morale.

In continuing his war of maneuver, Grant slid his army farther to the south after his assault on Cold Harbor, crossed the James River, and focused his full force against Petersburg. As the troops and supplies poured through City Point, the Fifth Cavalry finally received orders to prepare for battle.[9]

To restore the fighting units of the 18th Army Corps to full strength after the losses at Cold Harbor, Grant committed the black soldiers under General Hinks to its battle line. On June 15, 1864, the corps crossed the Appomattox River and marched down the City Point Road, approaching Petersburg from the north. A cautious commander, made even more so by the carnage at Cold Harbor, General William F. Smith carefully approached the Confederate position at Battery 5, a linchpin in the city's defenses. Finally ordered to attack at 7:00 P.M., Smith's troops won a decisive victory, with the newly added black soldiers capturing the battery's six guns and taking numerous prisoners. Quickly joined by additional white troops, the integrated Federal force pushed the

Confederates back even farther, so that by late evening Smith's forces held critical segments of the last line of defense before Petersburg. Ever cautious, Smith refused to continue the advance.

As they entrenched themselves that evening, there existed a general feeling among the 18th Corps that the black troops had acquitted themselves with the highest honor. As Lieutenant N. H. Eagerton, a white officer who had led them in battle, wrote to his training instructor: "You have doubtless read and heard much of their [the black soldiers'] conduct during the engagement of June 15. But," Eagerton asserted,

> as a general thing the newspapers give but a partial view. To appreciate fully what they did one must remember that it was not a charge made suddenly on first-finding the enemy and while all was enthusiasm. But that for five long hours they were subjected to a heavy cannonade of shot and shell. All the time cautiously approaching—walking, creeping, *crawling,* in the *very dust.* — By regiment, by company and almost man by man. Five hours were spent crossing an open and almost level field a quarter of a mile in width. But under all this fire they remained [disciplined] and when the order to charge came they were as ready to obey and as enthusiastic to rush on as any soldiers could be.

In taking these fortifications, which marked the farthest Federal advance until the following spring, the black soldiers under Hinks's direct command won widespread praise. The white soldier, General Smith later said, "so long prejudiced and so obstinately heretical on this subject, stands amazed as they look at the works captured by negroes, and are loud and unreserved in their praise."[10]

Praise and a newfound respect accrued to the black soldiers of Hinks's division in the aftermath of the battle. Lieutenant Eagerton thought the bill equalizing military pay for black soldiers—which had just been passed—had been favorably received in part due to the valor of these men. "Congress has acknowledged the worth of our Troops as soldiers," he wrote, "and [they] are one step nearer to owning their rights as men."[11]

But for Amos Webber and his men, this postbattle praise contained another, more bitter message. Following its first engagement of the war the Fifth received at best mixed reviews as a number of their officers, including their divisional commander, sharply criticized their efforts.

Christian Abraham Fleetwood, a black sergeant major with the Fourth Regiment, United States Colored Troops (USCT), who would receive the congressional Medal of Honor, also fought at Baylor's Farm on the outskirts of Petersburg that June day. As he recalled within days of the battle, his regiment "[w]ent into action early [and] charged out of woods." The intense Confederate fire "cut up badly" the Federal troops and Fleetwood's regiment "broke and retreated." In the confusion they were "[f]ired into by 5th Mass," which was advancing behind them. Yet, Fleetwood noted, the Fifth regrouped and, together with other regiments, "took the battery." Captain Charles P. Bowditch, who had doubted the character of the men of the Fifth in training, agreed with Fleetwood's analysis. The Fifth "rushed on over a long open plain," he wrote his sister three days after the battle, "on which they were exposed to a cross-fire from three batteries and charged the centre fort." The successful assault on the center forced the right and left Confederate batteries to fall in succession. In a second letter written the same day, this to his mother, Bowditch described how the Fifth Cavalry, on emerging from the woods, confronted Fleetwood's regiment "running helter skelter back upon them. . . . Our men behaved very well indeed," Bowditch thought, "though it is not the most favorable way of going into first action with another regiment breaking through them."[12]

A week later, the correspondent for the *Army and Navy Journal* publicly echoed these private evaluations. At Baylor's Farm, he wrote, "the 22d and 5th colored regiments gallantly carried the enemy's works, capturing one of the guns and turning it promptly on the enemy."[13] But General Hinks, a Massachusetts man and abolitionist sympathizer who strongly endorsed the use of black soldiers, nonetheless had some harsh words in evaluating the conduct of the Fifth Cavalry. In his report of the battle to General Smith, he wrote:

In forming line of battle in the morning, for the attack upon enemy's works near Baylor's house, I placed the Fifth Massachusetts Cavalry (dismounted) on the left of the second line of

battle, and its awkwardness in maneuvering delayed my movement fully three-quarters of an hour, and finally when it advanced, though nobly and heroically led, it was but little other
than an armed mob, which was held up to its work by the almost
superhuman efforts of its officers. . . . [I]ts power to inflict injury upon the enemy was nominal. I could but commend its gal-
lantry, but considering its inefficiency, decided that to further
engage it with the enemy would be a reckless and useless exposure of life to no purpose.

The majority of the forces Hinks committed were, like Fleetwood's regiment, all trained infantry veterans while, in contrast, the
Fifth, as Hinks wrote in another report on the battle, "is also composed of new recruits, and not drilled in infantry formations."[14]

Sergeant Webber would later imply a different interpretation.
Fourteen years after the battle at Baylor's Farm, Webber penned a
detailed "Chronology Of the Rebellion between the *North and
South*," and noted that by June 17, 1864, the "[d]esperate but unsuccessful attack upon the rebel line before Petersburgh" had concluded. The failure to advance was General Smith's and this
proud veteran never accepted the blame his commander assigned
to the Fifth Cavalry.[15]

Hinks understood clearly why he thought the Fifth ineffective in
battle. The "dismounted cavalry regiments," he told General
Smith, "labor under disadvantage of being transferred to a branch
of the service with which they are entirely unacquainted." Yet,
unwilling to consider the testimony of his junior line officers, or to
consider the implications of the lack of training, Hinks stood by
his report, which relegated the Fifth to a distinctly inferior standing. Replaced in the line of battle by black infantry veterans on
June 18, the Fifth was shortly reassigned to guard duty at Point
Lookout, Maryland, a major detention center for Confederate
prisoners of war. While there may have been a certain "just
retributive providence" in this assignment, as a contemporary
Worcester historian noted, in that "the subject race were placed as
guards over those who had held them or their brethren in
bondage," there was also widespread disappointment. "I never
knew why this [reassignment] was done," Captain Bowditch recalled years later, "for our men had been discharging their duties

very well." As an officer Bowditch could ease his disappointment by resigning his commission that August. But black noncommissioned officers and enlisted men had no such option. They had to endure their disappointment, and the negative opinion of the regiment held by many officers and men alike, for the remainder of the war and beyond.[16]

The battle of Baylor's Farm was, in the overall picture, a minor engagement in a far larger movement orchestrated by Ulysses S. Grant. With the failure of the Federal forces to push beyond the line established on June 15, Grant ceased his war of maneuver and instituted a strategy of siege instead. With few exceptions, both sides now dug their trenches deep around Petersburg and limited hostile contact largely to sharpshooters and the occasional artillery barrage until the following spring. For Amos Webber, William Curtis, and the other men of the Fifth Cavalry, however, the opportunity to alter official negative opinions remained elusive. Increasingly employed as laborers "digging, throwing up entrenchments and so on just what white soldiers dislike to do," in the approving words of one white Pennsylvania private, the men of the Fifth Cavalry had no chance to prove themselves in battle throughout the remaining year.[17]

ON JULY 1, 1864, the Fifth Cavalry arrived at Point Lookout to replace the 36th United States Colored Troops, who were being sent to join General Butler's Army of the James. A large depot, Point Lookout could hold upward of 14,000 Confederate prisoners. Since the opinion of General Hinks was widely known throughout the ranks, the Fifth's morale must have sunk even lower when they recognized the other Federal troops on guard duty. With few exceptions the remaining guards at Point Lookout were members of the Veterans Reserve Corps (known as the Invalid Corps until March 1864) and other reserve units composed of soldiers ill equipped, due to age, infirmity, or other disability, to serve at the front. The healthy men of the Fifth understood Hinks's message; but if it eluded some, the very prisoners they guarded made the point repeatedly. As the Confederate prisoner A. M. Keiley wrote in his diary on July 1: "[T]he Fifth Mas-

sachusetts Colored Cavalry and another black regiment ordered
here, it is said, by Butler, for cowardice in presence of the enemy
(good joke for Butler)." The disdain Confederate troops held for
General Benjamin Butler, given his strong advocacy on behalf of
black troops, added a particularly mordant tone to the gossip
among the prisoners concerning their new guards. It was a bleak
moment for the men of the Fifth.[18]

Life at Point Lookout, as anywhere in the military, had its own
prescribed patterns. Reveille came between dawn and sunrise,
with the prisoners falling in by company to be counted. Breakfast
for prisoners followed, usually crackers and weak coffee. Within
limits, prisoners did as they chose until dinner, in midafternoon,
which consisted of a small ration of meat, more crackers, potatoes,
and a cup of watery soup. At sunset they formed into companies
for another counting. There was no supper meal. For the men of
the Fifth, encamped in tents a mile above the prison, this duty
brought its own rhythms. They stood guard on alternate days; on
off-days squads were detailed to accompany prisoner exchanges,
dig fortifications, and perform other menial tasks. This unrelenting routine grated on most soldiers but was especially burdensome
for the troops of the Fifth Cavalry, who hungered to prove their
worth once again.[19]

Holidays such as Thanksgiving temporarily broke the tedium.
As Webber excitedly recalled in a letter to the *Anglo-African* in
November 1864, this was the Fifth's "first holiday that we have
witnessed during the eleven months in service." An officers-only
horse race began the festivities, with the enlisted men gathered as
cheering spectators. The "sumptuous turkey dinner" followed:
Webber's Company D joined two other companies at a table
"about forty feet long," laid out on the main street of their camp.
"[T]he men were all seated around the table," Webber wrote, "eat-
ing away for life, on turkeys, oysters, turnips, onions, bread without butter, etc." Wines, however, were "excepted" from the menu.
Following the meal the men competed for prizes, especially the
valuable tobacco plug, in foot races, greased-pole climbings and
greased-pig chasings, "a Jig Dance," and sack races. White officers were honored with gifts, as was the black chief bugler of the
regiment; while "the band poured forth volumes of music from
their great horns" into the evening. For the men of the Fifth,

Webber thought, "the day was well spent in sport and pleasure to their satisfaction."[20]

In these rather insulting, even depressing, circumstances the men of the Fifth sought to maintain self-respect and to perform their duties with pride. But neither Webber's temporary elevation to acting first sergeant that July nor the enjoyable Thanksgiving celebration could permanently lift the general pall that enveloped the unit. They had been dismissed and denigrated, relegated to a military backwater usually the preserve of the infirm and recuperating soldier. The only major military challenge to the normal routine came early in the Fifth's time at the camp, when Confederate cavalry, under the command of General Jubal Early, were reported but four miles from Point Lookout. Placed on full alert the Federal troops stood down rather quickly when Early's broad attack on Washington failed to materialize.[21]

Central to life at Point Lookout was the daily struggle between the prisoners and their guards to define the terms of their interaction. A southern private, captured with Lee's forces during the battle of the Wilderness, etched one dimension of that struggle quite vividly. "The colored soldiers patrolled after nine o'clock along the avenues between the tents with six-shooters in their hands," Marcus B. Toney recalled; "and if they heard any noise in a tent, they would shoot into it, therefore, after 9 p.m., Point Lookout, with its army of ten thousand men, was nearly as quiet as a cemetery." Underlying this struggle to establish authority and, for the prisoners, to claim a degree of autonomy was a deeper racial tension. "Of course," Toney continued, "it was very humiliating to Southern men to be thus guarded by some of their former slaves."

This tension underscored the major daily contest between white prisoners and black guards, which occurred over the "dead line." A line marked in the earth within the prison fence around which the guards walked their beats, this "dead line" established the limits of the prisoners' physical mobility. Early one evening, Private Toney remembered, "a squad which had been on detail on the outside entered the prison, and quite a crowd rushed up to them to hear the news, and some of them were crowded over the dead line. Without hesitation the guard fired into the group, severely wounding two of our prisoners." As Toney and other prisoners quickly realized, daily life at Point Lookout involved its own kind of warfare. "Our ears," he wrote, "were frequently greeted with the expression from the colored guards: 'The bottom rail is on top now; my gun wants to smoke.' "[22]

It is hard to know how Sergeant Webber responded to these confrontations. His own sense of discipline and order and his application of a just moral law to all human beings make it difficult to imagine Webber as consistently motivated by a sense of vengeance. His status as a noncommissioned officer, with the responsibility to maintain discipline within the ranks, mitigated the expression of such feelings, for unbridled anger emanating from the sergeant would have undermined the ordered conduct military life demanded. Yet that same concept of discipline undoubtedly led Webber to enforce rules such as the "dead line," for it was those limits that established the central order at Point Lookout. Webber appreciated that not to enforce that order would both neglect one's responsibilities and undermine the new public role the war allowed black men to assume.

In command over prisoners who considered them less than human, the men of the Fifth took a certain pride and enjoyment in this major reversal of roles, but it was not only Confederate prisoners who wished to deny them this new recognition as soldiers and citizens. For every Charles Bowditch, who came to praise the courage and competence of the men under his command, there were many more officers in the Fifth who expressed a far more ambivalent attitude at best. The opinions of Lieutenant Colonel Charles Francis Adams, Jr., who assumed overall command of the Fifth upon the resignation of Colonel Henry S. Russell in February 1865, reflected this reality.

The grandson of President John Quincy Adams, son of the United States ambassador to Great Britain, and heir to a proud abolitionist tradition, Adams enlisted to end slavery and not, as most did, to preserve the Union. He joined the Fifth in September 1864, following a quite successful career with the First Massachusetts Cavalry, in part to further these abolitionist convictions. His first impression after a week at Point Lookout, Adams wrote his brother, Henry, was positive. While he thought the black troops "lack[ed] the pride, spirit and intellectual energy of the whites," Adams found them "sensitive to praise or blame"

John J. Omenhauser (1831–1877), original watercolor done in 1863 while the painter was a Confederate prisoner at Point Lookout, Maryland. The "dead line" carried powerful physical and psychological meanings to white prisoners and black guards alike. The original caption provided by the prisoner/artist read: "No. 1 Git away from dat dar fence white man, or I'll make old abe's gun smoke at you, I can hardly hold de ball back now. De Bottom rails on top now." *Courtesy of the Maryland Historical Society, Baltimore*

and possessed of an "immeasurable capacity for improvement." Reflecting a racial romanticism widely held among whites in both the United and the Confederate States of America, Adams insisted that black Americans would respond primarily to emotional appeals. "The rugged discipline which improves whites is too much for them. It is easy to crush them into slaves, but very difficult by kindness and patience to approach them to our own standard." This ambitious military officer and a leader of black troops worried that these qualities—although all he could expect from

Negroes—nonetheless provided little hope "either for my success individually or for theirs as a race."

In other letters throughout that fall and winter to both his brother and his father, Adams reiterated these feelings. Still an abolitionist in his self-perception, he nonetheless maintained his low opinion of black Americans. They lacked a self-reliant spirit, both father and son agreed, and Adams thought his experience in the Fifth explained why. Either the African race lacked the innate spirit found in both men and animals to resist oppression, he wrote, with the result that "they are as supine as logs or animals," or the experience "of that patriarchical type" of slavery had "left the race as a whole, not overworked, well fed and contented—greedy animals! Commanding a colored regiment, and seeing the ugly characters in it, I adopt the latter as the true explanation of this wonderful supineness." In his rejection of a biological cause for that presumed "supineness," Adams actually expressed a more progressive racial attitude than most whites held at that time. Yet that did not always mean very much for the black men of the Fifth.[23]

These attitudes on the part of white officers, coupled with the normal demands of military discipline, generated clashes with the enlisted men. In July 1864, for example, an unsigned story in the *Anglo-African,* written by a black soldier in the Fifth Cavalry, told of a private in Company L, punished for allegedly raping a freedwoman, hung until his thumbs separated from his hands. Condemning "this *gentlemanly* and *Christian* officer" who ordered the punishment, the soldier-reporter threatened that his comrades would turn "*our arms against these demagogues*" if the conduct of the white officer was not investigated. Within days, Major Horace Weld wrote the publisher of the paper, Robert Hamilton; while he did not deny the charges, Weld accused Hamilton of encouraging "a mutinous feeling among the enlisted men of this command" and demanded that Hamilton reveal the "name of your correspondent in order that proper steps may be taken in this regt. to prevent similar letters being sent to the press." Robert Hamilton and his brother, Thomas, refused, claiming they did not know the name of their reporter, which caused Weld to write the provost marshal of New York City on August 1 to ask for assistance in curtailing the paper's reporting. "The Anglo-African is extensively circulated in this regiment," Weld worried, "and if such letters are allowed to appear in it a few unscrupulous men may produce very great mischief in the command."[24]

Such potentially explosive incidents occurred frequently. Some directly involved the Fifth's enlisted men in clashes with commissioned officers, all of whom were white; in others the noncommissioned officers, all of whom were black, found themselves in the critical, tension-filled space between the officers and the men. In either case the racial dimension was never far from the surface. When Sergeant Webber's superior, Company D's Second Lieutenant John W. George, slapped Private J. W. Hackett of Company K across the head with the flat of his saber for not forming ranks properly, Hackett brought his rifle to the "charge bayonets" position and declared: "God damn you! You would not strike *me* that way." A military court sentenced Hackett to six months in prison. In a second explosive situation, Corporal George Butler— whose immediate superior in Company D was Sergeant Amos Webber—and another soldier allegedly assaulted and attempted to rape the women of a white Maryland farm family in January 1865. In a military trial with heavily conflicting testimony, the female slave who cooked for the family testified that it was not Butler but his companion who "hugged [Mrs. Eliza Carnes] and wanted to feel her breasts" and who then asked the daughter, Anne, to sleep with him. The military tribunal, however, was more impressed with Anne M. Carnes's testimony, especially when she stated that it was Butler who "had hold of my arm, the same as if he had been white." Butler's twenty-year sentence was especially harsh in light of his alleged accomplice's minor punishment of a reduction in pay and the fact that the conflicting testimony of the white and black women hinted at the importance of racial stereotyping in the judgment of the tribunal.[25]

Whatever Webber thought of the merits of these cases, the tensions generated in such instances demanded that he as a noncommissioned officer both caution and counsel the men under his command. This required tact, sympathy, and a leader's capability to focus attention on ultimate goals amid quite immediate conflicts.

In some instances at Point Lookout, however, it proved impossible for black noncommissioned officers to balance the demands of those contradictory positions. In two particular cases during the winter of 1864–1865 this inherent tension burst openly among the men of the Fifth. When Private Joseph Stafford of Company F refused an order to "fall in" by Sergeant William Carter of Company C, the sergeant, a black carpenter from Gardner, Massachusetts, near Worcester, struck the private. The other enlisted men, Carter later testified, declared that "if I struck [Stafford again] they would shoot me." As Carter wrestled with Stafford, a second black private, rifle slung over his shoulder, pulled Carter away. An uncontrollable Stafford still refused to obey the sergeant's order but, as Carter testified, instead "kept walking along close beside me, cursing me, and calling me a 'damned yellow nigger, etc.' " He would not "fall into rank for white officers," Stafford exclaimed, and, Carter acknowledged, "he wouldn't for me." For some enlisted men, black sergeants and corporals were part of a military hierarchy they perceived as hostile. Rather than easing those tensions, their shared racial standing could, on occasion, exacerbate them. The prejudice of white officers melded with antebellum antagonisms over status, color, and position among blacks, making life for black soldiers of whatever rank even more complex.[26]

This became sharply evident again in December 1864, when Private Abraham H. Williams reported drunk for Company F's drill and expressed "contempt and disrespect toward his superior officers." As Williams was brought under escort to the regimental guardhouse, Colonel Henry Russell, the commander of the Fifth, instructed another white officer, Lieutenant A. I. Mallory, also of Company F, to "handcuff the Prisoner, and gag, and tie him up so that his toes should just touch the ground." As the lieutenant approached the private with the handcuffs, the prisoner, a Massachusetts shoemaker in civilian life, yelled that "[n]o God-damn white son-of-a-bitch shall put irons on me." By his own admission Mallory then swung the cuffs at Williams, causing a bloody wound to his head. Quite quickly Mallory found himself standing over the bleeding Williams while surrounded by a crowd of armed and angry black troops who had been brought there by Private James Finley of Company H. Finley had witnessed the lieutenant's beating of Williams; he had immediately returned to his tent, armed himself, and declared to all in the vicinity: "Come, boys, get on your equipment; I'm going to the Guard House to release that man." To make matters even more complicated for Mallory, just after Finley left to arm himself, Sergeant James H. Cornish, also of

Company F, addressed his superior officer directly: "Mallory," he demanded, "don't strike that man [again], don't you touch him." The astonished lieutenant later testified that Cornish gave the order "as if he expected to be obeyed."

The situation eventually calmed, but by the time the bugler played taps a black sergeant and two black privates stood charged with various degrees of mutinous conduct, and many black soldiers had experienced again that particular solidarity born of mutual anger and shared, spontaneous, and dangerous action. Neither the whites nor the blacks of the Fifth Cavalry would quickly forget just how close they had been to the flash point.[27]

Although away from the front, the Fifth Cavalry's service at Point Lookout was not without its peril. Each noncommissioned officer had been in Sergeant Carter's position, instilling military discipline, slapping or pushing a recalcitrant private. That discipline, and the military success it foretold, was a central component of the broadly accepted quality of manhood, which in turn promised self-respect and communal esteem. For black soldiers, evidence of manly qualities carried an additional burden: military success, many hoped, would vindicate the race in the eyes of whites. In such an atmosphere each small daily encounter that threatened those expectations demanded a forceful response from the sergeants and corporals.

Yet regardless of their relatively high degree of discipline, most noncommissioned officers also shared Sergeant Cornish's motivations when he ordered the lieutenant to cease beating the prisoner. By early 1865 the men of the Fifth—sergeants, corporals, and privates alike—had already experienced a pattern of cruel and arbitrary treatment at the hands of their white officers. The *Anglo-African*'s report of the previous July and the court-martial hearings that followed over the next seven months attested to the widespread regimental belief of prejudicial treatment. But still these soldiers remained committed to securing the personal respect and freedom for the race that would accrue, they expected, to those who fought to destroy slavery. That common faith structured the military experience of most and provided some guidance in handling the severe tensions encountered daily.[28]

This faith was neither uniform nor one-dimensional, however. The experience in the military sharpened the contrast between ex-

pectation and reality, leading some black soldiers to distance themselves from many northern political leaders, white and black alike.
"Many of our intelligent colored men believe in Mr. Lincoln," an
anonymous soldier of the Fifth Cavalry, who signed himself
"Africano," wrote the *Anglo-African* in August 1864; "but *we*, who
have studied him, know him better." Alluding to Lincoln's earlier
support for colonization, which would sever colored Americans
"from the ties we hold most dear," this soldier endorsed Republican John C. Frémont for president in the fall elections. Lincoln's
racial policy "has always been one of a fickle-minded man," he argued; and while "we thank Mr. Lincoln for what the exigencies of
the times forced him to do, we also censure him for the non-
accomplishment of the real good this accursed rebellion gave him
the power to do." Had he utilized this power, the soldier insisted,
"instead of bartering human sinews and human rights with slave-
holding Kentucky," Lincoln would have been recognized "as the
magnanimous regenerator of American institutions, and the
benevolent protector of human freedom."[29]

DURING THE NINE months that the Fifth spent at Point Look-
out the fortunes of the Confederacy declined precipitously. In
September 1864 Atlanta fell to Federal troops under General
William Tecumseh Sherman; by Christmas, as a result of his
"March to the Sea" through the heart of the Confederacy, Sherman had captured Savannah and devastated southern morale. Although less dramatic activity occurred around Petersburg,
Federal troops did occupy the last open road to the city and took
control of all but one of the railroad lines supplying Lee's army.
Webber was but one of many soldiers in that theater of the war
who returned home for a week's leave early in March 1865.[30]

By the time Webber reported back to his unit on March 11,
Grant had already begun preparations for the final assault on the
Confederacy. Gathering every available soldier in Virginia under
his direct command, the general also assembled the largest force of
black soldiers ever to confront the enemy—the 25th Army Corps,
the military's only all-black corps. As part of this mobilization,
Grant asked the commander of the military district that included

James M. Trotter (1842–1892) of Boston. Born in Grand Gulf, Missis-sippi, Trotter relocated to Boston after the Civil War. A musician, au-thor, and Civil War veteran of the 55th Massachusetts Infantry, Trotter clerked in the Boston post office. His and Webber's paths crossed in a number of organizations. Taken in 1865, the photograph reflects Trot-ter's recent promotion to second lieutenant, a rank a few black soldiers were granted in the last days of the war. *Courtesy of Division of Rare and Manuscript Collections, Carl A. Kroch Library, Cornell University*

Point Lookout if the Fifth Cavalry could be spared. Major Gen-eral Christopher C. Auger responded positively but requested in-struction: Should the regiment be sent immediately or should it first be supplied "with a compliment of horses. They are armed with muskets. Shall they be furnished with carbines instead? Shall they take wagons with them?" Grant, continuing the pattern es-tablished the year before, ordered Auger to "send the Fifth Mas-sachusetts Cavalry as it is, transportation and all."[31]

Lee, fearful that Grant would encircle his army, attacked on the night of March 24. Momentarily successful, Lee's forces held their positions for only a few hours before Grant's troops pushed them back deep within their original lines. Spread thin and highly vulnerable, Lee's battalions had lost some 5,000 men and were now outnumbered more than two to one by Federal troops. Grant

William H. Dupree (1838–?) of Boston. Born in Petersburg, Virginia, Dupree relocated in Boston after his service with the 55th Massachusetts Infantry. Beginning as a postal letter carrier, he rose to become supervisor of a substation of the U.S. Post Office in Boston. A political activist on behalf of equal rights and a fraternalist, Dupree and Webber were friends and co-workers in the decades following the war. This photograph, also taken in 1865, reflects Dupree's promotion to Second Lieutenant at the war's end. *Courtesy of Division of Rare and Manuscript Collections, Carl A. Kroch Library, Cornell University*

moved quickly. On March 29 he attacked Confederate forces southwest of Petersburg. Overwhelmingly successful, Grant ordered a full assault along the entire front. On Saturday, April 1, the Fifth Cavalry, under the command of now Colonel Charles F. Adams, stood before Richmond. At dawn the following Monday, they marched toward the city. Finding the Confederate positions deserted, the regiment continued to the city itself. By 10:00 A.M., in conjunction with other elements of the Army of the James, the Fifth Massachusetts (Colored) Cavalry liberated the heart of the Confederacy without firing a shot. Petersburg fell the same day.[32]

In the columns of the Fifth an indescribable joy and fierce pride propelled them that morning. Their profound faith in the larger meaning of their military service found its echo in the hosannas of the city's black populace that greeted them as they smartly marched into the Confederate capital. It was a moment of self-definition beyond words, the memory of which would reverberate in these men for decades to come. One white officer of black troops at Petersburg described similar scenes and thought he would never again "see so much wild joy as was manifest by both Soldiers and Union citizens as on that morning[.] The Slaves of the city," Robert Dryer wrote his father, "could not find expression to their happiness - it seemed to them to good to be real."[33]

The fervent collective faith, shared by black soldiers and freed slaves alike, was most powerfully evident when Abraham Lincoln visited Richmond only hours after it fell. As the President walked the streets, massive crowds of black men and women overwhelmed his small military escort, shouting, singing, and jostling to see him and perhaps touch him. "I know I am free," one old woman exclaimed, "for I have seen Father Abraham and felt him." "There is no describing the scene along the route," the black reporter Thomas Morris Chester wrote. "The colored population was wild with enthusiasm. Old men thanked God in a very boisterous manner, and old women shouted upon the pavement as high as they had done at a religious revival." Although the black soldiers in the city struggled to maintain order and their military mien, they too were exuberant. It was a historic moment: to have partaken in the destruction of the slave system gave ultimate meaning to their sacrifices and raised great hopes for the future. For Amos Webber, as for many black soldiers, the meaning of his participation in that liberation would form the foundation of his public activity in the decades to come.[34]

IN RICHMOND AS IN PETERSBURG, where the Fifth moved on April 7, the soldiers maintained stern discipline. Amid the celebrations their task was to restore order, prevent pillaging, and remain alert against attack by the remainder of Lee's army. In neither city, Colonel Adams thought, did the "usual scenes of violence which had accompanied such captures abroad" occur; and he thought his troops "behaved admirably." Yet for the men of the Fifth Cavalry their joy proved short-lived. Within a week of their posting at Petersburg, the regiment stood accused of so many criminal depredations that even Colonel Adams complained that the charges did "me an injustice." In the confusing situation as power was transferred from Confederate to Union officials, some—civilians and soldiers, whites and blacks—took advantage of the civic disorder to rob, rape, and inflict violence at will. Despite the "heavy guard" Adams placed around his camp, the Fifth Cavalry was singled out again and its men charged with major responsibility for such crimes. As had happened nearly a year before, the Fifth could not remove the stigma imposed on it and could only watch despondently as Grant's staff detached it from the 25th Corps and placed it back in camp near City Point. By the end of April this dissatisfaction extended to the whole of the all-black corps, which was branded as "a very improper force for the preservation of order in this department." Major General Henry W. Halleck accused these soldiers of a "number of cases of atrocious rape" and thought the corps had a bad influence on freedmen and -women. He urged Grant to remove the soldiers; the following day Grant ordered the corps to "a camp of instruction . . . until some disposition is made of them for defense of the sea-coast."[35]

The demotion of these soldiers reflected the racist attitudes of many white officers, especially those who commanded white regiments, but there was another aspect as well. Halleck's concern about the soldiers' "bad" influence on freed blacks suggested an unease concerning the sympathies of black soldiers as the South, and the nation, began the process of reconstruction. As more than one white officer noted, black soldiers interacted freely and enthusiastically with the former slaves; and the soldiers expressed "very bitter feelings toward the rebels," feelings that reinforced those held by the freedmen. That intermingling of black soldier and former slave challenged white prerogatives, both military and civilian. At a time when the military planned to herd former slaves back to the plantations to work under their old masters—in "some labor system in the interior," Halleck thought—black soldiers symbolized an alternative for freedmen and -women. Many of these soldiers were themselves former slaves and deeply sympathized with the demands of the freed people—for mobility, for new work relations, and above all for land of their own. They were also incensed when these demands were largely rejected even before the national political debate began. But Grant agreed with

Halleck. The presence of black troops, clad in Federal blue and exuding the possibilities of a broader freedom, impeded the general's plans, and they too were swept aside.[36]

Swept aside, but not yet dismissed. In May 1865 the 25th Army Corps received orders to sail for Texas, to occupy the one Confederate state that had never felt the presence of Federal troops during the long war. Military officials originally intended to deny straggling Confederate forces a sanctuary in Mexico from which they might continue guerrilla warfare, but by early June this more glorious possibility had dissipated, replaced by a far more prosaic, if not demeaning, rationale. Speaking of Texas, a reporter for the *Army and Navy Journal* stated that Grant had no intention of sending "any Eastern troops of importance to that service at present, Weitzel's Twenty-Fifth (colored) corps being the only ones mentioned as likely to go."[37]

Webber's reaction to these orders is unknown. But on June 12 other black cavalrymen, arriving at Fortress Monroe, Virginia, to board the transport ships, mutinied. Announcing their "unwillingness" to serve in Texas, they brandished their weapons and refused their officers' orders to board. The military command immediately organized an overwhelming force of white Pennsylvania troops and forced the black soldiers to stand down. The very next day Amos Webber and the men of the Fifth arrived to board those same ships.[38]

Accompanied by "Sutch Bad Water to Drink" and a consequent "Diereah," the voyage to Texas took the better part of a month. On sighting land the troops, many of whom had never gotten their sea legs, undoubtedly felt elated. But when the troops alit on July 6 at Brazos Santiago, nine miles from the mouth of the Rio Grande, it was not certain that their situation had dramatically improved. A "wretched sand-bar [that] surpassed any desert I have yet encountered," thought one white officer, Brigadier General Samuel Chapman Armstrong; "a long, low island entirely destitute of verdure." Nor were the climate and geography the most pressing issues at first. "We get no fresh vegatable or vegatables of any kind," Armstrong continued, "and seldom secure fresh meat. . . . We seldom receive letters or newspapers—nothing ever happens." Discouraged yet again, the Fifth nonetheless assumed its duties as ordered.

Despite Armstrong's complaints, something clearly did occur on the island. The base of a supply system that would support some 45,000 troops—white and black—in the army of occupation, Brazos Santiago instantly became the depot for the supplies and munitions that soon arrived in enormous quantities. To unload these supplies, and to prepare them for transshipment to the mainland, the Army detached the Third Division of the 25th Army Corps, which included the Fifth Massachusetts Cavalry. It was here, at Brazos Santiago, working as manual laborers, that the men of the Fifth spent the majority of their remaining time in the military.[39]

Conditions were horrible. The physical labor was hard, the climate unforgiving, and the emotional strain enervating. Rare was the soldier who avoided sick call entirely. For Webber's own Company D, the Texas sojourn proved to be the most fatal of their service. Thirteen of the company's fourteen deaths were the result of disease; most occurred at Brazos Santiago. The heat, debilitating dehydration, widespread scurvy, a host of intestinal disorders, and a numbing workload wreaked havoc on these men. Where help might have been expected, the white officers of these black soldiers often exhibited instead a profound scorn for their condition. As Edward Woolsey Bacon, a white officer of the 25th, wrote his wife with uncommon frankness that July:

> Men sent from Camp to Hospital lie on a hard brick floor until they die or get well, while the [officers] of the different Head Quarters keep constantly corned in whiskey and mixed drinks. Indeed it is my belief that the Hd.Qrs. 25*th* Corps have not been sober since the evacuation of Richmond. In every department of the Corps—except that of subsistence—there appears to be most criminal incompetency.

"Of course these remarks are highly improper and must not be repeated," Bacon admonished his wife, "unless you wish me dismissed [from] the service."[40]

Amos Webber received his promotion to quartermaster sergeant during July and this welcome advance removed the thirty-nine-year-old soldier from the worst of the physical labor.[41] Nothing, however, could restore his hopes for a more just postwar world. The army's actions by now revealed a very different reconstructed

America than what Webber and his comrades had suffered to achieve, for the attitude of these officers in Texas echoed official government policy. Black troops were treated harshly, and overall military policy precluded any effective occupation of the state,[42] with disastrous results for the newly freed population. In the three years following the Federal occupation of Texas, 468 blacks, mainly males, suffered violent deaths, primarily at the hands of white civilians. So brutal were conditions throughout the state that Major General Philip H. Sheridan was moved to write in an 1866 report that "[i]t is strange that over a white man killed by Indians on an extensive frontier the greatest excitement will take place, but over the killing of many freedmen in the settlements nothing is done." But as Sheridan might have reflected, where the army did intervene, its actions frequently reinforced a climate supportive of such depredations. Military commanders in Texas enforced the Black Codes (which restricted the movement of former slaves and forced them to sign disadvantageous labor contracts or face severe penalties) and, in the words of Sheridan, joined with the provisional governor of Texas to order "all such freemen that they must remain at home; that they will not be allowed to collect at military posts, and will not be supported in idleness." As in Virginia the military perceived black troops as a troublesome labor force, whose ideas and attitudes could rile a presumed docile black population. Former slaves "are very ignorant," thought Major General David S. Stanley, and thus could not be responsible for the belief, "at one time almost universal among the negroes of Texas," that the plantation lands would be confiscated and redistributed to them. "I do not know how they got the idea," Stanley told a congressional hearing,

but [I] have no doubt that our own soldiers put them up to it sometimes out of mischief. Soldiers are very apt to do such things, and I have no doubt the negro soldiers particularly gave them the idea. A negro community is very much like a system of telegraph wires; what one knows the whole State knows in a very short time.[43]

Following the pattern established that spring, Grant acted quickly to remove the alleged troublemakers. In order to prevent more "difficulties" with the black civilian population, he pressed the War Department to immediately muster out all black regiments raised in the northern states, regardless of the time left on their enlistments. By January 1, 1866, twelve of the twenty-nine black regiments, including the Fifth Massachusetts Cavalry, had departed Texas; four months later an additional eight regiments returned home. The already inadequate military presence, consisting of some 45,000 troops in September, had shrunk by almost 75 percent. This was not exactly disturbing news to many of those white military men who remained in Texas. Writing to his in-laws from headquarters at Hempstead, Texas, General George Armstrong Custer applauded the rapid withdrawal of the black soldiers: "I trust this will continue until they can lay down musket for shovel and hoe," he wrote. "There are white men, veterans, anxious to fill up the Army, to whom preference should be given."[44]

It had been only a few short months since Sergeant Amos Webber and his comrades in arms had liberated Richmond and gloried in the presence of Lincoln himself. Now that memory must have been painful, impaled as it was on such common, everyday experiences.

Yet for Webber and the men of the Fifth, their early separation from the service was welcome for other reasons. No leaves had been granted since the previous spring, and the men had received no pay between March and September. Their concern for their own families was intense. But despite the past months of physical, political, and personal disappointments, the men of the Fifth boarded the transport ships on October 22 to return to Boston, by way of New Orleans and New York City, in basically good health and, the Fifth's commanding officer judged, in even better spirits as they envisioned the pay yet due them and "their speedy return to their homes." A month later, during the Thanksgiving season, the Fifth finally arrived at Boston and, after accounting for army equipment in their possession, they received their back pay and their discharge papers.[45]

A final ceremony awaited them. Three days before Christmas, fifty members of the Fifth Cavalry, under the command of Charles Francis Adams, Jr., donned their uniforms once again to march through Boston's streets. They were joined by contingents

from almost every regiment raised in the state and, proudly flour-
ishing their battle standards—embroidered now with the name of
each of their engagements—the line of soldiers paraded for more
than two hours before a large, appreciative crowd until they
reached the State Capitol. There they were to present their standards to the state's ranking general, who, in turn, would pass them
to Governor John Andrew. As the Fifth approached, with the inscription "Baylor's Farm" visible on its standard, they presented
their banner first to Major General Darius Nash Couch, the same
officer who in June 1863 had refused to accept black soldiers for
the defense of Pennsylvania against Lee's then powerful Army of
Northern Virginia. Given all that had transpired since the Fifth
Massachusetts Cavalry (Colored) had assembled at Readville, it
was a fitting, if ironic, ending.[46]

IT HAD BEEN a difficult and troublesome period between the time
Amos Webber reported to Camp Meigs and his separation from
the military twenty-two months later. For Webber and his comrades of the Fifth, sustained racial tension, denigration by their
own commanders, and the studied withholding of the equipment
needed to perform their duty marked their service experience.
These accumulated insults took their toll on the men, to be sure,
but a profound pride also gripped them as well. Few experiences
could match what they felt on entering Richmond. That memory
affirmed a faith in and legitimized demands on a political culture
that, at its best, remained deeply ambivalent over the presence
of an engaged, free black citizenry. In ways that none could fore-
see in November 1865, the memory of that experience in turn
informed many of the actions and attitudes of postwar black
Americans.

    More personally, Amos Webber and his fellow sergeants—
William Carter, William D. Curtis, James Cornish, and the rest—
found that they had changed dramatically. Their military service
drew from them leadership capabilities previously unknown.
They had negotiated the racial rapids with some success, maintaining in the process their self-respect and largely that of their
men as well; and they discovered anew the value of discipline and

order in the creation of a group pride. Tempered by these struggles, and by the sobering experiences faced by all soldiers during wartime, they nonetheless retained the hope that their sacrifice would provide a place for them and their history within the broader American mosaic.

When Amos Webber returned to Worcester, to his wife, Lizzie, and to his job at Washburn and Moen in November 1865, he was a different man from the one who had enlisted. It was not that he had become a new person: his rectitude and his reserve, to say nothing of his strength of character and his courage, remained his most telling attributes. But as a result of his wartime experiences, Amos Webber was now a man more confident in his abilities and more willing to assume a leadership position. He may have allowed himself a small smile as he observed his confidence reflected in the reactions of Worcester residents, white and black, as he resumed his civilian activities.

CHAPTER SEVEN

CIVIL DUTIES

Amos Webber kept no chronicle throughout the 1860s. He certainly could not have lugged his large ledger books across Virginia, Maryland, and Texas, even though many soldiers did carry pocket-size diaries. He chose not to, for reasons he never revealed, and his persistent silence is particularly striking when set against the enormity of the events he experienced. Neither the joy of vanquishing slavery, nor the normal difficulties of military life, nor the racial insults that accompanied the Fifth's activities found an outlet. As no private wartime letters have survived, this articulate man essentially remains without a recorded, reflective voice during these years. Nor did Webber revive his chronicle immediately upon returning to Worcester in 1865. Although he had the Philadelphia chronicle in his possession in Worcester, he would not begin the second volume until 1870, five years after his demobilization from the service.[1]

With the exception of his furlough the previous March, Webber had been away from Worcester for the better part of two years, living in the company of men. As they resettled in civilian communities, the bonds formed in the military continued to structure the lives of these veterans. In Worcester and elsewhere, many soldiers moved from prewar communities and established new residences in light of their war-related friendships in patterns that reinforced wartime roles: even twenty years later, Webber was still Sergeant Webber in this circle. But that postwar experience also vividly echoed the shared nature of their military past. These veterans helped one another with the often difficult transition to civilian status, witnessed for each other in their applications for disability

and pension benefits, and enjoyed the recognition and respect accorded them by other black residents. Many of them became active in the complex associational life within the black community.
The experience of the war had indeed instilled "a confidence in
taking hold of the problems of civil duties" that many had not felt
before.[2]

Wartime conditions—the absence of accustomed amenities, the
rigorous discipline, the pervasive stench of the sick, the dead, and
the dying—also contributed to the transformation of many rather
innocent civilians. Then too, there was the killing. To risk one's
own life to take another's transformed the psyche in often unimaginable ways.[3]

———————

IN PHILADELPHIA DURING THE 1850s, Webber had been an activist in his lodge, in his church, and in the related political world
of slave rescues and abolitionist agitation. These activities, and
the moral and religious principles that fueled them, marked him
as a member of that moral community. But Amos Webber had not
been a leader. He held no lodge office, no supervisory position in
his church, nor did he orchestrate the activities of the Underground Railroad. His relative youth at the time and his status as a
recent migrant to a city where leadership traditionally came from
a coterie of established families explained part of this, but the pattern continued after Webber left Philadelphia. In the three years
in Worcester before his enlistment, in a city with a black population 1 percent of Philadelphia's, Webber's name did not appear on
the lists of organizers, speakers, or committee members of the
various groups active among Worcester's black citizens. The war
transformed Webber, however, and he returned to Massachusetts
no longer content simply to participate.

Black Worcester remained a minuscule portion of the city's population in 1865, but its support of the war effort had accelerated its
own internal organization. In 1865, while Webber was still in the
military, blacks celebrated the passage by Congress of the Thirteenth Amendment, which abolished slavery, and sponsored public talks on the postwar role of Negro Americans by such
prominent black orators as John S. Rock, Frances E. W. Harper,

and Frederick Douglass. In July of that year, black citizens played a significant role in the city's Independence Day parade. Gilbert Walker (barbering), Isaac Mason (house cleaning), and J. J. Mobray (wallpapering) entered horse-drawn floats signaling their trades. The banner that surrounded Walker's float sharply announced the stand of many: "The black man has shed his blood for the Union; he claims equal rights before the law."[4]

Black Worcester also celebrated the anniversary of Lincoln's Emancipation Proclamation on January 1 during these immediate postwar years. On one occasion William Wells Brown, the former slave and author, addressed "this jubilee of the colored people" at Washburn Hall, although the refusal of the A.M.E. Zion Church to participate resulted in a meeting "very thinly attended."[5] And even as American emancipation received its notice, the antebellum tradition of celebrating the abolition of slavery in the British West Indies continued every August 1. In both 1865 and 1866, large celebrations at Webster Park, in the southwest section of the city, drew blacks from the city and the surrounding communities for a picnic, speeches, and songs that echoed earlier freedom festivals. The 1866 fete had "considerable éclat," the Worcester *Evening Gazette* thought, as a well-attended "social dance . . . which was kept up to the small hours of the evening" followed the picnic.[6] This activity reflected a growth in the local black population—over 500 by 1870—that sparked the development of new institutions. Lay leaders J. J. Mobray, Henry Johnson, and Henry Cooper established the Bethel A.M.E. Church, known in its early years as the Bethel Society, in 1867, and Reverend Joshua Hale became its first pastor. The church remained a peripatetic institution, meeting in private homes and rented rooms for over a decade.[7]

If the war transformed black veterans and residents alike, the city too had altered. The war-induced inflation had abated, and in 1870 Worcester's total population had increased by more than 60 percent to over 41,000 inhabitants.[8] Driving this growth was the continued expansion of Worcester's industrial capacity. Production of textiles, machine tools, and boots and shoes grew throughout the decade,[9] but the most dramatic expansion occurred in wire production, and specifically in Webber's old company, Washburn and Moen. An important part of the city's economy in 1860, the company came to occupy a premier position in the postwar economy of both the city and the nation. In 1865 it incorporated and absorbed William E. Rice's Quinsigamond Iron and Wire Works. Three years later Washburn and Moen capitalized itself at one million dollars, the first company in Worcester to reach that level; in 1869 the firm introduced a continuous rolling mill at its Grove Street plant, which allowed it to expand production while reducing costs. By 1870, the firm of Washburn and Moen ranked among the largest iron-producing corporations in the country, whose more than 600 employees turned out over 35 miles of wire daily.[10]

Growing pains accompanied these developments in both the firm and the city. Worcester had a reputation as a nonunion town where employer paternalism, backed by force if needed, marked industrial relations. Yet its working people were not supine. Washburn and Moen had experienced a short strike in 1864,[11] and the postwar years marked the gradual emergence of intense labor activity in the city. The Knights of St. Crispin and its female auxiliary, the Daughters of St. Crispin, each formed city locals among boot and shoe workers, and numerous other craft workers, such as the carpenters, also organized locals. In 1866 Worcester workers formed a citywide Trades Assembly, which, with the active support of such craft unions as the cigarmakers, tailors, bricklayers, and coachmakers, established a short-lived "co-operative produce store" in 1867. Working to encourage "a fraternal feeling among the workingmen," the Trades Assembly sponsored speakers and public forums on trade union issues.[12]

Perhaps most important, the Trades Assembly and its constituent unions sought to support other white workers in their strikes. Bricklayers, boot and shoe workers, city laborers, coal team drivers, hod carriers, masons, tailors, and others struck for wage increases or for union recognition during these years, often with the support of other unions. Occasionally successful, these strikes more often revealed labor's structural weakness in the city. Unions that offered assistance to other workers one year were themselves frequently extinct the next, a consequence of weak organization, employer resistance, or both. This was the experience of the small percentage of the Washburn and Moen workforce who struck in both 1868 and 1870. They had been active in supporting other workers, but these Washburn and Moen workers lost both strikes—in part because other workers in the firm did not support them—and were able to reclaim their jobs only if they promised "never again to engage in a similar movement."[13] Another failed strike at Washburn and Moen in these postwar years resulted in a concerted effort by strikers and other working people in the Democratic Party caucus to deny a company official nomination as a delegate to the state Democratic convention.[14] Such victories were rare, however, and did not challenge the city's basic economic structure.

Furthermore, racial distinctions sharply limited the development of the "fraternal feeling" the Trades Assembly promoted. When the black waiters at the Bay State House, Worcester's largest hotel and restaurant, struck in May 1868, just before the dinner hour, they received little sympathy then or in the days that followed from white workers. The waiters, who also boarded at the hotel, demanded five dollars more per month. They refused to tie on their aprons until their demands were met, forming "a long line of colored individuals standing shoulder to shoulder" in the dining room, while the guests awaited service. The proprietor, Major O. C. Hatch, a leader in the Third Ward's Republican Party and an activist in the Grand Army of the Republic, the veterans' organization, refused the pay raise and ordered the men back to work. They in turn refused, and the stalemate lasted until Hatch threatened to replace the waiters immediately. "This was a contingency that had not been anticipated," the local paper commented, "and after a moment's reflection, they silently donned their aprons."[15]

After the war Webber had returned to his position as a janitor in Henry C. Willson's tempering room at Washburn and Moen. Within a year his earnings, coupled with the last of his military pay, allowed him to purchase a lot and to erect a house at 25 Liberty Street—in the heart of the Second Ward's cluster of black families—where the Webbers would reside for most of the next four decades. A wooden single-family house in northeast Worcester, with a barn on the lot for horses and enough rooms inside to extend hospitality to visiting Philadelphia friends and to install a frequently used piano, the Webber residence stood apart on a block where most neighbors, black and white, lived in the multifamily dwellings known as triple-deckers. A modest house in comparison to the mansions of the wealthy that dotted the exclusive Salisbury Street area less than a mile to the north and west, possession of it differentiated the Webbers from the majority of black, and even white, Worcester.[16] Webber's wages suggested a similar demarcation. Among the lowest in Willson's department, his rate in 1869 of $2.25 per eleven-hour day, coupled with consistent employment (he worked some 255 days), produced a yearly wage of $573.75. Anything but lavish, the sum nonetheless equaled the average yearly wage of all workers, black and white, regardless of skill, in Worcester during the first half of the 1870s.[17] Within black Worcester, where wages were generally lower and employment less secure than among whites, Webber's salary and home ownership placed this workingman squarely within its upper ranks. This standing, and his newly discovered capabilities as a leader, led Amos Webber to an ever more public role in Worcester.

BEFORE 1868, Webber's name did not appear on the published lists of organizers and activists within black Worcester, although he undoubtedly attended some of the meetings and celebrations as a private citizen. It was perhaps ironic, if nonetheless understandable in light of his fundamental political commitments, that the first organization he joined was Worcester's previously all-white Grand Army of the Republic (GAR).

The GAR became the fastest-growing voluntary organization in the nation in the years following the war. Established in Decatur, Illinois, in April 1866, the GAR had but one requirement for prospective members: that the applicant be a former Union soldier with an honorable discharge. Economic distinctions, social background, and ethnic and racial identities received no formal recognition when members were inducted. The stated purposes of the GAR were equally direct. The veterans organized "to preserve and strengthen those kind and fraternal feelings" that had formed during the recent conflict; to aid former comrades and their families in need; and to instill a patriotism "based on a paramount respect for and fidelity to the national Constitution and laws . . . and to encourage the spread of universal liberty, equal rights, and justice to all men." To ensure against divisiveness within the group, all partisan political discussions were banned, as were group endorsements of candidates for political office. By 1870, the GAR had nearly 300,000 members nationally.[18]

Driving those more formal aims were often potent, powerful private needs as well. "I am more sorry than ever before that my home is not near yours or some of those of my friends in the Regiment," Harry Krebs wrote Worcester's Woodbury Smith in 1866. "I miss you more than I can tell you." Like so many soldiers, Krebs had also returned home to discover that the "one great friend" of his prewar life "is gone—Killed by a Traitor's *bullet*. . . . I loved him more than tongue can speak or *heart* can utter," he confided to his friend and former captain, "and in the midst of home and dear ones I feel a deep saddness, and a strange feeling of lonliness."[19] The GAR provided a context to assuage such pain.

Similar impulses led Worcester veterans in April 1867 to establish the George H. Ward Post 10, named after a fallen local officer. Meeting at first in rented rooms, the post soon purchased its own hall on Pearl Street, just off Main Street in the business district, across from the public library. The composition of the Worcester post reflected the official egalitarian ethos. Of the eleven men who organized the post, three were skilled workers (two machinists and a carpenter), four were clerks, while three were professionals and businessmen, and one, City Marshal James M. Drennan, was an elected public official. Classic Anglo-Saxon names such as Fordis O. Bushnell shared space on post membership lists with the names of more recent immigrants such as Dennis W. Meagher and Peter J. O'Marra. All, however, were white. By 1870, the post had enrolled an estimated 9 percent of Worcester's adult males, growing from a membership of 304 in 1867 to more than triple that size three years later.[20]

This was the post Amos Webber joined in 1868. How he joined and how the white veterans received this first black member remain unknown. But Webber's reasons for desiring membership were understandable and, on one level, quite pragmatic. The GAR had proclaimed its intention "to establish and secure the rights of these defenders of their country, by all moral, social, and political means in our control." And secure them they did. Nationally, GAR officials pressured Congress to broaden pension eligibility and to increase payments. In Massachusetts, state GAR officials would demand an exemption for veterans from civil service requirements. As early as 1868, Post 10 urged Worcester officials to give preference to veterans in filling positions in the public works department. In keeping with their culture's broad strictures, however, the men of Post 10 also turned to self-help to take care of their own. In 1867 they established a relief fund to support veterans and their families in need unless their "own immoral, or criminal conduct" was responsible for their difficulties. So rooted was this relief in a particular moral vision—a vision that resonated deeply in Amos Webber's own mind—that the post soon established a committee of three watchers in each of the city's eight wards to visit both applicants and recipients of the fund to determine their credibility.[21]

One of the GAR's most meaningful rituals was the annual Decoration Day observance on May 30. With his fellow members, Webber marched in solemn procession to the three city cemeteries holding the remains of the Union dead. For Webber such celebrations bespoke of a shared sacrifice in pursuit of a common national goal, tying him to an emerging concept of a national community. As one who had risked his life to forge a more inclusive meaning of citizenship, this black veteran—who had never thought of himself as without a country or lacking a history—now demanded subtly but quite publicly that white Americans recognize what he held as self-evident. This formal commitment to equality, sealed with the blood of soldiers, was a patriotism worth embracing.[22]

Perhaps because active military duty becalmed such concerns by immersing men in alternating bursts of bloodletting and boredom, the end of hostilities triggered in veterans an emotionally difficult transition back to civilian life. For some the GAR's egalitarian rules—open as it was to all who had shared honorably in the defining moment of maleness—were a sharp but welcome contrast to more competitive social relations beyond the post's four walls. A society of male equals, the post's historian thought, required that religious and ethnic identities, although reflecting an "individual adherence," be left behind at the post's door in favor of "a religious tolerance very different from the general attitude at

Interior of Post 10, GAR meeting room, GAR Hall, Worcester, 1895.
The post commander's chair and those of his aides face the flag-draped
altar at the center of the room and, in the foreground where the pho-
tographer stood, the seats of the Post's members. *Courtesy of American
Antiquarian Society*

the time." In this view, the post itself possessed an almost sacred
character, separating the men from the more secular and profane
everyday world, as well as from women, whose social roles had
greatly expanded during the war. In establishing the " 'form' of
'setting up the stations' of its various officers, the use of the altar,
and its ritual, both in wording and exemplification in 'floor-
work,' " Post 10 created a symbolic spiritual world that matched
its physical contours.[23]

Yet the rhetoric of fraternity had its limits. Nationally the
GAR soon overlooked discrimination toward black veterans, a
concession to the continued refusal of many white veterans to acknowledge the black soldier as a comrade. Black veterans in
Philadelphia, for example, as early as January 1867, held a convention of the Colored Soldiers and Sailors League to demand
"equality of rights with the white soldiers." Perhaps because
Worcester still had so small a group of black veterans in comparison with Philadelphia, no branch of the league was established in
the city.[24]

As the first black member of Post 10, Webber broke this segregated pattern, and his example led other black veterans to consider a similar step. Not all followed his lead; nor did white members necessarily welcome those who did. Thus it was not surprising that, even as he joined Post 10, Webber assumed a central role in another organization that pointedly addressed black Worcester's concerns. In the process, he provided himself with what would become the bedrock of his postwar public identity.

On August 1, 1868, Amos Webber convened the first meeting of North Star Lodge, No. 1372, of the Grand United Order of Odd Fellows. The names of the charter members have not survived, but Webber's central position was clear: in succeeding decades Odd Fellows repeatedly celebrated him "as the founder of North Star Lodge." An active member of the Order in Philadelphia, Webber had been without its fellowship since moving to Worcester. The pool of eligible black men in Worcester may have been too small before 1865 and Webber not yet sure of his abilities, but after the war black Worcester was larger and—like Webber himself—more energized. The arrival of the official dispensation from New York City's Philomathean Lodge in mid-August 1868, authorizing the organization of the North Star Lodge, marked an important turning point in the city's collective black life. Joining black residents of Boston and New Bedford (who had maintained lodges since 1846), black Worcester's new association reflected an additional commitment to collective organization and action.[25]

Neither the date of the founding nor the name of the lodge was selected accidentally. August 1 had long been observed by northern blacks to commemorate West Indian emancipation in 1834, and the North Star, of course, was both the astral guide of the fugitive slave and, when it appeared on the masthead of Frederick Douglass's newspaper in 1848, the political guide of the emancipated black citizen.[26] Those symbols, and Webber's action, also carried important meaning in relation to Worcester's white fraternal world. White lodges of the Independent Order of Odd Fellows, in Worcester as elsewhere, regularly ridiculed efforts by blacks to share in the values they held. The presence of North Star Lodge challenged such racial assumptions and claimed for blacks in Worcester a place in that broader fraternal world.[27]

Not unlike the GAR post, North Star Lodge had its meetings, its socials, and its public celebrations. But in a fashion quite different from those of Post 10, the lodge's celebrations were framed by American racial realities. Both groups sought to create an "inner Sanctuary," where universal values transcended social, economic, and religious distinctions, but unlike the veterans, who claimed to transcend (momentarily) even their ethnicity, black Odd Fellows remained rooted in their racial identity. The lodge became a self-conscious instrument of both individual and collective black self-help; with its meetings and socials, it bound together a leadership group that encouraged one another's attainments even as it offered assistance to those in need. Women were actively involved with the lodge from very early on, even before the establishment of the Worcester branch of the Household of Ruth, the female auxiliary; the realities of poverty and prejudice in black Worcester prevented these men from luxuriating in an exclusively male world unlike the more populous GAR.[28]

The establishment of North Star Lodge struck a responsive chord. Within three years it reported forty dues-paying members and a succession of men had assumed the position of grand master once Webber stepped down after a year. This rotation in office layered black Worcester with additional experienced leaders. The lodge officers were primarily working people—painters and gardeners, janitors and porters, with an occasional barber or minister as well.[29] Although most worked with their hands, collectively they formed a recognized leadership network within black Worcester, sharply differentiating them from more socially stratified black communities such as Philadelphia's.

Though closer to the world of the poor, these men and women were not themselves the most destitute. They could afford induction fees, monthly dues (as much as fifty cents for men and twenty-five cents for women), and further fees and frequent assessments for the Odd Fellows–sponsored mutual benefit society. Coupled with the cost of uniforms, regalia, and travel (including the loss of a day's pay for the numerous visits to other lodges), active membership in North Star Lodge and its female auxiliary was, as a practical matter, limited to a segment of the city's black working people. Steady employment at more than bare subsistence was all but a prerequisite for joining.[30]

Amos Webber's membership in both the GAR and the Odd Fellows suggests that he possessed a complex appreciation of his place in postwar America. In the GAR, Webber publicly claimed his rights as a veteran and as a citizen, as well as his right to define the meaning of the war in the nation's memory through his continued, uniformed public presence. But his involvement in the organization proved limited, in part by the coolness of white members toward black veterans and in part by the requirements for membership that excluded most of Worcester's black men.

In contrast, North Star Lodge—which, ironically, rented rooms in the GAR's Pearl Street hall—allowed Webber an outlet for his talents, provided a vehicle for the continued development of his leadership qualities, and established the setting in which he nurtured even his private sense of self. Given the relentless denigration of black Americans by whites, the creation of such mediating institutions was essential to counter potentially debilitating images. The individual growth and the group cohesion experienced in the lodge proved, as in Philadelphia, to be a precursor to more concerted, collective political action as well. The exchange of visits between the different lodges, forming as they did an intricate pattern that crisscrossed the centers of northern black urban life, reinforced a larger sense of collective purpose and in that exchange of information, discussion of group strategy, and formation of friendship lay the trellis that supported a great variety of northern black activism.

The need for this continued activism quickly became evident. During the administration of Andrew Johnson, who succeeded to the presidency following Lincoln's assassination, the conditions of freedmen and -women actually worsened in many areas. Although slavery had been abolished, in much of the South racial violence, fanned by the Ku Klux Klan and other groups, raged. Black voters were intimidated and worse; black farmers were run off their land; and schools for black children were underfunded or eliminated outright. Nor was the North a racial paradise. In the four years following Appomattox nine northern states rejected referenda that would place black male voters on a par with white men, and schools that accepted black children remained rare and poorly maintained in most northern states.[31]

In Massachusetts black men possessed the right to vote, although the existence of a poll tax created certain hardships.[32] Even in Worcester, with its liberal, abolitionist reputation, hopes remained largely unfulfilled. As Samuel May, the Worcester-area abolitionist, wrote in the summer of 1868, many in the North had "sympathized with the Slaveholders & the Rebels all through the war, [and] still sympathize with them." Writing to Edwin Connant, his former Harvard College classmate and at the time Worcester's Democratic Party leader in the Second Ward, May connected these national concerns with local Worcester politics as the city prepared for the November presidential election. These same northerners, among whom he included his correspondent, now sought by violence if necessary to deny black Americans their basic "human rights throughout the Southern States, and, for ought they know (or, I think, care) over every square mile of our country."[33]

Worcester's Republicans themselves bore out part of May's dire predictions within weeks of his letter to Connant. Ulysses S. Grant, the Republican candidate, ran in the national arena as the victorious general who had restored the Union and vanquished slavery, and as one who would defend the Fourteenth Amendment with its provision that all citizens possessed "equal protection" and "due process" under the law. In contrast the Democrats had nominated Horatio Seymour, the governor of New York who had publicly befriended the draft rioters in 1863; his running mate was Frank Blair, an unreconstructed white supremacist who openly attacked southern black political activists as "a semi-barbarous race of blacks who are worshippers of fetishes and polygamists."[34] In Worcester, as elsewhere in the North, local Republican parties trimmed their national platform to appeal to voters. Reminders of a war to abolish slavery and of the need for continued vigilance in defense of black rights had limited appeal even among Worcester's Republican voters.

Thus, while the Republican Party's national platform still supported black political rights, the local convention of Worcester Republicans prepared for the coming election in a different mood. They presented themselves as "the only true conservative party of the nation," and underscored their party's past defense of the Union "against all attempts at disruption." Worcester's white Republicans largely ignored the issue of protecting black rights, North or South; rather, they asked voters to measure their current role as preservers of the Union by their announced resolve to reject "all attempts at repudiation of honest debts contracted to save the life of the nation."[35] For many black voters, such a stance sharply diminished the political distance between the two parties and their candidates for the presidency.

In states with a larger black voting population (Massachusetts had only 1,400 black male voters in 1867), it was possible to consider institutional challenges to this form of white dominance. In Pennsylvania, for example, black residents created the Equal Rights League, which sponsored the founding convention of the short-lived Colored Soldiers and Sailors League. More successfully, a committee of Equal Rights activists led by David B. Bowser, the national grand master of the Grand United Order of Odd Fellows, lobbied the legislature and the governor to outlaw segregation on the state's railroad cars. In Philadelphia particularly, lodges of the Order enrolled *en masse* as locals of the Equal Rights League, in an effort to provide an independent base for black political organizing that might win concessions from local white Republicans.[36] The smaller numbers of blacks in Massachusetts prevented similar developments in that state and funneled most political energy toward the Republican Party, despite its tepid defense of black rights.

The 1868 presidential campaign in Worcester graphically captured the dilemma black residents encountered. The Republican Party refused to allow black voters to join regular party organizations and instead organized segregated Colored Grant and Colfax Clubs for black supporters. But even this proved too much for some whites. On the evening of November 2, 1868, Worcester's Colored Grant and Colfax Club, consisting of fifty uniformed men under the leadership of white officers, marched in support of their candidates as part of a large Republican torchlight parade. All along the way, hostile crowds, interspersed among Republican supporters, intermittently attacked the parading Republicans, but the principal target was the black Republican contingent. Three times the howling white mob attacked these marchers; three times these black men repulsed their assailants, effectively wielding their lit torches against the mob. Stones and bricks rained down upon the marchers, pistol shots frequently were heard, and one white attacker found himself chased through a store's large glass window by black Republicans. Miraculously, no one was killed, although both sides incurred injuries. With anger, but also with considerable satisfaction, Worcester's black Republicans finished their march.[37]

It is likely that Amos Webber was part of that group of black Republicans who aggressively defended themselves in 1868. His name did not appear in local press accounts, but his involvement in both the GAR and the Odd Fellows already made him a leader within black Worcester. That standing in the community would now demand of Webber an increased public presence and engagement.

ULYSSES GRANT WON THE 1868 PRESIDENTIAL ELECTION AND, for all the political tacking on the part of local Republican supporters, that was undoubtedly a better result for black citizens than if Horatio Seymour had been elected. A certain expectation permeated the politics of men such as Webber, as they hoped Grant's election signaled a more explicit public proclamation of equal rights for all Americans. Certainly popular perceptions of the Fifteenth Amendment, ratified in 1870, enhanced this expectation. The measure, the last of the Reconstruction-era amendments, prohibited either federal or state government from preventing any citizen from voting due to race. Despite its critical loopholes,[38] many northern blacks regarded the Fifteenth Amendment as the crowning legislative achievement of the Civil War decade, a major advance in their struggle for a race-free concept of citizenship.

In Worcester these hopes were overt and public. At a meeting on April 1, 1870, black residents voted to send a delegation and a marching band to join the massive demonstration in Boston to celebrate the passage of the Fifteenth Amendment. The citizens elected Amos Webber and Joseph A. Palmer, a veteran of the 54th Massachusetts (Colored) Infantry, to serve as marshals for the occasion. Two weeks later Webber and Palmer led the forty members of North Star Lodge, in military formation, wearing their official regalia, and preceded by a marching band, through Worcester's streets to the railroad depot. The marchers joined another forty-five black men and a "large number of lady friends" to fill four railroad cars for the trip to Boston. There, with thousands of others, white and black, they marched in the streets and listened to speeches by William Lloyd Garrison and Wendell Phillips, two of the nation's premier antebellum abolitionists.[39]

By 1870, Webber's position within black Worcester was widely acknowledged. Most whites might perceive him, when he was not simply invisible to them, as a janitor easily dismissed; but in black Worcester he was a man of regard who could be trusted with important public responsibilities. His qualities of command, his veteran's status, and his commitment to the Odd Fellows all promoted him in the eyes of others as one whose opinions carried meaning and upon whose involvement the success of major public ventures in part resided. Important in this calculus as well was the role of the Odd Fellows. In establishing North Star Lodge, Webber and his fraternal brothers provided a firm moral foundation for their public, political action. In a community where church membership was not universal (no church, for example, recorded Webber as a member at this time), the lodge's moral strictures and concern with individual responsibility and social order provided a secular standard that augmented that of religious leaders. In this fashion a moral politics, at once personal and public in its demands and expectations, framed the stance of a significant number of black men and women in the city.

Webber's membership in these associations provided him with forms of entertainment as well. Debates and discussions on numerous issues occupied a portion of North Star's frequent meetings, and the GAR post sponsored a large number of public events, such as the play *The Drummer Boy,* a heroic rendition of the battle of Shiloh, which it presented more than twenty-five times over the course of several decades as a fund-raiser for its charitable work among its more destitute members. One of the play's central characters was "Uncle Joe, the old darkey, who was in the right place at the right time." In keeping with the minstrel tradition, a white actor in blackface always played this role. At least twice during these years Webber was in the audience when the curtain went up. He also may have attended some of the lectures given under GAR aegis during 1868 and 1869. The topics varied: Anna E. Dickinson spoke on Mormonism, polygamy, and the degradation of women; Kate Field on life in the Adirondacks; Senator Charles Sumner on the origins of caste divisions; and William Denton, a local amateur scientist, on the development of mental culture.[40] Between the meetings of lodge and post, the entertainments sponsored by each, the demands of work, and his political activities, Webber's days were full, and though deeply rooted in black Worcester he nonetheless maintained, through work and through the local GAR, a significant involvement with whites as well. This reflected his fundamental political commitments—he was a soldier, a citizen, a black American—and allowed him to maintain his focus on the ultimate goal of a society whose public functions were thoroughly integrated. How troublesome, then, to Webber's larger purposes was the racially driven rejection of another black veteran by Post 10 but two months after the celebration of the Fifteenth Amendment's passage.

The rejected veteran was First Sergeant Bazzel Barker, Company B, Fifth Massachusetts (Colored) Cavalry, a friend of Webber's who was then a barber working in Worcester. He applied for membership in Post 10 in late May 1870, and on June 2 his application was rejected; he reapplied on the ninth, only to be rejected again. These rejections, apparently on racial grounds, instigated fierce debate within the post. The members then passed a resolution that brought the post into compliance with official national GAR policy in explicitly rejecting race as a condition of membership. Yet on June 16, following the passage of the resolution, Barker reapplied, only to be rejected again. At this point three of the officers, including the white post commander, A. C. Soley, resigned in protest. No record of the specific resolution of this dispute exists, but Bazzel Barker's name never appeared on Post 10's membership rolls.[41]

Amos Webber was an active member of Post 10 at this time and possibly participated in the heated debates over his friend's application. As the minute books of the post have been lost, and Webber did not resume his chronicle until six months later, it is impossible to know how he acted at that time. Yet the different experiences of Webber and Barker demand some explanation. Although Barker was a respected noncommissioned officer and longtime Massachusetts resident (he had been married in Worcester in 1850 and resided in Boston when he enlisted in January

1864), perhaps white post members objected to his Maryland birth, which they equated with a slave experience.[42] Equally plausible, the simple presence of this second black applicant may have exhausted the limits of tolerance for a number of white members. For some whites, moreover, Webber's association with white veterans at Washburn and Moen may have made him acceptable; in contrast, Bazzel Barker worked for a black barber in a small business that catered to a white clientele. That perception of servility clashed sharply with many members' protestation of their own manhood.

What is clear, however, is that Amos Webber did not passively accept these racial taunts. While his words remained unrecorded, his actions both before and after the debate over Barker suggest that, in concert with white supporters, Webber redoubled his efforts to establish a black presence in Post 10. Six months prior to Barker's application Webber, then the only black member, helped arrange for the participation of the A.M.E. Zion Church in the GAR fair. The church set up a "Fred Douglass table" for their baked goods, an activity that involved a broader segment of black Worcester than just church members. Six months later, Webber accepted election as Post 10's alternate delegate to the state GAR's convention the following year. Ultimately, white resistance evaporated, in part as a result of his leadership, and over the next two decades, more than twenty additional black veterans joined Webber as members of the post.[43]

The ultimate goal for Webber and this community of moral activists in Worcester remained a social order free of racial barriers. Few, however, were innocent enough in 1870 to think they had no need for organizations that specifically addressed the concerns of black Americans. Webber engaged in both black and white arenas, and his activities suggest he hoped, in time, to bridge the distance between them. The continued dissension over the role of blacks in a reconstructed America subjected these hopes to a sharp and painful test.

CHAPTER EIGHT

To Stand for Right

—————

SOMETIME BEFORE DECEMBER 1870, Amos Webber purchased another ledger book quite similar to the one he had used in Philadelphia. The cover and the title page marked the starting date as December 1, 1870, and Webber numbered the book, "1st *Vol.*" As he had years earlier, he simply titled his chronicle "Amos Webber Thermometer Book."

On the first page of this volume Webber entered the month, year, and the designation "Worcester." Just beneath that heading he titled the first section: "State of the Thermometer at 9° A.M. 3° P.M." As he had in his Philadelphia volume, he lined the page with vertical columns for each observation time, in order to enter the temperature, wind direction, and a commentary twice daily. On page 100, the halfway point in the book, he wrote across the top: "1870 Local Pages Worcester Mass". That done, he was again ready, more than a decade after his last entry, to give shape to his world.[1]

Webber's use of the term "1st *Vol.*" did not indicate that he had lost the Philadelphia volume. On December 30, 1870, when he recorded the month's lowest temperature (9 degrees), Webber added a note at the bottom of the first "Thermometer" page referring an imagined reader ahead to the "Local Pages" section, where he compared climatic conditions in Worcester for December 30, 1870, with Philadelphia's generally warmer weather on the same day between 1854 and 1859. His 1870 entry almost perfectly matched those originally made years earlier, and was most likely copied directly from the Philadelphia book. As Webber observed: "Thus we see a great different of the temperature = of the distance to 3 or 400 miles &c." He had clearly not lost any of his curiosity about the physical world or his drive to seek order in nature's phenomena; the term "1st *Vol.*" merely reflected a change in location.[2]

Webber never acknowledged the gap of more than a decade, and he never explained why he began again late in 1870. Always laconic when discussing his own motivations, he was totally silent about these points. Indirectly, his first entry in the "Local Pages" hinted at one possible catalyst: Washburn and Moen had just moved to new offices on Grove Street at the eastern tip of Salisbury Pond, a short walk from where Main Street merged with Lincoln Square.[3] As in Philadelphia, Webber kept his chronicle at work—"At the East Side of the W.M.Maf. C. [Washburn and Moen Manufacturing Company] office the thermometer stood at 6:15 4 Deg^s = 8 Ocl 6 Deg^s 9Oclock 9 Deg^s", he wrote when comparing Worcester and Philadelphia on December 30[4]—and thus a thermometer, perhaps not available in the old office, was included in the accoutrements of the new. Still, that convenience does not explain Webber's deeper motivations for resuming his writing. As his life became more complex, given his leadership in black political and fraternal organizations, he may have felt more intensely the need to use a chronicle to order and structure his thoughts. That purpose certainly infused his first volume. What can be said with confidence is that Amos Webber used his chronicle to develop ideas that, as a black man in a predominantly white society, he had limited opportunity to explore in more public venues. At the deepest level Webber told stories in his own particular narrative style because he found great personal satisfaction in knowing that the chronicle existed. His life, and the lives of his friends and associates, counted for something in this world; and his storytelling redeemed some of the pain, and preserved some of the pleasure, of daily life.

WORK REMAINED AN important theme in Webber's life. He mentioned the new office, a workingman who lost a finger in an industrial accident, a clerk who left the firm, and the return of one of the partners from six months of travel in England, "a sojourn" from the business in order to "expand the bump of knowledge to see strange sights and wonders of the world."[5] Events at work also tapped into Webber's scientific interests. When a steam pipe "bursted" at Washburn and Moen's new office, he blamed the worker who installed the radiator system for "not understanding the philosophy of steam, and going by directions but the direction, led to the bursting of the pipe &c=" Webber's emphasis on scientific understanding carried a specific charge for, and image of, the workingman: "Every thing should be made plain to person before acting alone= as a Mother says to her son, my son see me cut this apple into; Now you do the same= the act is done, the same by the child = which is correct . . . therefore every person before acting should understand the nature of their cases;="[6] Amos Webber, janitor, scientific enthusiast, annalist, and self-conscious chronicler, whose own employment profoundly underutilized his abilities, found the parent-child analogy quite appropriate in assessing the capabilities of at least some of the workers he cleaned up after in the plant.

In a different mood, Webber's interest in science and meteorology sparked a tight, almost coded social commentary. On December 16, Webber observed that although the temperature had fallen sharply, Salisbury Pond, a small body of water just west of Washburn and Moen, had yet to freeze. "The skaters are looking anxiously for this pond to freeze over, So they may have a gay time, at this amusement. both Ladies and Gentlemen.= both Rich & Poor." Webber's inclusion of economic criteria in describing "this amusement" suggested a recognition of social distinctions. More pointedly his evocation of the "gay time" that awaited all contained another, hidden meaning. Two years earlier Charles Bulah, "a colored chap," won a skating competition, the Worcester *Evening Gazette* noted, by showing "his competitors a 'a clean pair of heels.' " Overnight, charges were made that Bulah was not the recognized champion, that he was guilty of some unspecified, underhanded tactics, and the *Evening Gazette* now called for "a good square match, and see whose heels get out of sight first."[7] As Webber well knew, even simple pleasures could not escape the pervasive racism that prevented many whites from envisioning any black success.

Politics also occupied Webber's attention in December 1870. He happily recorded the election victory of incumbent Republican Mayor James B. Blake on December 12 by a three-to-one margin over his Democratic challenger.[8] But five days later, a "Terrible Explosion" wrecked the city's gasworks while Blake and a foreman were on the site; on December 18, the mayor died of the burns he suffered. Webber wrote a detailed account of the official funeral, including the different groups in the procession, and composed an original poem of four stanzas to mark the occasion.

As was often the case with Webber's social commentary, much remained latent. Of Blake's political career and religious fate Webber wrote openly; the meaning of the funeral procession he conveyed far more indirectly. Included toward the end of Webber's listing of the marchers were the city's fraternal orders. Henry C. Willson, Webber's foreman at Washburn and Moen, led some 200 white Masons; they were followed by "Quinsigamond Lodge I.O. of O.F. (White)," the national organization of white Odd Fellows; then came "North Star Lodge. G.U.O. of O.F. (colored) 30 men Also several other societies walk Germans French, & Irish=the bells tolling till after the funeral=" Webber's juxtaposition of the white and colored Odd Fellows recognized the reality of racial separation while simultaneously his inclusion of North Star Lodge as but one of many fraternal and voluntary societies who paid their respects claimed for black residents their right to transcend the racial divide by participating as equals in the city's pluralistic civic and political life. As in so many other instances, what Webber recorded he often participated in, and his commentary contained tiers of meaning he did not always develop explicitly. Perhaps most revealing, however, was the poem Webber wrote in Blake's honor. While it was a rather sentimental depiction of Blake's thoughts on leaving this life, it also contained a much less sentimental commentary on Webber's understanding of human existence. The last couplet of the first stanza read: "Since Jesus, has call^d me: I dread not the tomb, / But leave you all here, mid sorrow & gloom,".[9]

———— ——

WEBBER'S WORKDAY WAS quite long. As his entry comparing temperatures in Philadelphia and Worcester indicated, he could be at

Washburn and Moen as early as six-fifteen in the morning, and he was required to stay as long as one of his supervisors had need of his services. Although he still referred to himself as a janitor,[10] in reality his duties were broader than that title might suggest. In addition to his responsibilities in Henry C. Willson's tempering room, senior officials of the firm called on Webber to drive their horse-drawn carriages about town, deliver messages throughout the city, and make regular runs to the post office on Pearl Street. He often conversed with the company officials he drove about and also with employees at other firms where he stopped on business. These travels also enabled him to enjoy Worcester's street life, talk with friends, and conduct his own fraternal or political business. His familiarity with company executives occasionally conveyed other privileges as well: "Amos at home to day work in garden" was one workday's entire entry.[11]

Webber was not the only employee at Washburn and Moen who developed comfortable relations with foremen and supervisors. Throughout the 1860s, amid the occasional strikes and union organizing in the city, Washburn and Moen workers regularly participated in rituals honoring their foremen and supervisors. The tempering-room workers twice presented gifts—"a handsome goldheaded cane" in 1862, followed several years later by a pair of silver goblets—to their foreman, and foremen of other departments were given similar celebrations. In December 1869, all the employees of the firm held their first social at Horticulture Hall, which was deemed well attended by the local paper. Washburn and Moen workers were by no means unique in the city for these events. Workers in textile mills and machine shops and in the construction trades also partook in similar festivities, even as some also participated in the more antagonistic world of strikes and worker demands.[12]

When workers presented supervisors with gifts, the range of emotion governing such events was quite broad. Friendship, coercion, respect, fear, and the demands of an honorific ritual—all these and more could motivate the participants. From contemporary newspaper accounts it is almost impossible to distinguish among these possibilities, since the reports in Worcester's papers celebrated only a presumed harmony of interests between worker and foreman, between white and black. But early in January 1871

Employees in front of the Washburn and Moen Grove Street Plant, Worcester, 1874. Production workers, clerks, and even children are present, but none of the plant's black workers are clearly identifiable. *Courtesy of Baker Library, Harvard University Graduate School of Business Administration, Boston*

Webber himself participated in a series of such socials and left a firsthand account.

"The old hands of the tempering room . . . under Mr. Henry C. Willson," Webber began, carried two camp chairs to the home of George A. Barber, a co-worker in Willson's department, and his wife. "We found Mr. Barber asleep in the front room, as we walk in upon him. he was about to run, but we caught the gentleman as we caught him asleep in the 10th year of his marriage etc." As the Barbers recovered from the surprise, amid, no doubt, considerable jesting over George Barber's apparent lack of passion on his tenth wedding anniversary, "the chairs was presented to the said Mr. & Mrs. Barber by Mr. H.C.Willson & A.Webber in behalf of the men present etc etc". The Barbers then returned the compliment with an impromptu repast, which lasted until almost 10:30 P.M. As the Barbers finally retired for the night, "the crowd" sought yet more entertainment. Encouraged by rather mild seasonal temperatures, the revelers paraded through the Worcester night, escorting one of their number, Henry P. Haynes, "home to his bride, as he was tied in the Hymeneal and conjugal Chain the night before="[13]

Some two weeks later it was Henry C. Willson's turn to be feted. After twelve years at Washburn and Moen, Willson resigned to enter the undertaking business; or, as Webber's heavy humor noted, Willson left "so as to make a fortune by speculation of the Dead as well as the living (Undertakers business)". On a cold Wednesday evening, at eight o'clock, the workers of the tempering room met "at the foot of Laurel St.," three blocks from Webber's home, and from there walked to Willson's nearby house. The men carried with them a silver pitcher and salver as a gift, and "also 2 or 3 qt. of Oysters and cakes to have a Supper." George Barber made the presentation this night and, after Willson expressed his deep thanks, "the fun" began:

> Afterwards the company enjoy themselves with singing etc etc Miss Willson performing on the Piano of Piano Music = Mr. A. Webber accompanied the Singers on Church Music; On the whole we had a grand time then adjourn for *our respective* homes = *Author*"[14]

Eight days later the assistant foreman of the packing room received similar gifts from the men under his charge. The entertainment following the presentation that evening consisted of speeches "made by the men etc etc Mr. A. Webber by request made a Stump speech of which Mr. Otis Bean was sore 3 day after." Otis Bean was the longtime foreman of the packing room.[15] Webber's stump speech (whose substance he did not record) revealed another connection to American popular attitudes. The stump speech was a central part of the minstrel show in which the actor's wit, irreverence, and sarcasm produced a caustic, satirical social or political commentary, often in a heavy black dialect. That Webber familiarly adopted the stump speech to his own purposes reflected the pervasive attraction of this popular entertainment. How Webber responded to the racial imagery of the minstrel show he never indicated.[16]

There was no coercion in Webber's accounts of these festivities. The camaraderie evident as "the old hands" gathered, the apparent ease with which all joined in the entertainments, and the spontaneous extension of the fete to the newly married Haynes all suggest a great comfortableness. Workday hierarchies certainly existed, but those relations did not dominate these evening socials. Most striking was Webber's very participation in the festivities at all. Worcester's streets and workplaces had certainly seen their share of racial violence. Yet Webber accorded himself a significant role in each of the three socials, and never directly alluded to any racial tension.

Within the boundaries of these work-related socials a peculiar freedom developed. Participation in these celebrations neither challenged plant authority nor necessarily required recognition of social relations beyond the event itself. Perhaps not even Webber knew how far his inclusion softened racial distinctions among these specific workers, but given that ambiguity, Webber maintained a pattern—begun at Hart, Montgomery and Company in the 1850s—of sustained, work-related engagement with white men of all positions and social classes.

Only once in his account of these socials did Amos Webber draw a clean line between himself and the activities of the other men, and that was in his discussion of the party at Henry Willson's house. "Mr. A. Webber accompanied the Singers on Church music," he wrote, and it was significant that this rare distinction involved neither race nor economic status but rather the proper conduct of an observant Christian. Although he did not reject all forms of popular entertainment (in addition to his familiarity with minstrelsy, Webber went sleigh riding, celebrated St. Patrick's Day, and attended the circus in the months immediately following these socials),[17] a particular moral stance, developed in his youth and reinforced by the examples of his Philadelphia employer, Charles Wurts, and Elder Robert Jones of the Lombard Street church, structured his enjoyments.

Despite these evening entertainments, however, harmony between workers and their superiors in the firm did not always reign. Two months following these socials, Webber confronted the tension that also permeated Washburn and Moen's sprawling industrial world.

On Saturday, March 18, 1871, workers at the Grove Street mill of Washburn and Moen struck. Some months before, the company had reduced wages while retaining the eleven-hour workday. Now, collective anger boiled over. In a series of nightly mass meetings they demanded a ten-hour workday to match their reduced wages. Philip L. Moen and his associates, in turn, responded sharply. Following a policy implemented during the 1870 strike at the company's Quinsigamond branch, management at first refused to meet with the strikers. Even as they categorically rejected charges of unfairness, Washburn and Moen executives closed the Grove Street plant "to check this movement" and announced that what was in essence a lockout would not end until "the men are willing to go on without dissatisfaction or grumbling."[18]

The wire-drawers returned to work on March 27, and on the company's terms, much as had happened in a brief strike the preceding summer. But the anger remained. Four days later some 100 workers walked out, again demanding a reduction in hours. Webber commented: "Therefore by working 10 hours, the men think it will balance the account." But Washburn and Moen "was not ready for this act yet therefore the men went out to work for Mr. Street Walker." Over the next week the strike grew again, as the original group were joined by additional strikers from the Grove Street and the Quinsigamond plants. A meeting on April 8 proved ineffective, as the strikers refused the company's proposition to couple a reduction in hours with another reduction in pay. Two days later, the plant started up on a ten-hour schedule but what Webber called "the old hands" still refused to return. The final resolution of the strike is not known—it may never have been made public—but by April 17 all the men had returned to work. Webber thought that both sides had "all their troubles adjusted no doubt satisfactorily," but neither he nor the local papers noted whether a second wage cut accompanied the reduction in hours.[19]

Webber did not participate in the strike and while his reporting was decidedly nonpartisan, these events clarified his opinions about strikes in general. Among "that great congregation" of workers in these and other strikes, Webber noted, "some of them was thunder struck when they found that they had nothing in the house to eat. So much so it cause the Children to cry out for bread=Thus:

> "'Mother; i want a piece of bread,
> Another, say' mother, i want to go to bed,
> Another say' is thire no bread,
> Father say' Ill knock all strikes in the head.'"

Amos Webber's folk poetry captured here, as it had during the crisis over John Brown's raid a decade before, a central social issue in immediate and personal form. His repeated use of the family analogy reflected the power that image held for him, but at the core of Webber's analogy, at times presented in high romantic fashion, lay an important social commentary. "That is the end of all strikes, poverty, or they have no means of obtaining a livelihood without doing something else besides what they struck for." His concluding comments expressed as well some of his reasons for returning to his chronicle: "I studied well the nature of a Strike or the Philosophy of it. Therefore I guess 50 years from now the people will understand what a strike is without further comment."[20] An analyst and historian, Webber here was clearly anticipating an audience for his chronicles, and taking pride in what he might teach those who would follow. His engagement across time assured him a place in that future.

Webber's attitude toward strikes was not unusual for the period. Many a future trade union militant argued during the 1870s that strikes were inimical to attaining the professed goal of harmony with employers. Yet Webber remained rather pragmatic in his evaluation, not so much opposed to strikes as opposed to the devastation he thought they inevitably brought. In contrast, Booker T. Washington recalled a much harsher reaction. Writing of 1874, when he was a teenager, Washington remembered thinking that strikes "usually occurred whenever the men got two or three months ahead in their savings. During the strike, of course, they spent all that they had saved, and would often return to work in debt at the same wages, or would move to another [coal] mine at considerable expense. In either case, my observations convinced me that the miners were worse off at the end of the strike." While Washington's memory of the cause of such strikes—"professional labour agitators"—most probably reflected his later public self, neither in the 1870s nor after did the future leader of Tuskegee Institute express any sympathy for working people in their frequent struggles with employers.[21]

Webber's more evenhanded treatment of workplace tensions created no obstacles in his relationship with Philip L. Moen, now the firm's president. A shared commitment to abolition and to the Republican Party structured their connection, and while Webber could on occasion exhibit a wry sense of humor concerning the distance between himself and his employer—after noting the re-election of Moen as president at the annual stockholders' meeting in 1871, he signed the entry: "*A. Webber, Janitor=Well, Well*"[22]— he never questioned Moen's right to his position or his moral judgments in the management of the firm. Moen might well have disagreed with Webber's attitudes toward strikes and strikers, if he had known of them, but that would not have prevented Moen from calling on his employee to drive his carriage, deliver messages, or supervise the activities of his son, Philip W. Moen. When "Master Philly Moen" broke his wrist "[w]hile playing baseball" in June 1871, it was Webber, the thirteen-year-old boy's escort, who made certain the right doctor was called and the injured boy brought home. Webber also accompanied the younger Moen on horseback, trying to contain his teenage charge's penchant for "flying about our streets" on his pony. When the elder Moen decided Philly had outgrown the pony, he instructed Webber to deliver the animal to the railroad depot for resale in Boston. A rueful Webber hoped that another boy would quickly take to the animal. Young Moen "feels Somewhat Sad, at heart, on being separated from his pony," Webber observed, as he did himself: "I must admit when I led the pony on platform . . . I hated to give *up the Halter strap: to Let the pony go*."[23] This heartfelt affection for his employer's son must at times have caused Amos Webber to ache for his own Harry, who, had he lived, would have been but a few years older than "Master Philly."

———

WEBBER'S RELATIONSHIP WITH the Moen family deepened with time, and the friendship of men like Moen remained a needed pro-

Philip L. Moen (1824–1891). Abolitionist, Republican politician, philanthropist, president of Washburn and Moen, and Amos Webber's employer for thirty years. *Courtesy of Worcester Historical Museum*

tection in the often hostile racial atmosphere in Worcester. Dramatic violence was not a daily occurrence, but racial insults and segregationist policies were common enough. Irish waitresses at the Lincoln House in 1871 refused to serve the black guests, among them Amos Webber and Isaac Mason, celebrating the anniversary of the founding of the black Odd Fellows in America. A month later, the Temple of Honor, a national temperance society, made clear that blacks were not welcome as members or as sinners to be saved. Webber watched with growing anger and unburdened himself in his chronicle: "The speakers spoke of a great good that they were doing at large in the community in the way of saving men (White men) from the intoxicating drink = or cup." But these same speakers, Webber sharply complained, never noted that the group's constitution "was not in accordance with the 15th Amendment, which gives, all an Opportunity to do good unto his fellow= man, either Black or White." Entering in his chronicle what he could not then say in public, Webber invoked a God who demanded a more just social order to counter the segregationist present: "God will ask them, where is they brother Ethiopia, you see in the gutter drunk, and never lifted your hands to, raise them; they are my children too: *Webber*".[24] In this atmosphere ties to Moen provided concrete support and symbolized the hope for a more equitable society in the future.

It was in this spirit of commitment to a racially just America, promised by the sacrifices of the recent war, that Amos Webber maintained his involvement with the GAR. He proudly served as Post 10's alternate delegate to the state convention in January 1871.[25] Five months later, with an equal pride, he accepted appointment to the post's committee on arrangements for the GAR's major yearly event, the solemn Decoration Day observances on May 30. With reverence and patriotism, Webber emphasized the primary obligation he and his comrades shared, namely to place flowers "on the graves of the fallen comrades as a remembrance." To the city's three cemeteries, the "boys in blue" marched in formation, at each stop paying their respects and decorating the graves. At the Catholic cemetery, where the choir of St. John's Church provided the music, Webber pronounced "the chanting done well; to my satisfaction." But the most telling aspect of Webber's memory of that day found expression in his choice of language. Twice in his short entry he claimed the collective pronoun: patriotic women "so kindly gave us" the flowers to strew on the graves; and then, in his terse account of the march from Rural Cemetery, "we proceeded to the Hope Cemetery." He belonged, Webber announced, as a veteran, as a citizen, as a black American. His "I" was, at least for a moment, a universal "we."[26]

The Decoration Day observance also provided Webber with a less formal perspective on his superiors. With the temperature well over ninety by midafternoon when the public parade began, residents along the march offered lemonade, ice water, and other refreshments to the perspiring veterans. At one house, Webber joined as "the boys dipped well into the barrel of Lemonade"; it was "So Cooling." But his sharp eye also caught something else: "On takeing a bird=eye=peep, I saw the Commander and others came out from a house above as if the Lemonade was to Sweet for them; of course a little eye opener was accepted on a hot day." As he had at the wedding of Alexander Montgomery's daughter, Webber overlooked behavior he would not himself join—in this case, drinking hard liquor—when exhibited by men he thought possessed moral stature. Later that same month, he wrote that a referendum to ban liquor sales lost because "to many, temperance men; likes a glass of beer on a hot day." In contrast with the working people who flocked to the various saloons, "those good gentlemen, stop at home on business" in order to imbibe from their private stock.[27]

Despite his personal connection with Philip L. Moen and his membership in the largely white Post 10, Webber did not isolate himself from other black residents. He did not pursue these involvements with whites as his private solution to public racial tension, but instead remained deeply grounded in the broader collective activity of black Worcester. Webber's invitation to the national grand master of the Order to lead black Worcester's celebration on August 1, 1871, indicated just how intricately layered these bonds were. The grand master was none other than Robert Jones, the elder of the Lombard Street Central Presbyterian Church, where a younger Amos Webber had worshiped when he lived in Philadelphia. Webber and Jones had remained in contact over the eleven years since Webber had left that congregation, and they shared a common moral vision and a deep commitment to the Order. Webber met Jones at the depot near Washington Square and escorted him to his home on Liberty Street, where Jones would stay during his visit. Lizzie Webber prepared refreshments and then the grand master joined with Amos to lead more than one hundred black Odd Fellows in a public parade. The route stretched from North Star Lodge's rooms on Pearl Street north on Main, west on Highland, snaking through the streets of the Eighth Ward; on Pleasant Street, the parade turned east toward downtown, passed City Hall unnoticed, and veered northeast on Shrewsbury Street out to Lake Quinsigamond, on the outskirts of the city. It was a route calculated to avoid the greater part of immigrant, working-class Worcester. Following this celebration of Odd Fellowship, dinner was served at the lake and as the dishes were cleared Charles Bulah, a housepainter and the ice-skating enthusiast, introduced Robert Jones to the eager crowd.

Odd Fellows, Jones began, were superior to other fraternal orders because the Order's whole aim was to make "wiser and better men." Casting aside "the asperities of sects and parties," Odd Fellows sought to "inculcate charity and brotherly love [and to] invigorate all the relations of man towards himself, his family, his neighbors, his country and his God." Jones dismissed attempts at religious or political proselytizing in this fraternal context, and stressed that "men of every creed" might join "if they will . . . learn the lessons of love and truth there taught." But, Jones demanded, these "lessons of love" carried an incisive meaning for Odd Fellows, for they must apply "to all men, of every clime or color and condition." It was this divide that separated the white American Odd Fellows from the Grand United Order of England. Unlike the American branch, the British members "gave us our charter and honored us as men." As Jones recounted the Order's history, embedded in his narrative lay sharp contemporary meaning. Deriving institutional legitimacy from the British, "the progenitors of the Pilgrim Fathers . . . we prize it highly; coming from that people who years ago, on the 1st of August, declared that English soil should not be trod by the foot of slave and that from every such stepping on British soil the chains should fall. God be thanked," Jones prayed, "the people of this country, descendants of the Pilgrims, are fast treading in their footsteps."

In treating white American Odd Fellows as the prodigal sons of their British fathers, Jones underscored the central contradiction of the American democratic experiment. For the Americans to return to the true path marked by the British founders, they must cease defining democracy in racially exclusive terms. But Jones did not therefore reject the universal and humanitarian principles of the Order. If these principles were "allowed to exert [their] power, men of all creeds, and nations will sit together in friendship."

The descendants of Jacob, the followers of Mahomet, and the worshippers of Christ, commingle together with fraternal greetings, firm in their respective faith, but equally firm in the doctrine of the brotherhood of man, trusting to the Father of all, and the influence of love and truth, to win men from the error of their way into a faith and practice that will fit them for the Grand Lodge above.

"We want," Jones concluded, seeking again to tie his people's specific history with the fraternity's democratic promise, "not charity, but countenance and encouragement. I have faith in our destiny and would inspire you with a like faith. Reforms never go backward . . . but we must work out our destiny with confidence in the Father of all and Ruler of all." Jones then thanked the wives and daughters of the members "for their encouragement and assistance in the work of the order" and sat down.

Robert Jones captured well the central tenets of the Order. The fraternal call for religious tolerance, for example, did not undermine the recognition of a clear moral order; nor did the prevalence of racism among white Odd Fellows invalidate the Order's universalist principles. Indeed, there were few black members who did not relish the irony that their commitment to those principles in the face of exclusion actually provided them with a sense of moral superiority over those fraternal white racists.

Webber and others also spoke at the celebration, but no one recorded even snippets of their talks. Following the speeches the Odd Fellows regrouped and marched back to town to join in gala parties that evening honoring North Star Lodge, the Order itself, and the anniversary of West Indian emancipation. At Horticultural Hall, "those with music in their sole" danced the night away. At the Old Theater Building on Exchange Street "there was a festival, patronized generally by those who were opposed to dancing." Pluralistic as he was in the fraternal context, Robert Jones nonetheless remained most deeply a Presbyterian elder whose Calvinist sensibility was palpable. Given Webber's past association with Jones and his reluctance only months before to perform secular music at Henry C. Willson's home, it was quite likely that he and his wife joined Jones at the Old Theater Building festival.[28]

For Amos Webber, Jones's visit was an important, special occasion, but it was only one incident of many that he and his fraternal brothers participated in during the year. Webber averaged a minimum of two meetings a month throughout the early 1870s, and he aided in the organization of numerous trips—such as to Rhode Island beaches to celebrate August 1 with area Odd Fellows and to other lodges of the Order throughout the year.[29] Each March the Worcester members of the Order sponsored a dinner at a local hotel to celebrate the introduction of the Odd Fellows to America. As had Robert Jones in his August 1 speech, speakers at the March dinners recalled Peter Ogden's early efforts at establishing a lodge and the history of the Order among black Americans, and underlined the relationship between the Order's moral precepts and the rights and privileges claimed by black citizens. Webber himself gave the speech at the 1873 dinner.

The world possessed a natural and a moral order, Webber explained, which was "truly 'heaven's first law,' a rule of being stamped on nature at its birth, and recognized by men with the first dawning of a social life." To acknowledge and follow these rules would ensure a righteous life, but the temptations of the world made such recognition difficult. This explained why "Odd Fellowship had its birth." To strengthen the social bonds that encouraged the search for righteousness, Webber demanded of his fraternal brothers "a strict observance of [the] exhalted principles: 'Friendship, Love, and Charity,' linked like the symbolic chain." After defending the Order's ritual, Webber read an original poem dedicated to the women of the Order, thanking them for their aid. The speech, the reporter commented, was "well-received."[30]

The commitment to order that permeated Webber's fraternal address certainly owed a profound debt to Protestant religious beliefs, brimming as it did with intimations of the American Enlightenment in its use of such terms as the "All-Seeing Eye." Webber and his Worcester lodge retained close ties to black ministers, much as he had done in Philadelphia. In fact, a sharp divide between religious belief and fraternal practice was simply inconceivable to Webber or many of his lodge brothers. Nor were larger political issues ever far removed from discussions of the Order's moral precepts. Webber quite easily mixed moral imperatives with a recognition of the white Odd Fellows' claim of a history reaching back to the dawn of the Christian era—all the while inferring his right as a black member to that same heritage in accord with the Order's central principles.[31]

The experience of being black in a largely white world was never far from consciousness for these fraternalists, a point made most obvious almost every time they marched in public. On those occasions, the North Star Odd Fellows were often preceded by the Johnson Colored Drum Corps. Organized by Alexander H. Johnson, known when a teenage soldier as "the Drummer Boy" of the 54th Massachusetts (Colored) Infantry, the corps consisted of black men, not all of whom were veterans, who also provided martial accompaniment to a variety of other black groups and to the local GAR post as well. Johnson, an accomplished drummer who once boasted, "I dont take my hat of[f] for any man living that Tap the Drum," was a great favorite, and the sight of these men in uniform, in the streets of Worcester, proclaimed to all the meaning they attributed to their sacrifices during the recent war. Although

Alexander H. Johnson (1846–1930). Formal portrait taken after his service, possibly as a publicity photograph for his Colored Drum Corps. *Courtesy of Worcester Historical Museum*

he was not widely known among the city's white citizens, the very drum Johnson played—"Fort Wagner's historic drum," which he beat that bloody day in July 1863—made the point even more sharply to black Worcester.[32]

Equally ignored by most whites was the rich cultural life that members of North Star Lodge created for themselves and for black Worcester. Occasional speakers addressed the members; more frequently, members themselves read papers, held discussions, or performed dramatic skits. Periodically the lodge sponsored public debates on political or literary themes. The lodge also owned a pipe organ, and Amos Webber, an avid musician, performed as music director and for a number of years taught a singing class for lodge members. His students once surprised their teacher with the presentation of "a very fine folding chair."[33] In this fashion the fraternal lodge continued the tradition of the antebellum black literary societies that had so effectively combined self-help, self-education, and political and social activism.

This multiplicity of lodge activities allowed someone like Amos Webber an outlet for his varied interests that encouraged even stronger collective ties. The flexibility of the lodge's culture allowed for inclusion of brothers like Amos Webber whose curiosity and passion (Webber's musical reviews during these years ranged from reports on local performances of the Fisk Jubilee Singers[34] and of Boston's World Peace music festival,[35] to an obituary of the Scottish-born opera diva Euphrosyne Parapa Rosa[36]) led them to many idiosyncratic interests. In this fashion the lodge bound individuals together in a complex relationship around a core of shared values that also left room for considerable individual variation.

IN POST–CIVIL WAR AMERICA, politics was, among other things, a form of mass entertainment, marked by a high degree of popular participation in campaigns and in the actual voting. From this perspective, it was not unusual that in 1868 Worcester's black Republicans should have formed a political club, complete with military-style uniforms, to support Grant for president. But as the violent attack on those black Republicans in the 1868 parade indicated, political participation carried with it a charged meaning. Every black footstep marching in cadence down the city's streets

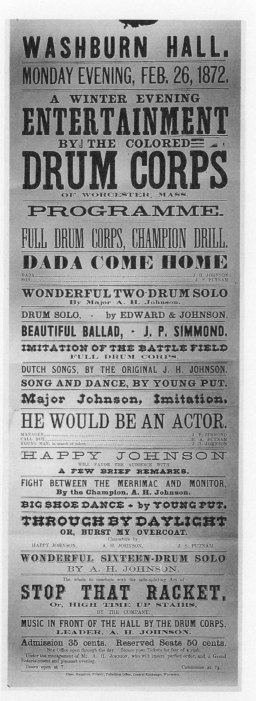

Broadside advertising Alexander H. Johnson's Colored Drum Corps entertainment at Washburn Hall. Johnson, who thought himself the equal to "any man living that Tap the Drum," was prominently featured in a variety show that played to integrated audiences. *Courtesy of American Antiquarian Society*

redrew the boundary lines that had previously truncated black Americans' public presence, and in a fundamental way such activity transcended the immediate issues, no matter how important they might be. For, at its core, to assert a public place for blacks in American life was an effort to redefine the meaning of the collective memory of the Civil War itself.[37]

In 1871, Amos Webber was forty-five years old, and his experiences had led him to equate ultimate black progress with the success of the Republican Party. The Democrats remained for him the party of demagogues who had controlled Philadelphia politics to the detriment of Negro residents, as well as the party that had encouraged Irish rioters to murder and mutilate black New Yorkers in 1863. Not surprisingly, then, Webber welcomed Republican electoral victories, such as in the governor's race in Connecticut in 1871, and boasted that "[t]he colored votes is what done the thing." Into the mid-1870s, Webber retained a sharp eye on elections in other states, applauding Republican victories and fretting over their losses.[38] A similar tone characterized his discussions of local city politics. The 1871 mayoralty race, which resulted in the defeat of the Republican candidate by George Verry, a Democrat running on the independent Citizens Party ticket, puzzled Webber. He compared Verry's majority of 2,116 with Republican James Blake's majority a year earlier of 1,511, and attributed the swing to a personal dislike of the more recent Republican candidate.[39]

A steadfast advocate of the Republican Party, Webber nonetheless maintained a complex understanding of how the party's internal political dynamics might affect black Americans. When Republican Charles Sumner, the senior United States senator from Massachusetts and a powerful advocate of racial equality, distanced himself in 1871 from President Grant's desire to annex Santo Domingo as a future colony for some American blacks, Webber worried that the split foreshadowed a coming Democratic presidential victory. Just as basic divisions within the Democratic Party had led to Lincoln's election, Webber argued in March 1871, "I think the President will go out . . . and the Democrats will put one in that Corner: A President." What bothered Webber the most, however, was the prospect that Sumner and what he stood for would become the minority position within the party.

"What Senator has stood more than he, for right=" Webber remembered how Congressman Preston S. Brooks, of South Carolina, had "tried to Kill him with a cane some years ago=but nay he is here yet." And Sumner's political presence remained crucial for black Americans: "We have other Brooks that has gizzards for hearts, their is Bully Brooks. Bully Fernando Wood, the Bullies of 1863 hanging Loyal Colored men to the Lamp Post &c." In siding with Sumner, Webber also distanced himself from Frederick Douglass, who had publicly supported Grant in this dispute.[40]

Events would prove that Webber misjudged Grant's reelection chances, but his deeper concern over the continued commitment of the Republican Party to equal rights proved only too accurate. A month later, in a discussion of Reconstruction in the American South, Webber examined the groundwork for his pessimism in a blunt analysis of conditions.

As in the past, a meteorological comparison provided Webber with an interpretative framework. "[T]his splendid light" of the aurora borealis "appeared last night," he wrote in April 1871, following his last entry on the Washburn and Moen strike. "[W]ith all its beauty imageable, [the Northern Heavens] was light up from sky to earth. With streaks of red fire tint of Blue; with flashes of light as if some one was at the other end throwing brush on the fire; & & c." "This strange phenomena" reminded Webber of a similar occurrence in Philadelphia in the fall of 1859. Then "[e]verybody said it was a sign of War, War; So we had War;". So too in 1871 Webber understood these supernatural manifestations as omens of quite real human tensions. "We see trouble again brewing in the Zodiac Sign of War," Webber suggested; "War with the Ku Klux Klan this Summer 1871. May they all be killed dead dead."[41]

Within days, continued Klan violence magnified Webber's anger. In Kentucky the policy of Berea College, "where they admitted Colored men as Students," proved "to much for these Villains." The Klan abducted a college trustee, beat him severely, "Stretch[ed] him across a Log, then Whipped him for a long time." Only because he left town did the Klan spare his life. In Florida, a former Federal captain of Vermont volunteers, John Quincy Dickinson, a public advocate of "the right of the Colored people to freedom and Education," was fatally shot by the Klan.

Offering "one more of Ku Klux Klan doings," Webber wrote of William C. Luke, a devout white Canadian Methodist in Alabama who established a school "towards Educating the Freedman." Harassed as "a Nigger teacher" by the Klan, he and four black men were arrested "on some frivolous pretext." That night the Klan abducted all five from the jail and hanged them from three separate trees just outside of town. Before his death, his murderers allowed Luke to write his wife and six young children:

I die to night. It has been so determined by those who think I deserve it; God knows I feel myself innocent. I have only sought to educate the negro; I little thought when leaving you so far away that we should then part forever; God's will be done; . . . God of mercy bless and keep you my dear, dear wife and children

Webber copied the heart-wrenching letter from a newspaper and concluded: "I have nothing to say but a melted heart: *Webber*".[42]

In choosing from among many these three examples of Klan violence, Webber's emphasis on incidents involving the education of southern blacks was not accidental. Freedmen and -women themselves stressed education's importance, and Webber understood the value of literacy and learning in his own life. If the race was to advance even in the face of white resistance, education would prove central. The Klan, Webber implied in 1871, understood the promised connection between education and social progress as much as he himself did.

As his reference to the aurora borealis indicated, Webber understood nature's upheavals as signs of God's presence on earth. In ways mysterious to humanity, an all-powerful God might use suffering to direct men and women toward certain ends.[43] But in true nineteenth-century Protestant fashion, Webber did not hold that this divine intrusion in human affairs absolved individuals of their responsibility. When the body of former Captain John Quincy Dickinson reached New York City from Florida on its way to Vermont, the captain's friends "held an indignation [meeting] against the doings of the Ku Klux Klan." Better, Webber thought, would have been a different kind of gathering, one reminiscent of the battle for Kansas in the 1850s: "They should of held a meeting to see how many muskets could be got to shoot them down."[44] Webber understood the underlying issues at stake in this violence, and was anything but squeamish in his responses.

Atrocities such as these, and the inadequate federal response, forced Webber to maintain a dual perspective on Republican politics. "There was a little blowing the other day among some politicians," Webber observed in May 1871, concerning the next presidential campaign. Webber read of trial balloons raised on behalf of Allan G. Thurman, Ohio's Democratic senator, but dismissed Thurman's chances out-of-hand. In a speech "sometime ago," Webber heatedly remembered, the senator called black Americans "darkies, [and] that word put the last nail in his presidential coffin." Remembering Thurman recalled as well William Seward, Lincoln's secretary of state, who himself had harbored presidential aspirations. "[B]ut in a speech he called the colored people Niggers = So down he fell from the high position he was looking for:". Rejecting any supine image of the black electorate, Webber instead claimed for black voters continued responsibility for such retribution. Had the successful Republican gubernatorial candidate in Connecticut, whom Webber judged had won due to the black vote, "made speeches as Thurman & Seward, He would not been elected, for most of the colored people would [have] voted" for the Democrat in the race, and "thought him quite as good" as the Republican. "The trouble is about the Republicans," Webber already understood in the spring of 1871, "half of them are always on the fence, you can never find them."[45]

Webber rarely analyzed the position of the local Republicans on any major issue but he did use his entries, and specifically his frequent obituaries of the famous, to define again the meaning of the war. The June 1871 death of Clement Vallandigham, the Indiana Democrat jailed for his pro-South sympathies during the war, drew from Webber the terse comment: "If he had been a true Union man, the country would of met *with a Loss: Otherwise it does not* - Webber". A month later Webber evoked far different emotions in his obituary of General Edward N. Hallowell, an officer in the 54th Massachusetts Infantry and brother to Norwood P. Hallowell. Hallowell, the son of the Bucks County abolitionist family that had aided Daniel Dangerfield's escape in 1859, had from the start of the war, advocated the use of black soldiers in the Union army. For Webber it was only appropriate that Wendell Phillips, William Lloyd Garrison, and an honor guard of black veterans accompany Hallowell's casket to "Mount Auburn Cemetery: Where he rests; with other brave men of the War; And remembered as an honored officer of a Colored Regiment - *Webber.*"[46]

Webber's avoidance of direct mention of the politics of race in Worcester clearly reflected the limited political alternatives and the hope, still evident in his mind in 1872, that the Republican Party would forcibly define black equality as central to a reconstructed America. To this extent the man who only a year earlier had complained about the Republican Party's untrustworthiness applauded that same party as it met in national convention to renominate Grant in Philadelphia in June 1872. In an enthusiastic entry, Webber paraphrased parts of Reverend James D. Lynch's speech to that convention. A black Mississippi Methodist and political activist, Lynch thought the Republican Party needed no elaborate presentation to black voters, and Webber agreed: "Its necessity to the country and mankind was as clear as that of the sun. . . . The colored men were born of the republican party and by it they stand. Opposition to Grant means Opposition to the triumph of the war." Of Horace Greeley, the newspaper publisher and candidate for the presidency on the Liberal Republican ticket, Webber, like Lynch, was dismissive: "Tell me not because Greely is Identified with the cause of Liberty that the colored people will find magic in his name They Know the name of Grant still more as he who carved out their path to freedom with the sword (Cheers.) they are bound to Grant by cords that can never be separated (Cheers.) & &c."[47]

But Webber's record of Lynch's address, for all its seeming repudiation of the Worcester veteran's earlier caution about Republican faithfulness to the principle of equality, in fact excluded two major themes in the original speech that sharply altered Webber's rendering of Lynch's meaning. Where both accounts recognized that black men and women "were born of the republican party," Webber tied that acknowledgment to a ringing endorsement of Grant as one who "with the sword" led the slave to freedom. In the same passage in the original speech, however, Lynch offered a different version of the black–Republican relationship. Rhetorically, he asked the overwhelmingly white delegates what guarantee they might have "of the fidelity of the colored men in the Republican Party? You have the same guarantee that fathers all over the land, wherever civilizations beams, have for the filial and faithful regard of their children."

Equally significant was Webber's omission of Lynch's defense of Grant's policy of expansion. While both speaker and scribe supported Grant, the former embraced the expectation that America, the "foremost in the family of nations, with its advanced intelligence and Christian morals exceeding any portion of the world—must soon make Mexico, the West Indies and Central America part of ourselves, as is Alaska." These lands could enrich the United States "beyond any country in the world, and they need the black man's muscle. Without the black man the cotton States cannot be developed." Lynch teetered on the edge of embracing antebellum southern white expansionist views, even though his purpose was to secure an economic foundation for freedmen and -women. This too Webber ignored, influenced as he was by his own support for Sumner in the senator's fight with Grant over annexation of Santo Domingo.[48]

What at first glance appeared to be a copy of Lynch's speech was, in reality, an adaptation of it that reflected Webber's own political evaluations. Intensely proud that a black man would play such a prominent role at the convention, Webber nonetheless maintained his distance from a number of Lynch's positions. Nationally prominent black politicians such as Lynch and Douglass might indeed support Grant's policies, but that did not therefore mean that men like Webber had to follow. But however independent Amos Webber might be, the limited nature of the alternatives he had constricted his practical political choices. The national Democratic convention that same year underscored this bleak reality.

The Democrats met in Baltimore that July and, in a stunning political gambit, chose as their candidate Horace Greeley, who had already been nominated by Liberal Republicans when they had met in Cincinnati. One of Greeley's most prominent supporters was Charles Sumner, who refused to back Grant for reelection. Greeley's advocates demanded that the Democrats adopt the entire Cincinnati platform, including the plank that opposed "any reopening of the question settled by the 13th 14th and 15th amendment of the constitution:". This, Webber thought, was "a bitter pill for the Baltimore Convention to swallow," and he doubted the sincerity of their conviction. Those "an=ti Greely men," Democrats who bolted the Baltimore convention rather than agree to those terms, Webber thought indicative of the party's deepest feelings: "they vomit the pills up (13th 14th & 15th Amd) and went out to hunt up another platform" upon which to stand.[49] His deep suspicion of the Democratic Party left him little practical alternative but to support, no matter his pointed misgivings, the Republican Party and its candidates.

The manner in which Webber and other Worcester blacks organized for this election may have made their limited choices more palatable. On August 23, 1872, the black residents of the city, led by William Brown and Amos Webber, held a mass meeting at Masonic Hall in downtown Worcester in anticipation of the coming campaign. Brown upbraided the crowd for its "past lack of enthusiasm and interest in practical political work" and urged an intensive effort to ensure a strong black presence at the polls. He then introduced the main speaker, J. F. Manning, of Boston, who developed the themes that Brown had outlined.

"Colored voters hold the balance of power" in this election, Manning argued, and he proclaimed a Grant victory essential to the successful reconstruction of the South and to the preservation of black rights nationwide. Horace Greeley, Manning thundered, deserved no support. That candidate had supplied part of the bond that allowed Jefferson Davis to leave prison in 1867, and his current presidential platform promoted local self-government that would, in effect, end federal reconstruction in the South. Greeley, moreover, urged Americans to "clasp hands across the bloody chasm" by finally forgetting the divisive events of the past decade—a slogan, Manning pointed out, that held little promise for black Americans, whose very freedom was advanced by engaging those tensions. Also ominous was the defection of Senator Charles Sumner, the abolitionist and defender of black rights, who had already announced for Greeley at the time of the Worcester meeting. In doing so, Manning claimed, Sumner marked the end of his political usefulness. Simply to gratify his personal hatred for Grant, Manning told the crowd, Sumner "had driven the nails into his own political coffin." Webber's basic fear—that divisions among Republicans would, if not lose them the presidency, further weaken the party's commitment to equality—appeared justified.

Other speakers voiced a sharper anger. Following Manning's address William H. Jankins, the local barber and former slave, took the floor to argue that as Sumner "has gone over to Greely, and Greely has gone over to Jeff Davis & Company . . . we cannot support either of them." Excoriating Greeley for his southern policy, Jankins asked the crowd: "Do we want such a granny as that for President?" Amid cries of "No" and "Never," Jankins concluded: "You are right, we don't want him and we will not have him. We are regarded as a power at the ballot box and our votes will tell." Before adjourning, the meeting did recognize Sumner's historic role as a proponent of black rights, but that did not alter this fundamental criticism.

Black Worcester took two other actions that evening. They voted not to organize a "colored battalion" to march in Republican Party parades, ward-level "flag raisings," or other campaign activities. Instead, these black men (there is no record of women being allowed any public role) intended to work within the city's regular (that is, white) party organization. The meeting also elected a committee of five to organize Worcester's black citizens to attend an even larger mass meeting at a national black political convention in Boston that September.

Webber did not address the Worcester meeting but he did play an important role. In addition to serving as recording secretary, he was one of a handful of men who signed the call to meeting that had appeared in the Worcester *Evening Gazette* on August 21; and the group elected him to the committee to prepare for the Boston meeting. Respected and given public responsibility, Webber was but one of thirteen local black men responsible for calling the August gathering. Four were veterans, including Cyrus Wiggins of the 54th Massachusetts Infantry, who attended in military uniform and from the floor denounced efforts to restore former Confederates to political power; four others, older men, had been active in local efforts to recruit black soldiers. These thirteen activists ranged in age from seventeen to the late fifties, and in occupation from porter and messenger to housepainter, boot crimper, and a variety of small businessmen. Only one, William Brown, a skilled upholsterer to Worcester's elite white families, could be considered even minimally wealthy. Their common political ground was the deep belief that the Civil War had redefined the meaning of American citizenship and that the Republican Party remained the only viable political option if they were to achieve full equality. The prediction of one speaker, that the "colored vote of Worcester will be cast solid for Republican candidates," thus echoed hope and doubt simultaneously.[50]

At the September 1872 Boston meeting, held at Faneuil Hall and addressed by Frederick Douglass, John M. Langston, and George T. Downing, the basic dilemma facing all black activists, the famous as well as the unknown, became apparent. The delegates praised Grant for urging on Lincoln "the proclamation of emancipation" and for his support of the Fifteenth Amendment, his appointment of "men of our color ministers plenipotentiary," and his administration's general policy toward the freed population. Gently urging him to continue "the work of checking and controlling this disloyalty" among southern whites, the delegates

William Brown's trade card, ca. 1870s. The complex social life of blacks living in small urban black communities is evident as all the references for this political activist's business are from elite whites. *Courtesy of American Antiquarian Society* closed their public letter to the President with the assertion that most Americans, white and black, would support such a policy and such a candidate.[51]

By any measure this was a most generous evaluation. Yet no feasible alternative existed, and it was with renewed hope that Webber, like many a black activist, greeted Grant's reelection that November.[52]

As central as the demand for racial equality was to Amos Webber, it was not the only issue of justice that engaged him. The development of the postwar economy brought with it a variety of tensions evident in factory management and in political affairs. In December 1872, for example, Webber celebrated the victory of Republican Clark Jillson over the incumbent mayor, George Verry, whose majority a year earlier had been a commanding 2,116 votes. Those votes and the election, Webber ironically suggested, "went with the Sewer Question."[53]

Worcester, like other growing communities during these years, undertook a series of improvements in the city's infrastructure, including the widening of streets and the creation of sidewalks. Sanitation became a major concern and the extension of sewer lines, to control disease and create an aura of urban progress, had been a major municipal expenditure over the preceding decade.[54] But the question of how to pay for such improvements remained contentious. In 1872, Worcester's Board of Aldermen voted a new sewer assessment that taxed the cheapest plots, largely the homes of working people, at a rate four times that of the wealthy. To add insult to injury, those with the resources to pay their tax bill within the month would receive an additional 6 percent reduction, while those who needed additional time faced a 7 percent penalty. The levy was, Webber pithily stated, but a scheme for "Makeing the poor pay more than the Rich;". Early on the morning of Independence Day that year, Webber watched as the General Studlefunk Brigade took to the streets "with all their Laughable paraphernalia on." A voluntary organization that participated in many local celebrations, always offering a satirical commentary on the issues of the moment, the brigade took on the sewer assessment and

Mayor Verry, who enforced the levy. "Verry-ly (*Mayor Verry*) I say unto you," Webber gleefully paraphrased the chant of the brigade on its march through city streets, "unto them that hath Shall be given. Unto them that hath not shall be taken away=" Six months of protest meetings and popular, public ridicule, which Webber thought "was very amuseing to the people" and in which he, as a home owner himself, participated at least as an observer and voter, resulted in the defeat of Verry.[55]

The moral structure of Webber's vision extended well beyond his interest in the electoral fate of local politicians. He believed that God's will infused the world, and that individual men and women had a corresponding duty to understand and follow that direction. In his chronicle Webber frankly assessed others in light of his morally driven concept of social justice. When James J. Fisk, Jr., the president of the Erie Railroad, died of gunshot wounds in 1872, Webber shed no tears. Shot by his mistress's other lover in New York City, Fisk lingered long enough for his wife to arrive from Boston to witness his death. In his account, Webber exhibited sympathy for her, for Fisk's elderly parents in Brattleboro, Vermont, and for his boyhood friends. Toward Fisk himself, however, Webber was disdainful, even cold. "He is no more the Great James Fisk Jr. of the Erie R. Road," Webber intoned; "He is no more the Great Colonel Fisk Jr. at the Head of his Regiment"—a sarcastic reference to Fisk's cowardly actions during the riots between New York's Catholic and Protestant Irish in 1871. "His works do follow him," Webber judged, and he dismissively concluded his review of Fisk's life: "Thus ends the excitement of James Fisk Jr."[56]

A year later the death of Oakes Ames, a principal in the Crédit Mobilier scandal that had rocked the Grant administration, drew a similar reaction. Ames "will be remembered in History as a schemer," Webber thought; and after reviewing the scandal in some detail he concluded: "Thus ends the life of Oak Ames; ==.Webber like that of Jas Fisk." For Webber, Fisk had become a symbol of immorality and its inevitable consequences.[57]

Men like Fisk and Ames were not the only ones whom Webber found at fault for their greed and irresponsibility. A freight conductor in Illinois who had missed a signal, thereby causing a disastrous accident, received no sympathy from Webber; nor did a New

Hampshire conductor fired in the aftermath of a similar accident. Comparable judgments applied to events closer to home. When Harry Morgan, a young machinist at Washburn and Moen and the oldest son of the wire mill's superintendent, had his leg "horribly mangled" while oiling the continuous rollers, Webber expressed sympathy and concern. He knew both father and son, but that did not keep him from insisting that "A little more care on his part no doubt might of saved him from the Accident."[58]

Nor did Webber flinch from judging the responsibility of employers for disasters that struck others. When an 1872 fire in a New York City hotel resulted in the deaths of more than twenty women servants where a single blocked exit left them, in the words of the New York *Times,* "shut up, as it were, in a box, to be suffocated and roasted to death," Webber recorded the horror and concluded with an admonition: "This will be a Lesson to Hotel Keepers, and Other large Buildings, where person are employed from the first (1st) story to the 6th or 7th story. Such Large places as these should be arrang So as to let out a multitude by Doors and windows, in a few seconds."[59]

When a poorly maintained elevator in a Worcester building broke, dropping a load of wrapping paper on young Frederick Knowlton and killing him instantly, Webber expressed both a deep sadness and a righteous approval of the coroner's verdict that placed responsibility on the building's owner for negligence.[60] When a blocked exit and the lack of external fire escapes resulted in the deaths of more than thirty women and children in Fall River's Granite Textile Mill, Webber again recounted the horrid details and demanded: "It is time for owners of large buildings to put in three (3) Large doors instead of one; then the occupants can escape out of some door;".[61]

Webber held that the imperative to individual moral conduct was a responsibility incumbent upon all, regardless of their station in life. To suffer racial prejudice or economic injustice did not ease this basic human responsibility, he thought, nor did the attainment of wealth and social standing. Webber's terse 1873 obituary of Stephen Smith's life drew from him a model to emulate. With great pride Webber retold this former slave's story, emphasizing Smith's rise from poverty to ownership of a lumber business that netted him a fortune of over $200,000. "By Energy and

Sharp tact," Smith "succeeded in raising himself to the front rank of the commercial community" in Lancaster County, Pennsylvania. Overcoming both racial prejudice and economic competition, Smith retired from the lumber business in 1841, "having secured what he though sufficient." The virtue of that moderation in turn rippled through the black community in both Lancaster and Philadelphia Counties, as Smith devoted his time and money to a series of charities. In contrast, the excesses of a Fisk or an Ames, of irresponsible workers or factory owners alike, offended Webber's sense of justice.[62]

As Webber's evocation of Smith suggested, his concept of a good life wedded individual moral responsibility to involvement with others to create a more just world. In the ability of Webber and his co-workers to stand for right in the face of sustained white indifference and resistance lay the best of nineteenth-century America's ideals. Between 1873 and 1877 this complex mixture of moral vision, social justice, and racial pride met its sternest test as the nation determined, for Webber's generation at least, the place of blacks in America after slavery.

CHAPTER NINE

LOYAL SON

THE POLITICS OF RECONSTRUCTION dominated Amos Webber's thinking in the years leading to the 1876 presidential election. Like many black Americans, Webber worried as southern white sympathizers of the recent rebellion successfully defeated Republican administrations in state after state in the South. These "redeemer" governments, as they were often called, returned to power leaders and defenders of the Confederacy in the region's statehouses and legislatures and promised to end, by whatever means necessary, black participation in the South's political life.

The terror that marked this often bloody struggle in the South made a deep impression on Amos Webber. In an April 1873 entry, he focused on Grant Parish, Louisiana, some 200 miles northwest of New Orleans, where two governments vied for control. One, recognized by the United States government and the federal courts, consisted of "the only Loyal men there, namely Colored men." The other government in the parish consisted of whites who opposed Reconstruction, and they were refusing to acknowledge the legitimacy of black assertions of civil and political rights. "These Loyal Sons," as Webber termed the black supporters of the legal government, occupied the courthouse and withstood an armed attack by their opponents. The attackers then set fire to the building and the smoke and flames forced the defenders to flee under a flag of truce. As the fifty-nine black loyalists left the building, Webber recorded with trembling anger, "each one of them was shot down, and thus murdered by these Villains with a white Skin; while they tried to retain the Loyalty of the Parish[.] The whites," Webber cried, "was more treacherous than the Modoc Indians, whose acts we have so lately and sadly read off:".

Webber's horror at the massacre did not distort his understanding of the fundamental issues involved. Slavery, he argued, "is dead, and the Old Slave-holding Rebels are dying out inch by in at the very thought of his slaves are men among men, and enjoying the right of the U.S.Gov; of which they fought for, against their Old Masters This is the=Bumble Bee, that sting him (The old master.) And that is why those colored men are murdered to day: Because of their Loyalty to the Union="[1]

In terming the black defenders of the Grant Parish courthouse loyalists, Webber expressed a central component of his political vision. They died to uphold the law, he wrote, to defend "Citizens rights" for all. Webber's obituary of Salmon P. Chase, the chief justice of the United States Supreme Court, a few weeks later reiterated the importance of the law in his political thinking. Chase had also been Lincoln's secretary of the treasury and "a great Anti=Slavery man [who] fought for the freedom of the slave, till the work was accomplish." With historical awareness and not a little sarcasm, Webber recalled that Chase, ascending to the Court, "took the place of that good Old Gentleman Chief Justice Taney whose Heart was in his Heels; and his Ideas in the sole of his boot." Roger Taney, of course, had authored the Dred Scott decision in 1857, which Webber accurately summarized as declaring "that colored men were not . . . anything that White men was bound to respect; & &c". In contrast, "Mr Chase look at the Law in its true light, which gave every man his rights, according to Law;".[2] This hope in the law, and in men like Chase to interpret it accurately, revealed the broad influence of American political culture on Webber's attitudes.

Webber's discussion of the Grant Parish massacre also suggested another way in which he was an American among Americans, even in the midst of his painful protest of an American atrocity. "We send troops to exterminate the Modocs," Webber had written, "but I say by strong reasons, **exterminate the race of disloyal treacherous White men of Louisiana**". The immediate context for Webber's strong language was the murder, also in April 1873, of General E. R. S. Canby and other American peace commissioners by a group of dissident Modocs near Tule Lake, in northern California. While the word "exterminate" did not carry a twentieth-century meaning, it was still not an innocent term in the 1870s. As Webber acknowledged by its very use, he knew well the intent of American policy toward Indians, for it was precisely that policy that he wanted carried out in Louisiana. In his descriptions of the murder of the peace commissioners—the Modocs "prove treacherous," he wrote, and hidden in "crevices in the rocks," they proceeded to "shoot our soldiers down from these places un=seen"—his identification with "our soldiers" was evident.[3]

Webber never doubted that the law deserved respect and honor, nor did he question the federal government's critical role in enforcing obedience to that law. Webber was not alone in this faith, as a gathering in Worcester on October 28, 1873, revealed. Webber and his black neighbors and friends convened at the A.M.E. Zion Church to discuss the proposed National Equal Rights Convention being called by Frederick Douglass. All who participated in the Worcester meeting endorsed Douglass's call to the December convention, to be held in the nation's capital, which announced as its major goal achievement of "equality before the law of all classes of citizens, and applications of the teaching of the Declaration of Independence." The assembled residents elected William Brown and Amos Webber to represent them as delegates at the convention.

Inexplicably, neither Worcester man attended the Washington meeting, nor did they or any other Worcester resident appear on the official convention list of delegates. It is unlikely that the cost proved prohibitive: Webber frequently made trips to Philadelphia during these years on Odd Fellow business, and Brown was one of the wealthier black men in Worcester.[4] The demands of work or illness may have intervened, but as Webber never discussed why he did not attend the convention, and did not note the convention itself that December, his reasons remain unclear. He did, however, miss the opportunity to meet friends such as David B. Bowser, a Pennsylvania delegate, and William H. Dupree, a Boston delegate and veteran of the 54th Massachusetts Infantry. He also missed hearing firsthand the speech of Cincinnatian Peter H. Clark, whose ideas Webber would have applauded. Commenting on the contemporary congressional debate over Charles Sumner's civil rights bill, the opponents of which were raising the specter of social and sexual intermingling of the races, Clark asserted: "I do demand social equality and I will define it. I demand the right to

"Amos Webber Thermometer Record and Diary," Volume II, April 17, 1873, page 182. *Courtesy of Baker Library, Harvard University Graduate School of Business Administration, Boston* qualify myself for the first-class manhood in the same institutions and under the same circumstances that the white man pursues, and when I have that leave it to ourselves whether we will mingle together or not."[5]

Despite stirring speeches and intensely debated resolutions, the Washington convention was unable to influence Congress to report out civil rights legislation during that session. But that did not mean that the convention was a failure, because—like so many other activities that white America mostly ignored—the process itself created for black Americans another vehicle for the discovery and recognition of broad common goals.

In the months surrounding the Equal Rights Convention, Robert Jones, this time accompanied by David Bowser, again visited Worcester to celebrate the anniversaries of West Indian freedom and the founding of North Star Lodge.[6] That November, the Prince Hall Masons, the national black Masonic organization founded by Prince Hall, inaugurated King David Lodge No. 16 in Worcester.[7] Early the next year George Lee, a black Odd Fellow, sponsored a meeting in his home to establish a black Baptist presence in the city. Although a congregation would not form for another decade, Lee and a handful of others continued to meet in one another's homes.[8] Also in 1874, Worcester witnessed the establishment of a local branch of the Household of Ruth, the female auxiliary to the Odd Fellows. Amos Webber founded the Worcester branch of the auxiliary and served as its secretary between 1874 and 1886. These activist women, whose bylaws required the presence of a designated male Odd Fellow for a quorum, counted Lizzie Webber among their approximately twenty original members, gave entertainments for the men, redecorated lodge rooms, and organized many of the dinners celebrating various Odd Fellow anniversaries. They also established their own relief fund for local use, and the money raised aided sick members and underwrote the purchase of regalia for those men unable to afford it themselves.[9]

What remains striking about Worcester's black residents is the level of organization they achieved with a rather small number of available adults. With a total population, including children, that was just under 600 individuals at mid-decade, Worcester blacks[10] supported two male fraternal groups, one female auxiliary, two

churches, and an informal prayer meeting—not to mention the
frequent political meetings called to support specific candidates,
discuss pending legislation, or elect delegates to regional or national conventions. This complex mixture of self-help, racial
pride and assertion, and political protest had to involve a near majority of the black adults in the city, even allowing for a significant
overlap in membership.

At the center of this activity was Amos Webber. By no means the
only leader, Webber nonetheless played a critical role in black
Worcester's public life. Rarely did a meeting open or the ritual of
a lodge function begin without his presence and involvement. As
befitted a man so frequently elected to officially represent his
neighbors, Webber also found himself called upon in more informal settings as well. When in 1874 the police arrested Charles W.
Anthony, a young black man, on charges of knowingly passing
counterfeit currency and transported him to Boston for trial, it
was Amos Webber who was "At U.S. Court: Boston" when the
trial began. Two weeks later, with Anthony sentenced to a two-
year term in the Worcester County jail, Webber acknowledged
that "U.S. Court—over." Much is unclear about this relationship,
but it is evident that Webber, one of Worcester's black leaders,
bore witness, and perhaps more formally testified, in behalf of
this young man.[11]

The death of another young man demanded a different public
role from Webber. Under his leadership the North Star Odd Fellows, the King David Masons, and the Johnson Drum Corps all
"turned out in full dress regalia," to commemorate Rudolph
Franey, an Odd Fellow, at his funeral. Webber led the marchers to
the Bethel A.M.E. Church, where Reverend A. N. Mason conducted the service. Reflecting on the funeral, Webber gave the
only explanation he thought necessary for this display of respect
and support: "Rudolph Franey was a young man that was much
respected by his odd-Fellow Brethern, and the community at
large."[12]

Not all of black Worcester shared Webber's particular energy or
perspective. Many were neither church members nor fraternalists,
and a low but persistent level of criminal activity ran through black
Worcester. Theft, assault, and burglary—crimes often associated
with poor people living under harsh conditions—frequently in-

volved black residents.[13] Nor was sin simply the preserve of those
outside one of the various organizations that honeycombed black
Worcester. In the years since Fort Sumter, such prominent church
and fraternal members as Charles Bulah, William Ebbitts, Alexander F. Hemenway, and Henry Washington had faced assorted
charges of bastardy, illegal liquor dealings, assault upon women,
and other criminal violations.[14] Given repentance, these community institutions expanded to absorb the temporarily wayward
member, thereby limiting further disruption to family, church, or
lodge. Webber himself may have done as much when Anthony
faced his trial; that ability to forgive and absolve allowed both individuals and their institutions the compassion to embrace the fallen.

It was out of this expansive network of community organizations that black Worcester drew its political activists. Not only did
these men and women work with one another in these various voluntary groups, but many appeared to share a common perspective
about their activities. Even as they built lodges and churches that
addressed specific spiritual and material needs, these activists also
persisted in their demand for full inclusion in American life. A belief in the law's ultimate goal, and of the value of their efforts to
achieve that promise, drew a surprising number in this small population into public social and political engagement.

THE FUNDAMENTAL ISSUE of the mid-1870s, the role of blacks
in a reconstructed America, carried renewed concern following the
death of Charles Sumner in March 1874. Despite the sharp disagreement with the senator over the 1872 presidential campaign,
Webber and most of black Worcester deeply mourned his passing.
In fact, Webber thought that the concern evidenced "all over the
country" had not been experienced "since the shooting of President Lincoln by Booth April 15th [sic] 1865;". Upon learning of
his death, Webber recapitulated in his chronicle Sumner's contributions, including his repeated public condemnation of the Fugitive Slave Bill, "the offensive Law," on first taking his seat in the
Senate in 1851 and his fierce and effective opposition to the extension of slavery to Kansas, for which he suffered a "cowardly and
brutal assault upon him with a bludgeon by Preston S. Brooks," the

U.S. representative from South Carolina. Sumner had always remained committed to the idea of justice and equality through law, and that deeply impressed Webber: "His last words were take care of the civil rights bill, which yet show*ed* his great interest in the colored people till the last; (breath;)". Others felt the same. Both the Zion and Bethel A.M.E. Churches held commemorative services in Worcester simultaneous with Sumner's funeral in Boston. It was one of the few times in these postwar years that black Worcester so honored a white politician.[15]

This ongoing commitment to the Republican Party was a product of both an intense optimism and the absence of viable alternatives as perceived by most black residents. There were in addition, however, a few tangible signs that support for the Republicans could translate into real benefits. That A. F. Clark and Isaac Mason served as vice presidents of Worcester's Republican Party may have been a symbolic honor; but the fact that "Augustus Murry (Colored) commenced his duties as Mail Agent . . . being the first colored man appointed to office in the New= England States"—a position obtained with the help of Worcester Congressman George F. Hoar—was an important pragmatic step.[16] A position at the post office or an appointment as a messenger attached to a city department or as a janitor at City Hall was a promise of a secure income, at least as long as the Republicans remained in office. Although Webber's own history testified to the individual abilities that these positions never tapped, it was also true that specific black families benefited from this security. In addition, each appointment raised hopes that it marked an advance for the race as a whole. Each new position, no matter how modest, offered evidence that some change was possible.

This much was enough for Webber to continue to look askance at opponents of the Republican party in local and state elections. Citizens tickets, usually composed of Democrats and disaffected Republicans, had some success in the city's mayoralty elections, and always received Webber's rather disapproving notice. Similarly, independent prohibitionist candidates weakened the Republican Party and drew his displeasure.[17] In 1874 Webber identified the Democratic optimism as a result of "so much dissention in the republican party, as to the question of prohibitionist and temperance." German voters, he thought, "have left the republican⁸, on account of the temperance question: and will cast their vote in favor of the Democrats."[18] A month later, when the Republicans met in Mechanics Hall in Worcester to nominate their state candidates, Webber again voiced his fears. The incumbent governor, Thomas Talbot, won renomination, a result "not satisfactory" to many delegates. Talbot had vetoed a bill to license (but not ban) the sale of liquor, despite the strong support it received among Republican legislators, in response to "the outside pressure of the prohibitionists . . . thus comes the feeling against the Candidate Mr. Tolbert- &c."[19] Webber also recorded the county and city nominating conventions of both parties, and particularly noted the five ballots it took for Philip L. Moen to win the Republican nomination for state senator from Worcester.[20]

Webber's forebodings proved accurate as the Democrat William H. Gaston defeated Governor Talbot in the November election. As Webber described it, the Republican Party was thrown "from the track yesterday on account of a broken Rail." It was not just that Talbot was voted out: George Verry defeated Moen for state senator by a slim but sufficient 251 votes. That Verry, who had fallen so low in public opinion just two years before as mayor during the sewer levy debacle, could rebound as he did made Webber uncomfortable; that Verry owed his margin of victory to the commanding majorities he garnered in the only three city wards he won (the heavily immigrant and working-class Third, Fourth, and Fifth Wards) reinforced Webber's unease. It was further evidence of the Democratic Party's adeptness in capitalizing on some workers' distrust of Republican employers and assertive blacks alike.[21]

Despite the fact that Republican candidates won other city and state elections, Webber thought even these results indicated a bleak future. George F. Hoar won Worcester's congressional race, for example, but he did so by only 500 votes over Democrat Eli Thayer, who ran on a platform that declared that "the settlement of the negro question should be left to the people of the South."[22] The growing strength of the Democrats, Webber feared, would influence local Republican policies, and the changing political demographics of Worcester all but made that a certainty. Black voters were, after all, a small portion of the electorate (in 1875 the black electorate in the city contained at most no more than 130 voters). Republicans could afford to bypass them, as their num-

bers were insignificant compared to the 10,854 officially regis-
tered voters in the city.[23] Furthermore, almost 29 percent of the
legal voters in the city in 1875 were foreign-born, and the overwhelming majority of these (78 percent) were Irish. These men
voted the Democratic Party, "the only hope and refuge to which
the oppressed of Ireland could flee," the Boston *Pilot,* the state's
Catholic newspaper, had explained, since the Republicans were
seen as elites who possessed an "open hatred for the rights of the
poor and laboring classes."[24] For Republicans wishing to overcome this antagonism and appeal to a portion of the Democratic
voters, a strong public endorsement of black political and civil
equality was not welcome.

These political realities caused Webber to fear for the future of
the Republican Party. Only too aware of the Republican ability to
straddle the fence, he was nevertheless more worried by the gathering Democratic forces who did not even possess a historical memory of a commitment to racial equality. Forced to choose between
growing indifference and rising antagonism, Webber reaffirmed his
allegiance to that party "which has been running over the course for
so many years." For himself, and for his imagined reader, Webber
then explained what propelled him, despite recent events, to continue to define the party as his own. The Republican Party had

> Done away with Slavery in these years.=Made four (4) Million;
> freemen in these years= Had a four year' War in these years Col-
> ored Senators and representatives was sent to Congress in these
> years, the 14th & 15th (15) amendments was made in these years.
> and many other things was done in these years.[25]

This dilemma was widely recognized. Frederick Douglass, the
preeminent example of a black Republican stalwart, understood
the party's ambivalence but nonetheless argued, much as Webber
hoped, that the "Republican party is still the party of justice and
freedom. It is, relatively, the black man's party."[26] With an evident
cynicism that undermined the hope Webber and Douglass professed, the Worcester *Evening Gazette* dismissed a fall 1874 black
protest meeting in Boston, which condemned white southern violence and voiced its lack of faith in Republican Party policy, with
the sneering: "To whom will the colored man look for support—

the Democrats?"[27] But while Webber and Douglass strained to retain their loyalty in the face of such attitudes, in part by evoking historical memory, other black activists explored a different path.

William Still, the antebellum leader of Philadelphia's black abolitionists, refused to be tied to a wavering Republican Party. Identifying the central task as improving the conditions of the race, he supported an independent Republican for mayor of Philadelphia in 1874. Attacked for this by other blacks, accused of "having 'deserted my principles' " for publicly acknowledging that a black voter might consider even a Democratic candidate, Still defended himself at a large public meeting a month after the election. In contrast to Webber, Douglass, and other northern blacks, Still did not consider political affiliation central to his people's identity or needs. He thought himself "simple enough to think that the acquisition of knowledge, the pursuit of business enterprises, good trades and comfortable homes . . . are of infinitely greater consequence than to be connected with politics." More worrisome than political positioning, he said, was the depressing fact that, in a city where many of the 30,000 black residents are "allied to one another in church, fellowship, various societies, etc.," few are encouraged to establish "shops, stores, trades and the like." Still, himself the owner of a coal business, recognized the role of white racism in excluding blacks from the trades, the professions, and entrepreneurial activity, but he stressed that equally troublesome was "the lack of enterprise among us, which for a long while has concerned my mind very deeply."

Having reordered priorities, Still then discussed politics. The argument that black voters owed the Republicans gratitude for the party's historic role in ending slavery he found both demeaning and erroneous. Such an understanding not only ignored the role of black abolitionists such as himself, but it also assumed that the children of the founding white abolitionist Republicans could profess the old faith without continuing their fathers' deeds. Still was only too happy to acknowledge gratitude for those "early, earnest, and self-sacrificing workers" in the movement, "[b]ut I rather think those old workers have been overlooked and forgotten in the midst of political excitement . . . in order to keep up party influences." To demand of blacks an unthinking loyalty to the party was the most insulting aspect of the situation. Still argued:

"I think that colored men who have been so long bound down under the yoke, and have been so long compelled to think and act only at the bidding of the dominant race, should be the last people on earth to institute or encourage this kind of political tyranny."

To deny black voters, under pain of social and political ostracism, the choice of voting for a Democrat, as leading black Republicans attempted, directly subverted the sense of liberty and the spirit of voluntarism that permeated American culture. "All private and public organizations," Still argued, "secular and religious are directly at variance with this idea." Nor did Still think that the Democratic Party in 1874 was, in Philadelphia at least, the same party as in 1860. Democratic judges now secured the right of blacks to serve on juries and, despite dire warnings, no frenzied mobs of irate immigrant Democrats greeted the desegregation of the city's streetcars after the Civil War. Still cautioned that a black citizen "cannot vote the Democratic ticket when the Democratic party is arrayed against him," but urged all black voters to look more closely at whether political realities were in fact changing, and to act accordingly. To exercise such a wise judgment was the only path that a people "landless and without capital" might take to avoid an even more "pitiable condition."[28]

Still's position generated intense opposition within black Philadelphia and ensured his future political insignificance, as leading stalwart Republicans such as Isaiah C. Wears and William Forten rose to places of prominence within Philadelphia's black world.[29] Although Webber almost certainly knew of Still's speech and the ensuing arguments (he spent a week in Philadelphia at an Odd Fellows festival two months later[30]), he did not discuss Still's ideas in his chronicle. Yet Webber would have disagreed with Still for at least two reasons. First, Webber did not share Still's emphasis on economic development. Where Still regularly encouraged young black would-be entrepreneurs by insisting that "instead of having to spend every dollar of our earnings in stores kept by others, we must manage to be found here & there conducting stores too,"[31] Webber never raised such possibilities. In part, Worcester's far smaller population made it difficult to envision the development of a black entrepreneurial class, whose success required access to credit and potential black customers with income enough to patronize such enterprises. In part, too, William Still was ahead of his time, anticipating by almost two decades Booker T. Washington's elevation of the businessman as a symbol for the race.[32]

Webber's second reason for disagreeing with William Still was his perception of his dual identity as a black American in a singular political fashion. The question of others' acceptance of his and his race's equality as citizens drove Webber in his political activities and, in the classic liberalism of the nineteenth century, he assumed that economic advance would somehow magically follow that recognition of equality. Robert Purvis, another black Philadelphia supporter of abolition, expressed this orientation succinctly in a letter he wrote after the Civil War. The ultimate goal of the postwar legislation was "*Equal rights for all Men, by virtue of a common humanity*"; and he proclaimed: "I scorn to claim rights by any standard less then [*sic*] my manhood."[33] By that standard, to put economic well-being ahead of equal rights seemed, quite simply, wrongheaded. Webber echoed Purvis when he wrote, shortly after his proclamation of adherence to the Republican Party, a tribute to the abolitionists who had died during 1874: "But memory we cannot forget," he concluded.[34]

THE CONTINUED COLLAPSE of southern Reconstruction, with its horrifying violence against black activists and the dwindling number of their white allies, precluded any change in Webber's political loyalties. The Republican commitment to equality may have continued to ebb, locally and nationally, but it was local Democratic leaders who led the armed and vicious white mobs against black voters across the South. Almost daily the news of yet more atrocities appeared in the press, and as before, events in Louisiana provided Webber with gruesome support for his position.

Resistance to Louisiana's Republican state government was led by the White League, described accurately by Webber as "a lawless military organization," containing "in it rank most of the able bodied conservatives of the state," whose "chief business is to overawe the State Government the police and Courts, and regulate the Election." In an armed confrontation in September 1874, the league attacked the governor's office and barred the governor and other state officials from entering. With "[s]everal . . . Killed and many wounded," the

Republicans appealed to Washington, and President Grant ordered the officials reinstated, threatening, Webber emphasized, to "take the field in person" if not obeyed within five days. Three days later, with the support of gunboats and 2,700 federal troops, the governor resumed his duties.[35] A few months later, with Grant's role in reinstating the Republican governor under attack as a usurpation of states' rights, Webber scornfully dismissed "the hue and cry . . . as if any Democrat President never used the military in State services." In 1854, he argued, Democrat Franklin Pierce authorized the use of federal troops in returning a fugitive slave, Anthony Burns, "back into Slavery again," and in 1857 Democrat James Buchanan had offered troops to settle the battle for control of the Kansas legislature; he did the same again to Virginia in 1859 "in time of hanging John Brown." If these Democratic presidents "had the power then to call troops," Webber wondered, "Why not a Republican President call now, for a greater demand."

His own answer was curt and understated: "The fact of the case is somebody meant mischief."[36]

The appointment of a congressional committee, chaired by Worcester representative George F. Hoar, raised some hope that the horrific conditions in Louisiana might spark renewed federal intervention. Webber's six-page discussion of the committee's report (taken either from the local press or from a copy of the document itself) was not so optimistic. As Webber was unable to point to new federal actions, his "little sketch of the report" emphasized the brutality that had already occurred. Accompanying the election of Grant in 1868, Webber wrote, a reign of terror swept the state, as "over two thousand persons were killed wounded, and otherwise injured." This violence was not indiscriminate, however, for the Ku Klux Klan had a plan: "Having conquered the republicans, Killed and driven off the white leaders the Ku=Klux captured the [white] masses, marked them with badges of red flannel, enrolled them in clubs, led them to the polls, made them vote the democratic ticket, and then gave them a certificate of the fact &c." "[C]olored men following their daily work," Webber cried, "were Shot down like dogs;". Overall, the statistics numbed the mind. Between 1866 and February 8, 1875, Webber reported (citing the evidence of General Philip Sheridan), 2,141 Louisianans were killed and another 2,115 wounded

"on account of their political opinions." Webber's extensive para-
phrasing of the committee's eleven resolutions could not obscure
the fact that even George Hoar thought it infeasible to call for either federal oversight of Louisiana's elections or a renewed and
sustained military occupation. The last rays of Reconstruction's
once bright light were sinking fast.[37]

Webber described the process of intimidation by the Klan and
the White League accurately enough, but a certain unrealistic optimism infused his understanding of those white masses. He did
not account for the possibility, so abundantly evident in his own
chronicle and in the testimony of the Hoar report, that most
whites shared a common purpose with the "able bodied conservatives" who led such groups. As the Hoar report made clear, few
whites voted Republican by 1875, and even those "more moderate" whites who opposed violence desired the same ends as the
Klan or the league, and thus "are powerless to restrain their more
violent associates."[38]

Two events that spring, each revealing the depth of northern
racial tension, further tested Webber's rather strained analysis of
dominant white attitudes. In part in homage to the memory of
Charles Sumner, Congress passed and President Grant signed the
Civil Rights Act in March. But it was a different bill from the one
envisioned by the Massachusetts senator. Where Sumner had
fought for a broad act with strong provisions to assure compliance,
Webber explained that the watered-down version that passed
"[s]trike out [from] the bill=going to School together (White &
colored) and not be buried in the Cemeteries together." The bill
did provide that "the White & Blacks may eat and drink together
in all public places, ride together in public conveyances, go to public Theaters together Sit on Juries together"—but it provided no
enforcement mechanisms for securing these civil rights.

On Thursday evening, March 18, black Worcester held its pub-
lic meeting on the bill at the Odd Fellows lodge on Pearl Street.
Chaired by Isaac Mason, the activists in attendance praised the
Republican Party and revered the memory of Sumner, whose
"faithful efforts . . . to establish national equality" kept him
"cherished in the hearts of those whom he has so nobly served."
The meeting also expressed its gratitude to the President and to
Congressman Benjamin F. Butler, the former Union general, for

their support. These ceremonies completed, the assembly unani-
mously passed two resolutions, supported from the floor in comments by Amos Webber, Gilbert Walker, and William H. Jankins.
The first, Webber recorded, "[r]esolved=That while we return
our thanks to those noble men, who by words and act have sought
to elevate us into equal citizenship, it is with regret the same does
not extend to the public schools." The second, striking that note
of cautious optimism, expressed the hope that "the prejudice of
the past," which was "still lingering in the hearts of some of our
distinguished men," might finally pass away. Webber concluded
his entry on a personal and more pessimistic note:

> It remains to see, how it will all come out; I think it will come out
> pretty rough & tuff; A bitter Pill to Swallow.
>
> Webber[39]

Some months later, on the occasion of the anniversary of the
first Prince Hall Masonic lodge in America, Webber considered
again the role whites might play in attaining racial equality. Black
Masonry "is the oldest colored organization in the United States,"
Webber noted; and he explained how, like Peter Ogden and the
Odd Fellows, Prince Hall, the Barbados-born free black of English, African, and French parentage, was denied a charter by
white Americans but received one from British members. Webber,
who joined Worcester's King David Lodge No. 16 sometime between its founding in November 1873 and this commemoration in
June 1875, described in great detail the Boston parade in which he
himself marched with Alexander F. Hemenway, Isaac Mason,
Francis A. Clough, and other members of the lodge.[40]

But Webber's purpose was more than just ceremonial. In an
1868 petition Lewis Hayden and seventy-two other black Masons
from Boston, New Bedford, and Springfield requested of white
Masonic officials: "since all men in our Commonwealth are equals
before the law, inspired by the spirit of the age, the genial and *truly
'cosmopolitan'* character of our fraternity, we are prompted to hope
that we may be permitted to establish our claim to masonic rite by
whatever means the Most Worshipful Grand Lodge may suggest." A year later, this basic claim to equality, referred to committee, was denied. Since the grand lodge had not recognized the

petitioners as legitimate Masons in the past, the committee ruled, they had no standing in the present. In a practiced bit of casuistry, the grand lodge officers affirmed that no racial discrimination permeated Masonry because no petitioners, "if 'worthy and well qualified,' are excluded from our fraternity, if they seek admission through duly organized Lodges."[41]

Denied but not defeated, Hayden and his fellow Masons raised, in the same year they chartered King David Lodge in Worcester, their hope that a reconstructing America might change white Masonic attitudes. "The *Dred Scott decision* did no more than express the American sentiment, which pervaded the whole country from its earliest history," Boston's Prince Hall Grand Lodge argued in 1873; and as long as that spirit dominated American life, they "considered it as useless" to press upon whites "our Masonic claims." "[B]ut now, possessed of all the rights of American citizens, we owe it to ourselves and posterity to present our claims." However, in response to the handful of northern white Masons

Lewis Hayden (1809?–1889) of Boston. Escaped slave, abolitionist, advisor to Massachusetts Republican governors, recruiter of black soldiers, leader of black Masons, and political activist, Hayden worked closely with Webber for more than twenty years. *Courtesy of Massachusetts Historical Society, Boston*

willing to allow a discussion of the petition, the grand master of the Texas Masons, John Bramlette, asked dismissively: "What miracle has been wrought with the black man, that has caused the change in the Masonic mind North in his favor?"

At the 1874 meeting of the Prince Hall Grand Lodge, Lewis Hayden rose to respond to Bramlette. These Texans were best, he thought, in working "to bring into being Ku Klux Klans for the purpose of devouring widows and orphans, and for crushing out whatever . . . love for equity and justice there may be found within the limits of that State. What are they and their lodges but 'whitened [sic] sepulchres, beautiful without, but full of dead men's bones within'?" Citing St. Augustine to the effect that "those are not societies whose supreme law is not justice," Hayden dismissed the Texas lodges as "great confederates of thieves. . . . What miracle?" he pointedly asked, responding to Bramlette's sarcastic query:

> We call attention to one: A regiment composed of Massachusetts negroes, on Texas soil, coercing Grand Master Bramlette and his Masonic brothers of Texas into obedience to the constitution and the laws of our common country. Has he not a short memory?[42]

The regiment Hayden referred to, of course, was Webber's own Fifth Massachusetts Cavalry.

Webber did not discuss all the details of this debate in his centennial commentary, but he was surely familiar with the issues. Since he was well acquainted with Hayden and with Worcester's black Masons, the reference to the Fifth Cavalry doubtless reached Webber's ears. More directly, Webber indicated he understood white Masonic duplicity at its heart. The original petition was denied, Webber wrote, "unless they became members of one of the White Lodges;". White Masons could claim this was possible, for no lodge enacted a "Law to *prevent* this, The fact is However; that an entirely unanimous vote is required for the admission of a member: This renders the chance of colored masons for membership=rather hopeless;". Still Webber was optimistic, noting that "many of our first Class White Masons are strongly in favor of admiting the Col^d masons as brethren of the Order;".[43]

More intimate reasons also led Webber to emphasize "first class White Masons." One of those undoubtedly included in that category would have been Henry C. Willson, Webber's longtime foreman and co-reveler in the work-related socials Webber enjoyed so much. A seasoned member of Montacute Lodge, the oldest of Worcester's four white Masonic lodges, Willson had served as lodge master between 1869 and 1871, at the height of the debate over the first petition presented by Lewis Hayden. Willson also regularly attended grand lodge meetings in Boston, and played an important role in state Masonic affairs.[44] Without question Willson knew of the petition and its denial, and perhaps even discussed it with Webber at some point. Willson's sympathetic words may have encouraged Webber, especially in the context of their broader relationship.

Whatever his relationship with Willson, Webber did get more than sympathy from a few other whites. For the preceding quarter century, such white men as Charles Wurts, Alexander Montgomery, Philip L. Moen, and numerous military superiors had employed Amos Webber and provided him with a certain economic security. Nor was the impact of these elite whites solely materialistic. His direct exposure to a Wurts or a Moen, as well as the example of the abolitionist Charles Sumner or the Hallowell family of Bucks County, confirmed in Amos Webber that core moral vision first developed in the Bethlehem Colored Methodist Church which stressed a universal human equality before a stern and demanding God. His undeniable rootedness in the structures that girded the urban black world of the North did not demand he reject the moral example of any human being. The public presence of Sumner, Moen, John Brown, and Isaac and Sarah Pugh, among others, hewing a path between their moral principles and the contentious politics of the moment, also allowed Webber to hope that white Americans could change their racial attitudes. Black Worcester could meet frequently and nurture a most important set of religious, fraternal, and cultural institutions; but if there was no hope of changing, however slowly, majority white attitudes in the city or the nation, basic political change remained impossible. That unrelenting need for coalition, for hope that would negate the despair that led to political paralysis, drove Webber's at times unrealistic evaluations.

There was a final element involved in framing Webber's broad political stance. Webber was, in his deepest public belief, a patriot. This was true in an obvious way—his military service to abolish slavery fostered a postwar public identity built around the concept of citizenship. This he never lost sight of, no matter how despairing he at times felt over white American intransigence. At the same time that he first included reports on the depredations in Louisiana and the protest over the Civil Rights Act in his chronicle, Webber also recorded the march of the veterans of the Sixth Massachusetts Infantry to Worcester's Rural Cemetery. These white veterans, mustered into the service before black men could serve, marched to honor their fallen comrades who "[f]ourteen years ago to day . . . pass^d through Baltimore, and was fire on by the Baltimore rebels; while marching to the Washington Depot" to defend the Union following the surrender of Fort Sumter.[45] Thus, even as most whites, North and South, would deny blacks an equal place in a postwar America, Webber recalled a more harmonious vision that could transcend their ignorance and hate.

Webber's patriotism contained another dimension as well, one that affirmed his deep allegiance to the central political imagery that infused American culture. His commentaries on the centennial of the start of the American Revolution, also made that spring of 1875, revealed both how deeply rooted he was in that political culture and how the racial categories demanded by white fellow citizens of necessity structured his fundamental attitude. He observed: "One hundred years ago to day the first blow was struck for freedom at Concord & Lexington by the colonist against the British Soldiers;". To commemorate that signal event, the President, his cabinet, military generals, "and all great men is there," reviewing a parade "said to be three hours long." The image of American freedom forged in struggle moved Webber deeply: "[T]he tongue cannot express the day^s doing" as large crowds of Americans celebrated "the Centennial of wonderful events in History."[46] Two months later the centennial of Bunker Hill occasioned "[t]he great Celebration" in Boston and Charlestown. Massachusetts veterans, including a small contingent of blacks, all under the command of Benjamin F. Butler, led the festivities, and they were joined by veterans from across the United States. On the whole, Webber thought, this evocation of the potent myths of national origin and identity "was a beautiful Sight." But among the thousands of soldiers and uniformed veterans in the Boston parade, Webber thought the "most noticeable feature of the procession" was the presence of Confederate veterans from Maryland and South Carolina regiments. Where the Boston *Globe* applauded this commingled celebration of the nation's revolutionary origins as marking "the heartfelt and sincere reunion . . . between the people of two sections so long and unnaturally alienated," Webber's response was more tempered. As he witnessed these Confederate veterans "who appear to receive all the Honor and applause" as "the Northern soldiers and Citizens, open their arms" to welcome them, Webber hoped to find in the Confederate demeanor the image of "the prodigal Son [who] with heartfelt thanks" returned to the fold. For Webber held there was much to atone for, not the least of which was the violation of the principle of freedom the centennial celebration itself commemorated: "It must be remembered that Charleston was the place where the first shot was fired against the union; But today they are here to make amends for that sorrowful day; which was received; & & c." Without that element of atonement, the presence of the Confederate veterans mocked the celebration, and the June 1875 reunion of these white former enemies signaled again that the struggle for equal rights may have rasped its final breath. What many white Americans considered alienation Webber embraced as the very lifeblood of efforts to protect black American rights.[47]

AT TIMES CONTRADICTORY and unrealistic, a response both to the increasingly depressing circumstances and to his own confusion, Webber maintained his concern with political issues during these days of waning hope. At the deepest level Webber's politics still flowed from a moral vision that owed much to religious influences, and he occasionally attended Sunday services in the company of his lodge brothers, though, for all his local prominence, Webber remained outside any known church fellowship. With his demanding standards, he distrusted surface impressions, and perhaps he never found a minister as commanding as Elder Robert Jones of the Lombard Street Central Presbyterian Church among

Worcester's religious leaders. But there was more to it than that. Although fundamentally sympathetic, he cast a somewhat skeptical eye on the efforts of integrated "praying bands" of local Christian women trying to win souls for temperance by entering Worcester's saloons to preach. The women drew large crowds but few converts, he thought, and after they left, the largely male audience "would go into the saloon to hear the news and take a drink Upon the whole they [the women] created more excitement on the Street, than it done good." The saloons, Webber added with a certain ironic tone, "done an excellent business." As Webber understood from many a parade or liquor-licensing referendum, the gap between public rhetoric and personal conduct could be wide indeed. Irony aside, he hoped that these efforts "may be as the bread cast upon the waters: Seen after many days:—*Webber*."[48]

Webber's 1875 obituary of William B. Astor, "the richest man in America," captured this duality more sharply. "It might be preposed that such a man died, the Heavens & earth would be shaken from Center to Circumarion [circumference]," Webber wrote, referring to the cultural prominence wealthy industrialists and financiers enjoyed in American life. "But, alas; there is no note of praise for him=" as moral stature, and not simply the accumulation of material goods, governed Webber's evaluations. Webber briefly noted the worth of Astor and of his father, John Jacob Astor, "said to be the richest man of that day," and delivered his own judgment of the deceased: "May he rest; It looks doubtful} Webber."[49]

This dual perspective was most evident in his reaction to the yearly religious revivals held at Sterling, some twelve miles north of Worcester. During the postwar years these interdenominational revivals grew in size and duration and the railroads added extra cars to transport to the site the crowds, black and white, variously estimated at from 5,000 to over 15,000. As the revivals grew, their tone changed. The days of fervent preaching in open fields propelled by the spirit of the Lord gave way to less spontaneous services and a concern to provide certain comforts. Individual Worcester churches built permanent structures at the Sterling Camp Ground for their members' convenience, and many of the city's prosperous Protestants built themselves vacation cottages on the grounds to better enjoy the yearly renewal.[50]

85

Local. Pages Worcester,

Camp Meeting

Aug. 26. The attendence at the Sterling
Junction camp-meeting to day is
said to be very large, the number are
variously estimated at from ten to
twelve thousand it is probably
upwards of ten (10.000) thousand
on the camp ground; all the
restaurants and boarding tents are
well filled: also at the lake Side
and at the tent on the Depot platform
: A very large congregation was at
the Stand in meeting hours;
the Morning Sermon was Preached by
the Rev. Dr. S Smidley of Lowell
text = Gal. 3: 13: = the exhortation by
the Rev: W. W. Colburn of Fitchburg;
afterwards the usual prayer meeting
was held in different tents; & &

The camp meeting of the Ye. olden
times were quite different as of our
times; when the Methodist people
would gather up their tent and straw
go in a woods near a Spring break
down the under-brush put up their
tents, — drive down two forked Sticks
put a Straight stick across; build
a fire; then hang the Pot on to cook
& & thus the Olden time people
use to enjoy themselves; according
to their Views; while now the Camp
ground must be decorated with cottage
built for Summer resort; also call it
Camp-meeting time; Have a good time
=end Thursday is the best day of the week.
when it brings thousands to camp-meeting
to see whatever there is to be seen, and
see who has betterd themselves by being
at Camp-meeting; To see how many young
people has professed Religion: At the first
dance next Winter — like a Stiff Wind = Gone; =
(A.Webber)

"Amos Webber Thermometer Record and Diary," Volume III, August
26, 1875, page 85. *Courtesy of Baker Library, Harvard University Graduate School of Business Administration, Boston*

For the most part, Webber noted this yearly event briefly, as in 1872: "Camp=meeting. Sterling" was the entire entry.[51] But the intensity of Webber's own beliefs surfaced in his discussion of the 1875 revival.

An eyewitness, Webber began his page-long comment as a reporter, providing information as to the crowd, "probably upwards of ten (10,000) thousand," and the facilities, "all the restaurants and boarding tents were well filled." The morning sermon, given by a minister from Lowell and based on that verse from Paul's letter to the Galatians that told of the possibility of human redemption because Christ had become "accursed for our sakes,"[52] Webber simply acknowledged, and he recorded that "afterwards the usual prayer meetings was held in differents tents; & &". But his entry quickly moved beyond mere reporting. Webber was in his fiftieth year that August, and his moral foundations lay deep in a sterner Calvinist tradition than that of the contemporary revival. "The camp meetings of the Ye olden times were quite different as of our times," Webber wrote with a specificity born of experience. "[T]he Methodist people would gather up their tent and straw, go into a woods near a spring break down the underbrush put up their tents,=drive down two forked sticks put a straight stick across; build a fire; then hang the pot on to cook & &, thus the olden times people use to enjoy themselves; according to their views;".

The contrast with the present could not have been more vivid. Now "the camp ground must be decorated with cottages built for summer resort." Webber expressed dismay at the motivations of current attendees, most of whom thought the revival meant

Have a good time and Thursday is the best day of the week when it brings thousands to camp = meeting to see whatever there is to be seen; and see who has bettered themselves by being at Camp = meeting: To see how many; young people; has professed Religion:= At the first dance next Winter = like a Puff Wind = Gone.= (Webber.)[53]

As an accurate summary of some 10,000 individual motivations, Webber's judgment may be too quick. But the certainty of his personal opinions revealed a critical component of his private spiri-

7

1875.   July.   Worcester, Mass

Thermometer 9 O'clock A.M.   3 O'clock P.M.

Week's Day	Day	Deg	Wd	Weather			Deg	Wd	Weather
Thurs	1	73	SW	Cloudy			74	SW	Cloudy
Fri	2	66	W	Clear			77	W	Clear
Sat	3	72	NW	Clear			80	SW	Hazzie
Sun	4	76	SW	Cloudy			78	SW	Cloudy
Mon	5	77	NW	Cloudy			87	SW	Cloudy
Tues	6	77	W	Hazzie. 4th of July. 76			88	SW	Clear
Wedn	7	76	SW	Cloudy			84	NW	Cloudy
Thurs	8	75	E	Cloudy Beecher; 83.			82	E	Cloudy
Fri	9	72	SW	Clear			80	SW	Hazzie
Sat	10	72	SE	Hazzie ———— xx LN.			76	SW	Clear
Sun	11	76	SW	Clear ———— xx LN.			78	SW	Clear
Mon	12	68	NW	Clear = Sovereign. 77			80	SW	Clear
Tues	13	70	SW	Clear New Depot. 77			80	SW	Clear
Wedn	14	70	NW	Clear C. Pike 77			83	NW	Clear
Thurs	15	73	N	Clear			83	NW	Clear
Fri	16	74	SE	Raining			71	SE	Raining
Sat	17	71	NE	Clear			80	NW	Clear
Sun	18	62	SW	Cloudy			66	SW	Raining
Mon	19	61	NW	Clear			71	NW	Clear
Tues	20	66	SW	Clear			72	SW	Hazzie
Wedn	21	64	SW	Clear			71	SW	Clear
Thurs	22	71	NW	Clear P.L. Moen vaca			81	NW	Clear
Fri	23	64	NE	Raining			66	NE	Cloudy
Sat	24	68	NW	Clear			77	NW	Clear
Sun	25	70	SW	Clear Lost; Page 78.			76	SW	Clear
Mon	26	74	SW	Clear = Proff. Donelson			82	SW	Cloudy
Tues	27	76	NW	Clear			83	NW	Clear
Wedn	28	66	NE	Raining			78	SW	Cloudy
Thurs	29	76	NW	Hazzie Page 84			80	W	Clear
Fri	30	68	SE	Clear A Johnson died			74	NW	Clear
Sat	31	66	N	ble. Harry Willard vac			74	N	Clear

July 19th on two weeks vacation: Frank Bullard
  "   "   one   "   "   Charles Bullard
  " 22 P.L. Moen and family at the W. Mountain
  " 26 Chas. Bullard returned
  " 31 on two weeks vacation: Harry Willard

"Amos Webber Thermometer Record and Diary," Volume III, July 1875, page 7. Courtesy of Baker Library, Harvard University Graduate School of Business Administration, Boston

tual world. Somewhere in his past Amos Webber had undergone a moment of moral transformation that structured his subsequent life. He may have come to Philadelphia after such a conversion, or experienced it there at the Lombard Street church. He never wrote about it, but the similarity of these comments with his 1858 critique of Philadelphia's revival participants suggests as much. In each instance the inner surety Webber carried (even as he might doubt his own worthiness) strongly pointed to such a singular conversion experience.[54] It was this inner conviction that allowed Webber access to the prophet's jeremiad, that gave him the felt urgency to call sinners to righteousness, that provided him with direction in his public life.

ON JULY 19, 1875, Amos purchased a burial plot, with provisions for perpetual care, in Worcester's Hope Cemetery, large enough for six graves. It cost seventy dollars. At some point in the months that followed, possibly that October, Amos and Lizzie had their son's body disinterred from Philadelphia's Lebanon Cemetery, removed to Worcester, and reburied in the new site. The parents erected a small marker, with the simple inscription "Harry J."[55] Amos did not mention these events and there is no record of his or Lizzie's emotions as they laid their sorrow to rest once again. The symbolic reunion of the family may have healed wounds still open seventeen years later.

Webber's world was not always so solemn. During the late spring and summer of 1876, for example, in addition to his close observations of the vacation habits of the firm's clerks and officers, Webber discussed a host of fires and other natural disasters that had impressed him, explained both dramatic crimes and the expansion of local railroads, and recorded the opening of the Centennial Exhibition in Philadelphia that May. He attended the Barnum circus when it came to town, marched in the Decoration Day parade, celebrated the American centennial in Worcester that July, again attended the camp meeting, and spent a week that September in Philadelphia, staying with friends while he (Webber does not mention his wife) visited the exhibition. Even with all this, he found the time to attend the numerous meetings of the lodges he

Harry J. Webber's gravestone, Hope Cemetery, Worcester, erected sometime after his mother and father had his remains transferred from Philadelphia in 1875. *Courtesy of the author*

belonged to and the funeral of William Jankins's daughter, and to discuss with friends, and then write about, how General George Armstrong Custer and approximately 260 soldiers "were massacred" at the Little Bighorn. Finally, during these same few months, Webber joined with Peter S. Hood, Roswell B. Hazard, and fellow veteran George H. Scott to establish Integrity Lodge No. 1768, the second black Odd Fellows lodge in the city, for which he served as recording secretary.[56]

Such a schedule—and we know but a portion of it—would have overwhelmed someone less driven than Amos Webber. What propelled this wiry, energetic man, even in many of his entertainments, was the complex moral perspective that had infused his first fifty years of life. In this, Webber made no distinction between public and private occasions, political events and public amusements, specifically black organizations and the promise of American citizenship: his hope, his faith, and his perseverance

City Hall, Worcester, Massachusetts, decorated for the Centennial of American Independence, July 4, 1876. *Courtesy of American Antiquarian Society*

drew their vitality from his internal moral sensibility. Precisely because this moral sensibility was grounded in a belief in the reality of evil, the inevitability of human sin, and the ultimate Christian promise of redemption, Webber possessed an inner conviction of final victory that protected him against the deepest despair. The 1876 presidential election, marking the final collapse of postwar hopes for true equality, tested his reservoir of faith most intensely.

That summer his reporter's eye detailed each of the seven ballots that resulted in the selection of Rutherford B. Hayes of Ohio as the Republican standard-bearer, while a paragraph, partisan in its brevity, reported that the Democrats required but one ballot to nominate Samuel J. Tilden of New York: "There being no further business: adjourned."[57] Throughout the fall Webber followed the various state elections, noting with pleasure when Republicans took the governor's office, as in Ohio and Maine, or in more somber tones when they lost: "West Virginia voted with the Solid South: A Dem; Majority."[58] It was with considerable anticipation, then, that Webber awaited the results of November's presidential balloting.

On November 8, the day after the voting, Webber reported that "excitement is great all over the country" as both parties "are putting every=thing to Elect their candidate for President." Hayes, he already knew, had carried Massachusetts, and Webber could record local results as well. There were reports that Tilden had carried New York—which, many thought, would have guaranteed the Democrat's election—and Webber noted that Republican papers in the East "have given up the contest." The following day he excitedly wrote that politicians of both parties now understood that Hayes could still win even without New York, as long as he carried three southern states: Louisiana, South Carolina, and Florida. But Republicans, Webber reminded himself, should "not count the Chickens before they are hatchs," especially as the white South "has gone into all kinds of frauds" to turn those states to Tilden. Because of the widespread use of the telegraph, in most elections the final results were usually in by this time. But 1876 was anything but a normal electoral year.

"Three weeks has gone and no President yet," Webber wrote on November 29. There was "trouble down in Dixie," as Republican electoral boards certified Hayes's victory in those three critical southern states and the Democrats refused to accept the results. Talk of a severe constitutional crisis was in the air, and some took up the slogan "Tilden or War." For Webber, this crisis again raised the central American tension, which had dominated his adult political life. "A physican generally by symtons tells the desease," Webber's folksy yet precise analysis began; "that old desease; of 1861 breaking out again; in 1860=61 certain of the Southern states openly repudiated the Constitution . . . and sett up a government of their own whose chief corner=stone was Slavery=" Although they lost the war, it was not too long before their leaders found their way back to Congress, where they served "in bad faith, for whenever a Republican proposed a measure of reconstruction, up rose the wild=fires (all there was of them at that time) and oppose any good bill;". This same political movement, grown now into a full blaze, would consume the national government. Wade Hampton, South Carolina's Democratic candidate for governor, Webber fumed, "who sets up as the champion of Law & order," himself intimidated black voters and encouraged his supporters in the belief that Tilden "must be President if they had to wade Knee=deep in Blood. . . . Such was the conduct of these empty headed fools."[59]

In the end, of course, Webber erred if he expected this tension would instigate yet another civil conflict. White Americans, the majority of whom would not support strong civil rights legislation, would certainly not go to war in 1876 to defend black rights. Instead, an electoral commission, the first ever in American history, awarded the presidency to Hayes. Generally enthused at the Republican victory, Webber emphasized the inauguration's "usual Pomp = and Show as in the days of Old." In his one specific political reference, he proudly noted Hayes's nomination and the Senate's confirmation of "Frederick Douglass (Colored)" as marshal of the District of Columbia.[60]

But Webber's hope proved short-lived. In less than a month Hayes awarded the contested gubernatorial election in South Carolina to Wade Hampton over the incumbent Republican Daniel Chamberlain, who had been a colonel in Webber's cavalry regiment. Webber's response revealed his appreciation of the *Realpolitik* that had surrounded the presidential election commission. South Carolina's electoral votes went to Hayes, Webber explained, "by Chamberlain having the U.S. troops present in protecting the Citizens in casting their vote, without Intimidation." But when Hayes ordered those same troops from South Carolina's statehouse, thereby giving the office to Hampton, Webber recognized that both Chamberlain and his supporters now lacked even a minimal level of protection and that this national Republican administration would not respect black rights. Three weeks later, a wiser Webber wrote of another contested gubernatorial election in Louisiana. As in South Carolina, Hayes also ordered federal troops withdrawn, thereby giving the state over to the Democrats. "[T]hus ends the Military: Rule & c" was Webber's final comment.[61]

What Webber might not have recognized until Hayes's actions in South Carolina and Louisiana was the extent of the compromise the Republican Party had accepted. As a condition of winning the contested national election, Republicans agreed to end Reconstruction and to withdraw any federal oversight of the southern states' compliance with constitutional and congressional law. Webber's 1871 description of the party as untrustworthy— "half of them are always on the fence, you never can find them"— seemed more true than ever. In the remaining six and one-half volumes of his chronicle—his record of the next twenty-eight years following the 1876 election—Webber never mentioned Reconstruction, its demise, or the hopes he had once entertained. As the violence in the South continued, as white mobs lynched black men and women throughout the nation, and as Republican support of equal rights all but disappeared, Amos Webber was silent. In the privacy of his chronicle and in his public actions, he remained a loyal son of the party of Lincoln, but his own critique was, as it had always been, checkmated by the specter of even worse alternatives.

To this extent a powerful voice, one that reflected the tones of numerous other black voices in Worcester, was tempered. Webber would remain active in local affairs over the following two decades, but the national transformation he so fervently desired could no longer be realistically envisioned. Of necessity his attention turned to other aspects of his life: to local politics, to other discussions of social justice, and to nurturing the small yet numerous organizations that enabled black residents to create rewarding communal lives from the dilemma white America imposed.

PART THREE

To Be Honorable
in the Community:
1877–1904

CHAPTER TEN

The Kindness of Brethren

THE COLLAPSE OF RECONSTRUCTION, with its different yet equally depressing meaning for black Americans North and South, did not transform Amos Webber into a cynic, nor did it create in Webber or in his friends a paralysis of their political will. They remained engaged, active, and concerned in electoral politics and in building the social institutions that were the foundation of black Worcester. What had changed was their expectations of the political system. Although Webber remained committed to a belief in ultimate justice, he struggled to find a viable political expression for this commitment. In this way Webber's rich social activities now assumed even greater importance in his life.

WEBBER'S WORKDAY HAD NOT CHANGED dramatically since his promotion from his janitorial duties in Henry C. Willson's department some years earlier. He remained a messenger, assigned to the front office, where he interacted daily with the clerks and the leading officers of the firm. He probably had a desk where he awaited assignments, and where he could keep his ledger books. He drove Washburn and Moen officials about town, made daily runs to the post office, and performed other deliveries as needed: "Please send by Amos as many blank licenses as you think should be taken west by Mr. Washburn," one company official requested of another when the firm's vice president prepared to visit Washburn and Moen's Illinois plant. Each fall, Webber helped to drain and clean the office steam pipes for the winter, and he shared responsibility for lighting the gas lamps at dusk each day. Most important, Webber aided, in whatever fashion they desired, the leading officers of the firm, and particularly the Moens, father and son. As before, Webber kept his chronicler's eye focused on the vacations, meetings, and deaths among the white-collar officials and selected foremen.[1]

Despite the long hours, the flexibility of his workday enabled Webber to maintain his varied social commitments. His travels about the city allowed him to visit with lodge brothers, drop in on William Brown at his shop, or exchange information and opinions at one of the barbershops run by such friends as Francis A. Clough, William Jankins, or Alexander F. Hemenway. At the office Webber had the time to enter his temperature records twice each day, and to give free rein to his interests and curiosity in both the temperature and "Local Pages" sections of his chronicle. In spring 1877, for example, Webber wrote of a "mesmerist" charged with the rape of a local clergyman's daughter after "he exerted his mesmeric influence over her"; the Russo-Turkish War; the opening of the second year of Philadelphia's Centennial Exhibition, which Webber thought was "almost as grand as the 10th of May/76 (see page 115.)"; and the death of Edward Earle, a former Worcester mayor.[2]

Interspersed with these entries were accounts of two men killed in a sewer trench in the city and a three-page listing of all the presidents of the United States to that point, including their terms in office, their political party, and the date and year of their birth and death. Ulysses S. Grant's reception in England received another three-page discussion, but Webber gave Decoration Day a rather subdued treatment. Twice during this period Webber recorded the efforts of "Miss Von Hillern the great Walker" as she attempted to achieve feats of endurance by walking 100 miles in twenty-eight hours in Mechanics Hall and, a month later, 50 miles in twelve hours.[3]

Numerous entries in his chronicle—those about the Russo-Turkish War, for example—clearly demanded a familiarity with the local and, perhaps, Boston and New York press. As at Hart, Montgomery and Company during the 1850s, the travels of the Worcester firm's officers and salesmen provided Webber with access to other newspapers. The clippings that he inserted in his chronicle indicated that Webber had occasional access to *Scientific American, Leslie's Illustrated Newspaper, Massachusetts Ploughman,* untitled newspapers from Detroit and upstate New York, and the New York *Tribune,* as well as Worcester's *Daily Spy* and *Evening Gazette.* In addition, of course, the city's Free Public Library contained over 60,000 volumes and subscribed to almost 260 newspapers and periodicals in the early 1880s, all of which Webber had access to during or after working hours.[4]

His was not the schedule of a workingman held to close account by his supervisors. He had his work to accomplish, undoubtedly, and his hours could be long. But even on the longest days, his schedule contained flexibility and his relations with superiors remained cordial, if not actually friendly. The man who had so enjoyed the social gatherings of "the old hands" from the tempering room retained similar feelings about work relationships upon his promotion to the front office. Amos Webber's experience provided none of the grist for the protests that affected other industrial workers during these years. Even as the firm grew into a national concern, spurred by its control of the patent for barbed wire,[5] with 3,000 workers in Worcester and additional plants in Connecticut and Illinois, Webber's wages enabled him to maintain a home and a busy schedule of lodge-related travel. As had been true in Philadelphia, simply owning the house on Liberty Street placed him among a distinct minority of all manufacturing workers, white or black, in the entire county.[6] For Webber, being the "personal attendant and messenger" to the Moens, as one former executive remembered him, had its very tangible rewards.[7]

Despite his personal circumstances, however, Webber did not ignore the sharp tensions that accompanied industrial development, though he was quite moderate in any conclusions he drew. In 1877 members of a secret organization of Irish miners, calling themselves the Molly Maguires, who fought sheriffs, mine owners, and judges throughout the coal districts of Pennsylvania, were finally arrested and tried. Eleven were sentenced to death by hanging, but Webber had little sympathy for them. "[T]his desparate organization overawed sheriffs and the whole community," he argued, reflecting his faith in the law's ability to achieve justice. He praised the undercover detective James McParlan for his signal role in bringing the leaders to trial, and explained with a certain precision exactly where each of the accused was hanged. "Thus ends the lives of these men," Webber pronounced, "who thought nothing of others lives."[8]

His moral imperative established the parameters of acceptable behavior for industrialist and worker alike. As Webber could criticize a James Fisk, the railroad president, or an Oakes Ames, the financial speculator, for his irresponsible conduct, so too did he with equal severity condemn workers who violated that standard. But as in his discussions of the struggle for racial equality, individual transgressions of that moral code did not therefore diminish concern for a more inclusive and just society.

"The Great Rail=Road Strike" (which was the title of a long, signed entry on July 27, 1877) began July 20, when "the engineers and fireman on the Baltimore and Ohio Rail=road" quit work in Martinsburg, West Virginia, to protest "the reduction of wages which took effect July 1st 1877." The strike quickly spread to other railroad workers in Martinsburg and then to other railroad centers as well. "Five (5) States were under arms," Webber explained in the second week of the strike, "and the fury spread from one town to another." After listing some of the cities that experienced strike activity, he depicted in the horrific tones of the popular press scenes of urban violence. Large mobs, Webber wrote, "fought the Soldiers, and burnt the round House at Pittsburgh, 125 Locomotives destroyed and 3500 cars burned, between 2 & 300 lives were lost; in different towns and places, were the scene of Riot occurred In Chicago a terrible Battle took place between the rioters and the Soldiers, the mob is said to be 10,000 person Strong;". The violence continued in places, although Webber thought that now "some of the roads are running," if with "a considerable dissatisfaction" from the railroad workers.

More than a chronicler of this strike,[9] Webber turned to a discussion of the central issue that the strike raised. The Baltimore and Ohio Railroad workers complained "that the Directors of the Road, do them injustice" by reducing wages "when the road is in a prosperous Condition=The Directors," on the other hand, claimed, with freight rates "so Low, they could not afford to pay the present wages." Scouring the newspapers and journals for information to help him develop an informed judgment, Webber framed the central problem. News reports, citing the railroad's corporate records, reported net earnings of more than $4 million in 1876. If the figure was accurate, Webber thought, "Why, Somebody Lies=" for there were ample funds to maintain wages. A fourth of the earnings, he estimated, would subsidize a dividend of 10 percent. The remainder of the profit, Webber argued, went to pay loans five and ten years before they were due and to augment the surplus fund, "which was already largely in excess. . . . If all this be true," this messenger for Worcester's leading industrialist asked, "what was the reduction for. only because they held the power over their employees thus comes the, trouble. of strikes. etc". Webber honed his analysis in an appended dense paragraph, entitled "Railroad Surplusage," in which he explored the way in which such surplus funds were often used to reward neither the majority of stockholders nor the workforce in the industry—but were instead used to reward a handful of executives who surreptitiously bled those funds of their value.[10]

Two days later Webber focused his attention on how the strike spread to the New York Central Railroad. The president of the railroad, William H. Vanderbilt, estimated that but 500 of the 12,000 operating employees actually struck and in a written statement issued on July 31 (and recorded by Webber the following day), Vanderbilt praised his workforce for protecting the road's property, for fulfilling their duties "except when overcome by outside violence," and for their "example [which] has tended greatly to allay the excitement" caused nationally by the strike and ensuing violence. Wishing to offer "some marked recognition of your Loyalty & faithfulness," Vanderbilt announced that he had set aside $100,000 as a bonus to be divided, "according to their positions on the Pay-Roll," among the operating employees. Executives, department supervisors, and clerical workers were explicitly excluded from this bonus. Vanderbilt also announced that those who did strike "cannot remain in, or re=enter" his employment; and he concluded with the diffident promise to the remaining workers that "[y]our pay will be increased, the moment the business of the country will justify it."[11]

Webber's reaction to Vanderbilt's plan reflected a sophisticated assessment of both the plan and the larger moral issues at the core of "the Labor Question." "The gift itself," Webber's barbed response began, "show that Mr. Vanderbilt has a spark of humanity." The plan was "a thoughtful Idea," but was perhaps less generous than at first glance for "the amount is Small, between 12000 men." Webber acknowledged that "the spirit of the gift" suggested "a better feeling towards the employed," and he hoped that it would bring about "a more confident [relationship] to both the employed & employers." More important, however, Webber did not accept William Vanderbilt's suggestion that out of his appreciation of the workers' loyalty he freely bestowed the bonus. Vanderbilt, Webber noted, referring partly to the wage cuts of July 1, had generally followed "this oppressive rule" established by other railroads in dealings with their workers. "But he found that it would not do, to go against that great force of Strikers; hence he stop it and consider^d In doing so it is evident he wants to do the right thing with his employees: etc."

In the railroad industry as elsewhere, Webber continued, some corporations had to reduce wages, given the prolonged depressed state of the economy. "[T]he workman never grumbled, when he knew that it was an honest reduction." But the cause of the recent strikes lay elsewhere. "The great trouble with some the officials of Corporations is the love of having their own way," regardless of the discomfort it caused others. "Instead of endeavoring to cultivate a friendly feeling between themselves, and their employees, they repel them by their haughty overbearing and arbitrary conduct," arousing such "a feeling of hostility of which the recent outbreaks are the fruits." Webber's proposed solution reflected some of the deepest currents in nineteenth-century popular protest:

> It should be understood by employers that a man is not a machine, that he has feelings and aspiration of his own and certain rights which ought to be respected; When men see that this fact is appreciated by employers, and no disposition to crowd them, and grind them down, the labor troubles will disappear[12]

Webber's opinions now differed sharply from his thinking six years earlier, when Washburn and Moen workers struck. Where he then had stressed the loss of money strikes inevitably brought, he now emphasized the collective power of strikers in pursuit of justice and the corresponding possibility that employers might

violate fundamental moral law. To this extent Webber acknowledged strikes as an occasionally necessary tactic in the search for
that "friendly feeling" between employers and workers. Because
he never contrasted his attitudes in 1871 and 1877, precisely how
his thinking developed—or how it reflected the thinking of other
workers in the firm—remains an open question. It seems likely,
however, that Webber still considered Washburn and Moen's corporate leaders a breed apart from the executives he chastised in
1877 and, in fact, when Washburn and Moen workers met in May
1877 to consider calling a strike to protest a 15 percent wage cut,
Webber never even noted the meeting.[13] Perhaps Webber considered this wage cut "an honest reduction."

Adams Express Company teamsters, Worcester, ca. 1868. Like messengers and janitors, the nature and pace of these men's work also allowed
for conversation and discussion on a variety of topics during the workday. *Courtesy of American Antiquarian Society*

Webber also left no record of any discussions about these issues among Worcester's black working people. Conversations in the lodge rooms, in the barbershops, and in people's homes undoubtedly took place, and Webber's long entries suggest something of the impact the strike had on individuals far removed from the actual events. But Webber's silence leaves few clues as to how his friends and fellow activists may have influenced him. In his emphasis that "a man is not a machine," but rather an individual who possesses "certain rights which ought to be respected," there is an echo of the language utilized by Worcester's black defenders of racial equality. How self-conscious this echo was and how widespread its appeal among Worcester's black wage earners is unknown.

What is evident, however, is the authority with which Amos Webber evaluated these issues. What could be only briefly glimpsed in his discussion of the 1871 strike and inconceivable from the author of those terse antebellum entries now fully emerged: Webber as an informed analyst, confident of his opinions, and direct in his expression. Where he had earlier dissected the causes of southern, antiblack violence, Webber now directed his considerable energy toward understanding the meaning of justice in another social setting. The sureness exhibited in his judgment marked his maturity and self-command. Given this authority, where this fifty-one-year-old chronicler still remained silent suggests a deliberate act rather than a simple omission.

———————

WEBBER'S POLITICAL VIEWS remained consistent throughout this time. He never noted the fact that, locally or nationally, the Republican Party enrolled many industrialists in its ranks. Indeed, this sympathetic observer of the 1877 strikes opposed independent labor candidates as contributing to "the cause of the victory for the Democrats."[14] Webber also closely followed the Massachusetts governor's race following the strikes, exulting when the Republican candidate won; with equal fervor he covered Worcester's mayoralty campaign that December. As before, the issue of racial equality framed Webber's politics, and the passing of the abolitionist generation caused him deep concern. "One by

One they go and leave us," he wrote in his obituary of Oliver H. P. T. Morton, the abolitionist and steadfast Republican.[15]

Webber took no note of a Boston meeting that October where blacks from Massachusetts and throughout the nation roundly castigated both President Hayes's southern policy and Frederick Douglass and other "so-call leaders of the colored race" for their uncritical endorsement of the Republicans.[16] So committed was Webber to his political perspective that, in his New Year's message for 1878, he enumerated as the most important domestic events of the past year the peaceful inauguration of Rutherford B. Hayes and the "retrenchments; with Business men; they have Suffered much privation and hardship;".[17] The conditions that the depression that began in 1873 created for working people, white and black, went unnoticed, and Webber remained incapable of envisioning a political alternative to the Republican Party, despite his earlier criticism of it.

The Massachusetts gubernatorial election in 1878 highlighted the inflexibility of Webber's position. Running against the Republican and Democratic nominees was Benjamin F. Butler, the former army general, Republican congressman, and staunch defender of black rights who, but three years before, had received black Worcester's public thanks for his support of the Civil Rights Act. Now running as an independent Democrat, Butler represented himself as the spokesman for the state's workingmen. In a protest against the Republican Party's southern policy that echoed the critique of William Still and other northern blacks, Wendell Phillips, the former abolitionist and staunch Republican, supported Butler.

Butler's candidacy received an additional boost from a different quarter that summer when Dennis Kearney, the leader of the anti-Chinese movement in California, arrived in Boston to support him. At a rally at Faneuil Hall in August, Kearney received an enthusiastic welcome from, among others, Charles Lichtman, a well-known labor organizer, and P. J. McGuire, a socialist organizer of carpenters. Workingmen had to organize against corrupt politicians and "capitalist thieves" alike, Kearney warned, and he particularly stressed the success of his state's white workers in defeating their employers' attempt to use Chinese workers, whom he termed "a band of leperous Chinese pirates, . . . as a knife to cut the throats of the honest laboring men of the state." A month later Kearney brought his racist message to Worcester, predicting not only that Butler would win but that those same "honest" white workingmen would soon "rule the country."[18]

The choices facing the Commonwealth's black voters were not simple. If neither the regular nor independent Democratic candidates offered a fair racial policy, it was unclear that the Republican candidate, former Governor Thomas Talbot, was significantly different. An uninspiring politician, he would not challenge his party's persistent drift away from its historic defense of equality. In Worcester, black voters generally favored the Republican, but there was a growing number who favored Butler. J. J. Mobray, a leader among black Butlerites, addressed numerous rallies during that campaign and at each predicted that "the colored men are going to vote for General Butler."[19] Black Republicans also held a series of meetings, in part to counter the first substantial electoral defection from the Republican standard among black Worcester voters. At a public meeting on October 24, presided over by Isaac Mason and with Webber as secretary, a speech by a white Republican, Edwin H. Hill, led city Democrats to charge that Republicans intimidated black voters with the threat that a vote for the "Democratic or Butler ticket [was a vote] to enslave the colored people again." The following day, in a letter to the local press, Webber responded: "Now, sir, no such statement was made by Mr. Hill," he began, and then offered his account of Hill's speech:

> It was simply this: The question had been asked, Why the colored men in the South were shot down and persecuted. Mr. Hill, in reply, said that the same party who were forming the rifle club were the very men who held them in slavery and put the shackles upon their limbs, and would do so again had they the power. He then asked the question, are the members of those rifle clubs Republican; are the men who are burning school-houses and prosecuting the teachers, Republicans? No; they are the same rabble who are in Worcester today, cursing "the nigger," as they term the colored people.[20]

If the choices confronting Amos Webber were not simple, they were also not very difficult. In the legacy of the Republican Party as he encountered it, Amos Webber understood the memory of his own experience. To forget that memory would be to erase two decades of public political life, with its powerful personal meaning. That he simply refused to do.[21]

In contrast with William Still, Alexander Crummell (a black minister and political activist), and others in the aftermath of Reconstruction, Amos Webber never broke with the Republican Party. If his steadfast allegiance to the party of Sumner, Lincoln, and Douglass made sense in an imperfect world, the unrelieved celebratory tone that now accompanied his political analysis of the Republican Party marked a sharp contrast with the past. Gone from his private commentary was the critical evaluation of policies that gave his earlier support a sustained, independent base, as if this dual perspective simply became untenable following Hayes's inauguration. Webber's ideas continued to develop; he remained as curious as ever about the world around him; and he was politically active in the Republican cause. But the end of Reconstruction established parameters that would not be challenged in the near future. To rail against that force seemed futile to Webber, and to this extent an eloquent yet not unusual political voice chose silence.

Benjamin Butler lost the statewide election to the Republican candidate, Thomas Talbot. In the Worcester wards most heavily populated by the foreign-born, however—particularly Wards Three, Four, and Five—Butler won by at least a two-to-one majority. Little wonder that Webber was concerned. "It was conceded," he wrote that election day, "that Butler would get all the Workingmen vote," due to his promises concerning taxes, monetary reform, and efforts to "make business good for the laboring class. . . . However," a relieved Webber announced, "the majority that was given to the Republican candidate showed that the people voted for the best policy."[22]

THROUGHOUT THE 1870s, a small but steady number of southern blacks trickled northward, some even to Worcester, to escape oppressive conditions. Following 1877, larger numbers of rural southern blacks, in an organized grass-roots movement, began a migration west into Kansas. Fleeing white violence and an atmosphere in which, as one supporter of the migration explained, "the colored man is not recognized here as human, but, as Tom Paine asserted, as a species of the monkey,"[23] blacks from Louisiana and Mississippi traveled first to St. Louis and then to Kansas to establish communities free from the worst of southern conditions. Known as the Exodus, this migration proved divisive for black Republicans, in part because it became an informal referendum on the Republican Party's Reconstruction policies.

Frederick Douglass represented one side of this debate. He sharply opposed the Exodus and repeatedly reminded southern blacks of their duty to remain in the South. Conditions had been "flagrantly and incomparably worse" only a few short years before, Douglass argued, and he insisted the rights now dismissed by southern whites "will revive, survive and flourish again." This required the continued presence of southern blacks, however, to support the few black congressmen still in office throughout the South.

Douglass added two other arguments. Where, he wondered, would the migration stop? In a reference to Dennis Kearney, Douglass asked what would prevent "some 'Sand Lot Orator' . . . as in California [to] take it into his head to stir up the mob against the negro, as he stirred up the mob against the Chinese? What then? Must the negro have another exodus?" Douglass also repeated a theme developed some years earlier by James D. Lynch. A South shorn of slavery was the best "field of labor" for freedmen and -women, since the "negro . . . is preeminently a Southern man," Douglass wrote. The black laborer "has a monopoly of the labor market" because the plantation owners "must have his labor, or allow their fields to go untilled." Migration, Douglass incomprehensibly argued, would reverse this relationship and "send the negro to the towns and cities [of the North] to compete with white labor. With what result, let the past tell." Other black Republican leaders, such as Blanche K. Bruce, P. B. S. Pinchback, and Isaiah Wears, also opposed the Exodus and, like Douglass, were motivated by a concern for their personal or their party's standing, as well as by a fear that large-scale migration into northern communities would upset the delicate racial atmosphere.[24]

Douglass's opinions generated intense disagreement. A delegate to a New Orleans convention sarcastically asked whether Douglass himself had not escaped the South. A Nashville meeting called to discuss the Exodus resolved "to pay no heed to such men as Fred. Douglass and his accomplices." At a New York City fund-raiser for the migrants, the mention of Douglass's name drew hisses and catcalls. Black leaders such as Henry Highland Garnet, John M. Langston, George T. Downing, and Richard T. Greener all supported the migration, as did white former abolitionists William Lloyd Garrison, Wendell Phillips, and George F. Hoar.[25]

Amos Webber never directly criticized Douglass for his stand on the Exodus, but he clearly sympathized with those who did. Ignoring its effect on the Republican Party, Webber placed the Exodus within the central tradition of black protests for freedom. "In the time before the War, the Slaves took to the North . . . and Started for the land of Freedom . . . in the free States and the Canadies; This Spring," he wrote in 1879,

> witnesses a renewal on an extensive scale of the flight of the colored people from the hardships and injustice in the South; in search of Liberty and the opportunity that are to be found in the North Star

In contrast with the tortured rhetoric of national black Republican leaders, Webber understood the migrants' motivation quite clearly. In Kansas, "they would not be Killed; burned and Shot down, like dogs. . . . They have had enough: of Ku=Klux, White league,= and raiding enough of bulldozing = and fraud enough of exorbitant Land rents, and oppression & &c".[26]

Webber considered these men and women as latter-day fugitive slaves worthy of the same help he had given the original fugitives twenty years earlier, and so did a majority of black Worcester. Building on a tradition of fund-raising for clothes, farm implements, and school supplies for southern blacks,[27] Worcester's black community again swung into action. The local press listed contributions from William Brown, Isaac Mason, Charles Bulah, D. T. Oswell, and Amos Webber, among others. Even a year later William Brown still coordinated efforts to send clothing and supplies to those migrants now living in Kansas.[28]

Thus, for Webber and other black activists in Worcester, the softened tone of their public evaluations of the Republican Party's racial policy did not signal abandonment of their southern brothers and sisters. In a manner that necessarily reflected post-Reconstruction politics, their earlier commitments remained firm.

―――――   ―――――

DURING THESE YEARS, Webber commented on a full range of topics in his chronicle. Snowstorms, railroad accidents, and other natural disasters received attention, as did the arrival of Ulysses S. Grant in "Tokio" in 1879. A fierce heat wave that summer sent Webber back through the first two Worcester volumes of his book to record the hottest day in each of the past nine years and to observe that "[a]s a general rule after an accessive heat it would be accompanied with a Severe Thunder Storm &c."[29] Five times that year he noticed major walking matches in New York City with significant prize money at stake. Two of the matches involved female athletes and one, for the Astly Belt and a $26,000 purse, included among the competitors one "Hart (The colored Boston boy)." Hart twisted his ankle during the race but still completed 482 miles for fourth place and over $2,300 in prize money, Webber explained with considerable pride.[30]

One of the topics that attracted Webber's attention, and which warranted one of the longer pieces throughout all of the nine volumes, concerned the demolition of Worcester's Union Church, a cavernous neo-Gothic structure on Front Street, in the city's business district. Housing a Congregational denomination that retained more than just the memory of a stern Calvinist tradition, Union was also the place of worship of many of the city's elite industrial and commercial families. As separate as he was from this social stratum, Webber nonetheless had an obvious connection to the congregation, since among those elite families attending were the Washburns and the Moens. Indeed, Philip W. Moen, the "Master Philly" whom Webber once tried to keep from harm's way as he raced his horse through city streets, now served as superintendent of the Sunday school.[31] Now, observing the final services in the old church building, Webber revealed the depth of his involvement with this congregation.

At that final service, which took place on the evening before the church was razed, "the members of said church came together to bid the Old Church Good Bye;". The occasion, Webber thought, "brings back many a scene of Olden times, and we give way to tears for the departed; Thus the members and congregation of Said Church feels the same way to depart from the Old Church. . . . Of which they have had so many a happy hour in praising their God, in Love and Truth;". In commemoration he offered an original poem of ten stanzas. Adapting the persona of a longtime church member, the poem's narrator reflected on "[w]hen this Old Church was new." At that time more than four decades earlier (the church was built in 1836), "Our grandsires; Spirit renewed / Through cold, heat, rain, hail & Snow." Dressed in plain "lindsay [linsey] and tow," wearing homemade socks, they lived with "No jar of cars, passing by / Or sounds, of the whistle blew"; rather "They Swung the scythes; not machines / Be drawn by a horse or mule." That generation's purpose had a pristine quality, the poet thought, one he clearly admired: "The Grand-sires sing Hallelu—u / Their songs and praises to Thee." In contrast this was a different era, which Webber found disquieting:

> Now this Old Church to Old
> For the fashion and the young
> O, what love it has unfold
> And many a psalm tune sung.

> Good Bye Old Church good bye
> Like life your days are number[d]
> Down with the steeple that stood high
> With its walls torn assunder.

The poet then claimed his work with the flourish: "By A. Webber."

Webber recalled the congregation's history in considerable detail. Union Church had been an abolitionist stronghold and provided the religious grounding for many of the elite white men who proved so important in Webber's life. The first minister had remained little more than a year following his installation in November 1836, resigning when the majority of the congregation voted to open the church to antislavery meetings. Webber (who never commented on similar tensions involving Reverend Stephen Gloucester following Philadelphia's 1842 race riot) here applauded the congregation's social traditions. The pastor's departure was quickly accepted because "he was not the kind of stone for the building as it is seen to day that the Union Church took the right course and Sees the Glory of the same."[32]

The laying of the new building's cornerstone that summer symbolized for Webber the church's attractive mixture of traditional theology and social activism. The master of ceremonies that afternoon, who also served as the chairman of the building committee and the leading layman of the church, was Philip L. Moen.[33] For Webber, his employer represented a religious tradition that emphasized the charge to live a moral life, encompassed abolition as a central component of its practice, and embodied these beliefs in political life in a particular image of the Republican Party. The 1880 search for a new pastor, which Moen also chaired, reinforced these connections once again.

Moen, speaking for the committee, recommended Reverend Henry A. Stimson to the congregation. Born in New York City in 1842, son of an early railroad president, Stimson clerked in business and then spent the war years as a student at Yale. Following graduation, he studied at Union Theological Seminary in New York at a time when orthodox New England Calvinism, with its belief in predestination and the literal veracity of the Scriptures, still shaped the curriculum.[34] Enamored of the American West, which he believed was unique in "[i]ts energy, its resources, its hospitality, its intelligence, even its religion," Stimson had accepted the call in 1871 from the Plymouth Church in Minneapolis.[35]

The most dramatic moment of Stimson's ministry came in a sermon he gave on July 9, 1876. Amid the tremendous excitement over the American centennial had come the news of General Custer's crushing defeat in battle against Sioux Indians led by Sitting Bull. White reaction was swift, built as it was on a long disdain for native Americans. "In the train and on the street corner," Stimson preached, "you hear it bitterly repeated, 'It were well if they could be exterminated.'" While the minister shared the grief of the families who lost their men at the Little Bighorn, he held his Minnesotan congregation and his country to a broader standard: "We are a Christian nation," he insisted, "and we, my hearers, are of the church of Christ within this nation." Therefore, "by virtue of our citizenship" in accord with each individual's measure of influence, we "shall be brought to account before God for this day's proceedings."

As he warmed to his point, it quickly became clear how starkly Stimson's ideas contrasted with popular opinion. At the very center of the national myth, on "the morning after the Pilgrim Fathers landed on Cape Cod," he argued, the "policy of faithlessness and plunder which has been followed to this day" began. Although Indians could be Christianized and would thus, in Stimson's understanding, be eligible for full citizenship, white avarice and racism had instead dominated almost every contact with Native Americans over the previous 250 years. Stimson warned his parishioners that their racial assumptions were spiritually demeaning, and although he could not envision any corrective but increased efforts to Christianize the Indian in preparation for citizenship, Stimson nonetheless framed the issue in terms rarely heard in public discourse at the time. Speaking self-consciously as a committed Christian and as a patriot, Stimson insisted that "[i]t is a mockery to boast of our [missionary] work across the sea while this lies undone at our door. I verily believe that our national life is at stake in the Indian as in the negro. God has given us this great charge, and he will hold us to a strict account."[36]

Four years later, Moen invited Stimson to Worcester to "look the ground over in person." He stayed at Moen's home, "a handsome place in the suburbs," Stimson wrote his wife, and was touched by Moen's interest and kindness. He was also impressed by the congregation, "a pleasant good people many rich—but 'self-made' pretty generally . . . with opinions of their own." Like Charles S. Wurts, Philip L. Moen, and Amos Webber, Stimson appreciated the accumulation of wealth within a framework that stressed individual effort and a corresponding moral responsibility. Worcester's wealthy men had "not only made their own fortunes but have created the business by which it has been done, building it up by successful inventions, or by prolonged & patient labor, from nothing." Stimson's vision allowed little room for the well-placed marriage or inherited position (a perspective he shared with Webber) and reflected his culture's homage to the self-made man.[37]

Stimson accepted the call from Union Church and at his October 1880 installation professed a belief in the innate sinfulness of all men, in the consequent need of all for salvation, and in Jesus Christ as "a personal savior."[38] These beliefs focused sharply on the individual penitent; but as Stimson's 1876 sermon indicated, he embraced Union Theological's emphasis on the idea of "the church as a company of faithful people, vitally united to Christ, living for Him, and doing His work in the world."[39] A pleased Amos Webber witnessed the ritual.[40]

Quite quickly Moen's expectations of the new minister were fulfilled. His preaching proved efficacious, and his social activism welcome. The Sunday school expanded and the women of the congregation organized to visit more than 320 families in the central city. This involvement with "city problems" soon led to more structured forms of support. Bedeviled by the poverty and unemployment of so many, Union Church opened a day nursery and kindergarten "for the care of infants and little children whose mothers would be competent to support their families if their hands might be left free during the day time." The nursery enrolled thirty children, including native-born blacks and whites as well as immigrants. The churchwomen selected the children based on home visitations, and those families received regular monthly visits as well.[41]

Amos Webber's silence about the activities of the city's predominantly black churches was stunning. Never once in the years on either side of 1880 did Webber note the presence of the Bethel or Zion A.M.E. churches, their pastors, or their congregations, despite the many friends and associates he had in each church. The laying of the cornerstone for Bethel in 1878, the dedication of the new church two years later, the three-day revival conducted by Bethel's pastor, Reverend Elijah P. Greeniage, in the summer of 1880 (before integrated but largely white crowds of between 800 and 1,000)—none of these events received Webber's attention. Even the conviction shared by Greeniage and Webber, that religious practice in 1880 paled before the experience of their youth, drew no response.[42]

Nor did he chronicle events at work beyond brief and occasional notations on the travels of the firm's officers. When a black worker on the night shift at the Grove Street plant was knocked "senseless" in a fight with an Irish co-worker in the summer of 1880, Webber neither recorded the incident nor acknowledged the newspaper report that the injured man remained "in a semi-unconscious state and . . . delirious" for days. His silence continued in November when a court found the black worker, Henry Johnson, guilty of vagrancy and released him "on the condition he leave town at once."[43] Similarly, Webber also ignored disturbing collective action by the firm's workers. A forty-five-day strike of 250 workers at one of Washburn and Moen's satellite plants in Worcester, begun in December 1880 to resist a wage reduction, won no notice from the commentator who had sharply analyzed the 1871 strike at the firm.[44]

Perhaps most striking is the way in which Webber ignored most personal events in his book. On January 1, 1880, he mentioned his wife for the first time in almost a decade: "Mrs. Webber & Mrs. Hazard goes to [Ayes?] in the Sleigh"[45] But that is all he said. That October, an equally cryptic entry appeared: "Webber gone to Richmond Va."[46] Whether he traveled on business for the Moens, or to deliver clothing and supplies to that city's poor black families, or for another reason altogether, Webber never stated. Indeed, although he kept his temperature pages daily throughout 1880, Webber's "Local Pages" entries that year totaled only four pages. As no evidence exists that he was sick, this pervasive silence for one so articulate is puzzling.

AMOS WEBBER UNDOUBTEDLY spent a considerable portion of his nonworking time in black Worcester's fraternal lodges. By 1880 he was already a member of the Odd Fellows' Patriarchical Lodge and Masonry's Mt. Zion Commandery, the two regional leadership groups in the respective fraternal worlds.[47] During the postwar decades, 126 individual men are identifiable as members in one of Worcester's black fraternal lodges.[48] Since the entire adult black male population in the city never totaled much more than 300 individuals before 1900, this reveals that black fraternalism in Worcester was not the preserve of a restricted elite.[49]

Of the 126 lodge members in Worcester, 54, or 43 percent, can be identified in the 1880 federal census. Half of them were born in southern slave states. Some, like Isaac Mason, had migrated to Worcester before the Civil War; others, such as William Dominis, a machinist, and William Ringolds, a day laborer, may not have come until after freedom. Two thirds of them were in their twenties and thirties, and less than 10 percent were sixty or older. Webber, at fifty-four in 1880, was of an older generation within the lodges.

Forty-six of the 54 in the sample were married and living with their wives, children, and occasionally, additional relatives; three of the single men lived with parents or relatives, while another three boarded with black families. Two lived alone. With the exception of Charles P. Dyer, a twenty-nine-year-old coachman married to a Massachusetts-born white woman, these men married within their race and, if the perceptions of the census enumerator can trusted in this regard, most wed women of similar skin color as well. Overall, 70 percent of these men were described as black, while the remainder were designated mulatto.[50]

Occupationally, half of the identifiable lodge members performed either personal service or unskilled work. Another third were skilled workers, with barbers the largest component in this category, while 13 percent were semiskilled. There was one clerical worker, the letter carrier Roswell Hazard, and two professionals, both clergymen, who may have also held other jobs. In a society that frequently favored mulattoes over darker-skinned Negroes, the opposite may have been the case in Worcester. All three of those in white-collar positions, eight of the eleven barbers, and five of the eight in service were reported as black. If anything, a disproportionate percentage of those perceived as mulatto were concentrated among the least skilled positions. Forty percent of both the semi- and unskilled workers were mulatto, while only 19 percent of the skilled workers were so designated. Recent migration to the city did not channel these lodge brothers disproportionately into unskilled positions. Those fraternalists born in the slave South accounted for just more than half of the skilled and unskilled workforces in the sample, and more than 70 percent of semiskilled group. In the one exception to this pattern, eight of the ten personal and domestic workers, the majority of whom were coachmen living on the property of the white families they worked for, were northern-born.[51]

In some nineteenth-century black communities, Masons were often considered the most elite fraternal group, due to their earlier

origins and their studied avoidance of the mutual benefit and insurance provisions so important to the Odd Fellows.[52] In Worcester, perhaps because the small male population simply did not
allow for such stratification, both fraternal orders possessed quite
similar characteristics. In each, nearly half of the members identified were born in the South; in each, blacks outnumbered mulattoes by better than two to one; and in each, nearly two thirds of the
members were not yet forty years old. Both Masons and Odd Fellows lived in stable nuclear or extended families. Occupationally,
half of the members in each organization performed unskilled or
service work (the small difference—12 percent—in skilled workers between these groups represented but two men). Most significant was the fact that in each order the majority of skilled workers
were barbers, a group whose economic condition varied greatly
over a career but whose social role, placed as they were at the hub
of black neighborhood life, remained of great importance.

The overall 1880 census returns for black Worcester differ in
certain characteristics from the portrait of the fifty-four fraternalists. Where half of the lodge members were born in the South, 80
percent of the entire black population was born in the North, half
of them in Massachusetts. The occupational pattern differed as
well. Of all the black residents who reported their occupations in
1880, only 20 percent were skilled workers (almost evenly divided
between mulattoes and blacks), with two thirds northern-born.
Unskilled workers accounted for 27 percent, the great majority
northern-born blacks, while service workers such as waiters and
carriage drivers, 39 percent of the workforce, were two thirds
northern-born and over 85 percent black. White families in the
city apparently favored northern-born blacks in such positions.
With almost 70 percent of Worcester's employed Negroes either
unskilled or in service occupations, the entire population was
probably somewhat poorer than the lodge sample.[53]

In other ways, however, these two groups reflected similar qualities. The census recorded two thirds of Worcester's residents of
African heritage as black, a figure close to that in the fraternal
world. More than 83 percent of Worcester's black families were
dual-parent households, and in only 7 percent of the families did
a single parent reside. The majority of marriages were between
spouses with similar skin color and from the same region of the

country.[54] Stable, traditionally structured families marked the experience of the fraternalists and the general black population alike, and, if marriage patterns are an accurate guide, each was rather self-conscious of differences in complexion, cultural background, and antebellum status.

This brief portrait of one central component of Amos Webber's world suggests that, while in their private lives lodge members remained conscious of differences in pigmentation and geographical and cultural background, in their public civic life they freely mingled across these divides. To this extent these fraternal organizations were democratic institutions. If a man was of good moral character, industrious and responsible, he was more than welcome into the lodge.

The governing structure of the Masons and Odd Fellows underscored this democratic ethos.[55] In both orders, the diffusion of leadership responsibilities involved a broad swath of men who administered the lodge and represented it in public. Between 1868 and 1879, for example, forty-three black men can be identified as Worcester Odd Fellows. Of these, over half held an office of some sort in the North Star or the Integrity Lodge, including at least seven who had been masters of one of those lodges. Another five who were not reported as officers also served on committees. During the 1880s, forty-four members participated in a similar pattern: sixteen serving as officers and another twelve active on committees. In each decade more than 60 percent of the identifiable members shared the administration of the lodge, and in this fashion the Odd Fellows in Worcester encouraged the development of a diverse leadership cohort with sustained organizational experience among many of the city's adult black males.

At the center of this group lay a core of leaders who, for a variety of reasons, played more dominant roles. Seventeen men were active in the Order throughout both the 1870s and 1880s. Three of these activists (Amos Webber, George Scott, and William Gardner) were Civil War veterans, and two others (Isaac Mason and William Jankins) had been important local military recruiters for the black regiments. At least four of them (Mason, Jankins, J. J. Mobray, and William Anderson) had been born in slavery. In these men both the Odd Fellows and the city's larger black population possessed seasoned, proven leaders. Residential longevity, a modicum of economic security, and a belief in the Order's values and purpose encouraged the development of this core leadership group.

Worcester's King David Lodge of the Prince Hall Masons reflected similar patterns. During the 1870s, when Masonry was not a large movement among the city's black men, only eighteen can be linked to the lodge. Not surprisingly, all served as lodge officers at least once. But during the 1880s, the lodge blossomed. Of the fifty-three identifiable members, twenty-eight were officers at some point, and six had been or were state or regional Masonic representatives. In the twenty years after its founding, fourteen different men are known to have filled the lodge master's chair, indicating another diffusion of leadership. Thirteen of seventeen known members of the Mt. Zion Commandery, Masonry's elite unit, including five of the eight veterans in King David Lodge (Webber, Charles Mero, John H. Waller, Amos F. Jackson, and R. D. Robinson), also served as officers.

As with the Odd Fellows, a definable leadership group emerged among these Masons. Of the eighteen members during the 1870s, fourteen remained active during the next decade; six were involved into the 1890s; and four men (Amos Webber, William Bostic, Percy Lethridge, and Primus Storms) maintained their commitment across four decades. Two older lodge members retained important offices throughout the 1880s: John H. Waller, a laborer, was treasurer and, with the exception of his term as master, Amos Webber served as secretary.[56] These two men provided the continuity that enabled others to grow into their own leadership roles.

Webber was not the only lodge brother central to the leadership of both fraternal organizations: in fact nine men (including Isaac Mason, William Jankins, and Roswell Hazard) were active in both the Odd Fellows and the Masons in the 1870s and 1880s. The activities of these men, whose ages ran from the midtwenties to the midfifties, allowed for a shared learning between the two organizations, reinforcing their collective responsibility to and for the black community of the city.

Amos Webber's leadership within this fraternal world reveals clearly the level of significance and influence he commanded within black Worcester. In his travels on behalf of both orders throughout the Northeast, Webber became part of a regional leadership network, exchanging information, discussing options, and sharing experiences on fraternal and other matters.

———————   ————

ON DECEMBER 1, 1881, Webber's journal entry was an understated "Amos Webber gone South"[57] This was not a short southernly jaunt, however; his destination was Florida.

We have no record of his trip, but Webber safely reached his destination, probably by train and then boat, and resided in the town of Palatka, Florida, for the next five months, possibly in the service of Philip L. Moen and his family. In the northeast quadrant of the state, fifty-six miles up the St. Johns River from Jacksonville and on a latitude similar to St. Augustine's, Palatka, the seat of Putnam County, was founded in the 1820s as a military outpost against the Seminole Indians. Palatka witnessed military action during the Civil War when Federal troops, including five companies of the 55th Massachusetts Infantry, fought an intermittent five-month battle for control of the town and the river.[58] After the war the town emerged as one of the premier resorts in Florida. "Palatka is full of northerners," one settler wrote in 1868, "invalids and tourists— sail boats and pleasure parties pass daily and they often call and visit us. There is plenty of life and stir on the river." The climate, the low land prices, and the St. Johns itself, which the Indians called "the String of Pearls" for its numerous lakes branching off from the river, attracted both northern entrepreneurs and wealthy vacationers. Orange groves perfumed the banks of the St. Johns; and northerners as famous as William Cullen Bryant, Grover Cleveland, Reverend DeWitt Talmadge, and Harriet Beecher Stowe wintered along the river. Palatka's resort hotels were renowned for their accommodations and their cuisine, and they vied with one another in pursuit of celebrities. The Putnam House bested its competitors in 1879 when, to open the winter season, it threw a grand ball for its honored guest, Ulysses S. Grant.[59]

Webber was not the only new resident that winter. The permanent population of Putnam County had grown in the preceding decade by more than 60 percent,[60] and one contemporary esti-

mated that the winter population grew fourfold, as wealthy northerners discovered the Florida climate. Such a seasonal population
influx required a large servant pool, the only way most whites
thought it appropriate for a black man to winter in Florida. As one
white sojourner at the Putnam House in 1879 reflected: "The po-
liteness of the servants, reminds us of the palmy days of the past,
when they were trained for use, and not permitted to roam, as
many do now, like untamed beasts, seeking something which they
can kill and eat, or steal and trade for money."[61]

If Amos Webber traveled to Palatka "for the benefit of his
health," as the Worcester *Evening Gazette* suggested in a brief notice of the farewell party his friends gave him, and not in the company of his employer, the community he selected was not chosen
idly. In 1880, 2,416 Negroes, more than three times the population
of black Worcester, lived in Putnam County, the majority in and
around Palatka. Like other black men and women throughout the
South, they had struggled with the meaning of freedom since
emancipation. White attempts to institute peonage, county chain
gangs, and formal segregation of social institutions brought a
sharp response from black Palatkans. By 1867 a black Union
League had formed to channel black political efforts into the Republican Party, and the county elected one black delegate to
Florida's constitutional convention in 1868. The forces arrayed
against them, however, were enormous. In fact, the promise of the
party of Lincoln was so tarnished that in February 1882, while
Webber was in residence, local black political activists met in
neighboring Gainesville to support an independent Democratic
candidate. Despite such efforts, black Palatkans could not stem the
torrent of Jim Crow laws or the systematic discrimination in private and municipal employment. Caught between overt Democratic racism and a corrupt, cynical Republican commitment to
black rights, they looked to survive until another era dawned.[62]

Central to that effort was black Palatka's intricate social structure. At the time of Webber's stay, Palatka had two black churches,
Mt. Tabor Baptist and Bethel A.M.E. As the community grew,
Jacksonville pastors, including Reverend James Randolph, regularly came to preach. Lodges of the Prince Hall Masons (possibly
affiliated, through the Jacksonville lodge, with the Massachusetts
grand lodge) and the Grand United Order of Odd Fellows were

active, and both fraternal orders maintained their female auxiliaries as well.[63] Webber thus entered a black world in Palatka more populous than he was accustomed to but similar in its intensity to his life in Worcester. Although he never referred to his daily regime in Florida, a banquet tendered him a few days before he returned to Worcester hinted at the fraternal bonds that structured his time there.

"Mr. A. N. Doyle, City Marshall," the report in the Putnam County *Journal* began, "gave a dinner Wednesday to quite a number of colored masons in honor of Mr. Amos Webber." With a clergyman as toastmaster, and with most of black fraternal Palatka in attendance, Webber listened as brother after brother stood to toast him and affirm their friendship. Webber responded "very affectionately, thanking the brothers for their kindness since he had been with them." As Webber continued, he grew more expansive, acknowledging "the kindness of his [local] Odd Fellow brethren, the Purcess boys [three black brothers active in political and fraternal affairs, and] members of Pride of Fairfield Lodge, No. 2115, G.U.O.O.F. of Winnsborough [*sic*], S.C." Following the dinner, "the company adjourned to escort Bro. Webber to the boat."[64]

This brief notice revealed additional glimpses of black social life within two decades of the Civil War. Fraternal membership provided a brother entrée into a new community, accompanied by a set of friends and acquaintances that were his to lose only through misconduct. A network similar to the regional one operated at this distance as well. Moreover, the reference to the Winnsboro lodge suggested how black fraternalists traveled, especially in the South, during these years. While the traveler could take a boat from New York, changing at Charleston for the steamer to Palatka, the trip taking about sixty hours, this itinerary was relatively expensive. It was cheaper to ride the train between New York and Charleston over some four days (if schedules were met), and then board the steamer to travel up the St. Johns River. It is probable that Webber thanked the South Carolina lodge for hosting him on his travels by train, and for providing safe and friendly accommodations.[65]

The banquet at Palatka, and one the following week celebrating his return to Worcester,[66] revealed the force of that fraternal bond in the lives of individuals. A source of moral, religious, and political activism, the fraternal lodge created thick local, regional, and even national networks in which brothers found in one another broadly similar values and concerns. Not all black fraternalists in Worcester traveled to the extent Amos Webber did, but all could participate in that network in the city. In the lodge they created an institution that structured their personal lives and nurtured their collective needs as well.

Webber may have considered describing this excursion to Florida. On his return to Worcester on May 3, 1882, he wrote: "Amos Webber arrived home from Palatka, Florida, P.   "[67] But he never filled in the page reference because he never entered a reminiscence of his trip. Nor did he ever mention his wife, Lizzie Webber. We do not know if she joined him in Florida, and Webber never discussed her reaction to his trip or his return. This silence, which permeated his chronicle, established one important boundary to understanding Webber's conscious identity. It was not that Amos thought Lizzie unimportant or that, after thirty years of marriage, he did not care for her. Rather, his formal distancing from her suggested the overwhelming maleness of the world he inhabited. In constructing a record of this world that largely ignored Lizzie, Amos bore witness to the powerful influence of an American culture he simultaneously struggled with and embraced.

CHAPTER ELEVEN

COMMON GROUND

AMOS WEBBER RETURNED to work in May 1882 as easily as if it were any Monday morning following his weekly day of rest, a fact that by itself attested to Webber's rather special relationship with his employer. His time in Florida had clearly enhanced his standing among his black neighbors. He was now one of the few northern-born free blacks in the city with experience in the deep South as a civilian and the insights garnered during his stay undoubtedly became the source of stories and commentary in the barbershops, lodge rooms, and social gatherings in black Worcester.

As was so often the case with Amos Webber, however, he acknowledged none of this in his chronicle. To judge solely from his writings, nothing had interrupted the flow of his life. During the first six weeks back at work he entered the data for the temperature pages for the five months he was gone from Worcester (either a co-worker kept the information for him or Webber used sources at the library to bring his records up-to-date). This laborious task indicated Webber's continued concern with order in the world and revealed just how seriously he took his scientific and meteorological responsibilities. His records for Worcester now stretched back in an unbroken line almost twelve years.

Even if he did not detail his own experience, shortly after his return Webber the chronicler hit his stride. His interest in accidents, natural disasters, and the obituaries of prominent local and national figures resurfaced, as did his appreciation of the role black men played in public life.[1] It was not politics themselves that engrossed Webber in the winter of 1882–1883, and although he noted the reelection of George F. Hoar to the United States Senate by the Massachusetts legislature in January 1883,[2] he ignored the 1882 state election, which saw Benjamin F. Butler finally elected governor, and Worcester's municipal elections. Instead, Webber focused on meteorology and history, drawing from them moral lessons for contemporary life. A story in the Hartford *Times* recalling the long, cold winter of 1779–1780, when wild turkeys froze in the forest and "domestic fowls fell frozen from their roosts," prompted Webber to explain that, given the absence of thermometers at that time, the accuracy of such popular, collective memory could not be trusted. "Human misery," he wrote, "is only fully appreciated when it can [be] measured." Yet, instead of dismissing this memory, it became the grist of a familiar morality tale. "The rich are prepared for all contigencies," he considered, "they can Seek warmer climates or Shelter themselves within thick walls, warmed by heated-air and Steam, It is not So with the poor; Let the rich Keep in rememberance of them;".[3]

Webber himself, of course, had sought those "warmer climates" the winter before. Whether his thoughts about justice reflected aspects of that Florida sojourn, he never mentioned. Instead, he followed with a twenty-three-page entry taken from the *Register of Pennsylvania,* which listed selected dramatic weather conditions in that state between 1681 and 1830.[4] Webber next recorded a four-page version of Philadelphia merchant Stephen Girard's 1831 will. He compared Girard's wealth to his own contemporaries such as railroad presidents and financiers William Vanderbilt, Jay Gould, and Mark Hopkins, but he was most impressed by the $2 million earmarked for the creation of a college "for the poor White male Orphans. . . . I suppose it was a disgrace in those days to let colored Children in a School house," Webber continued with a quiet dignity, "I wonder what the Old Gentleman would say now, if he were here, to view the progress of colored men, also to see the colored and white children playing together at School;—Webber."[5]

STILL RELUCTANT TO WRITE about himself, Webber was always enthusiastic to chronicle and interpret historical events that, however far in the past, seemed to have some relevance to his own life.

A 1722 petition to the Pennsylvania Assembly from white "day Labourers"—who described themselves as "poor and honest" men "who had emigrated from Europe for the purpose of obtaining a Livelihood"—to ban black laborers was the subject of one such entry. Webber gloried in the thought that these workers were "not Sharp enough for the Old Fathers"—the ban was denied—but never considered that a desire for an ample supply of cheap labor may have motivated those landholding legislators. An 1832 petition for a divorce also received Webber's close scrutiny. The petition of James Sisco, a black resident of Pennsylvania, precipitated a legislative debate as to whether black residents were also citizens of the state. If not, one representative asked, could the legislature grant a divorce to "a man who is not a citizen"? After considerable debate the legislature voted by a two-to-one margin to deny the petition for divorce without ruling directly on the issue of citizenship. The vote prefigured the formal denial of citizenship rights to black residents that occurred six years later. Webber, only six years old in 1832, sought fifty years later to rescue some positive meaning from this history, noting that two legislative leaders had "tried to get the bill to pass on principle." This act, Webber imagined, laid the groundwork for "a Sumner, Wilson, and other good men of our day;".[6]

Unfortunately for Amos Webber and for black America, history's lessons were not always that pliable, and the "progress of colored men" was anything but smooth. Benjamin Butler, the symbol of a white workingmen's electoral victory, sat in the statehouse in Boston. Throughout the nation, but especially in the South, the lynching of black men and women grew in depressing numbers, and other acts of violence largely went uncounted as white Americans sought to perfect their system of segregation. In this same period the U.S. Supreme Court ruled unconstitutional the 1875 Civil Rights Act that Worcester's activists had thought tepid.[7] Yet Webber's effort to project racial progress was not completely unfounded. Black and white children could attend school together a half century after Stephen Girard's death; the original Republican abolitionists had drawn on the example of earlier dissenters; and it was not unrealistic to imply that another reform cycle might reoccur. Twenty-five years earlier, reform efforts had helped abolish slavery.

Webber's entries on politics remained minimal in 1882 and early 1883. He wrote more about such events as the opening of the Brooklyn Bridge—with great attention to the scientists and engineers who overcame severe technical problems to create the world's most beautiful suspension bridge[8]—and about the death of Tom Thumb, long a fixture in P. T. Barnum's circus, whom Webber possibly saw perform in Worcester.[9] But whether he wrote about it or not, in the end politics was never far from his mind. When, in 1883, Lewis Hayden raised "a few hundred dollars" from Republicans to activate "in Boston, Springfield, Lynn, New Bedford, Worcester and other places throughout the state [the] many colored voters who are influential with all classes,"[10] Webber was ready.

The 1883 gubernatorial race pitted Republican George D. Robinson against Benjamin Butler. As the parties swung into action behind their standard-bearers, Worcester's black Republicans formed the Robinson Colored Republican Club and elected Amos Webber as their captain. On the night of October 19, Webber led the club on a torchlight march to attend a "Colored Republican" rally at Washburn Hall. Numbering perhaps forty men, the club wound its way through the streets while an ever-growing mob of white men, deemed "young hoodlums" by the local Republican paper, crowded from the rear, hurling racial epithets, slogans in favor of Butler, and rocks. At least one black marcher "was knocked down and made insensible for a short time." The presence of a white Republican militia unit forestalled further violence.

At Washburn Hall, Isaac Mason reminded all present that "it was their intention in coming together on this occasion to exercise their rights as citizens." J. J. Mobray followed, explaining how he had supported Butler until the Democrat had reneged in his support of black political and civil rights. Mobray, born a slave in Virginia in 1835, had unambiguous instructions for his adopted community: "The colored people can not afford to follow Gen. Butler and help him re-inaugurate the Democratic party in power."[11]

Webber publicly thanked the Republican militia unit the following day "for their escort duty last evening at the flag raising," and one week later he led his contingent of "Colored Republicans" in a parade of over five hundred, mostly white, uniformed Republi-

can militia. The usual advance guard of uniformed police was dispensed with this time, and reflecting either the general political
excitement or specific racial tension, more than twenty plain-
clothes policemen instead filtered through the crowd and the line
of march. This time no violence occurred.[12]

Despite the black Republican presence, a strain of Democratic
enthusiasm persisted among the city's black voters. J. J. Mobray
may have returned to the Republican fold, but other blacks were
active supporters of Butler in 1883. Two of them, Thomas H.
Henderson and Thomas Waples, had already suffered the consequences for having "voted the Straight Democratic Ticket." As
Henderson, born a slave in Virginia in 1850, explained in a letter
to Governor Butler, he and Waples, both "Poor Colored Carpenter[s]," were fired for their vote by their white Republican employer, George S. Clough. Waples brought suit in municipal court
but, the Democratic Worcester *Daily Times* asserted, the Republican district attorney did not forcefully prosecute and Clough's
foreman and friends pressured both the jurymen and the two fired
employees. The grand jury's refusal to return an indictment
prompted Henderson's letter and his pained appeal to the governor: "[I] want you as the Friend of the Poor Man do Something
With them. We have told nothing But the exact *Truth* about the
Matter and Can *Prove All* We *Say* in any Court Where there is
Justice for a *Poor Man*." Webber, himself a partisan of no little intensity, never commented on this dispute.[13]

Robinson won the election but carried Worcester by a plurality
of only 839 votes (of more than 11,000 cast), as Butler outpolled
Robinson in the city's immigrant wards by at least a two-to-one
margin. Webber concluded that Democratic overconfidence had
played an important role in the race. Large sums of money were
foolishly bet on Butler and the Democrats called "the Republicans
fools for paradeing the Streets in torch=light procession." But
Webber knew better, understanding his political activity, with the
physical risks he and other black Republicans endured, had made
a difference: "That is what drew out the republican vote, they did
not lay in the cradle of carnal Security, as if their man could be
Elected without trouble;". Butler's defeat, if not necessarily
Robinson's victory, allowed Webber and other black activists to
again claim a central role in public political life. They had made a

difference, their efforts counted. This proud feeling remained an important source of strength to black activists faced with mob violence in Worcester and increasing segregation nationwide.[14]

But two weeks after the election the contradictions inherent in Webber's unquestioning commitment to the Republican Party surfaced again. George L. Ruffin, a black graduate of Harvard Law School, received his appointment to the Charlestown Municipal Court, and Webber crowed in his chronicle that Massachusetts "[s]tands at the head of the column in according to colored men their rights and in recognizing a man upon his merits, without regard to his color." He marveled that following the swearing in "the business [of the court] went on as if nothing had happened," and concluded with obvious joy: "The Sun Still Shines in Massachusetts;".[15] What Webber never acknowledged was that Ruffin's appointment came with the assistance of the lame-duck Democratic governor, Benjamin Butler, and not as a result of the Republican victory.

The reality was that the few crumbs allotted to Massachusetts blacks by the state government would by and large fall regardless of which party held office. Massachusetts was not Mississippi, and the systematic violence that deprived blacks of the most rudimentary civil and political rights did not dominate the Commonwealth's political life. But it was also true that in Massachusetts, rewards to black activists were still greatly limited in number and lacking in obvious influence and power.

WEBBER ANTICIPATED THE 1884 presidential contest between Maine Republican James G. Blaine and Democrat Grover Cleveland with enthusiasm. As early as June 28, just three weeks after the Republicans nominated Blaine, Worcester's black Republicans organized a "colored battalion"—its segregated nature a concession to local white Republican racism. Isaac Mason, William H. Jankins, A. A. Clough, J. J. Mobray, and Amos Webber were but some of Worcester's black activists who became officers of the club. By mid-July, the group had more than fifty members and voted to adopt "the Continental Uniform, costing 75 cents per outfit," as their official dress. They elected Amos Webber captain of the battalion whereas Roswell Hazard, the thirty-four-year-old letter carrier who boarded with the Webbers, led the Colored Blaine and Logan Guards. Proudly wearing their uniforms, evocative of the American Revolutionary soldier and which the *Evening Gazette* thought "quite neat," these black Republicans soon numbered seventy men. They attended the party's opening campaign rally in late July in Mechanics Hall on Main Street, met almost nightly during August and September "for discussion and drill," and, as the election drew near, participated in a host of public parades in Worcester and in neighboring communities.[16]

On Saturday night, November 1, 1884, three days before the balloting, a massive Republican parade crowded the streets of downtown Worcester. Contingent after contingent strode past the reviewing stand, many uniformed as militia after the fashion of the day. These stalwart Republicans loudly and repeatedly proclaimed their support for Blaine and his running mate, John A. Logan. In the line of march, organized separately, were Worcester's black Republicans. The Johnson Drum Corps, under the command of Alexander H. Johnson, led the group; the Colored Blaine and Logan Guards followed with thirty-seven men, led by Roswell Hazard. The Colored Blaine and Logan Club marched next, totaling thirteen men under the command of Amos Webber, who had been designated the senior officer for the entire black phalanx. Two days later, on the eve of the election, many of these same marchers returned to the streets to greet the candidate himself as Blaine made a fervent final campaign swing through this New England city.[17]

Blaine lost the national election, however, and for the first time since 1856 the country elected a Democratic president. In Worcester, where 88 percent of the eligible men cast ballots, Blaine carried the four-way race with a comfortable 58 percent of the vote.[18] Webber blamed the Republican defeat on the party's internal disputes over reform and prohibition but if the politics of that election were important, the lack of significant differences between the candidates on racial matters softened the loss. Even in defeat, moreover, black Worcester again exhibited its own self-conscious, internal organization.[19]

Alexander H. Johnson (with drum), accompanied by an unidentified black banjo player and possibly a white piccolo player, in Worcester, ca. 1890s. Johnson regularly played for white organizations, as the racial composition of the crowd around him indicates. *Courtesy of Worcester Historical Museum*

IN 1885, BLACK WORCESTER totaled 836 individuals, having grown a modest 9 percent in the preceding five years. Although another 500 blacks lived in the surrounding county, black residents remained a distinct minority in a city with more than 68,000 residents. In that same five-year period, for example, the number of foreign-born residents increased almost 30 percent and accounted for just under a third of all inhabitants. Black Worcester, with slightly more than 1 percent of the population, was minuscule in comparison.[20]

Despite the small numbers, however, new black organizations formed in the 1880s and included a new generation of activists. The older fraternal lodges and the women's auxiliaries provided a model in their balance between new members and rotated leadership responsibilities. The new organizations—such as the Sixteen Associates Club, the B.P.T. Club, a social and charitable group consisting primarily of younger church members, and the Unknown Club—reflected a similar pattern by the mid-1880s. In addition to parties and dances, these clubs sponsored public debates on a variety of topical issues. The 1880s version of the Sixteen Associates was a reorganization of a long dormant club first founded in 1868. New Worcester residents such as G. Alfred Busby joined with original member Henry A. Bowman and the children of other original members to reconstitute the group. Some of the other clubs contained a larger number of younger residents, and all were committed to temperance and upright moral conduct.[21]

At this same time the Worcester Progressive Association formed. A joint stock company with a majority of members in their twenties and thirties, the association sold five-dollar shares, assessed an additional dollar per month in dues, and deposited the funds in a bank to invest after a year in "some branch of business." Although the association lasted for at least three years, and even reported "an upward tendency" in its stock in 1885, no collective investment was ever reported. Despite its intentions, it is probable that the association ultimately served more as mutual benefit association than a vehicle for collective economic uplift.[22]

Well before Booker T. Washington gained national attention in the 1890s, individual self-help was an important theme in black Worcester. Mrs. Mary Laws, who came to Worcester from Philadelphia in 1864, served as an example of such efforts in the eyes of at least one local black reporter. When Laws, a widow, took ownership of an apartment building in 1884, Peter Hood, the Worcester Odd Fellow and correspondent for a New York black newspaper, praised her achievement as it was "accomplished . . . single handed and by ordinary day's work. Her example may be profitably imitated."[23] Webber himself urged black residents to become home owners to avoid "paying exorbitant rents." In the absence of a viable local black alternative, he suggested two white-run cooperative building associations as sources for loans.[24] Other individual efforts to establish black businesses in the city were enthusiastically welcomed, even though the success rate remained quite low.[25]

Individual solutions were not enough, however, for a group without significant economic resources. At times those with positions could influence employers to aid others in obtaining work. George H. Scott, the Vermont-born veteran of the 54th Massachusetts Infantry and active Odd Fellow, had this reputation at the G. Henry Whitcomb Envelope Company, where he had worked since 1875.[26] Webber had a similar reputation at Washburn and Moen. By themselves, these men could not steer all who needed work into jobs; but, at Washburn and Moen, where Moen's liberal hiring policies allowed Webber some influence, the results were impressive. Although a pronounced minority among the 3,000 workers at mid-decade, perhaps as many as 10 black men (about 8 percent of the city's adult black males) held positions as janitors, messengers, and semiskilled wire-drawers at Washburn and Moen. Even more unusual, that firm was one of the rare manufacturers anywhere in the country that employed a black man, William Baker, as foreman of a large department with both blacks and whites under his control.[27]

WITH THE FORMATION of the Mt. Olive Baptist Church in 1885, Worcester's nineteenth-century black religious organizations were complete. In contrast to both the Bethel A.M.E. and the A.M.E. Zion congregations, Mt. Olive affiliated with the regional white Baptist association and at first held services at the white Pleasant Street Baptist Church. A white minister, Reverend Charles E. Simmons, who had led a mission among the city's black Baptists (including the remnants of the prayer group George Lee had organized eleven years before) and was widely esteemed in black Worcester,[28] initially served as minister. Within months of the church's founding, however, Simmons was replaced by Reverend Hiram Conway. Conway, born a slave in Virginia in 1850, had made his way to Worcester sometime after the war. The Pleasant Street Baptist Church underwrote the cost of his theological training at the Baptist seminary in Richmond, Virginia, during the 1870s, with the understanding that he would eventually return to Worcester. When Conway assumed the pulpit he faced a congregation of perhaps twenty-five adults, the majority of whom were, like him, of southern birth. In less than a decade membership grew to more than one hundred.[29]

Taken together, the three black churches formed the largest voluntary self-help organization among black residents. As a result, pastors occupied positions of great influence within the community, though they also proved highly transitory: in the last three decades of the century, Bethel installed a minimum of thirteen ministers and A.M.E. Zion at least eight. Not surprisingly, then, an active lay leadership emerged. To be the superintendent of the Sunday school, church sexton, janitor, musical director, or organist was to occupy a position of trust within the community. While the musical positions required a specific skill that usually ensured a long tenure, the other positions, based more on character and a willingness to shoulder responsibility, frequently rotated. During the three years in the 1880s when the name of Bethel's Sunday school superintendent is known, three different men held the position. A similar pattern developed in the other churches, including the appointment a few years later of Georginia Hawkins as Zion's superintendent, the first woman to hold that position in any of Worcester's black churches. Church leadership was dispersed in other ways as well: elders or local preachers (a term reserved for congregants who assisted the ordained minister at weekly services and revivals) provided further layers of leadership. The minister himself remained important, but always operated within a lay framework, and responsibility for the church as an institution was shared by many in the congregation.[30]

As the solitary example of Georginia Hawkins suggested, most of these visible leadership positions were held by men. But churchwomen were not dormant during these years. There was not a dinner-dance given, a festival held, an entertainment offered, or a debate scheduled that was not organized and staffed by a committee of female congregants. These tasks rotated among a large group, thus ensuring a broad female involvement in church affairs. While Bethel's Ladies' Aid Society and the Baptist Ladies Sewing Circle were led by older and more established women, a younger generation of women became active in the Bethel Literary Society, the Mt. Olive Young People's Society, and the more secular B.P.T. Club.[31]

These church clubs provided women with an important social network within which they could explore their talents, ambitions, and leadership skills. Their activities also served a set of pragmatic needs as well. When the Bethel Ladies held a "ring cake and cane election" or the stewardess of Zion gave a "leap year oyster supper" in January 1884, the money raised went to support the church. Carpets were bought, fixtures replaced, and, at both Bethel and Mt. Olive, money was often deposited in the church building fund.[32] Equally important were the fund-raisers earmarked to supplement the pastor's salary. At times these efforts took the form of socials, as when "a party of 61 persons," the majority from Bethel and Zion, feted Bethel's Reverend Greeniage "with many useful and valuable articles." The profits from festivals, concerts, and suppers improved the pastor's finances, dispersed the cost of his maintenance across the larger population, and affirmed again the close mutual ties between any given pastor and a portion of black Worcester broader than his own congregation. In this sense the word "community" had a very specific, concrete meaning for black Worcester's activists and their families.[33]

The work of churchwomen alleviated the suffering of many in these generally poor congregations. The sum of $83.40, the proceeds of a four-day fair organized by Zion women in 1885, may not have seemed all that much, given the tremendous effort required to run the event. But Laura Allen, a mother of two who had just lost her husband, appreciated how that money enabled Mrs. Joseph Peaker, Lizzie Clough, and Zion's pastor, Reverend Frank K. Bird, to visit her home "ladened with good and substantial presents." The aid societies in all three churches, in conjunction with the Odd Fellows' mutual benefit provisions, saved many from the most dire consequences of poverty. Nor was it lost on these men and women that the material assistance offered by both church and lodge was one concrete expression of a deeper spiritual concern. The overlapping membership of church and lodge underscored this common vision.[34]

Women also taught biblical morality and literacy in the Sunday schools, attended services, and staffed the numerous committees that gave the churches their visible presence in the community. Women were particularly active in church temperance movements,[35] and at times they also assumed roles in church affairs traditionally dominated by men. In 1884 Lydia Dyer was appointed Zion's only "accredited sollicitor" for its repair fund; while in Bethel's severe financial crisis that same year Annie Maddox, although only recently arrived in Worcester, proved to be "an important accession" for the battered congregation: "She seems to see the needs," Bethel member Peter S. Hood reported in the New York *Globe,* "and endeavors to supply them as far as lies in her power."[36] For these women, their acceptance of male religious leadership did not prevent them from creating their own network within the church. In this fashion black Worcester's churches and its fraternal lodges complemented each other. The men formally controlled both arenas, but they only dominated the lodge meeting. The church committee or the prayer meeting represented a unique sphere of female activity.

Despite the sparse records available, 133 church members are identifiable during these postwar decades. Of the 86 men, 34 percent were also members of one of the black fraternal lodges, and two thirds of these were Odd Fellows. Membership figures alone, however, understated these ties. Using more realistic criteria that would include kinship networks, 41 percent of the men and 44 percent of the women were either fraternal brothers, sisters of the Household of Ruth, or living with immediate family members in one of those organizations. Almost half (42 percent) of church activists had familial connections with fraternalism, indicating that the pathways between these organizations were quite well traveled. The prevalence of these links revealed that while men and women may have occupied overtly separate spheres, just beneath that public surface they shared a thicket of personal and organizational responsibilities, rooted in the recognition of similar moral and material interests.[37]

Amid the reports of the churches, lodges, and auxiliaries in both the black and white press, only brief, tantalizing glimpses of Lizzie Webber are possible. One Sunday in February 1884, the Worcester *Evening Gazette* reported, Lizzie Webber drove a horse-drawn sleigh accompanied by Jennie T. Oswell. More than a quarter of a century older than the twenty-nine-year-old Oswell (who was the daughter of Worcester's preeminent black orchestra leader), Lizzie Webber may have befriended her companion in the manner of an older female family friend assuming an aunt's role with the younger person. The sleigh, "swinging around on the ice," caused the horse to bolt onto Worcester's New Common, and Lizzie Webber suffered a gash over her eye.[38]

Two months later Lizzie Webber joined with Martha Brown, Lucy Hazard, Rachael Bostic, and Adeline Oswell to plan and sponsor a "Ladies Leap Year Party" for the night of May 1. Under their leadership the dinner-dance was a great success, attended by almost 100 couples and lasting until three o'clock in the morning: "The gentlemen were in full evening dress and many of the ladies' costumes were very handsome," the *Evening Gazette* reported, "and the affair was the most successful of the kind in the city since 20 years ago last night, when a similar ball took place." It is unknown whether Amos Webber joined in the dancing that evening, but Lizzie Webber's role is, for once, more apparent. She and her co-workers—all older married women, most of whom were church activists from established free-born black families— provided younger, single black women such as Carrie Gimby, Estelle Pickney, and Isabelle Hazard the opportunity to participate in managing a large social event. In this way these older women passed on to the next generation the lessons of organizational leadership, much as the men did within the fraternal lodge.[39]

Beyond this, however, little is known of Lizzie Webber's life in the two decades following the Civil War. She associated with church activists, but there is no evidence that she was one herself; and her name appears only infrequently in the social jottings in the press. She was reported in the 1880 census as "at home" (that is, without an occupation), and there is no evidence that she worked for wages within the Webber household, making dresses or shirts, or taking in laundry. Perhaps, given the numerous visitors to Worcester generated by her husband's fraternal and veterans' involvements, Lizzie Webber's duties to entertain them in her home, make their beds, and cook at least some of their meals occupied much of her time. Occasional long-term boarders such as Alfred and Sarah Edwards or Roswell Hazard also required daily attention. But whether she attended church or not, the residential pattern in her neighborhood suggests her involvement with a number of religious-based women active in a variety of organizations.

Of the more than 8,500 individuals living in the city's Second Ward, the overwhelming majority were native-born whites. The approximately 150 Negroes accounted for less than 2 percent of the ward's population; even the Irish-born residents, who were concentrated elsewhere in the city, outnumbered black inhabitants by better than two to one in the Second Ward. Thus it would not be surprising to discover that Lizzie Webber entertained daily, close social relations with some of her numerous white neighbors.[40]

A closer look at the ward's residential grid reveals a second, more textured pattern to the neighborhood. Rather than being dispersed randomly among the white majority, black residents concentrated themselves on a handful of blocks. Sixty-eight of the ward's blacks lived on Liberty Street or its contiguous blocks; another 48 lived on an additional six streets, none more than a three-block walk from the Webber home on Liberty Street. More than 75 percent of the ward's black residents lived in this cluster of blocks in and around Liberty Street, in a pattern that appears conscious and purposeful.[41]

Thus Lizzie Webber did not live isolated from other blacks. When her husband walked to work in the morning or went out to an evening meeting at one of his lodges, she may have remained at home, but that home existed among the residences of numerous black families with whom she and her husband shared a host of associational connections. Next door to the Webbers was a tripledecker[42] occupied by three black families. On the first floor Albert Smith, a carpenter, lived with his wife and three children. Emancipated slaves, they arrived in Worcester from Mississippi just prior to 1880, a small ripple from the larger wave of migrants into Kansas. John Stewart, a waiter and an Odd Fellow, and his wife, Martha, both of whom were active in Bethel A.M.E. Church, occupied the second floor; whereas the veteran Amasa Peters, his wife, Alice, and their two children resided on the third floor. Two doors farther up lived Isaac and Annie Mason, community leaders and A.M.E. Zion Church members. The family of William Edwards occupied the second floor of the Mason house. Born a slave in the nation's capital, Edwards migrated to Worcester with his wife and two children in the late 1870s; he was a janitor, an Odd Fellow, and the superintendent of Bethel's Sunday school. Across the street was Gilbert Walker, now an aging widower but long a leader in the black community. On adjoining blocks were the families of the Bethel's Reverend Elijah Greeniage, former boarder Alfred Edwards, veteran Cyrus Wiggins, and veteran and Zion activist James Harris.

None of the married women who lived within this cluster listed any occupation outside their homes with the census enumerator, although some may have taken a variety of work into their homes. But it was precisely that they were home each day, doing chores, caring for children, preparing meals, that proved important. With many of them active in church and fraternal organizations, the overlapping organizational ties and the daily dependencies of urban living encouraged the creation of a supportive social network. Such a network drew Lizzie Webber into the very heart of black Worcester's female activists and organizers.

As BASEBALL WAS ACHIEVING a wide popularity in the 1880s, Sunday schools from both Bethel and Zion fielded teams, and Bethel's Frederick Gimby managed the team sponsored by the Puritan Social Club, another black social organization. Black teams proliferated to such an extent that some sponsors of these games, who had to raise enough to cover expenses, adopted another aspect of the popular culture for that purpose. "Drum Major [Alexander H.] Johnson," the *Evening Gazette* reported in June 1884, "with a trio of assistants, driven about town on a Tally-Ho coach, is the newest base ball game advertising scheme."[43]

Amos Webber never commented on baseball, but he was concerned about the proliferation of organizations in the community. The size of the community and the limited economic resources most of its members possessed suggested caution, this experienced elder thought, and he publicly opposed efforts to establish a black Knights of Pythias lodge in 1886. The existing social and fraternal organizations, he thought, were "about as much as we can sustain and pay our honest bills, and be honorable in the community."[44] The younger men ignored Webber's advice, and in time Webber even joined the lodge, which feted its onetime critic on numerous occasions in the first years of existence.[45]

The growth of these institutions did not occur in a vacuum. While whites generally ignored the intricacies of black social life, blacks were both aware of the patterns in their own community and increasingly conscious of a connection to other black communities throughout the nation. Church and lodge networks fostered this, and in the 1880s developments in the black press created new avenues that encouraged such perceptions. In Worcester, two papers were of particular importance. Throughout the 1880s, T. Thomas Fortune edited from New York City a succession of weekly newspapers, named the New York *Globe, Freeman,* and *Age.*[46] He employed agents working on commission in black communities throughout the country to boost the papers, and these agents frequently served as correspondents whose reports on local activities collectively filled a page or more each issue. In Worcester, Peter Hood filled this role. Hood, a fifty-one-year-old porter in 1886, Pennsylvania-born and married to a Louisiana-born woman, was an Odd Fellow, Bethel member, and an activist in black Worcester's civic and political affairs. He was also a neighbor of the Webbers, living around the corner at 5 Palmer Street in a two-family house shared with Charles and Sarah Bulah. Hood's reports, coupled with those furnished by others across the nation, enabled the city's black residents to understand their own activities in a broader context and also to take pride in the public recognition of their lives.[47]

Another newspaper that reflected local events within a broader regional framework was the Boston *Advocate,* also a weekly. Started in 1885, its Worcester agent was William Edwards, one of the Webbers' immediate neighbors. The *Advocate* incorporated the local report as a major feature, but in Worcester the tasks of agent and reporter were separated. While Edwards sold the weekly papers, the column was written by a mysterious correspondent, under the pen name "D D," who was, in fact, none other than Amos Webber. Webber averaged two brief columns a month in 1885 and 1886 and his public writing contained none of the fascination with white elites, natural disasters, or spectacular crimes that marked his private chronicle. Nor did his column in the *Advocate* confront the central issues before American blacks in this decade (though by then he had largely ceased such discussions in his chronicle as well). Rather, the form and purpose of the column demanded brief accounts of social and civic events in black Worcester. Webber's public columns preserved an essential aspect of his private writing in that rarely did he mention himself by name, nor did he ever mention his wife. Amos Webber never noted the paper or his column in his own private chronicle. So we do not know what "D D" meant or what Webber made of his experience as a public reporter.[48]

But despite this familiar silence, both Webber's and Hood's columns offered further testimony on the role that community organizations, with their overlapping and intertwined memberships, played in the social structure of black Worcester.

BACK IN OCTOBER 1885, Webber had convened a meeting in Worcester of a small group of black veterans. Four other Worcester men attended—George Bundy, William De Lancey, Alexander Hemenway, and Alexander H. Johnson—as did veterans from Boston, New Bedford, and the Connecticut cities of New Haven, Hartford, and Norwich. Representing all three of the Commonwealth's Civil War black regiments, they gathered that evening to create a regional Colored Veterans Association. "It has always been a wonder to us," the editors of the Boston *Advocate* wrote in anticipation of the Worcester meeting, why black veterans "had not taken this step before, to keep alive a spirit of patriotism created during the triumphs and defeats of the great grand army." Such a reunion, the paper predicted, would be "prolific of much good."[49]

Contrary to the *Advocate*'s thinking, there had been efforts to organize black veterans right after the war, but they proved short-lived. Some blacks joined the GAR, but with few exceptions this group of largely white veterans proved less than hospitable to black former soldiers.[50] As news of a national meeting of black veterans, held in Washington, D.C., in December 1884, filtered back to Worcester, Webber and his comrades decided to form the Massachusetts Colored Veterans Association of Worcester, intending to sponsor a reunion of former black soldiers the following May. The response from black veterans throughout New England was enthusiastic.[51] Through the winter and early spring of 1885–1886, the Worcester committee developed their local Massachusetts Colored Veterans Association. They coordinated with other groups of black veterans throughout New England, including such famous compatriots such as William H. Carney of New Bedford, winner of the congressional Medal of Honor for his exploits at the battle of Fort Wagner, and former Lieutenants William Dupree and James Monroe Trotter of Boston.[52]

On the morning of Friday, May 28, 1886, Sergeant Amos Webber, still trim at age sixty, gaveled to order the first business meeting of the Massachusetts Colored Veterans Association of Worcester at the GAR hall on Pearl Street. As he looked out over the podium at the more than 125 veterans, many of whom, like himself, had donned their Federal blue uniforms, he must have been extremely proud. At ten o'clock veterans from New England, New York City, and Delaware—all of whom had served in one of Massachusetts' three black regiments—opened their brief business meeting. With Amos Webber presiding, they endorsed a plan for a national reunion of black veterans, and established an executive committee, consisting of Dupree, Trotter, Carney, Webber, and six other veterans to form a permanent state organization. Following the meeting, the veterans formed ranks under the command of Chief Marshal Webber and paraded through Worcester's streets under clear skies and a comfortable temperature in the low sixties.[53] Webber also presided at the dinner later that afternoon, also in the GAR hall. The main speaker was a white former officer of the 55th Massachusetts Infantry, Colonel Norwood P. Hallowell, whose commitment to racial equality had been tested even before he led his troops into battle. His family had aided the fugitive slave Daniel Dangerfield through Bucks County in 1859, and neither in abolition nor in military service had he been found wanting. He was, the Boston *Advocate* suggested, an "unassuming, intrepid leader."[54]

The colonel's speech suggested why these black veterans still held him in such esteem. He would not, he explained to his rapt audience, simply recall certain glories of a golden age long past; nor would he focus on the very real military exploits of these regiments. Rather, Hallowell addressed "the moral victory won by our regiments in the matter of their pay." He retold the familiar story of blacks recruited with the promise of equal conditions only to discover that their pay was well below that of white recruits. When the Commonwealth of Massachusetts sought to make up the difference in 1863, the men of the 54th and 55th regiments refused on principle: "They would be paid in full by the United States," the colonel explained, "or they would not be paid at all. They were soldiers of the Union, not of the state." As the veterans murmured their approval, the speaker recalled a critical turning point in this battle for equality. "At times our regiments were driven to the verge of mutiny," he remembered, and some units of the 55th "did stack arms one morning, unable to endure any longer the galling sense of humiliation and wrong." Ultimately, "the patriotism and inate good sense of the men, and the patience, tact and firmness of the officers" prevailed, and "a grand catastrophe was averted." This in turn allowed the central moral drama to unfold:

Seven times were the 54th and 55th mustered for pay. Seven times they refused, and pointed to their honorable scars to plead their manhood and their rights. During 18 months they toiled on and they fought on without one cent of pay. At last they won; won through long suffering and patient endurance; won through a higher and rarer courage than the courage of battle; won through the manly attributes of self-respect and self-control—a victory that is not inscribed on their flags by the side of Wagner, James Island, Oloustee [sic], Honey Hill and Petersburg, but which none the less fills one of the noblest and brightest pages in the history of their regiments.

Like the men he addressed, Hallowell did not live in the past. Evoking those comrades who lay buried on southern battlefields, Hallowell stressed that neither they nor the survivors had lived or died in vain. "So long as an atrocious massacre" of black citizens can still occur with regularity in America; "so long as public sentiment grows hot with indignation when political fraud is attempted in New York and Ohio, but grows cold and apologetic" when utilized to deprive southern blacks of their rights; "so long as the avenues of labor are closed against citizens of African descent, because of race prejudice, there is work to be done by those who revere the lives of John Brown and of Colonel Shaw." As the applause ebbed, Hallowell shared with these black veterans his correspondence with officials of the Brotherhood of Locomotive Engineers. The colonel had written Peter M. Arthur, head of the Brotherhood, to ask whether black men, themselves railroad engineers, might join the organization. An aide replied for Arthur, explaining that as the Brotherhood's constitution limited membership to whites, " 'a black man would not therefore be eligible for membership.' " With biting sarcasm, Hallowell then asked his audience: "What do you suppose is the motto of this labor organization? You could not guess. It is the Golden Rule."

Hallowell then inverted the reigning categories of late-nineteenth-century social thought. He acknowledged the central role of engineers and other railroad workers in the culture—they were, he stated, "the heroes of the day"[55]—and he praised their reputed "coolness, courage and discipline." To the extent that they achieved those qualities, however, railroad engineers, brotherhood members, were but "worthy to be compared with the soldiers whose memories we now commemorate":

> The locomotive engineers have yet to learn the very first principles of the dignity and the rights of labor. They are an organized tyranny. Their cornerstone is selfishness. They preach, they do not practice the Golden Rule. We all remember the steamer "Planter" which carried us back and forth across Light House Inlet during the seige of Fort Wagner. The steamer was run out from Charleston, and was delivered to the federal fleet by Robert Small, her pilot and a slave.[56] Has Chief Engineer Arthur done anything better than that?

As "a grand round of applause" rolled across the hall, Hallowell reminded these veterans that, twenty years earlier, "[y]ou were equal to the crisis." The implication for the present, if not the specific strategy, was obvious to all.[57]

Other speakers followed, among them another white colonel, Charles Fox, and black veterans Carney, Trotter, Dupree, and George Fisher, the commander of New Bedford's black GAR post. Amos Webber concluded the evening's speeches. Pleased at seeing "so many of his old comrades," he "thanked the comrades and officers for their attendance" and led the men as they rose, joined hands, and sang "Auld Lang Syne." With that the reunion came to a close.[58]

It was not unusual that the Worcester papers reported the colonel's words but barely recorded even a full sentence spoken by the black veterans. Interestingly, Amos Webber followed the same format in his column in the Boston *Advocate*, emphasizing Hallowell's speech and including a verbatim citation of the exchange of letters between the colonel and the brotherhood officials. Webber did note that he and former Sergeant Bazzel Barker—the same veteran who had been denied membership in GAR Post 10 in 1870—had both looked "especially notable" in their army blues, taking occasion to praise himself, in writing, for one of the few times in his life: "Chief Marshall Webber, through whose untiring efforts the reunion was held," gave the final speech. Webber expressed no discomfort at having Hallowell's public words stand for his sentiments as well, and even in his chronicle Webber never softened Hallowell's stinging critique of organized labor. Indeed, this prolific writer barely mentioned the reunion at all in his own chronicle, a brief notation in the temperature section standing as his only comment.[59]

Amos Webber was proud of the day's events. He had orchestrated the reunion and led each segment of it, and the rare praise he allowed himself marked the level of his pleasure. Webber understood the collective meaning of the reunion as well: the black veterans who built the association over the year, the black families who housed the visitors, and the black residents, interspersed with some whites, who lined the parade route signaled a sophisticated level of organization unimaginable in Worcester twenty years before. Webber had not created this community by himself. Service in the military, the growth of the fraternal lodge with its regional network, the emergence of the church as a central institutional presence—many men and women had participated in this community raising and were themselves transformed as a result. But

Webber might have allowed himself a moment of sheer joy as he reflected on the interlocking network of community organizations that he had done so much to create and which had contributed so greatly to the success of the reunion.

And then there was the colonel's speech. To have one's courage on the battlefield accepted as common knowledge and to have a prominent white speaker publicly emphasize the moral stature and sense of dignity evident in the troops marked an important moment in the lives of all the assembled veterans. Listening as Hallowell then applied their history to the present in a pointed discussion, challenging the pseudo-scientific racial categories that dominated most whites' thinking, Webber and his comrades must have been immensely proud. Hallowell's message, which harnessed self-denial, moral courage, self-respect, and self-control to a political activism that drove the struggle for equality, echoed one of the deepest strains in nineteenth-century black collective thought: God did rule the world, justice and right would prevail in the end, and a political activism infused with moral principles formed the path to ultimate liberation.

These ideas were Webber's deepest beliefs. They had guided his transition to manhood and structured his expansive and increasingly self-confident adult sense of himself in the world. Surrounded as he was that May day by men and women with whom he had created a community and from whom he gained strength even as he provided leadership, Webber indeed may have exulted in what he had accomplished.

A MONTH LATER Webber took to the city streets once again to lead King David Lodge in celebrating St. John's Day, a major Masonic festival. Delegations of black Masons came from New York, Philadelphia, and throughout New England. As a leader of the Mt. Zion Commandery, the elite Masonic organization, Webber again had a central public role.[60] He and Isaac Mason accepted a banner on behalf of the commandery that was presented by the "lady friends" of the organization. The women had commissioned David B. Bowser, Webber's longtime Philadelphia friend and current national leader of the Odd Fellows, to design the banner, which was inscribed with Masonic symbols and the words "In hoc signo vinces." Webber proclaimed his friend as "one of the greatest colored artists that we have." In the parade that followed, Chief Marshal Webber led his own group of thirty men, who were followed by contingents from other cities. Marchers and spectators alike then gathered for the day's oration as Webber introduced Reverend Miles Vanhorn, a Mason and minister from Newport, Rhode Island.[61]

Vanhorn touched on some familiar themes in black fraternalism. "Masons of varied nationalities and tongues on all continents meet together to day upon common ground," he explained, "as if all nations were invited to clasp hands and impart the feeling of true fellowship." The minister also echoed themes that the colonel gave voice to a month earlier. The Masonic emblems adorning Bowser's banner taught "right living, good citizenship and broad manhood," principles that "stand for loyalty and fraternity and they teach men to believe that what has been done others can do; that by teaching the truth, men will be made free. We find we must learn from others. There is very little in this world that is original. We must profit by the experience of others."[62]

This combination of moral uplift and personal rectitude, tied as it was to a sharp-edged, yet tempered, call for freedom and equality, recalled similar orations in Worcester by Robert Jones, Isaac Mason, Amos Webber, and many others. That integration of moral vision and pointed social commentary served for Webber as his basic religious belief, and the involvement of female church activists, the crowds of city blacks who lined the streets, and the delegations from near and afar attested to the collective strength of this belief.[63]

That strength was continually tested. Before the black Masons marched, the four lodges of white Masons in the city pointedly left on early-morning trains for Plymouth, Massachusetts, the site of the Pilgrims' landing in 1620. No clearer statement of the racial exclusivity these men attached to Masonry or to America's heritage could possibly be given.[64]

Yet black Worcester persisted. Webber and his comrades—men and women, Masons, veterans, Odd Fellows, and church activists—knew well the hostility they faced from most whites in the city. They remained committed, however, to the coming of a just society, where racial barriers no longer existed, even as they took the necessary measures to protect themselves in the meantime. The organizations immeasurably strengthened the ability of specific individuals and families to withstand the poverty, the insults, and the intended humiliation that befell them so frequently. They created a free space to develop one's skills and talents, to retain and nurture in collective memory the meaning of the struggle for freedom, and to pass that history on to the rising generation. This was done, moreover, largely without romanticizing the reality of racism or the desire for acceptance, finally and forever, as Americans with full civil and political rights. Particular tactics in this multigenerational battle at times caused dissension. What was rarely questioned was the commitment of Amos Webber and his comrades, male and female, to contain such contradictory strains and to build so rewarding a collective life on such a fundamental dilemma.

CHAPTER TWELVE

FOR THE RACE

As Amos Webber grew older, there was no dramatic change in his views on "the Labor Question." Issues of basic justice remained central but, unlike the majority of white working people then organizing the first national unions, his commitment transcended narrow racial categories. He wove together criticism of unbridled economic power along with a fierce resentment of racial prejudice.

Just a few months before the black veterans' reunion, Webber wrote about a strike by the Knights of Labor, the national workers' organization, against Jay Gould's railroad. Of this part of a wave of strikes occurring "all Over the country in every Mill, Factory, and Corporations,"[1] Webber saw the cause in the fact that "in Olden times Men were Satisfied with from 50, to 100,000 dollars and considered themselves rich and paid Laborers, good pay for their work, and let them live. But now if Men do not have from 1,000,000 to 200,000,000 they get it by cutting down their employees. hence come all of these Strikes, turning the World upside down, The Rich Men battleing the Poor Men;". Of Gould specifically, Webber was dismissive. Estimating Gould's worth at more than $2 million, Webber directed the reader to "[s]ee him engaged in fighting the Laboring men to get more added to his wealth;".[2]

Webber's image of the correct relations between workers and employers remained grounded in his experience with Charles Wurts, Stephen Smith, the black merchant and philanthropist, and Philip L. Moen. Capitalism and industrialization were in themselves perfectly acceptable economic systems and Webber took as a given the structures of authority within a firm, as long as they were not oppressive.

Webber continued to see Worcester's industrialists as a class apart, whose political affiliations, private philanthropy, and benevolent employment practices elevated them in his mind above the Fisks, the Goulds, and the Vanderbilts he frequently criticized. But contrary to Webber's thinking, the town's major industrialists had created a work atmosphere quite hostile to unionization. Paternalistic programs, aggressive antiunion regulations, and artful manipulation of entrenched ethnic sensibilities among workers constituted the employer response to organizing efforts. Some Worcester workers persisted, however, and the Knights of Labor gradually attracted perhaps as many as 6,000 members in a variety of trades and occupations. Nevertheless, as Peter Hood wrote in the New York *Freeman* just before the veterans' reunion, "the labor movement has struck this city in rather mild form." He emphasized the continued prominence of liquor licensing—not labor—as the most volatile political issue.[3]

Mild as it may have been, when the Knights organized the city's barbers, some black barbers attended the meeting. The extent of this interracial cooperation was not clear since, in those mercurial days of labor organizing, the group lasted but a short time. Some months later the *Freeman* asked, "what has become of the Barber's Union of this city among the colored workmen?" No one provided an answer.[4]

It would not have been unusual for Webber to herald the prospect of such biracial cooperation, but in this case he remained silent. His faith in Worcester's leading industrialists contributed to this; so did his reading of the larger political climate. Many of Worcester's leading Knights were Irish[5] and many of the Worcester meetings were held at Hibernian Hall—suggesting a strong Irish immigrant presence in the labor union. Given what that meant in political terms (Webber's Republican candidates inevitably lost by overwhelming margins in the wards of the Democratic, Irish working classes), his silence may have indicated his pessimism over the long-term prospects of such interracial cooperation.[6] But Webber did not stereotype the Irish. He particularly worried about the fierce violence in Ireland and America between Protestant and Catholic Irish, and in his chronicle asked: "When will this hatred ever cease;".[7]

ON NOVEMBER 27, 1887, Amos Webber acknowledged for the first time in his own writing the importance of the black church, recording in some detail the centennial of the origins of the A.M.E. denomination. "Bishop [Richard] Allen drew out of the White Methodist Church" in 1787 because he "conceived the Idea that their were to much prejudice against the colored members that belong to their Churches= Hence caused the come out." Webber stressed Allen's courage and the positive effects of his actions for black Americans across the century, but the entry carried no private musings about how, through Attleborough's Bethlehem Colored Methodist Church, Allen's stand had affected a younger Webber. The centennial also led Webber to try again to understand racism. Identical attitudes that led Allen out of the white Methodist congregation, he argued, "exist to day in the White Churches as to colored members; more or less, though they try not to Show it, but it will peep out somewhere; at times So as to be notice." As he had once before in his discussion of Louisiana during Reconstruction, Webber at times presented white racism as the product of elite imposition on poor and working people: "The poorer white receives a portion of prejudice from the richer members, of the Church & &c".[8] This approach preserved the hope that other elites who were not racist might reverse the process. Justice, he implied, would come in part through such efforts to influence popular white attitudes and through the preservation of black community institutions such as Richard Allen had founded.

But justice would not be quick in coming, and the powerful tensions of being both black and American surfaced again in August 1887 when Massachusetts' black veterans convened their national reunion at Boston's Tremont Temple. William Carney acted as chief marshal while Webber, a member of the planning committee, was his aide-de-camp. Another Worcester veteran, Alexander F. Hemenway, led a company of the 54th Infantry. More than 300 men attended the two-day meeting as delegates, although an estimated 4,000 people—mainly black and drawn primarily from throughout the Northeast—attended the evening ceremonies. So electrifying was the rendition of "The Star-Spangled Banner," as performed by Mrs. Nellie Brown Mitchell and a choir of fifty, that the "veterans shouted themselves hoarse" and, when the artist offered an encore, "4,000 people stood up on their feet and joined her in singing two more verses." The business meeting proved equally spirited. Evoking their past sacrifices, these veterans demanded federal guarantees for "full and equal protection of the laws" and resolved to support in elections only those who "have ever been faithful" to the Reconstruction amendments. They called for a monument in the nation's capital to the black veteran, and sharply criticized a Louisiana GAR commander for "refusing a charter to colored veterans." Specifically, they reminded "white comrades and . . . our white fellow-citizens" of *their* duty as Americans to ensure that "the patriotic negro soldier and his kin who came to the rescue of an imperiled nation, are allowed, and protected in, that freedom and full citizenship which they so nobly earned in the dark days of rebellion." Finally, these men acknowledged the recent spate of "fraternizing" between Federal and Confederate veterans, and expressed misgivings similar to Webber's a decade earlier: "Conciliation and peace with enemies are grand," they resolved, "when coupled with justice to faithful allies they are sublime."[9]

The concluding ceremonies further revealed the veterans' fundamental political expectations. They traveled by steamer to Hingham, Massachusetts, where a predominantly white local GAR post, in full uniform, and a detachment of the Sons of Veterans, greeted and escorted them to a reception. In formation by unit, black and white, the veterans then marched to the grave of Governor John A. Andrew, who had commissioned these black soldiers twenty-three years earlier. In speeches and with flowers, they honored his memory and decorated his tomb and in so doing they acknowledged the truth of what one of the reunion's speakers had stated the previous day. "I know well that when you enlisted in the war," General A. S. Hartwell explained,

you did what a white man could not do. You knew that the flag which you fought did not wave o'er the land of the free and the home of the brave, but that it waved over enslaved millions of your own people. And yet you went to work and never went back on that old flag.[10]

SIXTY-TWO YEARS OLD in April 1888, Amos Webber had to consider his future. If his terms of employment were generous, Web-

GRAND
REUNION OF COLORED VETERANS,

—UNDER THE AUSPICES OF THE—

54th and 55th Infantry, and 5th Cavalry Regiments, and Sailors,

MASSACHUSETTS VOLUNTEERS,

In Boston, August 1st and 2nd, 1887.

* * * " You will never part with that FLAG so long as a splinter of the staff or a thread of the web remains within your grasp." * * * GOV. JOHN A. ANDREW, *on presentation of flag at Readville, Mass., May 18 1863.*

" The old FLAG never touched the ground, boys ! " —SERGT. WILLIAM H. CARNEY (*severely wounded*), *on the parapet of Fort Wagner, S. C., July 18, 1863.*

BOSTON, Mass., June 1, 1887.

Comrade,—

DEAR SIR, — There will be a reunion of the surviving Veterans of the 54th and 55th Mass. Vol. Infantry Regiments, the 5th Mass. Vol. Cavalry, and Massachusetts Sailors, in Tremont Temple, Boston, August 1st and 2nd, 1887.

The Executive Committee extend a hearty invitation to the reunion to all colored Soldiers and Sailors of Massachusetts and the United States, and sincerely desire to make the occasion a most enjoyable and successful one : renewing old acquaintance, and reviving fraternal feeling among all the old comrades of the country.

You are, therefore, earnestly requested to join with us, and to do all in your power to create an interest among comrades, and also to make every effort for a grand and memorable reunion.

The Committee of Arrangements respectfully and earnestly request that all commissioned officers appear in uniform (coat and hat or cap); non-commissioned officers, (coat or blouse, and hat or cap) ; privates, (blouse and cap or hat, or G. A. R. uniform.)

All comrades are requested to send their names and addresses at once to Lieut. WILLIAM H. DUPREE, *Chairman of Executive Committee, Station A, P. O. Boston, Mass.,* in order that they may receive a circular-programme, later on, containing full information.

Various Sub-Committees will be appointed as soon as a sufficient number of names, from the different localities, are received.

The Executive Committee would further suggest for the Convention a programme as follows : —

Flyer announcing the 1887 reunion of black veterans. The reunion had originally been proposed at the 1886 Worcester veterans' reunion. Largely excluded from the "campfires" of the white veterans, these reunions allowed black veterans to share their memories, recall their

Aug. 1.—First Session.—Tremont Temple, at 10 A. M.

1.—MUSIC, BOSTON BRASS BAND, ALSO FIFE AND DRUM CORPS.
2.—CALLING THE CONVENTION TO ORDER BY THE CHAIRMAN OF THE
   EXECUTIVE COMMITTEE.
3.—PRAYER.
4.—MUSIC.
5.—ADDRESS OF WELCOME BY THE PRESIDENT.
6.—MUSIC.
7.—ADJOURNMENT AND COLLATION.

At 2 p.m., formation on the Common for a parade through the principal streets, which will probably be reviewed by the Mayor of Boston, and the Governor of the Commonwealth. The route will be published in the newspapers and printed on the programmes, which will be distributed in the Temple.

Aug. 1.—Second Session.—Tremont Temple, at 4 P. M.

Addresses to be delivered by commissioned officers and others of the different regimental organizations, also remarks will be made by other invited guests.

Aug. 2.—Third Session.—Tremont Temple, at 10 A. M.

Addresses by commissioned officers and non-commissioned officers of the several regiments, also representatives of the sailors.

A business meeting will be held at Tremont Temple before adjournment, to effect a permanent organization of all colored veterans in the United States.

Company L., 6th Regiment, Mass. Vol. Militia, will be invited to do escort duty for the parade.

The Executive Committee has under consideration an excursion to "Camp Readville," and a sail down Boston Harbor, *visiting and decorating with flowers the grave of Massachusetts' Great War Governor*, JOHN A. ANDREW, at Hingham.

" I will never give up the rights of these men while I live, whether in this world or the next."—*Gov. Andrew's appeal to Government for equal pay.*

" I know not what record of sin may await me in another world; but this I know :— I was never mean enough to despise any man because he was ignorant, nor because he was poor, nor because he was black."—*Gov. Andrew.*

Let the comrades of nearly twenty-five years ago respond to the call of the *Executive Committee*, and meet once more in one grand camp-fire, and revive the memories of our old campaigns

EXECUTIVE COMMITTEE.

Lieut. WM. H. DUPREE, 55th, Chairman, Boston, Mass.
   Sergt. BURRILL SMITH, 54th, Secretary, Boston, Mass.
      ISAAC S. MULLEN, U. S. Navy, Corresponding Secretary, Boston, Mass.
         Lieut. CHARLES L. MITCHELL, 55th, Treasurer, Boston, Mass.

Lieut. JAMES M. TROTTER, 55th, Washington, D. C.
Sergt. WM. H. CARNEY, 54th, New Bedford, Mass.
Sergt. AMOS WEBBER, 5th Cavalry, Worcester, Mass.
Sergt. GUSTAVUS BOOTH, 5th Cavalry, Hartford, Conn.
Chaplain SAMUEL HARRISON, 54th, Pittsfield, Mass.
Sergt. CHARLES W. LENOX, 54th, Watertown, Mass.
Sergt. GEORGE T. FISHER, 5th Cavalry, New Bedford, Mass.
Sergt. WESLEY J. FURLONG, 54th, Boston, Mass.
Lieut. STEPHEN A. SWAILS, 54th, South Carolina.
JAMES H. WOLFF, U. S. Navy, Boston, Mass.
Lieut. FRANK M. WELCH, 54th, Bridgeport, Conn.
Sergt. J. H. BATES, 5th Cavalry, Wilkes Barre, Pa.
WM. HAZARD, 54th (of John A. Andrew Post, G. A. R.), New York City.
WM. B. DERRICK, U. S. Navy, New York City.
Sergt. JOHN DAVIS, 5th Cavalry, Carlisle, Pa.
Sergt. ROBERT M. DORSEY, 55th, Washington, D. C.
Sergt. SAMUEL J. PATTERSON, 5th Cavalry, Wilkes Barre, Pa.
Sergt. E. GEORGE BIDDLE, 54th, Worcester, Mass.
GEO. E. HICKS, U. S. Navy, Boston, Mass.
Sergt. BENJ. W. PHOENIX, 5th Cavalry, Boston, Mass.
Sergt. GEORGE E. LEE, 54th, Wellesley, Mass.
JOHN LITTLE, 55th (of Wm. Lloyd Garrison Post, G. A. R.), Brooklyn, N. Y.
Lieut. GEO. E. STEVENSON, 54th (of Wm. Lloyd Garrison Post, G.A.R.), Brooklyn, N. Y.
WM. H. JARVIS, U. S. Navy, Lynn, Mass.

Comrades in organizations of 25 to 500, and over, can get discount from regular rates of 10 to 50 per cent. by applying to " General Passenger Agents " in their localities.

" BOSTON ADVOCATE " Job Print (Grandison & Powell), 65 Hanover Street.

sacrifices, and publicly assert their place in the national memory of that war. Webber's name is among those listed on the executive committee.
Courtesy of Massachusetts Historical Society, Boston

ber, like most Americans, still lacked insurance protection against illness, a pension, or other retirement benefits. Although he had not complained of his health since his trip to Florida in 1881, Webber took advantage of his age and his past military service to apply for a federal pension. He claimed that when on duty at Point Lookout in March 1865, he "contracted continuous colds . . . with chills," and that as a result of that illness he was now "in great part disabled." Philip L. Moen witnessed Webber's declaration, attesting to its truthfulness and accuracy. Nonetheless, federal officials denied the application. Two years later, following the passage of the Dependent Pension Act, which granted a pension to every honorably discharged soldier unable to work, regardless of how he had incurred the disability, Webber reapplied. He described his ailments as a "constant cough with expectoration," weight loss, and heart palpitations "on walking fast or going up stairs, etc." The surgeon who examined him corroborated the outlines of Webber's diagnosis, emphasizing the veteran's chronic laryngitis, weakened heart, and the general complaint that Webber was no longer "able to do hard day's work." The doctor recommended a five-ninths disability pension. This time Webber's petition was accepted, and starting in 1890, he received a pension of twelve dollars a month.[11]

The passage of the Dependent Pension Act was a testament to the lobbying power of the GAR. A generous act beyond even the dreams of many of its proponents, it was the result of a decade-long effort by the GAR, whose membership grew sharply in the process.[12] Worcester's Post 10, whose membership had fallen from a high of 1,200 in 1874 to 350 in the early 1880s, numbered 877 in 1890 after a decade of successful organizing.[13] At least 47 black veterans relocated in Worcester during these postwar decades, and almost half joined the local GAR. Those black veterans who had joined the GAR usually continued their affiliation with the white group even after the formation of the Massachusetts Colored Veterans Association, since the two organizations had different functions and quite distinct institutional purposes.[14]

As these men aged, access to veterans' organizations proved even more valuable. The local GAR post and the Colored Veterans Association were repositories of advice, information, and support about pensions and other benefits. But, as in the fraternal lodge and the church meeting, activities that on the surface paralleled those of whites contained a deeper meaning when understood through the prism of race. The process of receiving a pension suggested why.

Pension applications required corroboration of witnesses, and filing a pension therefore became something of a community effort. For black applicants, GAR connections were only one part—and a rather small one at that—of this support system. Of the 115 men and women who gave testimony for Worcester's black veterans or their widows in pension cases, 30 percent of the men were themselves veterans, almost all black; a third were members either of the black Masons or Odd Fellows; and 8 percent of the women were members of the Household of Ruth, the female auxiliary to the Odd Fellows. Less than 7 percent of the witnesses who gave affidavits for black veterans were white.[15] Access to the GAR's Post 10 might provide needed information but, given the segregated nature of the military experience itself, most black veterans relied on affidavits from other blacks.

Webber's relations with whites in the GAR and at work were important, if only because they affirmed his belief in an ultimately just, biracial society, but they never formed the core of his daily life. The interconnected layers of association apparent in the pension files did. Often obscured due to Webber's reticence, these social intimacies usually lacked drama, especially in comparison with the disasters Webber relished recording. But precisely because they formed the backdrop of common, everyday experience, they formed the very essence of his existence. In this intricate network were his friends and acquaintances the institutions they created, and the recognition of community they nurtured and protected. For all his emphasis on individual responsibility, Amos Webber drew a considerable portion of his essential strength from this communal world.

INEVITABLY THE PASSAGE OF TIME began to transform that world. In 1887 Sergeant Bazzel Barker died, as did Zion's longtime organist and Masonic brother, Asa E. Hector, and church activist Rachael Bostic. The next year, Charles P. Dyer, a fraternalist, passed away, and succeeding years claimed Martha Brown, Gilbert Walker, and Annie Mason.[16] The coming of age of a new generation had begun.

Webber still remained a respected leader. In 1889 both the Masons and Pythians in Worcester commemorated his sixty-third birthday. He became a thirty-second-degree Mason, among the highest recognitions possible, was elected second-in-command to Reverend Miles Vanhorn in the New England regional Masonic Commandery, and was appointed a deputy to Charles F. A. Francis in the first statewide Masonic "Colored Consistory."[17] But another event that year underscored the broader transformation already under way.

On Sunday, April 7, in Boston, Lewis Hayden died. The long-time "messenger in the Secretary of State's office," Hayden had been by turns a slave, a leading abolitionist, "one of John Brown's friends and the first-man to Know the plans of the Hero at Harpers Ferry," a recruiter of black troops, and a political and fraternal figure of considerable importance. He was also a friend of Webber's, an older man whose example and influence Webber had felt throughout the postwar decades. In his private obituary Webber stressed Hayden's courage in the struggle for freedom, and particularly underscored how the "Veteran Colored Messenger" wielded power with white elites: "The words of Lewis Hayden always had great weight with Gov. Andrew" during the war years. As Webber recalled, the governor asked the messenger early in the war what course "should the Government pursue to bring this terrible War to a Successful termination." Hayden's answer was direct: " 'Put colored troops in the field Sir.' " This response propelled Andrew to approach Lincoln, who, Webber reported, "[i]n due time . . . issued his call for the enlistment of colored Soldiers;".

Webber's account was clearly wrong: the struggle over black recruits was far more complex and prolonged than this heroic account indicated. But Webber's tale of Lewis Hayden's influence duplicated his own most private hope: that he achieved a parallel level of effectiveness with Philip L. Moen. As had Hayden, Webber saw himself as a principled black man, willing to risk penalties for violation of immoral laws, who could also work in sustained legal fashion with white elites to achieve, through suasion, justice for black Americans. In his eulogy for Hayden, Webber had drafted a coda for his own life as well.

Webber, who attended the funeral as a member of the Masonic grand lodge, reported on the presence of the sitting governor, aging abolitionists such as Lucy Stone, and other dignitaries. But Webber situated the funeral services squarely within the collective life of postwar northern blacks. Meticulously he listed the black organizations with representatives attending the funeral, among them the Prince Hall Masons, Knights of Pythias, and black veterans. He proudly displayed the complex associational life that honeycombed the black community.[18]

Another sense of generational change emerged when a new political organization appeared. Under the leadership of Lieutenant William H. Dupree, Webber's friend and supervisor of one of Boston's postal stations, representatives from black communities throughout the Commonwealth founded the Massachusetts Citizens Equal Rights Association in the fall of 1889. The following June the association established a Worcester branch and the identities of its leaders indicated the sea change then under way. Isaac Mason participated, but neither William Brown, William Jankins, nor Amos Webber represented the association to the public. In their place stood the pastor of Mt. Olive Baptist Church, Reverend Hiram Conway; G. Alfred Busby, the Barbados-born tailor who had come to Worcester five years earlier; and Walter M. Coshburn, another recently arrived small businessman. The association sought to obtain "to all Americans the full right and enjoyment of the natural, essential, inalienable rights guaranteed to them by the constitution of the United States," and "to celebrate the Anniversary of the Emancipation Proclamation with a Public Entertainment." The association soon grew to more than forty members locally and served as a vehicle for some activists in the younger generation to enter politics. With its support, G. Alfred Busby organized his six unsuccessful city council races on the Republican ticket during the 1890s.[19]

Events in the white community reinforced this sense of change. For Webber, none was more personally significant than the death of Philip L. Moen in April 1891. Sick that winter, Moen had gone to Winter Park, Florida; still failing, he moved to St. Augustine on the Atlantic and then traveled inland, up the St. Johns River, in search of the elusive restorative climate. Returning home early in April, he resumed work, only to suffer a stroke a week later. Within ten days he was dead.

Webber's obituary of his longtime employer filled three closely written pages. After recounting Moen's last illness, Webber provided a brief biographical sketch of "the Great Manufacturer." It was tersely written, as if the author feared that too evocative a word might unlock the dammed emotions that swirled within him. Webber recalled the death of Moen's first wife and recorded that his three children, a son and two daughters, followed his second marriage. Turning to the public man, Webber emphasized that his old employer had been "engaged in most of our Public Institutions" and listed some of Moen's involvement as trustee or director of banks, life insurance companies, and charitable institutions.

The biography was but prelude to what Webber termed the "Obsequies of Mr. Philip L. Moen." He described the scene on April 24, the day following Moen's death, when his body lay at rest at his home, awaiting viewing by mourners. A short walk away, "At the Grove St. Works, all was silent; Hush; Be Still; The great Engine was stop^{ed}; The steam was gone, not a ripple, or an Echo sound was heard; the great Flag swayed to and fro, at half mast To inform the inhabitants that a great man had died;". Shortly before 10:00 A.M. the force of clerks, numbering more than sixty, entered the Moen residence from the side, slowly marched past the body of their employer, and then exited through the front door. At 10:00 A.M. precisely, the working men of the mill began to assemble for their march to the house, which they reached "as the rear part of the clerks were passing out." For the next few hours, 2,400 employees—most from the shop floor— passed through the parlor, in two rows alongside the body. At 3:30 that afternoon, the funeral itself commenced, before "a large gathering of the people, many of them had grown up with Mr Moen; and Show^{d} Signs of Old age." Webber briefly acknowledged the ministers who officiated, and took some notice of the floral tributes from groups on whose behalf "Mr Moen had done some kind act." The young men's bible class at Union Church sent lilies that formed the word "Teacher"; the flowers from the Armenian church proclaimed, "Our Helper."

Following services the cortege formed outside the Moen residence, with the official funeral party consisting of ten carriages. Webber carefully recorded the passengers in each, and their order in the procession behind the hearse bearing Moen's body. Slowly the cortege proceeded to Lincoln Square, at the top of Main Street, where it wended its way through the square until it veered right, onto Grove Street, toward the Rural Cemetery on the far side of the Washburn and Moen plant. All along the march "the crowd was hushed into silence and every mark of respect was paid to Mr Moen." As the cortege approached the front door of the wire works the clerks "filed out 2 by 2 in front of the hearse, as an escort; 'Guard of Honor.' " Already in place, the more than 2,400 production workers lined each side of Grove Street from the office to the gate of the cemetery: "The procession pass^d on its solomn way through the double line of employees, they with lifted Hats; as we passed through &c." At the cemetery the clerks carried the casket to the grave site and, following prayers, lowered it into the earth. The recessional, Webber recorded, was "Oh, how sad we feel, when we return without *Thee*."[20]

Typically, Webber did not list himself among the passengers in the official carriages, but he was there, perhaps as a driver, in one of them. In this case, even had he not used the collective personal pronoun to describe the procession past the workforce, it would be safe to assume his presence. Webber's relationship with his employer extended back at least thirty years and encompassed far more than their daily exchanges over work assignments. The lives of the manufacturer and the messenger intersected politically, in efforts to hire additional black workers, and not the least in Moen's astounding generosity in allowing Webber to adjust his workday to his personal and organizational needs. Webber, in turn, as his obituary made so clear, treated Moen with respect and reverence, and saw in his career the model of an exemplary self-made man. The obituary indicated again Webber's fascination with order and authority. The honorific and hierarchical structure of the funeral and the procession, where each social component had a specific place in a visible order, Webber appreciated and participated in without hesitation.

Six months later, observing the death of another Worcester industrialist, George S. Barton, Webber expressed more directly his sense of a generation passing. He thought it appropriate that Barton's employees attended the funeral *en masse* to take "the last view of their Employer," and he offered a eulogy for a generation of industrialists who had now largely gone: "He [Barton] was a fine type of business men of Worcester, and was ever a corner stone as the, Crompton; Knowles; Moen; now Barton; Will men of like worth, again, figure in the every day work of Worcester;".[21]

Amos Webber's embrace of these businessmen and easy acceptance of the icon of the self-made man reflected a commanding characteristic of American culture. But it was also based on experiences that had begun, at the latest, with Webber's encounter with Charles S. Wurts's "Strict rules."[22] In his relations with elite white employers over a long work life, Webber had found men whose commitment to racial equality, relative to that of most white Americans, proved heartening. He also had found in these employers virtues worth emulating. Webber had not a little of the Horatio Alger within him, and the virtues he attributed to these men—morality, industry, and perseverance—infused his own personal and collective activities. His concern with their passing, then, also carried a public, political meaning.

As WEBBER EDGED closer to his seventieth birthday, important changes already under way further altered the tone of his chronicle. Webber had always been interested in public affairs, in acts of God, and in the newsworthy people involved in these events. Increasingly, however, his once critical perspective on politics lost its focus. Webber spent more time recording sporting events, the activities of Queen Victoria, and the comparative wealth of American millionaires than he did politics. Webber noted his friends more frequently than he had in the past because their deaths and funerals were newsworthy to him. In contrast, he never once mentioned G. Alfred Busby's numerous attempts to win office as Worcester's first elected black councilman.

In certain ways this tone was not new. Since Rutherford B. Hayes's inauguration in 1877, Webber had not commented in depth on national Republican politics. Benjamin Harrison's 1888 victory over incumbent Democrat Grover Cleveland brought pleasure but no substantive discussion. Four years later, when Cleveland achieved "a complete 'over turn' " in the rematch, Webber's only comment held that "the Republicans got picked as bare as a Buzzard; &&".[23] Broader issues of justice increasingly received one-dimensional treatment as well. When Jay Gould (the man whom Webber had excoriated for his role in the 1886 railroad strike) died, Webber provided an uncritical, celebratory eulogy: "The history of Jay Gould from the bare=footed boy, who wandered over the rough hills of Delaware county [New York] to the Railroad King whose wealth is estimated $100,000,000 is one of the most remarkable among American Self=Made Men." Absent was Webber's analysis of precisely how Gould had made his fortune, as was any critical comment when Gould's probated will revealed no provisions for charity. What remained evoked nineteenth-century America's most dominant cultural icon: the visage of the self-made man.[24]

The opening of the World's Fair Columbian Exposition in Chicago the following spring drew another expression of celebratory faith in the promise of American life. Americans primarily regarded the fair, which drew contributors from throughout the world, as a celebration of their proclaimed cultural and technological superiority. Webber unabashedly joined in the self-praise. "The american people are everywhere telling themselves to day that this is an exposition of the material glory of our age; but there is a moral significance inestimable in the great work" as well. "We are honestly proclaiming in all our ceremonial of the occasion that the courage, faith, intelligence, heroism, of this our day, are the children in lineal decent of the faith that gave columbus the honor of to day; The memorial nature of this celebration . . . reminds us that the rush for wealth has not torn from the minds of the age the remembrance of its parentage, 'Columbus.' " Such a sentimental invocation of history as moral antidote to an unchecked materialism proved a weak reed even for Webber. Where in the past a telling critique of the irresponsible use of such material plenty might have followed, perhaps with reference to James Fisk or Oakes Ames, Webber instead rather exuberantly embraced America's unique position in the world's quite material affairs:

In every phase of the great crowning fete of the 19*th* century there lies Glorification for the United States, the Capital of the Kingdoms of commerce, art and science has been set up in Jackson Park, Ill. of the great American progress that has been made in the 19*th* century or 400 years ago. The Eagle has a right to

Scream; at his loudest [to]day, and every American is proud of this Eagle.[25]

Despite the grammatical confusion, no stronger evocation of American nationalism and patriotism was possible.

But, in a very real sense, that celebratory tone had always been an aspect of Amos Webber's vision. When he wrote of the "Loyal Colored men" who had lost their lives to an enraged mob during New York City's draft riots in 1863 or when he described the brutal assassinations of nearly sixty "loyal sons," defenders of the legal government in Grant Parish, Louisiana, his repeated use of that term revealed a telling point. For the America he gave his loyalty to, he had few criticisms. Even as he participated in building social and cultural institutions that reflected the northern black experience, the values that reinforced those institutions revealed deeply American origins. Nevertheless, without a dissenting perspective, Webber's nationalism almost threatened to become a caricature of its former self.

Almost, but not quite. Although less frequently than twenty years before, sparks from earlier discussions flared again even in the 1890s.

The death of Sitting Bull, the great Sioux leader, provided one such moment. The Sioux victory at the Little Bighorn actually proved devastating to the Indians, as the army's retaliation inaugurated a decade of flight, exile to Canada, and ultimately Sitting Bull's forced acceptance of the hated reservation system. In 1890, government troops and Indian police at North Dakota's Standing Rock reservation killed the Lakota Sioux chief, his son, Crow Foot, and other supporters as Sitting Bull prepared to leave his reservation to visit Sioux spiritual leaders on the Pine Ridge reservation to the south. The five Indian policemen who died in the battle received a Christian funeral with "full military honors"; in contrast, Sitting Bull was buried "in a deserted corner of the Military Cemetary without any ceremony."[26]

This treatment of "the mighty medicine man of the Sioux" grated on Webber. "[V]ainly have we, [looked] for a word of praise for the old chieftan," Webber complained a week later. "Page after Page" in the press listed Sitting Bull's "long life of cunning and craftiness and his hatred for the Whites; His cowardice and his

121

Local Pages, Worcester. Mass, 1893;

The World Fair at Chicago, Illinois,—
The Opening; The Sights Were Wonderful; All Nations
Races, and Religion were Represented
800,000 Persons is supposed to beheld the great Opening,
May 1st — Representative of all nations. Elbowed one another
in broad avenues of the great white City to day
even the "Esquimaux. Children of the frozen North, Sau-
=nted through the road-way gazing curiosly at the Japanese
whose home is at the Equator,; It was a congress of Nations
    The President of the United States (Grover Cleveland)
Open the Columbia exposition by an address, and
pressing the Button, which caused the machinery to be put
in motion, through out the building; On this, the Exposition
was declared Open; As an account, taking of the actual
progress of the worlds Fair, it is not a new thing, since the
first World fair, held in London nearly half century ago
the self consciousness of the age The American people
are everywhere telling themselves to day that this is an exposition
of the material glory of our age but there is a moral signif-
=icance inestimable in the great work that has made the
Columbia exposition a great gift in America; We are
honestly proclaiming in all our ceremonial of the occasion
that the courage, faith, intelligence, heroism, of this our day,
Are the children in lineal descent of the faith that gave
columbus the honor of to day; The memorial nature of this
celebration is not only its unique feature but it is one
of its features which reminds us that the rush for wealth
has not torn from the minds of the age the remembrance of
its parentage "Columbus," In every phase of the great crowning
fete of the "19th century there lies Glorification for the
United States; the Capital of the Kingdoms of commerce,
Art, and Science has been set up in Jackson Park, All
of the great American progress that has been made in the
19th century or 400 years ago; The Eagle has a right to
Scream at his loudest-key, and every American is proud
of this Eagle;

"Amos Webber Thermometer Record and Diary," Volume VII, May 1,
1893, page 121. *Courtesy of Baker Library, Harvard University Graduate School of Business Administration, Boston*

mischief breeding nature etc. But never has there been a word of cheer for the Old redskin. Not a tear has been dropped to slip along a pale face . . . in remembrance of the mighty Warrior;". This Webber took as a mark against American culture: "It is a Knock-out-blow to our boasted humanity, and the rising tide of 'civilization.' " This inability to recognize a foe's greatness nettled him, as did the army's refusal to bury Sitting Bull according to Sioux custom. "Even after death," Webber complained, "the medicine man has been taken out of the beaten path, of his ancestry;".[27]

Webber's description sharply highlighted the duality he himself embodied. His sympathy for "the Old redskin" jostled with another image, the absence of tears "along a pale face," and suggested that Webber well understood the racial dimension at the center of the press treatment of Sitting Bull's death. Yet Webber could not deny his own identification with the dominant culture: it was "our boasted humanity" that suffered as a consequence. The man who had expressed no concern over the treatment of the Modoc Indians in 1873 had clearly broadened his views. But Webber remained a black American, living a social and cultural duality that at times he dimly understood and never could independently control.

Webber's economic analysis also reflected none of his earlier power. "The first strike since March 31st 1871 (See 1st volum P 110) was inaugurated this noon at the Grove St. Wire Works," he observed in 1892. Women now worked in the fine-wire department, in numbers that remain unclear, but male workers continued to perform the skilled tasks. When they were instructed to teach women the skilled task of hammering dies, some seventy to eighty men in the fine-wire department struck. When the men walked out, Philip W. Moen (once the young "Master Philly," now grown into a thirty-four-year-old corporate president) fired them, which caused additional men to strike as well. Interestingly, some of the female wire-drawers also struck, explaining to the local paper that "they did so partly through sympathy and partly because they did not think it [the skilled work] a proper kind of work for women."

Within a week the strike was settled: Moen backed down from his ultimatum, the men returned to work, and the women would henceforth be excluded from skilled work. Perhaps in an earlier year Webber's commentary about the strike would have been critical and curious, but now the strike raised no disturbing issues of justice denied. "The strike is amicably settled between the Workmen and the Corporation," he reported on March 11. "All hands returned to Work, with the understanding they are not to teach, the Girls to hammer dyes."[28]

Later that same year, during the steel strike at Homestead, Pennsylvania, Webber accepted the Carnegie Corporation's argument that its wage reduction resulted directly from a lowering of the market price for steel billets. Although he noted the military preparations made by the company, and the ensuing violence, the

Philip W. Moen (1857–1904). Amos Webber's "young Master Philly" as one of Worcester's leading industrialists. *Courtesy of American Antiquarian Society*

economic cost of the strike to both workers and the company impressed Webber most: "Those who cannot get back [i.e., get rehired], are in a bad fix; as the relief funds will be stopped and many hundreds of them have nothing to live on." The company, Webber estimated, lost more than $4 million. At no time did he mention that Alexander Berkman, who attempted to assassinate Carnegie leader Henry Frick during the strike, had lived in Worcester.[29]

Even the great Pullman strike two years later, which pitted the American Railway Union against the railroad industry and which Webber called "the greatest battle between capitol and Labor that has been inaugurated in this country," drew surprisingly little overt judgment. His analysis, particularly in noting the active involvement of many corporations and the critical role of the federal government in their support, was accurate; but despite a sympathetic mention of strike leader Eugene V. Debs and the insertion of a newspaper portrait of Debs into his chronicle, Webber refrained from discussing the moral and political issues in a strike he excitedly termed "the most gigantic war in the Worlds History."[30] The keen analyst of the 1877 railroad strike was nowhere to be found.

Only racial issues generated flashes of the honed critique that had once dominated his political thinking. Webber praised the former slave and current congressman from South Carolina, George Washington Murry, for his 1893 speech in support of an election bill (introduced by a Massachusetts representative, Henry Cabot Lodge) that—had it passed—would have enabled voters to request federal supervision of elections. Murry, Webber thought, "speaks with a flaming tongue on the freeman's Election bill and race."[31] Later that same year, in his eulogy of A.M.E. Bishop Daniel Payne, Webber touched on the relationship of religious faith to the needs of the race. The bishop had "Godly parents" and under their influence "the mind of the young Daniel received that sacred bias which led him to act the part; which so distinguished him through the course of his life." Even as it infused Payne's spiritual life, Webber saw how "that sacred bias" permeated the secular world as well: "He has done wonderful work for the Church and for *the race, and generations yet unborn will cherish his name;*".[32]

During 1896 Webber participated in three public ceremonies that together symbolized the direction of his thinking at this time. Like that of many individuals, his vision encapsulated powerful crosscurrents.

The first occurred in March, when William W. Rice died. A Republican political activist and legal advisor to Worcester's industrial elite, Rice deeply influenced Webber's own political thinking. As Webber wrote after attending Rice's funeral: "In Him the Slave had a friend whenever they appear[d] in Worcester; He Battled against the Slave=Holder till the last; and sent the slave to Canada to the Land of the Free, out of the grip of his Old Master &c." In addition to Rice, Webber remembered, the "earnest and fearless advocates of Freedom to the Slave" included Adin Thayer, P. Emory Aldrich, "and others young men [who] made a phalanx of young professional men who were not afraid to make Known their Opinion at any time or any Occasion."[33] Webber's involvement with that "phalanx of young professional men" had long framed important aspects of his political activism, and Rice's passing was another reminder of the changing political atmosphere.

The second ceremony took place on August 13. The white majority of Worcester's GAR post invited black members to tell their stories for the first time in the post's twenty-nine-year existence. Nine black veterans, including Amos Webber, addressed "one of the largest audiences of the season," gathered "to listen to the stories of the Colored Veterans." For white veterans these "campfires" had been a frequent post entertainment that allowed former soldiers to relive their army experiences, sharing again the camaraderie and the horror of those events, and in the very retelling, relieve the pain still present in their memory. Following the black veterans' stories (which have not been preserved), two white members rose to praise the black veterans, and Reverend J. Sulla Cooper, pastor of the A.M.E. Zion Church, spoke as well. The evening ended with selections from the Zion choir. Although they had to wait nearly three decades to address the membership, the black members of Post 10 turned the occasion into a broader celebration of their collective history.[34]

Finally, that fall, Webber's attention turned again to politics. He saw in Republican William McKinley's nomination "a great Glory for the people: the Rich and poor gave one consent to the great name of McKinley."[35] In the defining parade of that presidential campaign in Worcester, 15,000 Republicans massed for McKinley on the night of October 31. Marching through the city by battalions, organized by nationality and work group, the parade went long into the night. While the thirty "colored waiters of Rebboli & Sons, caterers . . . attracted much attention," the most impressive single contingent was the 2,500 men of Washburn and Moen, who constituted the fourth battalion. The office clerks all wore "gold bugs something over six inches long," and "all the employees carried yellow wire canes of various designs"—each made by the firm for the occasion to symbolize support for McKinley's defense of the gold standard. In addition, many of these marchers "wore knots of red, white and blue ribbon, either as neckties or in the lapels of their coats." At the head of this massive column was its commander, Philip W. Moen, assisted by nine aides. One of those aides, undoubtedly attired in gold pin and cane, standing close to "Master Philly," was the seventy-year-old Amos Webber.[36]

When McKinley defeated William Jennings Bryan, carrying Worcester by almost three to one, and Webber's own ward by better than five to one, the Washburn and Moen messenger exulted. The city's streets "were all ablaze with lights to celebrate the great victory," he recorded. "Brooms carried to sweep all the bad popocrats into the Pacific Ocean," he crowed, in his one reference to the Populist-Democratic fusion movement that supported Bryan. A proud Webber marched in the Republican victory parade a few days later, feeling that "the Heart of the commonwealth throbbed with renewed patriotism at the celebration of the victory of sound money and National Honor."[37]

Webber's politics remained Republican, and he no longer questioned that loyalty in light of the party's actual racial policy: political options proved elusive in this era of legal segregation and racial violence. But neither he nor other black activists completely lacked alternatives. In his recognition of men like William W. Rice and in the particular manner in which black veterans finally participated in the campfires, Webber and other black citizens in the city reaffirmed their understanding of the meaning of the war for freedom, asserted its contemporary moral relevance as clearly as they could, and transmitted those values to a rising generation. This neither eliminated political contradictions nor could transform a race-based public culture, but it did allow these men and women to create in their time against immense odds a sustained consciousness of themselves as a community defined.

———

As AMOS WEBBER entered his eighth decade, his days remained as full as they had been years earlier. His commitments to the three fraternal orders continued to occupy his time, as did meetings of the GAR.[38] He attended the dedication of the new Union Church and Chapel, the latter in commemoration of Philip L. Moen, and he reported that Maria Moen's will continued her husband's charity with a contribution to his scholarship fund at Hampton Institute in Virginia.[39] Webber celebrated Isaac Mason's seventy-fifth birthday, Queen Victoria's Diamond Jubilee, and the Fitzsimmons-Corbett prizefight, and more solemnly commemorated the thirty-second anniversary of Lincoln's assassination.[40] He brought suit in Worcester court, charging Charles E. Martin with breach of contract in a dispute over Webber's purchase of a horse, and won the case.[41] He recorded the temperature daily, noted fires, drownings, and disasters, and preserved a wry humor. "The saloons were empty all night," he explained during a particularly heavy snowstorm, "that is a sign the storm was a bad one."[42] On Labor Day in September 1897, Webber applauded the "1500 Worcester wage earners, every man a King who marched in the parade . . . Old Glory was conspicuous everywhere."[43]

Through all this activity Webber still reported to work daily. Observing the opening of the new post office building that year, he proudly wrote: "First Mail from the Wire Mill by A. *Webber* Messenger."[44] But then, with no warning, on October 1, 1897: "Left Washburn & Moen Service to day." So abrupt a notice after thirty-six years of employment. On the last day of October, another terse note: "Went to Rutland Massachusetts consumptive Hospital".[45]

Webber's thoughts on retirement, the nature of his illness, or the extent of his stay in the hospital, some fifteen miles northwest of Worcester, all remain unknown, lost in the silences between his words. He did keep up his notations and his entries and probably went to the Grove Street plant each day to record his data and pass part of his days. Those days, however, demanded that this lifelong eulogist turn his attention more and more to his friends. In recent years death had claimed William Brown, Charles Bulah, Francis A. Clough, A. F. Clark, Alfred Edwards, William H. Jankins, Alexander F. Hemenway, Tower Hazard (father of Roswell), and Matilda Waller, the wife of John. For each he had at least a comment.[46] In 1898 Isaac Mason, one of Webber's oldest Worcester friends, died. Webber memorialized him with the inscription "Born in Slavery; Dies a Leader;". The following year William Anderson, Mason's brother, passed away. The Webbers, friends and neighbors to this charter member of North Star Lodge for more than thirty-three years, both sent wreaths, and the chronicler proclaimed of Anderson: "Born a slave, die a Citizen."[47]

From one perspective Webber's life seemed to be unraveling. The death of friends surrounded him, his health grew frailer, and his politics seemed irrelevant. The same year he boosted William McKinley, for example, the U.S. Supreme Court, by a seven-to-one vote, affirmed as constitutional the "separate but equal" doctrine that devastated efforts to provide common schooling for white and black children. The majority decision in *Plessy* v. *Ferguson*, written by Justice Henry Billings Brown (a Republican appointed by Benjamin Harrison), laid waste to Webber's hopeful 1883 commentary on the segregated provisions of Stephen Girard's philanthropy. Racial progress and school integration appeared far more difficult after the Court enshrined racial distinctions as the law of the land.[48]

But the actions Amos and Lizzie Webber took in the years that followed suggest that, if political influence lay beyond their reach, they could use what resources they possessed to assist black Worcester in creating additional institutions to counter the effects of racial segregation. Spurred perhaps by the gradual disintegration of the local branch of the Massachusetts Citizens Equal Rights Association, a group of Worcester's black women formed the Women's Progressive Club in 1898. Rooted in the A.M.E. Zion congregation, the club encouraged "cooperation among its members [and] mutual improvement," and made plans to establish a day nursery for children and a home for the needy.[49] Two years later, many of these women formed the Lucy Stone

Club, named after the famous and fiery suffragette, to raise money to establish a home "for old folks and orphans of our race." Lizzie Webber and Estelle Pickney Clough served as vice presidents, and Mrs. Walter Coshburn presided. Amos Webber and the husbands of the other women officers formed a board of advisors. When the Women's Progressive Club incorporated in 1900, it also absorbed the Lucy Stone Club. Each had already affiliated with the Federation of Colored Women's Clubs of America. (That group had held its first national convention in Boston in 1895, where, under a large portrait of Lucy Stone, the more than 100 delegates had elected Mrs. Booker T. Washington president.)[50]

These black women and their men threw themselves into the effort to found a home for the aged. Perhaps none were so actively involved as the Webbers. In July 1900 the couple sold "the Webber homestead" to the Lucy Stone Club and their property of thirty-four years became the home "for aged colored people and homeless girls of the colored race." A well-received fund-raising drive was even then in progress, and counted among its supporters many of the city's white elites. But the Webbers, who continued to reside in the house, involved themselves more deeply in the project: "Both Mr. Webber and his wife are interested in the work," the *Evening Post* reported "and will assist in the starting of the home and its maintenance." Without children themselves, the Webbers utilized their resources to further the commitments of a lifetime.[51]

Managed by the Women's Progressive Club, the home filled an important need. The intention of these women reflected a clear recognition of the significantly higher death rate of black children in the Commonwealth, while elderly blacks had few options in late-nineteenth-century Massachusetts beyond family.[52] Meeting monthly, the women attended to the business of the home, held fairs, raffles, and other benefits to raise money, and hired a matron to operate the residence. Day care was provided for children, a few older residents were fed and housed, and an occasional woman used the home as a way station following hospitalization for a serious illness. For a number of years following the death of her husband, William, Mary Anderson, a community activist, neighbor of the Webbers, and "our oldest inmate"—in the words of the club's secretary—resided in the home.[53]

Lizzie Webber remained quite active in the club, even into her seventies. Three times in 1904, when she was seventy-five years old, she hosted the monthly meeting of the club, which usually followed a prescribed format. The president, Jane B. Collins, generally opened the meetings with the hymn "Blest Be the Tie," which was followed by the Lord's Prayer. The business meeting came next, with monthly reports of the funds solicited by members. The Worcester women often read papers "in regards to club work" written by delegates to national meetings, and they prepared for a local convention of black clubwomen by holding a salad supper and other fund-raisers. Rooted in the church, and connected to a secular yet church-based national organization, these women maintained their local organization, ran the home, and constantly solicited black Worcester for funds. As with the fraternal lodge and the church, black residents responded in support of an organization they collectively held in great esteem.[54]

Inevitably, time itself exerted its demands on this still active couple. In the fall and winter of 1903–1904, Amos Webber's seventy-seven years and his ailments gathered their forces once again, and this time he lacked the resiliency to respond. In September 1903, weakened in body and spirit, he penned his last full entry in the chronicle he had begun half a century earlier, a brief obituary of Elijah B. Stoddard, a former mayor of Worcester. With a noticeably shaky hand he maintained his temperature records through February 1904, and recorded his last comment on February 22: "Gen[l] Washington Born 1732." During this same month he clipped from a paper a notice of the death of Senator Mark Hanna, a Republican stalwart and former campaign manager for William McKinley.[55]

On Thursday, March 24, 1904, at 2:30 P.M. on the afternoon of his fifty-second wedding anniversary, Amos Webber died, at home, after a short bout with pneumonia. That evening Webber's death was reported to the weekly meeting of Post 10, GAR, where a dwindling group of veterans discussed the meaning of this, the thirteenth death of a member since the start of the new year.

On Sunday, March 27, his widow received mourners at her home. For four hours, between 10:00 A.M. and 2:00 P.M., Lizzie Webber received "a large number" of friends, lodge brothers, co-workers, and neighbors. "The house was filled with people," one reporter noted, all of whom filed past the open coffin, paying their last respects and offering condolences to his wife. Surrounding the casket were wreaths sent by Lizzie Webber, the city's black fraternal organizations, numerous black friends, and the two living officials of the old Washburn and Moen firm, Philip W. Moen and Charles W. Washburn. Charles Clark, a black veteran, was present, at attention.

In the open casket lay Amos Webber, dressed in the uniform of a grand commander of the Knights Templar, the exalted Masonic organization. Over the edge of the casket lay draped an American flag, and on it rested the regalia of the Knights of Pythias. Near the casket, on the floor, was Webber's violin with a string "broken and hanging." At 2:00 P.M., Reverend J. Francis Lee, pastor of the A.M.E. Zion Church, offered the opening prayer. He was followed by Reverend Charles E. Simmons, the GAR chaplain and white Baptist minister instrumental in organizing Worcester's black Baptist congregation, who officiated at the funeral service. Simmons "read the scripture and spoke briefly of the notable life of Mr. Webber."

At the conclusion of the service, the mourners bore the body to a waiting horse-drawn hearse, escorted the widow to a carriage, and themselves entered carriages for the nearly four-mile trip to the Webber burial plot in Hope Cemetery. Wearing the regalia and bedecked with the artifacts of his intense moral and political commitments, Amos Webber took to the city streets for the last time.

From Liberty Street the cortege made its way west a few blocks to Main Street, and it followed that gently curving central artery south to Webster Square, past the lodge rooms, meeting halls, businesses, and many of the churches Amos Webber had frequented in his forty-three years in Worcester. A left onto Webster Street brought the procession, after half a mile, to the cemetery's Chapel Gate. A short distance up the hill was section 37, and the Webber grave site was located on the hill's eastern slope, adjacent to the roadway.

The day was mild and clear as the mourners surrounded the site. Reverend Hiram Conway, pastor of the John Street Baptist Church (as the Mt. Olive church had been renamed), gave the graveside prayers. His friends then lowered Amos Webber into the grave on the far right of the plot, one removed from his son's resting place. The mourners filled in the grave and the widow may have taken one more moment of silent prayer before the cortege made its way back to Liberty Street.[56]

Some weeks later, in a ceremony we have no record of, stonemasons placed a small, simple granite marker at the head of Amos Webber's grave. Its only ornamentation was a shieldlike border that framed this proud and dignified man's lasting affirmation of his life's meaning:

Q. M. Sgt.
Amos Webber
CO. D.
5 MASS. CAV.

Lizzie Webber mourned her husband of more than half a century but took solace in the support of friends and especially of her co-workers in the Women's Progressive Club. Six weeks after the

Amos Webber's gravestone, Hope Cemetery, Worcester. *Courtesy of the author*

Lizzie S. Webber's gravestone, Hope Cemetery, Worcester. *Courtesy of the author*

funeral, the club held its meeting at Mrs. Webber's home, an act of support for this widow in her painful transition. But Lizzie Webber too was ailing, and on September 12, 1904, she passed away. Not surprisingly, no obituaries appeared in the press. The front page of the next day's *Evening Post* mourned the sudden death of the forty-six-year-old Philip W. Moen, once the "Master Philly" her husband shepherded through Worcester's streets. But even had that odd coincidence not blurred notice of her passing, the public silence about her death followed the contours of her life in Worcester with her husband. But she was remembered. Her friends in the Women's Progressive Club memorialized her privately and tenderly: "The club will mourn the loss of a dear and faithful member of the club, Mrs. Web[b]er. Her death is the first one since the club's existence."[57]

On September 14, Lizzie Webber's cortege followed her husband's path to Hope Cemetery. There her body was lowered into the middle grave, between son and husband, uniting the family in death as she had given it a private sustaining cohesion in life. Her gravestone, erected some weeks later, possibly by her club friends, affirmed her complex, basic commitment:

LIZZIE S.
wife of
Amos Webber
1829–1904
Gone but not forgotten

Epilogue

***

AMOS WEBBER'S ARTICULATENESS in examining his world can not obscure the fact that major portions of that world are comprehensible only in his silences. His persistent moral emphasis over a lifetime assumed a fuller meaning against the backdrop of what he did not discuss. Never did he explore the dislocation that poverty, prejudice, or what he would have termed immorality caused black individuals and their families. Nor did he ever recognize in his chronicle that subculture of saloons, brothels, and street life, except infrequently to draw from a particularly lurid incident a moral tale to remember. He was not unaware of the existence of this other world. He gave testimony at a church trial in 1857 and a Boston criminal trial in 1874, and it is inconceivable that in Worcester's small and tightly interwoven black community he could have remained oblivious of the failures and peccadilloes attributed to others in the lodge and the church. Indeed, the moral code that infused his thoughts and actions derived its social meaning from the existence of such persistent difficulties. The lodge and the church, those voluntary institutions in which members freely submitted to trials and an ensuing discipline to achieve social and spiritual redemption, were bulwarks against such forces. He chose not to record the dangers but to emphasize the path to individual and collective strength.

In similar fashion Amos Webber's insistent emphasis on the maleness of the world he inhabited assumed its specific tone in the silence about women in his chronicle. In this he was not unique among nineteenth-century American males. In Frederick Douglass's various autobiographies, to take but one example, Douglass never discussed his family life and mentioned his first wife, Anna

Murray Douglass, only honorifically. Unlike her husband, Anna Douglass shunned public life and, in sharp contrast to his eloquence, she remained illiterate until her dying day.[1] Lizzie Webber was also an illiterate woman married to an articulate man (she signed her 1904 affidavit for a widow's pension with only her mark),[2] and she too was largely absent from her husband's memoirs. But the comparison ends there, since, however limited her husband's testimony, Lizzie Webber's pronounced involvement in fraternal and church circles in both Philadelphia and Worcester allowed her to assume a central responsibility for maintaining and nurturing the institutions her husband took the more public role in directing.

If we knew nothing else but that Amos and Lizzie Webber were married for fifty-two years, lost a child early in that marriage, and worked together as closely as they did to the end of their lives, we would have cause to doubt that his silence about her indicated the lack of a bond between them. Rather, he chose that silence for other reasons. His was not an introspective diary and his conceit was that the world he inhabited was a world directed and propelled by men. But his silence about women could not fully obscure the complexity of his relationship with his wife and with the women so active in the community organizations he led.

This need to probe the shadows of Amos Webber's world, to explore the dualities found there, is also evident concerning his religious beliefs. In a chronicle that spans half a century, he rarely placed himself in church. Yet definably religious values structured his life. His sharp criticism of contemporary revivals underscored the possibility that he had experienced a youthful conversion himself. But he never said so, just as he never discussed the numerous sermons he heard preached when, in their finest regalia, he and his lodge brothers attended a black church. Perhaps the war and its horrors led to his withdrawal from the church; perhaps the intensity of a conversion experience, reinforced by his close association with the stern Robert Jones, led him to distrust less rigorous religious practices. As he again chose silence, we do not know. But he remained close to the black church, drew on its tradition of biblical prophecy and morality, and erected a moral structure to order his life that owed much to its influence.

In the construction of this moral universe, however, the influences on Amos Webber were multiple. Even before Robert Jones had become an elder, Webber had met, lived with, and been affected by Charles S. Wurts. To the extent that we know, Wurts's influence and that of other whites reinforced attitudes and lessons he had absorbed as far back as Attleborough, in the Bethlehem Colored Methodist Church. Yet while they reiterated certain values, they also opened up to Webber another world, the world of a white America not totally dominated by racists, one that he encountered again at times in the military and in Worcester. These varied influences, from whites and blacks, from lodge and church, never brought him back to church membership,[3] but in fraternalism he found a structure for his moral imperatives that allowed him to draw on both the spiritual values of the religious tradition and the more secular and universal elements of the American political tradition.

It was of this last influence that Amos Webber wrote most freely. He rooted his demand for inclusion in American political and civic life in a moral vision that evoked both the God of wrath and the promise of the Declaration of Independence. Although the collapse of Reconstruction caused a different tone to develop, he always claimed a full place for black Americans and pointed to their military sacrifices, their persistent loyalty, and their rights as citizens as justification. His demand for inclusion encompassed a belief in the essential goodness of American society, or at least of its promise. Despite the racism he well understood, he had little disagreement with his society's economic system or its broad cultural values. Where he did find fault, he pointed, as a solution, to the principles of social justice he thought embedded in the country's political tradition. These beliefs precluded other options even then apparent among some black Americans. Physical or cultural separatism from whites never appealed to him, in part because he identified so deeply as an American. The world of saloons, loose conduct, and weakened family structures he found morally offensive—he thought it marked a path toward political paralysis and personal degradation.

Amos Webber had another option as well. Aware as he was of the pressures confronting black Americans, he might have chosen a more private solution to this public, political problem. In his connections with elite whites, he could have sought the security and comfort only they might provide to selected black individuals. This he demonstrably refused to do. His life was a whirlwind of parades, meetings, speeches, and trips whose purpose was to organize and galvanize his fellow black Americans to confront the problems before them. His community involvements were not a springboard for personal gain. His relationship with Philip L. Moen was undoubtedly beneficial to him, but he never used it to distance himself from other blacks.

It is when we consider Amos Webber's persistent demand for equality in concert with his refusal to opt for a more private accommodation that we approach the complexity of this man's public sense of self. He demanded equality and developed connections with elite whites even as he remained centrally rooted in the culture and in the institutions of the black community. More the leader in Worcester than in Philadelphia, he provided moral and institutional leadership in both cities; in each he drew from his associations a personal strength and social recognition that formed the core of his identity. As a leader who never held himself above others, as a proud black man who was also a proud American, he worked incessantly to build organizations that transmitted to the next generation the values embedded in the history, rituals, and moral tales of the black American experience.

Collectively, however, neither Amos Webber, black Worcester, nor black America could provide the solutions for what bedeviled them in their communities. Their numbers remained a distinct minority, and political disfranchisement in the South, accompanied by systematic violence over decades, reduced the public black political presence to a shadow of its actual self. Yet Webber's basic response never varied. From his 1855 witness at the trial of Jane Johnson's rescuers to his storytelling at the GAR campfire forty-one years later, he asserted his right to full inclusion as an American even as he simultaneously participated in that intricate institutional overlay among black men and women. His ability to maintain both perspectives enabled him to appreciate the critical role that black organizations performed regardless of what white Americans did, even as he claimed the broader America as his own. Belittled as a porter, a janitor, and a messenger in the eyes of so many whites, he was in fact a man who could embrace an act of faith in the future and work intensely for its fulfillment. That he did not live to reach it himself reflected a lack neither of vision nor of effort.

This was Amos Webber's world. He took what he was given, built with it what he needed, and throughout lived in close connection with other blacks and with the few empathetic whites who cared about the dilemma. It was a world that remained astoundingly hidden from whites, although he explored the pathways between the black and white worlds. But too many whites thought that blacks as a people lacked a collective history or a social structure, and they therefore assumed that a man like Amos Webber was just a janitor. He knew better, and his act of faith in projecting that knowledge continued to bear fruit even eighty years after his death. As Ellen L. Hazard, the eighty-three-year-old historian of the Hazard family of Worcester County and a descendant of the Roswell Hazard who had boarded with the Webbers a century earlier, explained to an interviewer in 1984: "We all got history. Some of us just don't know it. But it's there. Just got to look for it."[4]

Amos Webber had much to do with the development and with the transmission of black Worcester's history, but his larger contribution to American life remains his chronicle, his record of the complex pain and joy of being both black and American. Through the imprint he left, we can appreciate the simple, common courage that informed his daily actions in a world he sought to engage and to change. His was not a national stage, and he was never the subject of editorial comment or headlines in the press. Yet his life, for all its quiet firmness and unspectacular valor, reveals more sharply than the lives of many more famous people how the web of daily interaction, association, and commitment bound individuals one to another in this community of principled men and women. The memory of that reality, Amos Webber affirmed time and again in his chronicle and in his life, "we cannot forget."

ACKNOWLEDGMENTS

The debts I have incurred in writing this book are sharp reminders of the collective nature of a human activity that is most often considered solitary.

Central to any scholar's work is the aid offered by librarians and archivists. While the staffs of the libraries listed in the notes were immensely helpful and supportive, three individuals stand out particularly. Richard Strassberg, archivist at the Labor-Management Documentation Center and Associate Director of the Catherwood Library at Cornell University's School of Industrial and Labor Relations, pointed me toward this book as I benefited from his thorough, professional advice in constructing another research project altogether. Florence Lathrop, the director of the Baker Library, Harvard University Graduate School of Business Administration, greatly supported me in this work. It was in that library that I first found Webber's chronicle, and first shared with Florence our common marvel at what the archives had released. Over the years she has facilitated my trips back to the Baker Library, helped in obtaining illustrations for the book, and was supportive in innumerable ways that made my task that much easier. In Philadelphia, Philip Lapsansky, the Research Librarian at the Library Company of Philadelphia, was absolutely indispensable. His vast knowledge of Afro-Americana in his and other collections, his joy in sharing it, and his irrepressible sense of the ironic led me in directions for which I am most grateful.

In addition to these professional librarians and archivists, five nonprofessionals gave me access to material held in private collections, without which this book would have been far poorer.

Walter W. Jacobs allowed me limited access to the records of the black churches in Bucks County, Pennsylvania. The late Joseph Boulware, grand secretary, and Hilda Spence, historian, of the Grand United Order of Odd Fellows, welcomed me, were generous with their time and resources, and provided me with important insights into that organization. In Worcester, Mr. and Mrs. Stanley Gutridge allowed me to read the papers of the Women's Progressive Club and spent the considerable portion of a morning sharing with me their perspectives on the development of black Worcester.

At a very early stage of the research, my friend and former chairman at the College of the Holy Cross, William Green, persisted in inviting me to return to that campus to talk about Amos Webber. My lecture was not very good, but his insistence forced me toward a deeper understanding of my subject. Other talks followed, and I learned much from the sharp queries and encouraging comments offered by audiences at Harvard University's Du Bois Center; the State University of New York, Binghamton; University of California, Davis; Emory University (twice, no less!); the Newberry Library, Chicago; Massachusetts Institute of Technology; University of California, Berkeley; and Cornell University's School of Industrial and Labor Relations.

At a critical point in an early stage of my first draft, four rough chapters received an intensely frank yet ultimately encouraging read from James R. Grossman, A. Gerd Korman, Roy Rosenzweig, Clarence E. Walker, and Shane White. Their understanding that the pleasures of friendship include such open exchanges enriches both aspects of our relationship. Comments on individual chapters, and on papers delivered at conferences drawn from those chapters, also were quite helpful, and I would like to thank Randell K. Burkett, Ileen DeVault, Tony Fels, Joseph Glatthaar, James Green, Janet Grogan, David Hackett, Robert Hutchens, Harry Katz, Roger Lane, Daniel Letwin, Walter Licht, Gary Okihiro, Richard Polenberg, Jonathan Prude, Albert Raboteau, Michael Salvatore, Katherine Stone, Joe Trotter, and Margaret Washington. The penultimate draft of the book received a most helpful read from Robert Hutchens, Harry Katz, A. Gerd Korman, Leon F. Litwack, and Roy Rosenzweig. After all this aid, I can only thank them and accept responsibility for the errors that remain.

Despite how it sometimes feels, scholars do not live solely on such intellectual exchange. Essential support of another kind was provided me by a National Endowment for the Humanities grant for a year's research, and by the Library Company of Philadelphia/ Historical Society of Pennsylvania for a summer's immersion in their rich collections. My home institution—the New York State School of Industrial and Labor Relations, Cornell University— has been wonderfully supportive. Dean David Lipsky and Direc- tor of Research Ronald Ehrenberg have provided research support for a host of purposes and have been consistently encouraging. Through their efforts I received support from the Smithers Foun- dation and the Theodore Kheel Affinity Group. They also pro- vided the funding that enabled me to hire the research assistants whose efforts proved so useful to me: Robert Bussel, Scott Nash, Rafael Olazagasti, Jonathan Sachs, and Marcy Sacks. In addition, Eileen Driscoll, director of computing, and Tim Nolan, a member of the superb computer support staff at the school, were indis- pensable as I tried to more clearly understand nineteenth-century black Worcester through the daunting methods of late-twentieth- century social science. I was also fortunate in having two superb secretaries. Lynette Malone typed the major part of the first draft, and I benefited both from her skill and from her abiding interest in Amos Webber. Laura Drysdale handled successive drafts with her accustomed skill and ability, and with a sense of humor that de- fused many a crisis. Her demands for the next chapter were a great encouragement.

The seemingly interminable research trips were made im- mensely pleasurable by the warm welcome I received from friends. In Boston Martin Blatt, and James Green and Janet Gro- gan, allowed me to all but move into their homes, as did Leonoid and Sima Kustinovich in Worcester and Roy Rosenzweig and Deborah Kaplan in the Washington, D.C., area. Michael Salva- tore and Rose Murphy in New York and Walter and Lois Licht in Philadelphia made slightly shorter stays immensely enjoyable.

My friend Bill Serrin, a journalist and professor, did not read any of the manuscript. But over the years his constant interest in and excitement about this project has encouraged me; and it was he who brought me and the project to the attention of his editor at Random House. Peter Osnos, now the publisher of Times Books, proved more than patient as I inevitably ignored the unrealistic deadline for which I had foolishly contracted. He was enthusiastic about Amos Webber and found innumerable ways to give me the same advice: "Just get it down." Henry Ferris, my initial editor, was quite helpful, and Geoff Shandler's insights have been enormously important in my preparation of the final manuscript.

During the writing of this book, my older daughter, Gabriella, became an adult and my second daughter, Nora, entered full teenagehood. While I know they learned more about Amos Webber than they ever bargained for, their support and understanding of both my physical absences and my preoccupations with the nineteenth century were more than I could ever ask for. As for the woman to whom this book is dedicated, there are no words to describe what she has brought to this book and to my life.

Notes

For full facts of publication of books and articles cited in these notes, see the bibliography.

The following abbreviations are used in these notes:

AB Abraham Barker Papers, Historical Society of Pennsylvania, Philadelphia

ACP Association of Colored Peoples, Record Books (personal possession of Stanley H. Gutridge, Worcester)

AH Alexander Henry Papers, Historical Society of Pennsylvania, Philadelphia

AHB Alexander Hamilton Bullock Papers, American Antiquarian Society, Worcester

ANTS Special Collections, Andover Newton Theological School, Newton Centre, Mass.

ASR A. S. Roe Contemporary Biography Scrapbooks, American Antiquarian Society, Worcester

ASW American Steel and Wire Collection, Baker Library, Harvard University Graduate School of Business Administration, Boston

AWT Amos Webber Thermometer Record and Diary, American Steel and Wire Collection, Baker Library, Harvard University Graduate School of Business Administration, Boston

BCHS Bucks County Historical Society, Doylestown, Pa.

BF Brown Family Papers, American Antiquarian Society, Worcester

BFB Benjamin F. Butler Papers, Library of Congress, Washington, D.C.

BGW Bert Green Wilder Papers, Division of Rare and Manuscript Collections, Cornell University Library, Ithaca, N.Y.

BTW Booker T. Washington Papers, Library of Congress, Washington, D.C.

CAF-LC Christian A. Fleetwood Papers, Library of Congress, Washington, D.C.

CAP Philadelphia City Archives, City Hall Annex, Philadelphia

CCW Caleb Cresson Wister Collection, Historical Society of Pennsylvania, Philadelphia

CGC Cephas G. Childs Notebooks, Historical Society of Pennsylvania, Philadelphia

COW Worcester County, Massachusetts Papers, American Antiquarian Society, Worcester

CPRW Worcester County Probate Records, Registry of Probate, Worcester County Court House, Worcester

CSW Wurts Family Papers, Historical Society of Pennsylvania, Philadelphia

CW Worcester, Massachusetts Collection, American Antiquarian Society, Worcester

DF Dryer Family Papers, New-York Historical Society, New York City

DJ Duncan-Jones Collection, New Hampshire Historical Society, Concord, N.H.

EC Edwin Conant Papers, American Antiquarian Society, Worcester

EWB Edward Woolsey Bacon Papers, American Antiquarian Society, Worcester

FD-LC Frederick Douglass Papers, Library of Congress, Washington, D.C.

FD-SC Frederick Douglass Papers, Schomburg Center for Research in Black Culture, New York Public Library, New York City

FPR Franklin P. Rice Collection, Library of Congress, Washington, D.C.

GAR-NYHS Grand Army of the Republic Collection, New-York Historical Society, New York City

GAR-WHM Grand Army of the Republic Scrapbooks, Worcester Historical Museum, Worcester

GFH George Frisbie Hoar Papers, Massachusetts Historical Society Library, Boston

GUOOF Grand United Order of Odd Fellows Archives, Philadelphia

HACW Home for Aged Colored Women Papers, Massachusetts Historical Society Library, Boston

HAS Henry Albert Stimson Papers, New-York Historical Society, New York City

HAW Henry Alexander Wise Papers, American Antiquarian Society, Worcester

JAA John A. Andrew Papers, Massachusetts Historical Society Library, Boston

JAJ John Albert Johnson Papers, Schomburg Center for Research in Black Culture, New York Public Library, New York City

JDL John Davis Long Papers, Massachusetts Historical Society Library, Boston

JR   Jonathan Roberts Family Papers, Library of Congress, Washington, D.C.

JRB   John Rutter Brooke Papers, Historical Society of Pennsylvania, Philadelphia

JW   Joseph Watson Papers, Historical Society of Pennsylvania, Philadelphia

LES   Leverett E. Seymour Papers, New-York Historical Society, New York City

LG   Leon Gardiner Collection, Historical Society of Pennsylvania, Philadelphia

LHC   Louis Henry Carpenter Papers, Historical Society of Pennsylvania, Philadelphia

LSC   Lucy Stone Club Collection, American Antiquarian Society, Worcester

LSCPC   Lombard Street Central Presbyterian Church Collection, Presbyterian Historical Association, Philadelphia

PAS   Pennsylvania Abolition Society Collection, Historical Society of Pennsylvania, Philadelphia

PHA   Presbyterian Historical Association Records, Philadelphia

PSCC   Pennsylvania State Constitutional Convention Scrapbook, Historical Society of Pennsylvania, Philadelphia

RGD   R. G. Dun & Company Collection, Baker Library, Harvard University Graduate School of Business Administration, Boston

RG15   Record Group 15, Civil War Pension Files, National Archives, Washington, D.C.

RG94   Record Group 94, Records of the Adjutant General's Office, Civil War Military Records, National Archives, Washington, D.C.

RG153   Record Group 153, Records of the Judge Advocate General's Office, U. S. Army, National Archives, Washington, D.C.

SB   Samuel Bell Papers, New Hampshire Historical Society, Concord, N.H.

SMC   Society Miscellaneous Collection, Historical Society of Pennsylvania, Philadelphia

SPC   Salmon P. Chase Papers, Historical Society of Pennsylvania, Philadelphia

USA   United States Army, Worcester District: Civil War Draft Records, American Antiquarian Society, Worcester

VCC   Vigilant Committee Collection, Historical Society of Pennsylvania, Philadelphia

WAW   William Augustus Willoughby Papers, American Antiquarian Society, Worcester

WBP   City of Philadelphia, Will Books, microfilm, Historical Society of Pennsylvania, Philadelphia

WG   Warren Goodale Papers, Massachusetts Historical Society Library, Boston

WH   William Hamilton Papers, Library of Congress, Washington, D.C.

WHM   Miscellaneous Collections, Worcester Historical Museum, Worcester

WMD   William Morris Davis Correspondence, Historical Society of Pennsylvania, Philadelphia

WSLB   William Still Letterpress Book, microfilm, Historical Society of Pennsylvania, Philadelphia

WSP   Woodbury Smith Papers, Haverford College Library, Haverford, Pa.

Introduction

1. Boston *Advocate,* June 5, 1886; New York *Freeman,* June 5, 1886; Worcester *Daily Telegram,* May 28, 29, 1886; Worcester *Evening Gazette,* May 27, 28, 29, 1886.

2. AWT, 5:35 (May 28, 1886).

1. Into the City

1. AW, death certificate [copy], RG15; AW, Company Muster Roll, Fifth Massachusetts Cavalry, January 29, 1864, RG94; U.S. Bureau of Census, Tenth Census of the United States, manuscript schedules, Worcester, Mass., 1880, entry for Lizzie Webber, 567-60883-6 [microfilm]; AW obituary, untitled clipping, March 24, 1904, ASR. Attleborough was renamed Langehorn in 1877. For information on Samuel Webber, I am indebted to Walter W. Jacobs, Jr., the historian of the Bethlehem Colored Methodist Church, whom I interviewed on June 28, 1989.

2. Stevenson W. Fletcher, *Pennsylvania Agriculture and Country Life, 1640–1840,* 116, 117; U.S. Census Office, *Fifth Census,* 8; Walter M. Jacobs, Jr., "Churches of the Black Communities in Bucks County," 53.

3. In contrast, the percentage of blacks in Bucks County in 1830 was 3 percent; in Philadelphia, on the eve of the great European migration, the figure was 8.2 percent. See U.S. Census Office, *Fifth Census,* 60–61; W. E. B. DuBois, *The Philadelphia Negro,* 49.

4. Thomas F. Gordon, *A Gazetteer of the State of Pennsylvania,* 20; J. H. Battle, ed., *History of Bucks County, Pennsylvania,* 450.

5. Sherman Day, *Historical Collections of the State of Pennsylvania . . . ,* 151. See U.S. Census Office, *Compendium . . . of the United States . . . Sixth Census . . . ,* 27; U.S. Census Office, *Statistics of the United States . . . Sixth Census . . . ,* 154–55.

6. Terry A. McNealy, "Sources for Black Genealogy in Bucks County," 4; W. Jacobs, "Churches of the Black Communities," 53; Milton C. Sernett, *Black Religion and American Evangelicalism,* 122–23; Clarence E. Walker, *A Rock in a Weary Land,* ch. 1.

7. W. Jacobs, "Churches of the Black Communities," 53–55; John W. Lee, *A Brief Sketch of the Presbyterian Church . . . ,* 4; Bucks County Society for the Promotion of Temperance, *First Annual Report . . . ,* 3; Walter W. Jacobs, Jr., "Colored Methodist Society of Attleborough, 1809–1817," typescript, African Methodist Episcopal Church Files,

BCHS; David E. Swift, *Black Prophets of Justice,* 32. For a brief account of AW's educational experience as a youth, see untitled clipping, March 24, 1904, ASR. See U.S. Census Office, *Fifth Census,* 60–61, for Middletown Township's population figures, by race, in 1830.

8. Edward H. Magill, "When Men Were Sold," 497–500; Minute Book, Vigilant Committee, December 4, 10, 1839, VCC; Charles L. Blockson, *The Underground Railroad in Pennsylvania,* 36; William W. H. Davis, *The History of Bucks County . . . ,* 800.

9. Blockson, *Underground Railroad in Pennsylvania,* 35–36; W. Jacobs, "Colored Methodist Society of Attleborough," A.M.E. Church Files, BCHS.

10. Magill, "When Men Were Sold," 517–18.

11. C. Walker, *Rock in a Weary Land,* especially 15–18, 26–29.

12. For Philadelphia, for example, see John Henderson to [Joseph Watson], January 12, 1826, folder 4; Joseph Watson to J. W. Hamilton, February 24, 1827, folder 4; Joshua Bucher to Joseph Watson, January 17, March 23, 1827, folder 6; all in JW. See also John W. Blassingame, ed., *Slave Testimony,* 178–84; Solomon Northrup, *Twelve Years a Slave,* passim. On the decline in kidnappings, see Edward Raymond Turner, *The Negro in Pennsylvania,* 117–18; J. Thomas Scharf and Thompson Westcott, *History of Philadelphia,* vol. 1, 617.

13. Bucks County *Intelligencer,* March 10, 1874; Battle, *History of Bucks County,* 352; Blockson, *Underground Railroad in Pennsylvania,* 35–36; Janice L. Painter, "Looking Back," 64; Magill, "When Men Were Sold," 511–14; Joseph A. Boromé, "The Vigilant Committee of Philadelphia," 320–23.

14. Paul Finkelman, "*Prigg v. Pennsylvania* and Northern State Courts," 6–12, 17–21, 27–30; Turner, *Negro in Pennsylvania,* 236–38. In 1847, Pennsylvania enacted a law that prohibited state officials from enforcing the 1793 Fugitive Slave Act, and denied to masters the right of transmit for slaves through the state without altering their condition of servitude. Previously, slaves could reside in the state for up to six months without becoming free.

15. See Edward Price, "The Black Voting Rights Issue in Pennsylvania 1780–1900," for a discussion of black voting in Bucks and six other Pennsylvania counties. Philadelphia County, which contained the largest black population in the state, did not allow black men to vote.

16. Turner, *Negro in Pennsylvania,* 169–75, 188; Leon F. Litwack, *North of Slavery,* 84–87; J. L. Painter, "Looking Back," 65; [John Fox,] *Opinion of the Honorable John Fox . . . ,* 3–4, 8, 13; Lyle L. Rosenberger, "Black Suffrage in Bucks County," 29; Charles Brown, comp., Pennsylvania State Constitutional Convention Scrapbook, 1837–1838 (n.p., n.d.), PSCC. The Doylestown *Democrat* is quoted in Painter, 65.

17. Joseph John Gurney, *A Journey in North America . . . ,* 102.

18. Gary B. Nash, *Forging Freedom,* 134–36; Theodore Hershberg, "Free Blacks in Antebellum Philadelphia," 375. On the percentage born outside the city, see Edward Needles, *Ten Years' Progress,* 6–7. For the age and gender of the black population see U.S. Census Office, *Fifth Census,* 8, 64–65; Society of Friends, *A Statistical Inquiry . . . ,* 5; U.S. Bureau of Census, *Population of the United States in 1860,* 410–11.

Nash argues that the gender imbalance in the 1820 federal census was a result of the undercounting of black men. This is at least questionable, given the fact that successive federal census data and the 1847 Quaker census report similar percentile differences over the forty year period 1820–1860. See Nash, *Forging Freedom*, 135–37.

19. U.S. Census Office, *Compendium . . . of the United States . . . Sixth Census . . . ,* 24–26; Russell F. Weigley, *Philadelphia*, 280. The figure for Philadelphia (258,126) included the city proper and the county, which contained most of the manufacturing sites. In 1854, the city and county consolidated into one urban entity.

20. DuBois, *Philadelphia Negro*, 46, 47, 49.

21. The four wards containing most of Philadelphia's blacks were the Fourth, Fifth, Seventh, and Eighth; see U.S. Bureau of Census, *Population of the United States in 1860*, 431–32; Sam Bass Warner, *The Private City*, 55. On property holding, see Bruce Laurie, *Working People of Philadelphia*, 46; Society of Friends, *A Statistical Inquiry . . . ,* 12–14; Theodore Hershberg and Henry Williams, "Mulattoes and Blacks," 415–16. On free people of color living in white families, see Pennsylvania Society for the Promotion of the Abolition of Slavery, *The Present State and Condition of the Free People of Color . . . ,* 6; Society of Friends, *A Statistical Inquiry . . . ,* 5.

22. Scharf and Westcott, *History of Philadelphia*, vol. 3, 2236, 2238; Pennsylvania Society for the . . . Abolition of Slavery, *Present State and Condition of the Free People*, 12; Hershberg, "Free Blacks in Antebellum Philadelphia," 376; Statistics on Education and Employment of the Colored People of Philadelphia, vol. 2, 44, PAS; Benjamin C. Bacon, *Statistics of the Colored People of Philadelphia*, 13–15; Hershberg and Williams, "Mulattoes and Blacks," 409–10; Turner, *Negro in Pennsylvania*, 148; Charles Lyell, *Travels in North America . . . ,* vol. 1, 207; Union Benevolent Association, *Report of the Ladies' Branch . . . ,* 7–8.

23. Hershberg, "Free Blacks in Antebellum Philadelphia," 370–72; Hershberg and Williams, "Mulattoes and Blacks," 409–12, 422; Nash, *Forging Freedom*, 219. On the issue of crime, see Nash, *Forging Freedom*, 157–58, 213–14, and Roger Lane, *Roots of Violence in Black Philadelphia, 1860–1900*, passim.

24. *Register of Trades of the Colored People . . . ,* n.p.; Bacon, *Statistics of the Colored People*, 12–15; Hershberg, "Free Blacks in Antebellum Philadelphia," 376. On the important social role of black barbers see Edward S. Abdy, *Journal of a Residence . . . ,* vol. 3, 185–86.

25. Hershberg, "Free Blacks in Antebellum Philadelphia," 370–72, 382.

26. Society of Friends, *A Statistical Inquiry . . . ,* 12–14.

27. For broad overviews on the class structure in nineteenth-century black America, see August Meier, "Negro Class Structure and Ideology in the Age of Booker T. Washington," 258–66; Orlando Patterson, "Toward a Study of Black America," 476–86; Williard B. Gatewood, Jr., "Aristocrats of Color," 3–20.

28. Hershberg and Williams, "Mulattoes and Blacks," 395–98; Hershberg, "Free Blacks in Antebellum Philadelphia," 378–82.

29. Scharf and Westcott, *History of Philadelphia*, vol. 1, 624, 637–38, 641–42, 654–55; Turner, *Negro in Pennsylvania*, 146. Abdy, *Journal of a*

Residence . . . , vol. 3, 119, 183–84, 325–26, 330–31; Laurie, *Working People of Philadelphia,* 63–64; S. B. Warner, *Private City,* 128–29; Philadelphia *Public Ledger,* May 18, 19, 21, 22, 25, 1838; Ira V. Brown, *The Negro in Pennsylvania History,* 25–26; Committee Report on Philadelphia Race Riot, [1834,] box 42, folder 8, PAS.

See Leonard L. Richards, *"Gentlemen of Property and Standing,"* for an insightful analysis of the social composition of leaders and participants in these riots. In New York City's race riots of the previous month, the lit candle in the window also designated white residents. See Swift, *Black Prophets of Justice,* 68.

30. Philadelphia *Public Ledger,* August 2, 3, 4, 5, 6, 8, 10, 1842; Howard O. Sprogle, *The Philadelphia Police, Past and Present,* 77–78; Boromé, "Vigilant Committee," 326; Elizabeth M. Geffen, "Violence in Philadelphia in the 1840's and 1850's," 387; Donald Yacovone, "The Transformation of the Black Temperance Movement, 1827–1854" 294; Julie Winch, *Philadelphia's Black Elite,* 149–50; Frederick Douglass, "Pioneers in a Holy Cause," speech given at Canandaigua, New York, August 2, 1847, in John W. Blassingame, ed., *The Frederick Douglass Papers,* vol. 2, 72.

31. Philadelphia *Public Ledger,* August 4, 5, 1842.

32. Winch, *Philadelphia's Black Elite,* 150–51.

33. Frederick Douglass, "Intemperance Viewed in Connection with Slavery," speech given at Glasgow, Scotland, February 18, 1846, in Blassingame, *Frederick Douglass Papers,* vol. 1, 167–70.

34. Turner, *Negro in Pennsylvania,* 253; DuBois, *Philadelphia Negro,* 32, 46; Warner, *Private City,* 106; William Dusinberre, *Civil War Issues in Philadelphia, 1856–1865,* 20–21. It should be noted that even at 4 percent, Philadelphia's black population maintained a higher percentile ranking of any other urban black population in a free state. See Dusinberre, *Civil War Issues.*

In 1849, yet another white riot destroyed black property, and resulted in the deaths of four Philadelphians and the arrest of more than thirty. See Philadelphia *Public Ledger,* October 10, 11, 12, 13, 15, 1849; Geffen, "Violence in Philadelphia," 388; Sprogle, *Philadelphia Police,* 91–93.

2. Deeply Cherished Principles

1. Frank Willing Leach, *The Wurts Family,* n.p.; J. Thomas Scharf and Thompson Westcott, *History of Philadelphia,* vol. 1, 595, 604; "Harry Toplin Report," CSW.

2. U.S. Census Office, Seventh Census of the United States, 1850, manuscript schedules [microfilm], South Ward, Philadelphia, 156; Charles S. Wurts to "My Dear Son," August 10, 1854, CSW; Leach, *Wurts Family,* n.p.; *McElroy's Philadelphia Directory for 1859,* 786. On Wurts's economic standing, see his state and county tax bills for 1850, box 2, folder 5, CSW; Charles S. Wurts, "Will," book 42, 215–16, WBP.

3. AWT, 1:11 ([June 1859]).

4. Charles S. Wurts to "My Dear Son," August 13, 1844, box 2, folder 1, and Louisa Wurts to Charles S. Wurts, December 4, 1850, box 7, folder 23, CSW.

5. For Wurts's activities in the association, see untitled clipping, January 5, 1848, box 14, folder 10, and Wurts, draft of resignation letter, n.d. [c. 1850s], box 7, folder 42, CSW; Union Benevolent Association, *Nineteenth Annual Report . . . , 3.*

6. Untitled clipping, January 5, 1848, box 14, folder 10; Wurts, draft of resignation letter, box 7, folder 42, both in CSW; Union Benevolent Association, *Nineteenth Annual Report . . . , 5-6.*

7. AWT, 1:11 ([June 1859]). The entry was prompted by news of Wurts's death. For the official death report, see Death Register, vol. 30, 818, CAP.

8. AW to Bureau of Pension, March 12, 1898; Susan Beulah affidavit [1904]; Sarah Frances Middleton affidavit [1904], AW file, RG15. The 1880 federal census records Lizzie Webber as fifty-one years old, which would date her birth in 1829. In an affidavit filed following her husband's death in 1904, she listed her age as sixty-five. By this figure she would have been born in 1839 and was thirteen at the time of her marriage in 1852. The absence of any mention of such an early marriage by the Webbers or any of their friends over the years suggests that Lizzie Webber's age on the affidavit is probably in error. Susan Beulah's 1904 affidavit on behalf of Lizzie Webber supports this reading. Beulah testified that she and Lizzie Webber "were girls together" in New Jersey. Since Beulah was born in 1821, her description would make little sense if eighteen years separated the two women. See U.S. Bureau of Census, Tenth Census, manuscript schedules, Worcester, Mass., 1880 entry for Lizzie Webber, 567-60883-6 [microfilm]; Lizzie S. Webber affidavit, April 1, 1904; Susan Beulah affidavit [1904], both AW file, RG15.

9. Robert Jones, *Fifty Years in the Lombard Street Central Presbyterian Church,* 145–46; Records of Third Presbytery, Philadelphia, 120 (October 1845), typescript, folder MS P529, PHA.

10. On the role of the Gloucester family, see Rev. William P. White and William H. Scott, *The Presbyterian Church in Philadelphia,* 33; Andrew E. Murray, *Presbyterians and the Negro,* 32–35; Minutes of the Philadelphia Presbytery, 366 (March 9, 1824), 380 (June 8, 1824), 383 (July 22, 1824), typescript folder MS P529, PHA.

11. David E. Swift, *Black Prophets of Justice,* 109–10; Second African Presbyterian Church, *The Report of the Board of Trustees . . . for the Year 1842,* 3; Frederick Douglass, "Brethren, Rouse the Church," August 6, 1847, in John W. Blassingame, ed., *The Frederick Douglass Papers,* vol. 2, 92–93; Murray, *Presbyterians and the Negro,* 34; Jones, *Fifty Years,* 12–14; Julie Winch, *Philadelphia's Black Elite,* 157; Reverend John B. Reeve to A. P. Smith, May 23, 1911, folder MS R253s, PHA; Minutes of Session, 1:14–15 (February 26, March 7, 1845), LSCPC.

12. On Samuel and Leanah Webber, see Church Records, n.p. (March 11, 1853), Minutes of Session, 1:64 (March 11, 1853), LSCPC; on Templeton, see Statistics on Education and Employment of the Colored People of Philadelphia, 1:70, PAS; Jones, *Fifty Years,* 12–15; Reverend John B. Reeve to A. P. Smith, May 23, 1911, folder MS R253s, PHA; Affidavit of Sarah Frances Middleton [1894], AW file, RG15. AW had not yet begun his chronicle when his son was born. Limited information on the family's early years following Harry's birth can be found in AWT, 1:n.p.

(January 15, 18, September 15, 1855); Statistics on Education and Employment of the Colored People of Philadelphia, 1:70, PAS.

13. AWT, 1:n.p. (December 1, 1854).

14. Ibid.; Edwin T. Freedley, *Philadelphia and Its Manufacturers,* 372–73. For the firm's credit ratings, see Pennsylvania Book, vol. 132, 359; for Pugh's ratings, see Pennsylvania Book, vol. 131, 157, both in RGD.

15. Kathryn Kish Sklar, *Florence Kelley and the Nation's Work,* ch. 1; Ira V. Brown, *The Negro in Pennsylvania History,* 30.

16. This information is gleaned from the notations in the thermometer section of AWT, vol. 1. For information on John Walls, see AWT, 1:n.p. (November 1, 7, 1858); Death Register, vol. 29, 84, CAP.

17. See AWT, 1:1 (December 1854). This was the first entry in AW's "Local Pages" section; the very first entry in the book was the notation in the thermometer section, December 1, 1854, concerning his employment at Hart, Montgomery.

18. For the entry on the Market Street fire, see ibid., 1:17 (June 25, 1859). AW was not a co-owner of 839 Market Street; the "&" was his symbol for "etc."

19. For the entries for 1855, see ibid., 1:2 (September 1855), n.p. (January 6, 24, 1855).

20. Ibid., 1:n.p. (February 8, 1855), 2 (February 1855), n.p. (September, October, November, 1858). On John Largy (alternately spelled Largey), see ibid., 1:n.p. (January, June, July 1856; September 17, 18, 1857); on William H. Kimber, see ibid., 1:n.p. (November 3, 1856; August 7, 23, October 5, 1858; July 28, August 1, 8, 15, 1859). Kimber's entry is recorded in ibid., 1:18 (September 6, 1859); AW's comment in ibid., 1:21 (November 19, 1859).

21. Ibid., 1:13 (July 1859), 21 (December 12, 1859).

22. See, for example, Duran F. Kelley to "Dear Emma," December 30, 1863, as cited in Richard S. Offenberg and Robert Rue Parsonage, eds., *The War Letters of Duren F. Kelley, 1862–1865,* 86; on George Templeton Strong and his fascination with urban fires during the 1850s, see Allan Nevins and Milton Halsey Thomas, eds., *The Diary of George Templeton Strong,* vol. 2, 53–54, 59, 79, 139–40, 143, 146, 152, 180, 233, 260, 349. The quote is on 146.

23. On the transformation of work in antebellum America, see W. J. Rorabaugh, *The Craft Apprentice.*

24. See, for example, Twain's depiction of such attitudes in *Pudd'nhead Wilson.*

25. "Sketch of James Pollard Espy," 839–40; Paul H. Oehser, *Sons of Science,* 48; William Jones Rhees, comp., *The Smithsonian Institution,* vol. 1, 509–10; Donald Zochert, "Science and the Common Man in Ante-Bellum America," 22. Espy's 1842 directive is from the Milwaukee *Courier,* August 10, 1842, as cited in Zochert, "Science and the Common Man," 17. The quote is on 146.

26. Nathan Reingold, ed., *Science in Nineteenth-Century America,* 60–64, 92–94. Philadelphia remained the leading center of scientific thought well into the nineteenth century; see ibid., 64; Henry May, *The Enlightenment in America,* 65.

27. Reingold, *Science in Nineteenth-Century America,* 128–29; "Sketch of James Pollard Espy," 835–39; Rhees, *The Smithsonian Institution,* vol. 1, 507–11; H. A. Newton, "Memoir of Elias Loomis, 1811–1889," 217–19, 227, 254; A[rnold Henry] Guyot, "Memoir of James Henry Coffin, 1806–1873," 259–61; Oehser, *Sons of Science,* 48–50; James D. Dana, "Memoir of Arnold Guyot, 1807–1884," 325, 338.

28. See, for example, the diaries of William Armstrong, passim, WA; Sidney George Fisher, *A Philadelphia Perspective;* Nevins and Thomas, *Diary of George Templeton Strong.*

29. May, *Enlightenment in America,* 209–11.

30. Stanley M. Guralnick, "Geology and Religion Before Darwin," 118–29; George I. Chace, *The Relation of Divine Providence to Physical Law* (Boston, 1854), 6, as cited in ibid., 129.

31. AWT, 1:17 (July 1859).

32. Frederick Douglass, *My Bondage and My Freedom,* 186.

33. AWT, 1:12 (July 3, 4, 1859).

34. Ibid., 1:n.p. (January 24, February 11, 24, 1857; January 17, 1858).

35. On the introduction of gas on Anita Street specifically and Philadelphia in general, see ibid., 1:n.p. (April 12, 1860) and Cephas G. Childs, notebook 14, n.p., n.d., CGC.

36. For data on wealth and ward populations, see U.S. Bureau of Census, Eighth Census of the United States, manuscript schedules, vol. 49, 287–90; U.S. Bureau of Census, *Population of the United States in 1860,* 431–32; Theodore Hershberg and Henry Williams, "Mulattoes and Blacks," 416, 421; *McElroy's Philadelphia Directory for 1857,* 711; *McElroy's Philadelphia Directory for 1858,* 717; *McElroy's Philadelphia Directory for 1859,* 749. The black residents of Moyamensing were few but well organized: their temperance organization had infuriated white Philadelphians who then led the 1842 riot. See above, chapter 1.

37. AWT, 1:n.p. (May 24, 1858); Philadelphia *Public Ledger,* May 28, 1858.

38. AWT, 2:112 (April 19, 1871). In 1896, recording the death of a three-year-old girl, AW wrote that "[t]he parents are much affected by the sad accident of their only child." Ibid., 8:110 (June 2, 1896).

39. Ibid., 1:n.p. (February 6, 11, December 23, 25, 1858); Robert A. Warner, "Amos Gerry Beman . . . ," 217. On middle-class male culture in the mid-nineteenth century, see Elliott Gorn, *The Manly Art,* and Mark C. Carnes, *Secret Ritual and Manhood in Victorian America.*

40. AWT, 1:8–10 (June 1, 1859).

41. On gender roles and perceptions thereof, see Ann Douglas, *The Feminization of American Culture,* and Carnes, *Secret Ritual and Manhood.* For an example of AW's concern with temperance and with intemperance as a cause of individual and familial dissolution during the 1850s, see AWT, 1:n.p. (September 28, 1858), 7–8 (April 29, 1859), 14 ([July 1859]). A fuller account of the parade of the Temperance Cadets briefly discussed in AW's entry of September 28, 1858, can be found in Philadelphia *Public Ledger,* September 29, 1858. On the role of temperance in antebellum black Philadelphia, see *The Liberator,* November 10, 1848; Roslyn V. Cheagle, "The Colored Temperance Movement," 68–70; Winch, *Philadelphia's Black Elite,* 148.

42. AWT, 1:8–10 (June 1, 1859).

43. Ibid., 1:9 (June 1, 1859).

44. Ibid., 1:24 (April 7, 1860).

45. AW notes the sale of the firm in ibid., I:n.p. (September 17, 1860).

46. Ibid., 1:n.p. (March 13, May 16–17, 1860), 25–26 (June 1860) [emphasis in original]. For a brief account of the visit of the Japanese, see Scharf and Westcott, *History of Philadelphia,* vol. 1, 734; Russell F. Weigley, *Philadelphia,* 381–82.

3. A Sense of Worth

1. William T. Catto, *A Semi-Centenary Discourse . . . ,* 105–10, contains reported membership figures for the city's black churches in 1857; see Presbyterian Church, *Minutes of the General Assembly . . . ,* 1830, 88–89, for earlier membership figures.

2. David E. Swift, *Black Prophets of Justice,* 7–8; Andrew E. Murray, *Presbyterians and the Negro,* 33.

3. Murray, *Presbyterians and the Negro,* 89, 120, and ch. 4, passim; Swift, *Black Prophets of Justice,* 145, 149; Bruce Laurie, *Working People of Philadelphia, 1800–1850,* 35. On Garnet, see Joel Schor, *Henry Highland Garnet;* Sterling Stuckey, *Slave Culture,* ch. 3. Suspicion of the Presbyterian faith remained evident among black Philadelphians well after the Civil War, the Reverend Matthew Anderson reported in the late 1870s. The black residents he encountered were "prejudiced" toward Presbyterianism, a feeling he thought "inherited, being associated in their minds with the church which encouraged slavery, also, as being cold, aristocratic, pharisaical, and which had no use for the Negro more than to use him as a servant." See Anderson, *Presbyterianism. Its Relation to the Negro . . . ,* 29.

4. For examples of this dependency, see Board of Trustees, First African Presbyterian Church, to Second Pres. Church, September 13, 1813 (P533.Af 83); "Recommendations of the Presbytery of Philadelphia to Their Churches" (flier), April 19, 1837, both in PHA; "Petition, F.A.P.C. to Board of Missions of Presbyterian Church," March 30, 1850, box 4G, folder 1; "Minutes, F.A.P.C.," September 17, 1853, box 4G, folder 1, John M. [?] to Jacob C. White, n.d., box 4G, folder 4; Rev. A. Sellers May to Board of Trustees, F.A.P.C., July 5, 1886, April 4, 1887, box 4G, folder 2, all in LG. See also Murray, *Presbyterians and the Negro,* 40–41; Anderson, *Presbyterianism. Its Relation to the Negro . . . ,* 78–81.

5. AWT, 1:n.p. (April 18, 1858), 17 (September 1, 1859).

6. Ibid., 1:n.p. (March 12, 18, 20, 1858, and entry, undated, at bottom of March 1858 page), 16 (August 28, 1859). For other discussions of these revivals, see Philadelphia *Public Ledger,* July 31, 1855; March 11–24, March 29, 1858; Jeremiah Asher, *An Autobiography . . . ,* 209–10. Russell E. Francis argues erroneously that blacks were not seriously involved in the revivals of 1857–1858; see Francis, "The Religious Revival of 1858 in Philadelphia," 74.

7. Catto, *A Semi-Centenary Discourse,* 105–10; Robert Jones, *Fifty Years in the Lombard Street Central Presbyterian Church,* 11–18; Murray, *Presbyterians and the Negro,* 35; William P. White and William H. Scott,

The Presbyterian Church in Philadelphia, 77; John W. Lee, *A Brief Sketch of the Presbyterian Church . . . ,* 10–11. Opposition to Gloucester's political stance emerged within the congregation in 1848, but it was resolved. Gloucester neither moved to excommunicate the dissenters, led by Charles H. Bustill, nor did the dissenters seek another church. See Julie Winch, *Philadelphia's Black Elite,* 212–13 (n. 15).

8. Minutes of Session, 1:23–24 (March 10, 1848), 24–25 (May 10, 1848), 26 (July 14, 1848), LSCPC; White and Scott, *Presbyterian Church in Philadelphia,* 77. On problems of finances and leadership in the 1850s, see Minutes of Session, 1:61 (January 17, 1853), 62 (January 31, 1853), 98 (December 17, 1855), 100 (March 14, 1856), 105 (June 12, 1856), 110 (December 3, 1856), 128 (February 9, 1858), LSCPC. For the notice of Garnet's visit, see ibid., 1:133 (June 13, 1858). On John B. Reeve, see ibid., I:159 (January 14, 1861); Alfred Nevin, ed., *Encyclopedia of the Presbyterian Church in the United States of America,* 747–48; Charles Ripley Gillett, comp., *Alumni Catalogue of the Union Theological Seminary . . . ,* 117; Edgar Sutton Robinson, ed., *The Ministerial Directory . . . ,* 1:449.

9. Jones, *Fifty Years,* 51–52, 58; Minutes of Session, 1:60 (December 7, 1852), 80–81 (August 7, 1854), LSCPC. Robert Jones was an elder from July 1844 to June 1904; see the Church Register, 1844–1922, p. 2, LSCPC.

10. Minutes of Session, 1:116 (April 27, 1857), 116 (April 29, 1857), 118–19 (May 1, 1857), LSCPC. Burton formally reapplied for membership and was readmitted in December 1857. See ibid., 1:125 (December 1, 1857), 126 (December 6, 1857).

11. Ibid., 1:40–41 (March 28, 1851), 42 (May 8, 1851), 79 (June 1, 1854).

12. For cases involving sexual conduct, see ibid., 1:46–48 (December 3, 1851), 49–50 (December 17, 1851), 55 (March 3, 1852), 60 (December 7, 1852); see also the case of G. W. R. Hall and his wife, I:152–53 (July 30, 1860), 154 (September 18, 1860), 155 (September 26, 1860).

13. On Eliza Howe, see ibid., 1:97 (January 14, 1856), 99 (February 27, 1856), 100 (March 14, 1856). On aldermanic justice in Philadelphia, see Allen Steinberg, *The Transformation of Criminal Justice,* 43, 45–55.

14. AWT, 1:17–18 (September 3, 1859). For a discussion of the relationship between morality and political action among black Presbyterians, see Swift, *Black Prophets of Justice,* 30–31, 64–76, 109–10, 285–86; Schor, *Henry Highland Garnet,* 29–33. Julie Winch notes the difficulties this combination of religious and secular concerns created for black elites when, despite such conduct, whites nonetheless engaged in vicious racial riots and excluded blacks from employment. However, she does not recognize the broader support for this approach among many of the churchgoing working poor in black Philadelphia. See Winch, *Philadelphia's Black Elite,* 148–51. On the antislavery activity of church members, see Charles L. Blockson, *The Underground Railroad in Pennsylvania,* 13, and below, chapter 4.

15. Nancy Lester to William Still, June 4, 1858, box 9G, folder 17, LG. On religious and secular reform in antebellum America, see Timothy L. Smith, *Revivalism and Social Reform . . . ;* Robert H. Abzug, *Passionate*

Liberator; Bernard A. Weisberger, *They Gathered at the River,* especially ch. 4, 5; Martin E. Marty, *Pilgrims in Their Own Land,* especially ch. 10, 11, 12. For mention of the leadership of the First African Presbyterian Church, see Arthur Truman Boyer, comp., *Brief Historic Sketch of the First African Presbyterian Church . . . ,* 4; Tony Martin, "Race Men, Bibliophiles, and Historians," 3, 6.

16. Jones, *Fifty Years,* 58; Minutes of Session, 1:106 (July 6, 1856), 114 (April 15, 1857), 118 (April 29, 1857), 119 (May 1, 1857), LSCPC. For a related case, where the accused rejected the session's assertion that public dancing was sinful, see ibid., 1:121 (June 14, 1857).

17. Jones, *Fifty Years,* 27, 51–52; Minutes of Session, 1:7 (August 9, 1844), 48 (December 10, 1851), 60 (December 7, 1852), 75 (March 27, 1854), 165 (April 8, 1861), LSCPC.

18. Minutes of Session, 1:112 (December 26, 1856), 114–15 (April 15, 1857), LSCPC.

19. Mary Still, *An Appeal to the Females of the African Methodist Episcopal Church,* 5–7. For another example of black women's organizational involvement in the church, see *The Prologue and Constitution of the Sisterhood of the Good Angels. . . .*

20. Minutes of Session, 1:148 (May 15, 1860), LSCPC.

21. AWT, 1:n.p. (May 13, 1855); D. W. Bristol, *The Odd Fellows' Amulet,* 153–57. On the regalia, see Chas. H. Brooks, *The Official History and Manual of the Grand United Order of Odd Fellows . . . ,* 26.

22. Stevens, *The Cyclopedia of Fraternities,* 235–36; Brooks, *Official History and Manual,* 12–13, 18, 64, 84; Dorothy B. Porter, "The Organized Educational Activities of Negro Literary Societies, 1828–1846," 564; Minute Books, Sub-Committee of Management, 1:2 (March 20, 1844), 4 (May 14, 1844), 16 (December 18, 1844), GUOOF.

23. Minute Books, Sub-Committee of Management, 1:9 (September 10, 1844), 26 (July 8, 1845), 34 (November 11, 1845), 70 (December 29, 1846), GUOOF.

24. Ibid., 1:59–60 (September 18, 1846).

25. Ibid.; Leonard P. Curry, *The Free Black in Urban America, 1800–1850,* 210–11; Brooks, *Official History and Manual,* 26, 28, 31–32; Theodore Hershberg and Henry Williams, "Mulattoes and Blacks," 423.

26. Hershberg and Williams, "Mulattoes and Blacks," 422–23.

27. James B. Browning, "The Beginnings of Insurance Enterprise Among Negroes," 422.

28. Minute Books, Sub-Committee of Management, 1:21 (March 8, 1845), GUOOF.

29. Material compiled from ibid., 1:85 (July 26, 1847), n.p. (June 1, 1848), GUOOF; *McElroy's Philadelphia Directory for 1847 and 1848;* Statistics on Education and Employment of the Colored People of Philadelphia, 2 vols., PAS. On the dedication of the hall, the public parade and ceremonies that accompanied it, and the stirring sermon by Reverend Henry Highland Garnet, himself an Odd Fellow, see Philadelphia *Public Ledger,* September 3, 4, 1857. The citywide figures on black literacy (54 percent) are taken from Benjamin C. Bacon, *Statistics of the Colored People of Philadelphia,* 11. These figures are inevitably inflated, since they are based solely on assertions made during a onetime visit by

enumerators for the Quaker census of black Philadelphia; in contrast, the GUOOF figures on literacy were supported by daily experience within the Order. Thus the difference in literacy rates between Odd Fellows and the adult black population was probably larger.

30. On nineteenth-century black leaders, see Winch, *Philadelphia's Black Elite,* passim; Emma Jones Lapsansky, "Friends, Wives, and Strivings," 5–6, 23–24. On J. J. G. Bias, see Statistics on Education and Employment of the Colored of Philadelphia, 1:39, PAS; Biographical Sketch, box 2, JAJ; Daniel Alexander Payne, *Recollections of Seventy Years,* 72–73, 142; on Smith, see AWT, 2:198–99 (November 22, 1873); Philadelphia *Public Ledger,* November 15, 1873; on White, see Jacob C. White, Jr. et al., to the Session of the First [African] Presbyterian Church, April 16, 1859, box 4G, folder 1, LG; Boyer, *Brief Historic Sketch,* 12; Jacob C. White, Jr., to AW, January 1, 20, July 8, 14, 1874, Lebanon Cemetery Records (microfilm), PAS; on Bowser, see Grand United Order of Odd Fellows, *General Laws Now in Force . . . ,* 9; Brooks, *Official History and Manual,* 70–90.

31. Roslyn V. Cheagle, "The Colored Temperance Movement," 68–71; Donald Yacovone, "The Transformation of the Black Temperance Movement, 1827–1854," 296; D. B. Porter, "Organized Educational Activities of Negro Literary Societies," 557; Edward Price, "The Black Voting Rights Issue in Pennsylvania, 1780–1900," 362; *Minutes of the State Convention of Coloured Citizens of Pennsylvania . . . 1848,* 3; Joshua Woodlin, *The Masonic National Union . . . ,* 129; *Proceedings of the Colored National Convention . . . 1855,* 6–7.

32. Minute Books, Sub-Committee of Management, 1:34 (November 11, 1845), GUOOF; on Jones's role in the GUOOF, see Brooks, *Official History and Manual,* 96, 113, and Grand United Order of Odd Fellows, *General Laws,* 10.

33. Statement of the African Temperance Society, *The Northern Star and Freedmen's Advocate,* February 17, 1842, as cited in Cheagle, "Colored Temperance Movement," 22; Douglass is quoted in Yacovone, "Transformation of the Black Temperance Movement," 290. See also the account of the black women's temperance convention in Philadelphia, organized by Mrs. Eliza A. Bias and Mrs. Stephen Smith, and addressed by Reverend Henry Highland Garnet, in *The Liberator,* November 10, 1848.

34. On the role of moral reform during the 1830s, see *Minutes and Proceedings of the First Annual Convention of the People of Colour . . . 1831,* 14 and passim; *Minutes and Proceedings of the Third Annual Convention . . . 1833,* 17 and passim; *Minutes of the Fifth Annual Convention . . . 1835,* 8 and passim. For a broader discussion of moral reform, see Winch, *Philadelphia's Black Elite;* Swift, *Black Prophets of Justice;* Lapsansky, "Friends, Wives, and Strivings"; Yacovone, "Transformation of the Black Temperance Movement"; Frederick Cooper, "Elevating the Race." Dale R. Vlasek presents an interesting discussion of E. Franklin Frazier's argument that nineteenth-century blacks had only American cultural sources upon which to draw; see Vlasek, "The Economic Thought of E. Franklin Frazier." Further discussion of these and related issues can be found in Wilson Jeremiah Moses, *The Golden Age of*

Black Nationalism, 1850–1925; Stuckey, *Slave Culture;* Roger Lane, *Roots of Violence in Black Philadelphia, 1860–1900;* and Nick Salvatore, "Two Tales of a City: Nineteenth Century Black Philadelphia."

35. For accounts of the Order's parades in Philadelphia, see Account Book, 1854–1855, n.p. (November 1, 1854), GUOOF; AWT, 1:n.p. (September 2, 6, 1857); Philadelphia *Public Ledger,* September 3, 4, 1857. For an even larger parade the Order held in New York City in 1856, which contained a large Philadelphia contingent and which Garnet also addressed, see New York *Times,* September 5, 1856; New York *Tribune,* September 5, 1856; New York *Herald,* September 5, 1856.

36. Eliza Cope Harrison, ed., *Philadelphia Merchant: The Diary of Thomas P. Cope,* 468; Philadelphia *Public Ledger,* June 25, 1859. Susan G. Davis's interpretation, insofar as it emphasizes a "unified community" whose parades suggest that intent "to collectively reduce white perogatives," is misleading. Davis overlooks both the meaning of the parades for a community that was anything but unified and misses the public protection offered black marchers, even if in the name of public order rather than racial equality. See Davis, *Parades and Power,* passim, especially 156; see also William Dusinberre, *Civil War Issues in Philadelphia, 1856–1865,* 22–23. For other examples of parades of blacks, see Philadelphia *Public Ledger,* June 25, 1856, June 25, 1857; AWT, 1:n.p. (June 24, 1856), n.p. (June 21, 1857).

37. The establishment of the Household of Ruth can be followed in Brooks, *Official History and Manual,* 78–79, and Albert C. Stevens, *The Cyclopedia of Fraternities,* 237. See AWT, 1:10 (June 2, 1859), for the account of the lodge's anniversary.

38. See, for example, AWT, I:n.p. (September 11, 1855; March 17, October 9, 1856; June 1, October 4, 1857; March 17, August 30, 1858; March 17, 1859). On the fox chase, see ibid., 1:n.p. (June 22, 1856).

39. Ibid., 1:18 (September 17, 1859).

40. Ibid., 1:n.p. (June 15, 1857; September 1, 1858); Philadelphia *Public Ledger,* June 15, 1857. On the question of popular and elite culture, see Lawrence W. Levine, *Highbrow/Lowbrow.*

41. Robert F. Ulle, "Popular Black Music in Nineteenth Century Philadelphia," 21–28 (Watson is quoted on p. 23).

42. AW noted his first Greenfield concert in AWT, 1:n.p. (November 30, 1856); he recorded a second Greenfield concert in ibid., 1:n.p. (May 30, 1857).

43. James M. Trotter, *Music and Some Highly Musical People,* 68; Rayford W. Logan and Michael R. Winston, *Dictionary of American Negro Biography,* 268–70; Darlene Clark Hine, *Black Women in America,* 499–501; [Elizabeth Taylor Greenfield,] *The Black Swan at Home and Abroad,* 4–14, 23, 48–49; Eileen Southern, *The Music of Black Americans,* 103–4. Mrs. Stowe is quoted in Greenfield, *Black Swan,* 42.

44. George G. Foster, *New York by Gas-Light and Other Urban Sketches,* 142. For an example of the music a black street vendor sang to sell his wares in Philadelphia, see Southern, *Music of Black Americans,* 124.

45. For sharply different views of this youthful subculture in Philadelphia, see Gary B. Nash, *Forging Freedom* and Lane, *Roots of Violence.*

46. Payne, *Recollections of Seventy Years,* 93–94; Southern, *Music of Black Americans,* 127–29; Jacob C. White, Jr., et al., to the Session of the First [African] Presbyterian Church, April 16, 1859, box 4G, folder 1, LG.

47. Foster, *New York by Gas-Light,* 145–46; Southern, *Music of Black Americans,* 101, 105–6, 107, 109–10; Russell F. Weigley, *Philadelphia,* 264–65; Vera Brodsky Lawrence, *Strong on Music,* 131–32; Levine, *Highbrow/Lowbrow,* passim. Johnson's music is currently available on *The Music of Francis Johnson and His Contemporaries: Early Nineteenth-Century Black Composers,* Musicmasters (D 193198). My thanks to Gerd Korman for bringing this to my attention.

48. Caleb Cresson Wister, journal entry, May 16, 1866, p. 66, CCW; Ulle, "Popular Black Music," 21. On ticket prices for a variety of concerts in New York City in 1849, see Lawrence, *Strong on Music,* 581, 597, 600, 604, 607.

49. Greenfield, *Black Swan,* 11–12.

50. Nancy Lester to William Still, June 4, 1858, box 9G, folder 17, LG.

4. In the Cause of Liberty

1. William Still's account of this case can be found in his *The Underground Rail Road,* 86–97; a discussion on the number of fugitives assisted is found in Dusinberre, *Civil War Issues in Philadelphia, 1856–1865,* 52–54; Pennsylvania Anti-Slavery Society, *Fourteenth Annual Report . . . 1851,* 10. On the personal liberty law, see Paul Finkelman, "*Prigg v. Pennsylvania* and Northern State Courts," 27; Edward Raymond Turner, *The Negro in Pennsylvania,* 238–42, 244–45. For a detailed contemporary account of the Johnson case, see Philadelphia *Evening Bulletin,* December 31, 1855. For another contemporary account that focuses solely on Williamson, see Sidney George Fisher, *A Philadelphia Perspective,* 249–51 (July 24, 26, 28, September 11, 14, 15, 17, October 15, 1855). Ralph Lowell Eckert, "Antislavery Martyrdom," 521–23, is also of interest.

2. AWT, 1:n.p. (August 8–10, 1855).

3. Philadelphia *Public Ledger,* July 30, August 9, 20, November 5, 1855; AWT, 1:n.p. (November 3, 1855); Eckert, "Antislavery Martyrdom," 528–29. On Kelley's marriage to Pugh's adopted daughter in 1854, and on the hearing before Judge Kelley in 1855, see Kathryn Kish Sklar, *Florence Kelley and the Nation's Work, 1830–1900,* ch. 1.

4. William M. Davis to Henry K. Brown, August 21, 1855, WMD.

5. For discussions of black dissatisfaction with white abolitionists in general, see David E. Swift, *Black Prophets of Justice,* 93, 121–24; William H. Pease and Jane H. Pease, "Antislavery Ambivalence," 314; in Philadelphia, see Charles L. Blockson, *The Underground Railroad in Pennsylvania,* 16–17. For the history of the Vigilant Committee between 1838 and 1860, see VCC, passim, especially May 31, June 4–December 31, 1839, December 14, 1840, December 28, 1843; Bucks County *Intelligencer,* March 10, 1874; Joseph A. Boromé, "The Vigilant Committee of Philadelphia," 323, 351; Larry Gara, "William Still and the Underground Railroad," 328–29; Russell F. Weigley, *Philadelphia,* 387–88. A

thorough history that nonetheless needs to be used carefully as to some of its details is W. Still, *The Underground Rail Road*.

6. Boromé, "Vigilant Committee," 351; James L. Smith, *Autobiography . . .*, 48–50; Journal C of Station No. 2 of the Underground Railroad (Philadelphia, William Still, Agent), microfilm edition (series 5, reel 32), July 24, 1854; Vigilance Committee of Philadelphia Accounts, 1854–1857, microfilm edition (series 5, reel 32), 331, both in PAS.

7. Philadelphia *Public Ledger*, March 21, 1839, as cited in Allen Steinberg, *The Transformation of Criminal Justice*, 283 (n. 33); see also ibid., 21. For examples of collective action by blacks, see W. Still, *Underground Rail Road*, passim; Turner, *Negro in Pennsylvania*, ch. 13; and below.

8. On the Douglass lecture, see AWT, 1:n.p. (October 21, 1855); Ira V. Brown, *The Negro in Pennsylvania History*, 30.

9. Swift, *Black Prophets of Justice*, 7–8, 69–70, 120.

10. AWT, 1:n.p. (August 1, 1860), 15 (August 1, 1859). See also *The Liberator*, August 20, 1858; [?] Leiree to Mr. White, July 9, 1842, box 4G, folder 21, LG. In 1841, Stephen Gloucester and Robert Purvis of the Vigilant Committee raised funds in black churches on July 4 for the committee's work and to assist these congregations "to make suitable arrangements, for the first of August." Entries, June 14, September 2, 1841, VCC.

11. AWT, 1:4 (May 1856).

12. John W. Blassingame, ed., *The Frederick Douglass Papers*, vol. 3, 223–24; William B. Gravely, "The Dialectic of Double-Consciousness in Black American Freedom Celebrations, 1808–1863," 303–11; W. E. B. DuBois, *The Souls of Black Folk*. For an insightful account of the interaction between freedom and bondage in the formative years of the nation, see Edmund M. Morgan, *American Slavery, American Freedom*. Gary Wills offers a brilliant discussion of Lincoln's use of the Declaration of Independence to reconfigure fundamental American ideals in *Lincoln at Gettysburg*.

13. Donald Yacovone, "The Transformation of the Black Temperance Movement," 282, 286–88, 295–96; Swift, *Black Prophets of Justice*, 246, 285–86, 292–96; Joel Schor, *Henry Highland Garnet*, 29. On the convention movements, see Howard Holman Bell, *A Survey of the Negro Convention Movement, 1830–1861*, passim. Black women were quite active in leadership roles in temperance societies but were less evident in political meetings and street demonstrations; on black women and temperance, see Roslyn V. Cheagle, "The Colored Temperance Movement," 68–70; *The Liberator*, November 10, 1848. For a different view of the emphasis on morality, see Julie Winch, *Philadelphia's Black Elite*, 21–22.

14. *Appeal of Forty Thousand Citizens . . . ; Minutes of the State Convention of Colored Citizens of Pennsylvania . . . 1848; Memorial of Thirty Thousand Disfranchised Citizens of Philadelphia. . . .* On the continued resistance to black suffrage, even after the Civil War, see I. V. Brown, *Negro in Pennsylvania History*, 50.

15. On black education, see Harry C. Silcox, "Delay and Neglect," 449–56; W. E. B. DuBois, *The Philadelphia Negro*, 85–87; I. V. Brown, *Negro in Pennsylvania History*, 52–53; Dusinberre, *Civil War Issues*, 20–21; Benjamin C. Bacon, *Statistics of the Colored People of Philadel-*

phia, 8–9; Pennsylvania *Freedmen's Bulletin,* December 18, 1866, 6–9; Eliza Cope Harrison, ed., *Philadelphia Merchant: The Diary of Thomas P. Cope,* 554–55 (April 25, 1848); A. Hurst to Joseph Watson, December 1827, JW; Esther Hays to William Still, January 2, 1858, LG. A brief summary of public school developments for whites can be found in Sam Bass Warner, *The Private City,* 116–18. For a contemporary account of Quaker educational efforts among the city's black population, see Samuel Breck, "Friends Public Schools in Philadelphia," 1840, box 10B, folder 2, SMC.

16. Bacon, *Statistics of the Colored People,* 8; Jacob C. White, Jr., "Address on the Reception of Governor Pollack," May 24, 1855, box 6G, folder 18, LG.

17. Pennsylvania Equal Rights League, *Proceedings of the State Equal Rights' Convention . . . 1865 . . . ,* 20. On the issue of race and education within the black community, see *Proceedings of the Colored National Convention . . . 1855,* 10–13; *Proceedings of the State Equal Rights' Convention . . . 1865 . . . ,* 19–21; on the elite's motives, see Emma Jones Lapsansky, " 'Since They Got Those Separate Churches,' " 69, although she places too much emphasis on the elite's "class" values in relation to white working-class racial antagonism. For another view that is occasionally very insightful, see Frederick Cooper, "Elevating the Race."

18. AWT, 1:4 (January 19 [?], 1858), 8 (May 1859). On the streetcar issue, see Roger Lane, *Roots of Violence in Black Philadelphia, 1860–1900* 48; Swift, *Black Prophets of Justice,* 279; James M. McPherson, *The Negro's Civil War,* 255–61. The most detailed treatment of this issue is Philip S. Foner, "The Battle to End Discrimination Against Negroes on Philadelphia Streetcars," Parts I and II.

19. AWT, 1:15–16 (August 16, 1859); Philadelphia *Public Ledger,* August 17, 1859.

20. William Parkman to Jacob C. White, Jr., December 9, 1861, October 10, 1862, box 6G, folder 17a; J. C. White, Jr., to Thomas Hamilton, November 6, 1860, box 12G, folder 15; J. C. White, Jr., Passbook with T. Hamilton, 1860, box 12G, folder 13; all in LG. For the *Anglo-African Magazine*'s position on Haiti, see especially vol. 1, nos. 8 (August 1859), 9 (September 1859), and 11 (November 1859). For a classic statement against emigration and against race distinctions of any kind, see Robert Purvis's letter to Parker T. Smith, February 22, 1867 [copy], box 2G, folder 14, LG. See also *Proceedings of the National Emigration Convention of Colored People . . . 1854,* 33–70, for a full contemporary discussion of the merits of emigration. For a more detailed historical discussion, see Stuckey, *Slave Culture,* 179–80, 184–85; Wilson Jeremiah Moses, *The Golden Age of Black Nationalism, 1850–1925.*

21. Philadelphia *Public Ledger,* April 4, 5, 6, 7, 1859.

22. AWT, 1:5 (April 1859), n.p. (April 6, 8, 1859).

23. See [Pennsylvania Anti-Slavery Society,] *The Arrest, Trial, and Release of Daniel Webster . . . ,* passim, especially 10–12, 27.

24. On Dangerfield's stationmasters, see Henry M. Minton, *Early History of Negroes in Business in Philadelphia,* 18; Norwood P. Hallowell, *The Negro as a Soldier in the War of the Rebellion,* 1. See also the account

of the organization of the Vigilant Committee in W. Still, *The Underground Rail Road*, 610–12.

25. On James Martin, see Philadelphia *Evening Bulletin*, April 10, 1856.

26. The Moses Horner case can be followed in the Philadelphia *Public Ledger*, March 28, 29, 30, 1860; J. Thomas Scharf and Thompson Westcott, *History of Philadelphia*, vol. 1, 734; Lane, *Roots of Violence*, 49. AW's only comment was "The Slave"; see AWT, 1:n.p. (March 29, 1860). For another large demonstration, one intended to save the freeborn James Valentine from being kidnapped into slavery, see *The Liberator*, March 24, 1860; on the leaders, see Blockson, *Underground Railroad in Pennsylvania*, 24; William Leonard to William Still, October 15, 1860, box 9G, folder 15, LG.

27. AWT, 1:n.p. (October 1, 11, 1859); on Canada's growing black population during the 1850s, see Robin W. Winks, *The Blacks in Canada*, 233–46, 484–96.

28. AWT, 1:19–20 (n.d.). It is possible that AW recorded this entry at more than one time between October 16 and mid-November, after the court issued its sentence. For another contemporary diarist's account of the Harpers Ferry raid, Brown's trial and execution, and the political meaning of each, see Allan Nevins and Milton Halsey Thomas, eds., *The Diary of George Templeton Strong*, vol. 2, 464–76 (October 18–December 9, 1859).

29. Henry Alexander Wise to William C. Whitcomb, November 17, 1859, HAW; Swift, *Black Prophets of Justice*, 313; the letter to Mrs. Brown is reproduced in Benjamin Quarles, ed., *Blacks on John Brown*, 16–19. The account of the Worcester meeting is in *The Liberator*, December 16, 1859.

30. AWT, 1:n.p. (December 3, 1859); Philadelphia *Public Ledger*, December 2, 3, 5, 1859; Dusinberre, *Civil War Issues*, 86. The selection from Isaiah 58 is from verse 6.

31. Robert F. Ulle, "Popular Black Music in Nineteenth Century Philadelphia," 21.

32. For such Union meetings in Philadelphia, see AWT, 1:n.p. (December 8, 1859); Fischer, *Philadelphia Perspective*, 339 (December 5, 6, 1859), 340 (December 8, 1859); Philadelphia *Public Ledger*, December 7, 8, 1859; *The Liberator*, December 30, 1859; Scharf and Westcott, *History of Philadelphia*, 732; Frederick Douglass to John W. Huon, June 12, 1882, FD-SC.

33. AWT, 1:22–23 (December 2, 1859). For a detailed discussion of these events, see Kenneth Stampp, *America in 1857*, and Stampp, *And Then the War Came*.

5. The Spark of Manhood

1. U.S. Bureau of Census, *Population of the United States in 1860*, 431–32; Secretary of the Commonwealth, *Statistical Information . . . 1865*, 658–59, 662–63, 676–77, 736, 760; Tilden G. Edelstein, *Strange Enthusiasm*, 135; Roy Rosenzweig, *Eight Hours for What We Will*, 11–14; Secretary of the Commonwealth, *Abstract of the Census of*

Massachusetts, 1865, 80–81; Dale Baum *The Civil War Party System,* 73. Of the 7,709 foreign-born in Worcester, more than 75 percent (5,892) were born in Ireland; see Secretary of Commonwealth, *Abstract of the Census of Massachusetts, 1865,* 80–81, 298.

2. On population figures see U.S. Census Office, *Fifth Census,* 18–19; U.S. Census Office, *Compendium . . . of the United States . . . Sixth Census . . . ,* 8–10; U.S. Bureau of Census, *Population of the United States in 1860,* 218, 220, 226, 431–32; Secretary of the Commonwealth, *Abstract of the Census of the Commonwealth of Massachusetts . . . 1855,* 60–61, 220; Secretary of the Commonwealth, *Abstract of the Census of Massachusetts, 1865,* 202, 217, 233, 300; Massachusetts Bureau of Statistics of Labor, *Thirty-fourth Annual Report,* 232.

3. See the listings for AW in the successive editions of the *Worcester City Directory,* 1861–1904. On his retirement from Washburn and Moen (as Ichabod Washburn and Company was soon renamed), see AWT, 8:37 (October 1, 1897).

4. Reynolds Farley, *Growth of the Black Population,* 43, 52–53; U.S. Bureau of Census, *Population of the United States in 1860,* 38, 90, 221–25, 246, 329, 378, 414; Kenneth L. Kusmer, *A Ghetto Takes Shape,* 10; David M. Katzman, *Before the Ghetto,* 61; Secretary of the Commonwealth, *Abstract of the Census of Massachusetts, 1865,* 54–55, 202. For the data on births among Worcester's black population, see Worcester *Daily Spy,* February 2, 1861, February 1, 1862, February 7, 1863, February 5, 1864, February 4, 1865; Worcester *Evening Gazette,* February 6, 1866; U.S. Bureau of Census, *Population of the United States in 1860,* 218, 226.

5. Worcester *Daily Spy,* August 30, 1861.

6. Franklin P. Rice, ed., *The Worcester of Eighteen Hundred and Ninety-Eight,* 289–90; Edna P. Spencer, "What Color Is the Wind?," 60–61; Charles Hersey, *History of Worcester, Massachusetts,* 334.

7. Worcester *Daily Spy,* November 5, December 6, 1862; Caleb A. Wall, *Reminiscences of Worcester . . . ,* 190; Alan Ira Gordon, "Political Elites in Worcester, Massachusetts (1855–1860)" 16, 34. See also Brooke, *The Heart of the Commonwealth,* for a more detailed analysis of Worcester's antebellum politics; for an account of the Republican Party's ascendancy, see Baum, *Civil War Party System.* For a brisk account of Worcester's abolitionist movement in the 1850s, see Edelstein, *Strange Enthusiasm,* 154–96.

8. AWT, 6:77–79 (April 24, 1891); John C. Rand, comp., *One of a Thousand,* 419; William T. Hogan, *Economic History of the Iron and Steel Industry in the United States,* vol. 1, 108–9; Charles G. Washburn, *Manufacturing and Mechanical Industries of Worcester,* 37–38; Paul R. Swan, "Personal Histories of Worcester's Social and Industrial Leaders with Certain Sociological Interpretations," 18.

9. Rosenzweig, *Eight Hours for What We Will,* 12–13; C. G. Washburn, *Manufacturing and Mechanical Industries,* 37–38; Hogan, *Economic History of the Iron and Steel Industry,* vol. 1, 49, 92.

10. The information on Washburn and Moen's internal structure is gleaned from the Worcester *Daily Spy,* 1861–1865, and the Worcester *Evening Gazette,* 1865–1870. On AW's employment record, see Payroll

Book, May 1868, vol. 32, ASW. (Company payroll records are not available for earlier years.) For the city's ethnic composition in 1865, see Secretary of the Commonwealth, *Abstract of the Census of Massachusetts, 1865,* 54–55, 80–81.

11. Worcester *Daily Spy,* August 26, 1863, February 2, 1864; Secretary of the Commonwealth, *Abstract of the Census of Massachusetts, 1865,* 298.

12. For biographical information on Francis Clough, see AWT, 8:48–49 (December 11, 1894); Worcester *Evening Gazette,* February 2, 1866, December 11, 1894; entry, 7:119, ASR. On Gilbert Walker, see entry, 5:99, ASR; Massachusetts, vol. 97, 634, RGD. On Alexander F. Hemenway, see entry, 9:17, ASR. On William Brown, see Alice Bush to "My Dear Son," [March 1849,] folder 1; "Business Card, W. Brown," [1865,] folder 1; Real Estate Mortgage, July 20, 1853, and Contract, Business Partnership, April 3, 1865, folder 2, all in BF; Worcester *Evening Gazette,* November 10, 1892. On Isaac Mason, see his *Life of Isaac Mason as a Slave,* especially 9, 45–52, 55–56, 67–74; AWT, 7:25 (January 1, 1894); 8:158 (May 15, 1897); 9:167 (August 27, 1898); Worcester *Evening Gazette,* March 20, 23, 1891; August 27, 29, 1898; entry, 10:110, ASR.

13. [Primary School Committee of Boston,] *Report of the Minority . . . ,* 13; Donald M. Jacobs, "The Nineteenth Century Struggle over Segregated Education in the Boston Schools," 423–31; Leonard W. Levy and Harlan B. Phillips, "The Roberts Case," 589–90; Edelstein, *Strange Enthusiasm,* 176.

14. "The Butman Riot. October 30, 1854," 89–90, 92–93; entry, 7:119, ASR; George F. Hoar, *Autobiography of Seventy Years,* vol. 1, 182–85; Albert B. Southwick, ed., *The Journals of Stephen C. Earle, 1853–58,* 28; Edelstein, *Strange Enthusiasm,* 167–71.

15. Figures for the number of Worcester blacks between twenty and fifty years old are approximate, derived from the 1860 county population figures given by gender and age, and the city figures, given by gender only; see U.S. Bureau of Census, *Population of the United States in 1860,* 218, 226. See also clipping, n.d., folder 4, BF; Bethany Veney, *The Narrative of Bethany Veney,* 40–41. On the connection between black Masonic organization and antislavery political agitation in Boston, see Donald M. Jacobs, "William Lloyd Garrison's *Liberator* and Boston's Blacks, 1830–1865," 260–61; Austin Bearse, *Reminiscences of Fugitive-Slave Law Days in Boston,* 4, 6; Archibald H. Grimké, "Anti-Slavery Boston," 458; William Schouler, *A History of Massachusetts in the Civil War,* vol. 1, 585; William H. Upton, *Negro Masonry . . . ,* 145.

16. *The Liberator,* August 19, 26, 1859. Mobray's name is variously spelled in the primary sources: J. G. Mowbray, J. J. Mabray, etc. I have followed the spelling as it appeared in the 1880 census.

17. On residential clusters, see Olivier Zunz, *The Changing Face of Inequality.* The data on residential patterns in Worcester is taken from U.S. Bureau of Census, *Population of the United States in 1860,* 226; Secretary of the Commonwealth, *Abstract of the Census of Massachusetts, 1865,* 54–55, 80–81; Bureau of Statistics of Labor, *The Census of Massachusetts: 1875,* vol. 1, 55, 283, 294.

18. *The Liberator,* August 26, 1859.

19. James M. McPherson, *Battle Cry of Freedom*, 264, 275.

20. Anonymous, "Civil War Diary 1861," [April 15,] April 17, 18, 1861, CW; Abijah P. Marvin, *History of Worcester in the War of the Rebellion*, 25, 130–33; Worcester *Daily Spy*, April 19, 23, 25, 1861; Charlotte Forten Grimké, *The Journals of Charlotte Forten Grimké*, 405; Lucy Sanders to "Dear Helen," September 21, 1862, WSP.

21. Schouler, *History of Massachusetts in the Civil War*, vol. 1, 177–87; Thomas Wentworth Higginson, *Massachusetts in the Army and Navy During the War of 1861–65*, vol. 1, 81.

22. Grant's letters are cited in William S. McFeely, *Grant*, 195–96, and McPherson, *Battle Cry of Freedom*, 502, respectively.

23. Jacob C. White, Jr., to Joseph C. Bustill, August 19, 1862, as published in Carter G. Woodson, ed., "Letters of Negroes, Largely Personal and Private," 82–83.

24. Selections from the Worcester press are taken from Worcester *Daily Spy*, November 7, December 10, 1861; January 31, February 5, March 17, 19, August 6, September 8, 1862; March 7, 10, July 17, 1863; April 6, 1865.

25. Ibid., July 31, August 4, 1862; January 2, 1863; January 1, 2, October 31, November 1, 2, 1864; January 5, 1865.

26. Ibid., May 20, June 28, 1862; William G. Hawkins, *Lunsford Lane*, 207–8. There are no known records of either of the black societies. Their activity during the war years may be followed in Worcester *Daily Spy*, December 5, 27, 30, 1861; January 6, February 5, 1862; January 2, April 27, 1864; January 22, 1865. On the Ladies Aid Society, see Marvin, *History of Worcester in the War of Rebellion*, 422–25.

27. Schouler, *History of Massachusetts in the Civil War*, vol. 1, 405, 509. See also Alexander H. Bullock, "Address Before the Literary Societies of Williams College," August 3, 1864, box 2, folder 4, AHB.

28. Sgt. G. E. Hystuns [?], Company B, 54th Massachusetts Infantry, to William Still, September 19, 1863, box 9G, folder 17, LG.

29. Jeremiah Asher, *An Autobiography . . . ,* 5. See also Joseph T. Glatthaar, *Forged in Battle*, 61–80.

30. *Anglo-African Magazine*, September 28, 1861, as cited in Alfred M. Green, *Letters and Discussions on the Formation of Colored Regiments . . . ,* 13–17. (The *Anglo-African* changed its name to the *Anglo-African Magazine* during the war.) Attitudes toward black enlistment are discussed in William Wells Brown, *The Negro in the American Rebellion*, 124–29, 142–46; Norwood P. Hallowell, *The Negro as a Soldier in the War of the Rebellion*, 6–7; Frank H. Taylor, *Philadelphia in the Civil War, 1861–1865*, 187; Dudley T. Cornish, *The Sable Arm*, 1–28; Glatthaar, *Forged in Battle*, 1–34.

31. Worcester *Daily Spy*, August 6, 11, 1862.

32. Ibid., August 20, September 12, 17, 1862; Marvin, *History of Worcester in the War of the Rebellion*, 138, 140; see also W. W. Brown, *Negro in the American Rebellion*, 146. On Gilbert Walker's role as a military recruiter, see his "General Affidavit," June 10, 1887, in George R. Rome file, RG15.

33. On the draft in Massachusetts, see A. M. Drummond, *The Union Army*, vol. 1, 158; Richard H. Abbott, "Massachusetts and the Recruit-

ment of Southern Negroes, 1863–1865," 209–10; Glatthaar, *Forged in Battle,* 63. Forbes is cited in Abbott, "Massachusetts and the Recruitment," 201. For discussions of government policy, see Thomas Webster to Edwin M. Stanton, April 27, 1864, AB; Cornish, *Sable Arm,* 29, 187–94; Frederick M. Binder, "Pennsylvania Negro Regiments in the Civil War," 383–84; Glatthaar, *Forged in Battle,* 1–11.

34. On the raising of the three black Massachusetts regiments, see Lewis Hayden to John A. Andrew, December 24, 1863, box 12, folder 16, and Hayden to White, January 8, 1864, box 13, folder 2, JAA; Massachusetts Senate Document No. 1, *Address of His Excellency John A. Andrew . . . 1865,* 74–76, 87–88; Schouler, *History of Massachusetts in the Civil War,* vol. 1, 392–93, 407–10, 491; Frank Preston Stearns, *The Life and Public Services of George Luther Stearns,* 285–89; Luis F. Emilio, *History of the Fifty-Fourth Regiment . . . ,* 11–12; Ira Berlin, ed., *The Black Military Experience,* 9, 12; Henry Greenleaf Pearson, *The Life of John A. Andrew,* vol. 1, 91–94. Gilbert Walker and his wife were assaulted on the street, possibly a result of his prominent role in recruiting black troops; see Worcester *Daily Spy,* February 19, 1863.

35. Worcester *Daily Spy,* February 18, March 12, 13, 21, 31, May 6, 13, 19, 29, 30, June 6, July 28, August 4, 1863; Marvin, *History of Worcester in the War of Rebellion,* 175. On Worcester's black volunteers and draftees, see Thomas D. Freeman to William Brown, May 8, [1863,] BF; Tally of Drafts, folder 1, USA; Enrollment Lists, 1864, box 5, folder 6, and "Worcester, Mass. Civil War Volunteers," box 5, folder 3, CW; Worcester *Daily Spy,* July 11, 13, August 17, 1863, May 21, 1864; Massachusetts Office of the Adjutant-General, *Record of the Massachusetts Volunteers,* vol. 1, 767–85, vol. 2, 848–83, 1057–78; Marvin, *History of Worcester in the War of Rebellion,* 284, 398, 546–47; Charles Barnard Fox, *Record of the Service of the Fifty-Fifth Regiment . . . ,* 123, 141; Murdock, *One Million Men,* 353. On federal bounty policies for soldiers, see Binder, "Pennsylvania Negro Regiments," 383–84.

36. For a brief account of the battle at Fort Wagner, see Cornish, *Sable Arm,* 152–56.

37. Muster Rolls, Company F, 54th Massachusetts Infantry, November–December, 1863, entry for Alexander Hemenway, RG94.

38. Worcester *Daily Spy,* July 17, 1863. For a strained revisionist account that stresses the class aspects of these riots, see Iver Bernstein, *The New York City Draft Riots;* for a compelling critique see James M. McPherson, "Wartime," 33–35.

39. AWT, 2:109 (March 10, 1871).

40. McPherson, *Battle Cry of Freedom,* 508–9, 686–88. Grant's letter to Lincoln, August 23, 1863, is cited in ibid., 687, fn. 26.

41. On the 1863 draft, see Worcester *Daily Spy,* July 11, August 17, 1863; Marvin, *History of Worcester in the War of the Rebellion,* 177–85, 239, 426–28; Drummond, *Union Army,* vol. 1, 158; Eugene C. Murdock, *One Million Men,* 306–7; McPherson, *Battle Cry of Freedom,* 606; James M. McPherson, ed., *Battle Chronicles of the Civil War,* vol. 5, 107–9. Provost Marshal Stone is cited in Murdock, *One Million Men,* 313–14.

42. On the difficulties recruiters of black soldiers encountered, see William Birney to Salmon P. Chase, July 21, 1863, SPC; Lewis Hayden

to John Andrew, December 24, 1863, box 12, folder 16, and Hayden to Andrew, January 8, 1864, box 13, folder 2, JAA.

6. Tempered in Struggle

1. Bound Regimental Record Books, Fifth Massachusetts Cavalry (Colored), "Orders," January 31, February 25, 29, April 28, 1864, RG94; Muster Rolls, Company D, Fifth Massachusetts Cavalry, entries for AW, January 29, February 29, April 30, 1864, RG94; Benjamin W. Crowninshield, *A History of the First Regiment of Massachusetts Cavalry Volunteers,* 326; Charles P. Bowditch, "The War Letters of Charles P. Bowditch," 472; Captain C. C. Parsons to First Lieutenant George F. Wilson, September 15, 1864, Regimental Papers, Massachusetts, Fifth Cavalry, box 1720, RG94; Massachusetts Office of Adjutant-General, *Record of the Massachusetts Volunteers,* vol. 1, 632–33, 766–67; Massachusetts Office of the Adjutant-General, *Massachusetts Soldiers, Sailors, and Marines in the Civil War,* 499, 507, 509. See also Joseph T. Glatthaar, *Forged in Battle,* passim, on racial attitudes of white officers in black regiments.

2. Thomas Wentworth Higginson, *Massachusetts in the Army and Navy During the War of 1861–65,* vol. 2, 261, 330; Ira Berlin, ed., *The Black Military Experience,* 440; Massachusetts Office of Adjutant-General, *Record of the Massachusetts Volunteers,* vol. 2, 855–56; Worcester *Daily Spy,* May 20, 1862; April 16, 1864.

3. Material compiled from Massachusetts Office of the Adjutant-General, *Massachusetts Soldiers, Sailors, and Marines,* 506–10; Bound Regimental Record Books, Fifth Massachusetts Cavalry (Colored), "Descriptive Books Cos A to M," Company D records, RG94. The total number of soldiers in the company varies slightly in each source but the percentages within any category are similar.

4. Bound Regimental Record Books, Fifth Massachusetts Cavalry (Colored), "Morning Reports, CO's A to M," March 12, 1864, RG94.

5. *Army and Navy Journal* 1 (April 23, 1864):577; Dudley T. Cornish, *The Sable Arm,* 173–76; James M. McPherson, *Battle Cry of Freedom,* 748; Glatthaar, *Forged in Battle,* 156–57; Higginson, *Massachusetts in the Army and Navy,* vol. 1, 166–67; Frederick H. Dyer, *A Compendium of the War of the Rebellion,* vol. 3, *Regimental Histories,* 1240; P. C. Headley, *Massachusetts in the Rebellion,* 497; Abijah P. Marvin, *History of Worcester in the War of the Rebellion,* 310. The Fort Pillow massacre remained sharply etched in black memory even after the war. "Remember Fort Pillow when you go to the polls," read one banner in a Tennessee parade of black Republicans in 1867. See Worcester *Evening Gazette,* July 18, 1867.

6. James M. McPherson, ed., *Battle Chronicles of the Civil War,* vol. 4, 14–27, 46–57; McPherson, *Battle Cry of Freedom,* 723–33; William S. McFeely, *Grant,* 164–73; Phillip Shaw Paludan, *"A People's Contest,"* 308. Major General H. W. Halleck to Major General Benjamin Butler, May 12, 1864, and Captain George S. Dodge to Colonel Shaffer, May 15, 1864, 1st ser., vol. 36, pt. 2, 688, 804, in U.S. Department of War, *The War of the Rebellion.*

7. Solon A. Carter, "Fourteen Months' Service with Colored Troops," 155; Robert Underwood Johnson and Clarence Clough Buel, eds., *Bat-*

tles and Leaders of the Civil War, vol. 4, 114–15, 146–47, 208–9; *Army and Navy Journal* 1 (May 14, 1864):630; William A. Willoughby to "My Dear Wife," [May 14, 1864,] WAW; Samuel A. Duncan to Julia Jones, May 7, 1864, DJ.

8. William A. Willoughby to "My Dear Wife," May 22, 1864, WAW; *Army and Navy Journal* 1 (May 28, 1864):659; J. H. Taylor to Major General Casey, May 11, 1864, Regimental Papers, Massachusetts, Fifth Cavalry, Box 1720, RG94; U.S. Department of War, *War of the Rebellion,* 1st ser., vol. 40, pt. 2, 224–26; A. M. Drummond, *The Union Army,* vol. 1, 215–16.

9. On Wilson's Wharf and the Confederate threat against black troops, see *Army and Navy Journal* 1 (June 4, 1864):675; Carter, "Fourteen Months' Service," 161; James M. Guthrie, *Camp-Fires of the Afro-American,* 592–93; *The Press,* August 25, 1864. On the Fifth Cavalry, see U.S. Department of War, *War of the Rebellion,* 1st ser., vol. 36, pt. 3, 181–82; Charles P. Bowditch to "Dear Mother," May 29, 1864, in Bowditch, "War Letters," 478–79. Grant's strategy is discussed in McPherson, *Battle Chronicles,* vol. 4, 43–44.

10. On the June 15 battle, sometimes known as Baylor's Farm, see McPherson, *Battle Chronicles,* vol. 4, 49–52; Hondon B. Hargrove, *Black Union Soldiers in the Civil War,* 182–83; Benjamin F. Butler, *Speech upon the Campaign Before Richmond, 1864 . . . ;* Higginson, *Massachusetts in the Army and Navy,* vol. 1, 125; Carter, "Fourteen Months' Service," 163–67; George W. Williams, *History of the Negro Race in America, from 1619 to 1880,* vol. 2, 336–38; Joseph T. Wilson, *The Black Phalanx,* 397–406; Cornish, *Sable Arm,* 272–73; Eagerton to Thomas Webster, June 27, 1864, AB; Colonel Louis Bell to "George," August 12, 1864, box 3, folder 7, SB; William Augustus Willoughby, diary entry, "Friday, June 17 (over 16)th 1864," WAW; Bound Regimental Record Books, Fifth Massachusetts Cavalry (Colored), Co. A, June 15, 1864, Co. L, June 15, 1864, RG94; Regimental Cards, May–June 1864, Service Records, U.S. Colored Troops, Fifth Massachusetts Cavalry (microfilm 594, roll 204), RG94. For a broad overview of Grant's massive campaign, see McFeely, *Grant,* 165–77; McPherson, *Battle Cry of Freedom,* 718–43. General Smith is cited in James H. Rickard, "Service with Colored Troops in Burnside's Corps," 7.

11. Eagerton to Thomas H. Webster, June 27, 1864, AB. Eagerton's timing was mistaken, as the bill was assured of passage before the battle at Baylor's Farm. See also Samuel Smith to "My Dear Woodbury," May 27, 1864 WSP.

12. Christian A. Fleetwood, diary entry, June 15–16, 1864, CAF-LC; Charles P. Bowditch to "Dear Mother," June 18, 1864, and Bowditch to "Dear Charlotte," June 18, 1864, in Bowditch, "War Letters," 479–82.

13. *Army and Navy Journal* 1 (June 25, 1864):721.

14. Edward W. Hinks to Major William Russell, June 26, 1864, in U.S. Department of War, *War of the Rebellion,* 1st ser., vol. 40, pt. 2, 460; Hinks to William F. Smith, June 27, 1864, in ibid., 489–91; Colonel John H. Holman to Captain Solon A. Carter, June 20, 1864, in ibid., vol. 51, pt. 1, 263–65.

15. AWT, 3:195 ([1878]). The full "chronology" can be found in ibid., 3:186–99.

16. Hinks to Smith, June 27, 1864, in U.S. Department of War, *War of the Rebellion,* 1st ser., vol. 40, pt. 2, 490–91; *Army and Navy Journal* 1 (June 25, 1864):722; Regimental Cards, July–August 1864, Service Records, U.S. Colored Troops, Fifth Massachusetts Cavalry (microfilm 594, roll 204), RG94; Marvin, *History of Worcester in the War of the Rebellion,* 311; addendum, written decades later, to letter of Charles P. Bowditch to "Dear Charlotte," June 27, 1864, in Bowditch, "War Letters," 484; Higginson, *Massachusetts in the Army and Navy,* vol. 1, 134–35, 298–99. On Bowditch's military record, see Massachusetts Office of the Adjutant-General, *Record of the Massachusetts Volunteers,* vol. 1, 766, vol. 2, 867.

17. McPherson, *Battle Chronicles,* vol. 4, 57; William Hamilton to "Boyd," June 28, 1864, WH.

18. Regimental Cards, July–August 1864, Service Records, U.S. Colored Troops, Fifth Massachusetts Cavalry (microfilm 594, roll 204), RG94. On Point Lookout, see William Schouler, *A History of Massachusetts in the Civil War,* vol. 1, 596; J. G. De Roulhac Hamilton and Rebecca Cameron, eds., *The Papers of Randolph Abbott Shotwell,* vol. 2, 119; McPherson, *Battle Cry of Freedom,* 801. On the Federal troops at the camp, see "Organization, 22nd Army Corps," July 31, 1864, in U.S. Department of War, *War of the Rebellion,* 1st ser., vol. 37, pt. 1, 545; Colonel A. G. Draper to Edwin M. Stanton, July 1, 1864, in ibid., vol. 40, pt. 2, 582; Captain J. W. DeForest to Brigadier General James B. Fry, November 30, 1865, in ibid., 3d ser., vol. 5, 543–67. For Keiley's comments, see his *In Vinculis,* 100. Marcus B. Toney, *The Privations of a Private,* 84–85, is also of interest.

19. On daily life in the camp for prisoners, see William Whately Pierson, Jr., ed., *Whipt'em Everytime,* 93, 109; Keiley, *In Vinculis,* 64–65; Toney, *Privations of a Private,* 86. On the experience of the Federal guards, see Captain J. W. DeForest to Brigadier General James B. Fry, November 30, 1865, in U.S. Department of War, *War of the Rebellion,* 3d ser., vol. 5, 564; Lieutenant Colonel Charles Francis Adams, Jr., to Charles Francis Adams, November 2, 1864, in Worthington Chauncey Ford, ed., *A Cycle of Adams Letters, 1861–65,* vol. 2, 217.

20. AW's letter dated November 26, 1864, appeared in *Anglo-African Magazine,* December 17, 1864, and is cited in Edwin S. Redkey, ed., *A Grand Army of Black Men,* 119–21.

21. On Early's attack, see Pierson, *Whipt'em Everytime,* 104; McPherson, *Battle Chronicles,* 4:70–83. AW's temporary promotion is recorded in Bound Regimental Record Books, Fifth Massachusetts Cavalry (Colored), "Morning Reports, CO's A to M," Company D, July 9, 1864, RG94.

22. Toney, *Privations of a Private,* 84–88. For similar expressions by Confederate prisoners, see Keiley, *In Vinculis,* 70, 96; Pierson, *Whipt'em Everytime,* 98, 108–10, 114; Mary Lindsay Thornton, ed., "The Prison Diary of Adjutant Francis Atherton Boyle, C.S.A.," 63–64; Reid Mitchell, *Civil War Soldiers,* 45. A. M. Keiley notes an occasional moment of respect between prisoners and guards, which he attributed to their common military service; see Keiley, *In Vinculis,* 113.

23. Edward Chase Kirkland, *Charles Francis Adams, Jr., 1835–1915,* 29–30; Glatthaar, *Forged in Battle,* 13, 18; Lieutenant Colonel Adams to

Henry Adams, September 18, 23, 1864, to Charles Francis Adams, November 2, 1864, in Ford, *Cycle of Adams Letters,* vol. 2, 194–96, 198–99, 215–16, respectively. For a similar hesitancy over the future of Negro Americans, expressed by a white abolitionist from Worcester and officer in a black regiment, see Samuel Smith to "Dear Children" [Woodbury and Helen Wheeler Smith], July 13, 1865, WSP. For a discussion of white racial attitudes, see Glatthaar, *Forged in Battle,* passim, especially 81–98; George Fredrickson, *The Black Image in the White Mind,* passim.

24. On the *Anglo-African* incident, see "Monstrous Barbarity in the 5*th* Massachusetts Cavalry," *Anglo-African Magazine,* July 16, 1864; and Major H. N. Weld to Robert Hamilton, July 18, 1864 [copy]; Thomas Hamilton to Major H. N. Weld, July 23, 1864 [copy]; Weld to Provost Marshal, New York City, August 1, 1864; all in Regimental Papers, Massachusetts, Fifth Cavalry, box 1720, RG94.

25. For Hackett's case, see "Proceedings, Findings and Sentence in Case of John W. Hackett," especially 4–7, 14–16, box 1071, no. mm 1940, March 23, 1865, RG153. Hackett was originally sentenced to six years at hard labor, a term later reduced by an appeals officer who accepted Hackett's explanation of his guilt: "I was in liquor." Butler's case can be followed in "Proceedings, Findings and Sentence in Case of George Butler," especially 18–19, 31, 45–47, box 1077, no. mm 1981, March 20–22, 1865, RG153, and in "Proceedings, Findings and Sentence in Case of William A. Underhill," 3–5, box 1071, no. mm 1940, March 22, 1865, RG153. Both cases are also discussed in "General Order No. 11," April 10, 1865, Regimental Papers, Massachusetts, Fifth Cavalry, box 1720, RG94.

26. On Stafford and Carter, see "Proceedings, Findings and Sentence in Case of Joseph Stafford," 5–6, 25, box 1071, no. mm 1940, March 25, 1865, RG153, and "Proceedings, Findings and Sentence in Case of Fielding Bolden, 14–16, box 1071, no. mm 1940, March 25, 1865, RG153; Massachusetts Office of the Adjutant-General, *Massachusetts Soldiers, Sailors, and Marines,* 503.

27. On the cases of Williams, Finley, and Cornish, see "Proceedings, Findings and Sentence in Case of Abraham H. Williams," 3–5, 17–19, box 1071, no. mm 1940, March 16–17, 1865, RG153; "Proceedings, Findings and Sentence in Case of James Finley," 4–5, 11, 18, box 1071, no. mm 1940, March 24, 1865, RG153; "Proceedings, Findings and Sentence in Case of James H. Cornish," 5–6, 15–17, 28, box 1071, no. mm 1940, March 15–18, 20, 1865, RG153. These cases are also discussed in "General Order No. 11," April 10, 1865, Regimental Papers, Massachusetts, Fifth Cavalry, box 1720, RG94. On discipline throughout the Federal forces, see Philip Van Doren Stern, *Soldier Life in the Union and Confederate Armies,* 95–112.

28. Cornish was found guilty of "contempt and mutinous language," reduced to rank of private, and compelled to forfeit three months' pay. The forfeiture was later commuted and Cornish returned to duty as a private. Williams was also found guilty of contempt and drunkenness, and his original sentence to a year's hard labor and forfeiture of pay was later reduced to just the forfeiture. Finley was found guilty of mutiny but the conviction was overturned. The appeals tribunal thought the

charge of mutiny unfounded, "although the language of the accused tended to incite mutiny." Finley, like Cornish and Williams, was released from the Guard House after four months and returned to duty. See "General Order No. 11," April 10, 1865, Regimental Papers, Massachusetts, Fifth Cavalry, box 1720, RG94. For another court-martial involving a black soldier from Worcester, see the trial record of Emory Phelps, Company C, 54th Massachusetts (Colored) Infantry, in Phelps, Military Records, RG94. Glatthaar, *Forged in Battle,* 99–120, presents an insightful overall analysis of such charges and trials.

29. Letter of "Africano," *Anglo-African Magazine,* August 6, 1864, as cited in C. Peter Ripley, ed., *The Black Abolitionist Papers,* vol. 5, *The United States, 1859–1865,* 277–78.

30. "Morning Reports, CO's A to M," Company D, March 3, 11, 1865, Bound Regimental Record Books, Fifth Massachusetts Cavalry (Colored), RG94.

31. Grant to Auger, March 20, 1865, Auger to Grant, March 21, 1865, Auger to General Barnes, March 21, 1865, Auger to Grant, March 22, 1865, and Grant to Auger, March 22, 1865, General Ord to General Weitzel, March 27, 1865, all in U.S. Department of War, *War of the Rebellion,* 1st ser., vol. 46, pt. 3, 58, 70, 71, 83, 212, respectively.

32. Brigadier General Charles Devens to Lieutenant Colonel Edward Moale, April 3, 1865, and General Ord to General Weitzel, April 4, 1865, in ibid., pt. 1, 567, 1211. See also Berlin, *The Black Military Experience,* 26; Adams to Charles Francis Adams, April 10, 1865, in Ford, *Cycle of Adams Letters,* vol. 2, 259–62; "Morning Reports, Co's A to M," Company A, March 27, 28, 1865, Bound Regimental Record Books, Fifth Massachusetts Cavalry (Colored), RG94; Frederick M. Binder, "Pennsylvania Negro Regiments in the Civil War," 415–16; Hargrove, *Black Union Soldiers,* 200; McPherson, *Battle Chronicles,* vol. 4, 125–48, 167–76; McPherson, *Battle Cry of Freedom,* 844–50.

33. Robert Dryer to "My Dear Father," April 5, 1865, DF; Warren Goodale to [?], [early April 1865,] WG. See also Samuel Smith to "Dear Woodbury," April 5, 1865, WSP, for an appreciation of the irony of black troops leading the Federal forces into Richmond.

34. Regimental Card, March–April 1865, Service Records, U.S. Colored Troops, Fifth Massachusetts Cavalry (microfilm 594, roll 204), RG94; McPherson, *Battle Cry of Freedom,* 846–47. Chester's description is from *The Press,* April 11, 1865.

35. Adams to Charles Francis Adams, April 10, 1865, in Ford, *Cycle of Adams Letters,* vol. 2, 262–63. Statement of Lieutenant R. M. Higginson, Company D, April 26, 1865, and Lieutenant Colonel Adams to Captain E. O. Brown, April 15, 1865, Regimental Papers, Massachusetts, Fifth Cavalry, box 1719, RG94; Edward Woolsey Bacon to "Kate," April 26, 1865, EWB; D. D. Wheeler to Major General Kautz, April 15, 1865, J. M. Howard to "Commanding Officers, Fifth Massachusetts Cavalry," April 18, 1865, Captain H. E. W. Clark to Major General Ferrero, April 23, 1865, Major General H. W. Halleck to Grant, April 29, 1865, and Grant to Halleck, April 30, 1865, all in U.S. Department of War, *War of the Rebellion,* 1st ser., vol. 46, pt. 3, 764, 827–28, 909–10, 1005–6, 1016, respectively.

36. Warren Goodale to [?], [early April 1865,] WG; Ord to Major General Hartsuff, April 16, 1865, Halleck to Grant, April 29, 1865, and Grant to Halleck, April 30, 1865, in U.S. Department of War, *War of the Rebellion*, 1st ser., vol. 46, pt. 3, 797, 1005–6, 1016; Berlin, *The Black Military Experience*, 734–36; James E. Sefton, *The United States Army and Reconstruction, 1865–1877*, 51–53. Grant is quoted in McFeely, *Grant*, 239–40.

37. *The Press*, May 16, 24, June 6, 1865; *Army and Navy Journal* 2 (May 13, 1865):600, (June 3, 1865):641–42, (June 3, 1865):649, (June 17, 1865): 680–81. On Grant's concern with the issue of Mexico, see Grant to Philip Sheridan, June 3, 1865, Major General Gordon Granger to Brigadier General R. H. Jackson, June 8, 1865, and Grant to Sheridan, July 1, 1865, in U.S. Department of War, *War of the Rebellion*, 1st ser., vol. 48, pt. 2, 743, 819, 1035. Broader discussion of this issue can be found in J. T. Wilson, *Black Phalanx*, 461–62; Berlin, *The Black Military Experience*, 734–36; McFeely, *Grant*, 221; Paludan, *"People's Contest,"* 276–77.

38. *Army and Navy Journal* 2 (June 24, 1865):689; Bound Regimental Record Books, Fifth Massachusetts Cavalry (Colored), Morning Reports, Co. A, June 12, 13, 1865, RG94; *The Press*, May 24, 1865.

39. Junius R. Roberts to "dear father," June 16, 1865, JR; Bound Regimental Record Books, Fifth Massachusetts Cavalry (Colored), Morning Reports, Co. A, June 16, 24, 27, 28, July 3, 6, 1865, RG94; Edward Woolsey Bacon to "Kate," June 25, 1865, EWB; Edith Armstrong Talbot, *Samuel Chapman Armstrong*, 125–26; *Army and Navy Journal* 2 (August 5, 1865):786, 3 (October 28, 1865):116; Capt. G. H. Beckwith to Leverett E. Seymour, July 23, 1865, LES; Sefton, *United States Army and Reconstruction*, 261–62; Philip H. Sheridan to Brevet Major General J. A. Rawlins, June 13, 1865, in U.S. Department of War, *War of the Rebellion*, 1st ser., vol. 48, pt. 2, 865.

40. Headley, *Massachusetts in the Rebellion*, 497–98; Glatthaar, *Forged in Battle*, 218–21; Massachusetts Office of Adjutant-General, *Massachusetts Soldiers, Sailors, and Marines*, 506–10; *Army and Navy Journal* 2 (July 8, 1865):729, 3 (November 4, 1865):162; Edward Woolsey Bacon to "Kate," July 10, 1865, EWB. See also Lt. Adam Kramer to William Jackson Palmer, January 5, 1866, in Brit Allan Storey, ed., "An Army Officer in Texas, 1866–1867," 243–46.

41. On AW's promotion to quartermaster sergeant, see Amos Webber entry, Company Muster Roll, August 6, 1865, RG94; for an account of life in the quartermaster's department, see Richard S. Offenberg and Robert Rue Parsonage, eds., *The War Letters of Duren F. Kelley, 1862–1865*, 22, 25; Warren Goodale to "Dear Children," July 8, 1865, WG.

42. On troop placements, see Lieutenant Adam Kramer to William Jackson Palmer, January 5, 1866, in Storey, "Army Officer in Texas," 245–46; Major General Philip H. Sheridan to Brevet Major General J. A. Rawlins, June 13, 1865, and Major General Gordon Granger to Sheridan, June 19, 1865, in U.S. Department of War, *War of the Rebellion*, 1st ser., vol. 48, pt. 2, 865, 927–28; Charles William Ramsdell, *Reconstruction in Texas*, 40–41; Ernest Wallace, *Texas in Turmoil*, 147; Thomas North, *Five Years in Texas . . .* , 183; *Army and Navy Journal* 2 (June 24, 1865):697, 3 (August 26, 1865):2.

43. On conditions in Texas, see U.S. Congress, Joint Committee on Reconstruction, *Report on the Joint Committee on Reconstruction*, pt. 4, 40, 47–48, 50, 150–67; Louis Henry Carpenter to "Dear Ned," September 14, 1866, box 1, folder 2, LHC; Elizabeth B. Custer, *Tenting on the Plains . . .* , 31; Ernest Wallace, *Charles De Morse*, 154–57; Austin Bearse, *Reminiscences of Fugitive-Slave Law Days in Boston*, 43; Randolph B. Campbell, *A Southern Community in Crisis*, 245–46; Major General Philip H. Sheridan, "Report," November 14, 1866, and Sheridan to Major General Gordon Granger, June 13, 1865, in U.S. Department of War, *War of the Rebellion*, 1st ser., vol. 48, pt. 1, 301, and pt. 2, 866–67, respectively; William L. Richter, "The Army and the Negro During Texas Reconstruction, 1865–1870" 12–13; Dudley G. Wooten, ed., *A Comprehensive History of Texas, 1685 to 1897*, vol. 2, 152. Stanley's testimony can be found in Joint Committee on Reconstruction, *Report*, pt. 4, 41.

44. Thomas A. Vincent, Assistant Adjutant-General to Commanding Generals, Departments of Florida, Virginia, Texas, Louisiana, and Arkansas, September 9, 1865, in U.S. Department of War, *War of the Rebellion*, 3d ser., vol. 5, 108; see also Sheridan to Rawlins, September 20, 1865, to Grant, September 21, October 7, 1865, in ibid., 1st ser., vol. 48, pt. 2, 1235, 1235–36, 1237–38; Sefton, *United States Army and Reconstruction*, 52, 261–62; Robert W. Shook, "The Federal Military in Texas, 1865–1870," 7–8. Throughout the South the Federal military presence dropped from over 185,000 troops in September 1865 to some 38,000 the following April, a decline of 80 percent. See also Custer to Mr. and Mrs. Bacon, October 5, 1865, as cited in Marguarite Merington, ed., *The Custer Story*, 174–75.

45. Bound Regimental Record Books, Fifth Massachusetts Cavalry (Colored), Morning Reports, Co. A, October 19, 1865, RG94; Colonel S. E. Chamberlain to Brigadier General William Schouler, October 22, 1865, and Chamberlain to Schouler, November 4, 1865, telegram [copy], Muster Rolls, Returns, Regimental Papers, Massachusetts, Fifth Cavalry, box 1719, RG94; Glatthaar, *Forged in Battle*, 218–21, 234.

46. On Couch's actions in 1863, see Alexander Henry to Governor A. G. Curtin, June 19, 1863, and Curtin to Henry, June 19, 1863, box 2, folder 2, AH; Worcester *Daily Spy*, June 18, 1863. On the December 1865 ceremony see Headley, *Massachusetts in the Rebellion*, 654–56; Higginson, *Massachusetts in the Army and Navy*, vol. 1, 149–50.

7. Civil Duties

1. See AWT, 2:103 (December 30, 1870).

2. Joseph T. Glatthaar, *Forged in Battle*, 238–50, Reid Mitchell, *Civil War Soldiers*, 209, and Phillip Shaw Paludan, *"A People's Contest,"* 222, discuss aspects of this transition.

3. See Mitchell, *Civil War Soldiers*, 56–64; Glatthaar, *Forged in Battle*, 236–37.

4. See Worcester *Daily Spy*, February 10, March 25, 31, May 27, 29, July 6, December 15, 1865.

5. Worcester *Evening Gazette*, January 2, 1867.

6. Worcester *Daily Spy*, July 22, 1865; Worcester *Evening Gazette*, August 2, 1866.

7. Worcester *Evening Gazette,* May 1, 1871; February 22, May 23, 1878. On Worcester's nonwhite population, see U.S. Bureau of Census, *Ninth Census of the United States,* vol. 1, *The Statistics of the Population of the United States,* 168.

8. Hattie Smith to "Dear Woodbury," February 25, 1866; Samuel Smith to "Dear Woodbury," March 25, September 25, 1864; Charles Sanders to "Dear Helen," July 11, 1865; all in WSP. On Worcester's population growth, see Secretary of the Commonwealth, *Abstract of the Census of Massachusetts, 1865,* 202, 233; U.S. Bureau of Census, *Tenth Census of the United States,* vol. 1, *Statistics of the Population of the United States,* 420.

9. Secretary of the Commonwealth, *Abstract of the Census of Massachusetts, 1865,* 658–59, 662–63, 676–77, 736, 760.

10. William T. Hogan, *Economic History of the Iron and Steel Industry in the United States,* vol. 1, 108–9; Charles G. Washburn, *Manufacturing and Mechanical Industries, of Worcester,* 37–38; Worcester *Evening Gazette,* January 25, August 19, 1868, October 4, 1869.

11. Worcester *Daily Spy,* May 6, 1864.

12. Worcester *Evening Gazette,* February 22, December 6, 18, 1866; January 31, April 13, September 21, 1867; July 24, August 13, September 29, 1868; September 30, 1869.

13. Ibid., March 3, July 19, 23, 1866, May 8, July 30, 1868, April 22, 30, May 12, June 21, July 10, 19, September 21, October 7, 18, 28, November 1, 1869, January 19, 1876; Massachusetts, *Eleventh Annual Report of the Bureau of Statistics of Labor,* 31.

14. Worcester *Evening Gazette,* April 27, May 19, 1868.

15. Charles Hersey, *History of Worcester, Massachusetts,* 426; Worcester *Evening Gazette,* May 14, 30, October 20, 1868.

16. On the house, see Worcester *Evening Post,* July 19, 1900; Lizzie S. Webber, Case #34448 (filed September 16, 1904), CPRW.

17. On AW's wages, see "Payroll, April 1868 to January 1870," vol. 32, n.p., ASW; Massachusetts, *Seventh Annual Report of the Bureau of Statistics of Labor . . . ,* 63. The yearly wage is for 1869.

18. Mary Harriet Stephenson, *Dr. B. F. Stephenson . . . ,* 43–55; Wallace Evans Davies, *Patriotism on Parade,* 33–35; Grand Army of the Republic, *Rules and Regulations . . . 1870,* 1, 2, 24.

19. Harry Krebs to "My Dear Woodbury," June 22, 1866, WSP.

20. Robert B. Beath, *History of the Grand Army of the Republic,* 405–6; Worcester *Evening Gazette,* September 23, 1867, July 10, 1868; Franklin D. Tappan, *The Passing of the Grand Army of the Republic,* 15–16, 20, 21, 97. See Tappan, ibid., 244–64, and Edward P. Kimball, ed., *Brinley Hall Album and . . . Post 10 Sketch Book,* 351–60, for lists of Post 10 members, 1867–1900. For the post's meeting halls, see Worcester *Evening Gazette,* October 8, 1868; AWT, 2:184–85 (May 30, 1873).

21. A. B. R. Sprague, *Address . . . ,* 5; Beath, *History of the Grand Army,* 415, 418; Tappan, *Passing of the Grand Army,* 22, 130–32; AWT, 2:176 (January 28, 1873).

22. For a superb discussion of this emerging new awareness, see George Fredrickson, *The Inner Civil War.*

23. Tappan, *Passing of the Grand Army,* 2–3; Beath, *History of the Grand Army,* 405–6.

24. Glatthaar, *Forged in Battle,* 256; on the Colored Soldiers and Sailors League, see Philadelphia *Public Ledger,* January 9, 1867; Philip S. Foner and George E. Walker, eds., *Proceedings of the Black National and State Conventions, 1865–1900,* 293–94. On the Worcester merger of the (white) Soldiers and Sailors League into Post 10 of the GAR, see Worcester *Evening Gazette,* September 18, 1866; April 12, 1867. In Philadelphia and other cities with large groups of black veterans, black-only GAR posts persisted. In 1883 Post 80 conducted the installation of its new officers at the Lombard Street Central Presbyterian Church, where Elder Robert Jones still supervised the congregation. See New York *Globe,* January 20, 1883. For similar developments among black veterans in Jacksonville, Florida, see New York *Age,* May 4, 1889.

25. On North Star Lodge and AW's role, see AWT, 2:134–35 (August 1, 1871); Worcester *Evening Gazette,* August 20, 1869, March 4, 1873; Chas. H. Brooks, *The Official History and Manual of the Grand United Order of Odd Fellows . . . ,* 30, 36, 66, 102. For Sergeant Alexander Hemenway's experience with the Prince Hall Masons, which he joined while with the 54th Massachusetts Infantry in South Carolina, see Joseph A. Walker, Jr., *Black Square and Compass,* 46.

26. See Worcester *Evening Gazette,* August 1, 4, 1868. The tradition of celebrating August 1 continued in Worcester into the 1940s. During her childhood, Edna P. Spencer recalled, Worcester blacks, joined by contingents from the black communities of Springfield, Boston, and Rhode Island, would hold picnics at Rhode Island beaches in commemoration of Emancipation Day. The GUOOF no longer remained a viable organization in Worcester, but the celebration was sponsored by another black fraternal association, the Elks. See Spencer's moving memoir and master's thesis, "What Color Is the Wind?," 63 and passim. Black communities in Kansas also maintained the August 1 celebration, at least into the 1880s. See *Western Cyclone* (Nicodemus, Kans.), July 8, August 5, 12, 1886; *The Benevolent Banner* (North Topeka, Kans.), August 6, 1887.

27. On the racial assumptions of the white Odd Fellows, see Worcester *Evening Gazette,* May 5, 1866; April 24, 1868.

28. For a partial accounting of the activities of North Star Lodge, see ibid., December 26, 1868; March 3, August 20, 1869; March 2, 3, December 22, 1870. Women could play a complex role in these male fraternities. Charles Sanders, a well-to-do white resident of Worcester, lamented his wife's death anew on the occasion of his lodge's annual banquet. "I did miss Lucy," he recalled, "much as she was instrumental in my joining that fraternity." Sanders to "Dear Helen," January 15, 1866, WSP.

29. *Worcester City Directory for 1870,* 51; AWT, 2:134–35 (August 1, 1871).

30. For the different dues for men and women in the GUOOF and the Household of Ruth, see Brooks, *Official History and Manual,* 101; Receipt, Gerrit Smith Lodge No. 1707, GUOOF to S. R. Roberts, 1889, 1890, 1891, Noblesville, Indiana, JR; AWT, 8:n.p. [placed inside back cover], membership contract, G.U.O. of O.F. Relief Fund Bureau, [signed] July 1, 1882; Massachusetts Bureau of Statistics of Labor, *Thirty-fourth Annual Report,* 282.

31. See Eric Foner, *Reconstruction,* passim, on the failure of southern Reconstruction and on equality in the North.

32. Dale Baum, *The Civil War Party System,* 10–11; Samuel Smith to "Dear Woodbury," November 11, 1864, WSP.

33. Samuel May to Edwin Conant, July 27, 1868, EC. For a contemporary wartime view of Worcester, reflecting similar perspectives, see Samuel Smith to "Dear Woodbury," July 31, 1864, WSP.

34. The national presidential candidates are discussed in E. Foner, *Reconstruction,* 337–45.

35. Worcester *Evening Gazette,* August 22, 1868.

36. On black voters in Massachusetts, see ibid., January 31, 1867. On the Equal Rights League, which also encountered resistance from many black Pennsylvanians, see National Equal Rights League, *Proceedings of the First Annual Meeting . . . ;* Joseph Wilt to J. C. White, Jr., December 29, 1865, box 2G, folder 2; Wm. M. Struthers to J. C. White, November 15, 1866, box 2G, folder 4; Wilt to White, [June 26, 1866,] box 2G, folder 5; [Aaron P.] Faucett to Jacob C. White, Jr., November 10, 1868, box 2G, folder 6; Oliver Reynolds to J. C. White, Jr., February 2, 1869, box 2G, folder 7, all in LG. On the Colored Soldiers and Sailors League, see Pennsylvania State Equal Rights League, Executive Board Minutes, 1864–68, 123 (November 13, 1866); on the Bowser committee's lobbying efforts, see ibid., 131 (February 19, 1867), 135 (April 9, 1867); on the affiliation of the GUOOF lodges, see ibid., n.p. (n.d.), all in LG (microfilm).

37. Worcester *Evening Gazette,* October 31, November 3, 1868.

38. The Fifteenth Amendment did not guarantee blacks the right to hold office, a concession to northern feeling; nor did it outlaw the use of race-neutral means of excluding blacks from electoral activity. Within a decade, especially in the southern states, literacy tests, educational attainments, and property taxes would be required, purportedly of all voters but in reality only of blacks. For an account of how this worked in Mississippi, see Neil R. McMillen, *Dark Journey.*

39. Worcester *Evening Gazette,* April 2, 12, 14, 15, 1870.

40. On *The Drummer Boy,* see Tappan, *Passing of the Grand Army,* 99–101, 105; AWT, 8:150 (January 2, 1897); 9:13 (January 10–15, 1899); Grand Army of the Republic, Post 10, *The Drummer Boy: Official Programme,* 7–9. On the GAR lectures and Denton, see Worcester *Evening Gazette,* January 8, 9, 29, June 28, 1868; February 1, October 29, November 13, 16, 17, December 4, 1869; January 5, 1870. On Post 10's activities, see Worcester *Evening Gazette,* February 24, 1868; January 1, 26, 28, February 23, June 26, December 3, 24, 1869.

41. Bazzel Barker's case is discussed in Tappan, *Passing of the Grand Army,* 23–25; information on Barker can be found in his application for a disability pension, December 22, 1883, and in the supporting affidavit of Francis A. Clough, December 29, 1883, in Barker's file, RG15.

42. See Barker, Marriage Certificate, Worcester, July 31, 1850; letter from War Department, December 22, 1883; and Death Certificate, September 15, 1887 (he died on September 9), all in Barker file, RG15.

43. Worcester *Evening Gazette,* January 28, December 30, 1870. For Post 10's members through 1896, see Kimball, *Brinley Hall Album,* 351–60, and Tappan, *Passing of the Grand Army,* 189.

8. To Stand for Right

1. AWT, 2:1, 100 (December 1870).

2. Ibid., 2:1, 103 (December 30, 1870).

3. Ibid., 2:100 (November 28, 1870). Although dated in November, both the form of this brief entry and AW's dating of this volume on the cover and title page suggest he recorded this entry between December 1 and December 5, 1870, the date of the next entry.

4. Ibid., 2:103 (December 30, 1870).

5. Ibid., 2:100, 103 (December 5, 22, 1870).

6. Ibid., 2:100 (December 14, 1870).

7. Ibid., 2:100 (December 16, 1870); Worcester *Evening Gazette*, January 28, 29, 1869.

8. AWT, 2:100 (December 12, 1870).

9. Ibid., 2:101–2 (December 17, 18, 22, 1870).

10. Ibid., 2:104 (January 3, 1871).

11. See, for example, ibid., 2:1–3 (December 1870; January, February, 1871), 120 (May 19, 1871); 3:91 (October 27, 1875); 6:167 (April 17, 20, 1889). For the quote, see ibid., 2:22 (September 19, 1872).

12. For descriptions of these work-related celebrations, see Worcester *Daily Spy*, March 5, 1862, February 11, 1864; Worcester *Evening Gazette*, January 14, 23, February 2, September 21, 1867, January 31, June 8, 1868, January 30, December 11, 1869. One Worcester firm, the Bay State Shoe and Leather Company, instituted an employee profit-sharing plan which, in 1869, apportioned $8339.20 among its workers. Two years earlier, these same workers had raised more than $400 at the annual company ball to purchase a portrait of William Lloyd Garrison. See Worcester *Evening Gazette*, February 1, 13, 19, 1867; January 15, 1869.

13. AWT, 2:104–5 (January 7, 1871).

14. Ibid., 2:105 (January 16, 19, 1871).

15. Ibid., 2:105 (January 27, 1871).

16. On the minstrel show and, specifically, the "stump speech," see Robert C. Toll, *Blacking Up*, passim and 52, 55–56.

17. AWT, 2:2 (January 24, 27, 1871), 4 (March 17, 1871), 5 (April 24, 1871).

18. Worcester *Evening Gazette*, March 20, 21, 1871. On the 1870 strike at the Quinsigamond plant, see ibid., November 1, 2, 5, 1870; Massachusetts, [*Second*] *Report of the Massachusetts Bureau of Statistics of Labor . . .* , 126–31.

19. The strike can be followed in Worcester *Evening Gazette*, March 29, April 1, 8, 10, 17, 1871; AWT, 2:4 (March 18, 27, 1871), 110–11 (March 31, April 4, 7, 8, 11, 17, 1871). A brief comment on the August 1870 walkout can be found in Worcester *Evening Gazette*, August 8, 1870.

20. AWT, 2:111 (April 17, 1871). For AW's reference to John Brown see ibid., 1:22–23 (December 2, 1859) and above, chapter 4. On the shoemakers' strike in Worcester, which AW briefly noted in his entry of April 17, 1871, see Worcester *Evening Gazette*, January 3, 4, 5, 7, 10, 13, 21, 22, 25, February 8, 9, 10, 11, 12, 15, 16, 17, 19, 28, March 10, 19, 22, 23, 1870.

21. Booker T. Washington, *Up from Slavery*, 65. On the theme of industrial harmony, see Nick Salvatore, *Eugene V. Debs*, ch. 1–3.

22. AWT, 2:104 (January 3, 1871).

23. Ibid., 2:127 (June 17, 1871), 129 (June 21, 1871). Eighteen months later, with the Moen family on extended vacation in Europe, AW and his young charge, Philip W. Moen, exchanged occasional letters. See ibid., 2:26 (January 1, 3, 1873).

24. Worcester *Evening Gazette*, March 3, 1871. The proprietor of Lincoln House, George Tower, quickly found other staff and fired those who refused to serve the black Odd Fellows. See also AWT, 2:115–16 (April 29, 1871).

25. AWT, 2:2 (January 18, 1871).

26. Worcester *Evening Gazette*, May 6, 1871; AWT, 2:123–24 (May 31, 1871).

27. AWT, 2:124 (May 31, 1871), 116 (May 2, 1871). See also his entry two months later, where he chortled that "temperance men can vote best in Cold Weather," ibid., 2:131 (July 3, 1871). On the use of liquor by Worcester's elites, see Roy Rosenzweig, *Eight Hours for What We Will*, 93. As the GAR local leadership was not solely composed of elites, it seems that the practice was widespread.

28. Worcester *Evening Gazette*, August 2, 1871.

29. See AWT, 2:26–28 (January, February, March, 1873), 39–43 (February, March, April, May, June, 1874). AW most often indicated a lodge meeting with a rectangular box, followed by the notation, "x x L.N." ("L.N." stood for "last night"). On the excursions, see Worcester *Evening Gazette*, August 1, 1872; August 2, 1873.

30. Worcester *Evening Gazette*, March 4, 1873. For an account of the 1872 dinner, see ibid., March 2, 1872.

31. On this, see also the letter read at the dinner following AW's speech in ibid., March 4, 1873.

32. On the composition of the corps, see New York *Freeman*, April 11, 1885; on the drum, see New York *Globe*, October 13, 1883. Early mention of the corps accompanying North Star Lodge can be found in Worcester *Evening Gazette*, July 24, 1874; February 10, 1875. See also Johnson to "Mr. B. G. Wilder," July 25, 1913, box 3, folder 4, BGW.

33. Worcester *Evening Gazette*, December 26, 1873, September 23, 1874, April 9, 1875, March 2, 1878, AWT, 2:46 (September 23, 1874).

34. AWT, 2:16 (March 27, 1872); Worcester *Evening Gazette*, March 26, 27, 1872.

35. AWT, 2:156 (June 17, 18, 19, 20, 1872). Although "no Colored bands" played, as AW noted, two black musicians, Frederick Elliot Lewis and Henry F. Williams, did play in white bands. See James M. Trotter, *Music and Some Highly Musical People*, 106–8, 184.

36. AWT, 2:199 (January 24, 1874). AW may well have heard Rosa when she gave a series of concerts in Worcester in 1869. See Worcester *Evening Gazette*, May 10, 1869. See also Stanley Sadie, ed., *The New Grove Dictionary of Music and Musicians*, vol. 14, 181–82, vol. 16, 191.

37. On postwar politics, see Michael E. McGerr, *The Decline of Popular Politics*, passim.

38. AWT, 2:118–19 (May 12, 1871). For examples of AW's commentary on other state elections, see ibid., 2: 151 (March 13, 1872), 152 (April 3, 4, 1872), 160–61 (August 8, 1872), 163 (September 5, 10, 1872), 165 (October 12, 1872), 180 (April 8, 1873).

39. Ibid., 2:146 (December 12, 1871).

40. Ibid., 2:109 (March 10, 1871). On the issue of Santo Domingo and American expansion in general, see William S. McFeely, *Frederick Douglass,* 276; Eric Foner, *Reconstruction,* 494–97.

41. AWT, 2:111 (April 18, 1871). For his comment on the aurora borealis in Philadelphia, see ibid., 1:n.p. (September 3, 1859).

42. Ibid., 2:113–14 (April 16, 1871). Although dated April 16, this entry followed his discussion of the aurora borealis (April 18). It is possible that AW entered the date of the newspaper or magazine from which he took at least some of his details of the events in Kentucky and Florida in March 1871.

43. AW wrote two months later that a devastating tornado that swept through Worcester County was "the Work of the Almighty Power, from God. with only one breath: from Him That Sits Upon The Throne;" See ibid., 2:125–26 (June 12, 1871).

44. Ibid., 2:113 (April 16, 1871).

45. Ibid., 2:119–20 (May 16, 1871); E. Foner, *Reconstruction,* 313–14. A month earlier the black expatriate and former Philadelphian Peter Lester had written to William Still that black Americans "are in the hands of a terrible [desperateness] with the Democratic party on the one hand, against you, and half-hearted Republicans on the other." Lester to Still, April 30, 1871, box 9G, folder 18, LG.

46. AWT, 2:130 (June 16, 17, 1871), 135–36 (July 28, 29, 1871).

47. Ibid., 2:155 (June 7, 1872).

48. Ibid.; New York *Times,* June 7, 1872.

49. AWT, 2:157–58 (July 10, 1872).

50. Worcester *Evening Gazette,* August 21, 24, 1872; see also AWT, 2:21 (August 24, 1872). The occupational information is derived from the manuscript returns for the 1880 federal census of Worcester.

51. Boston *Globe,* September 6, 1872; see also the account of Charles L. Remond's speech to the black voters of the sixth ward in ibid., September 4, 1872. Remond presided over the convention. For an account of an earlier Boston convention of black Republicans, chaired by Lewis Hayden and with William Brown representing Worcester, see ibid., March 29, 1872.

52. AWT, 2:167 (November 5, 1872).

53. Ibid., 2:173 (December 10, 1872).

54. See U.S. Bureau of Census, *Tenth Census of the United States,* vol. 18, *Report on the Social Statistics of Cities,* 338, 340, for an account of the installation of sewers in the city between 1850 and 1880.

55. AWT, 2:153 (May 6, 1872), 157 (July 4, 1872), 173 (December 10, 1872). On the Webbers' home ownership, see Worcester *Evening Post,* July 19, 1900.

56. AWT, 2:147–48 (January 5, 6, 9, 1872). For a contemporary account of Fisk's actions in the 1871 riot, see New York *Times,* July 15, 1871; for detailed coverage of Fisk's murder, see New York *Times,* January 7, 1872. In contrast to that newspaper, which viewed Fisk's conduct

as "loathsome exhibitions of depravity and cupidity" and his murder as "the natural consequence of a vicious life," AW was rather temperate. Four years later, when Fisk's murderer, Edward S. Stokes, was released from prison, AW noted this without comment, briefly recalled the murder, and referred the reader back to the earlier volume for the details; AWT, 3:130 (October 25, 1876). Fisk had traveled through Worcester in 1869 but there is no evidence that either Moen or Webber ever met him; see Worcester *Evening Gazette,* March 2, 1869.

57. AWT, 2:183–84 (May 9, 1873).

58. Ibid., 2:154 (May 1, 1872), 192 (August 19, 1872), 193 (August 23, 1872); 3:83 (August 1875).

59. Ibid., 2:174 (December 10, 1872); New York *Times,* December 11, 1872.

60. AWT, 2:188–89 (July 21, 1873).

61. Ibid., 2:66 (September 19, 1874); Boston *Globe,* September 21, 1874.

62. AWT, 2:198–99 (November 22, 1873).

9. Loyal Son

1. AWT, 2:182 (April 17, 1873). For another discussion of this event, following AW's reading of the *Congressional Record* about this and other atrocities, see AWT, 3:58–59 (January 29, February 24, 1875). Reconstruction in Louisiana is discussed in Eric Foner, *Reconstruction,* passim.

2. AWT, 2:183 (May 7, 1873).

3. On Louisiana, see ibid., 2:182 (April 17, 1873); on the Modoc Indians, see ibid., 2:181 (April 14, 1873), 186 (June 4, 1873), 196 (October 6, 1873). An editorial in the New York *Times* on April 13, 1873, specifically argued *against* a policy of extermination; for an account of the negotiations and ultimate murders, see New York *Times,* April 7, 8, 9, 10, 11, 12, 13, October 4, 5, 1873; Richard Dillon, *Burnt-Out Fires,* 188–276.

4. On AW's trips to Philadelphia, see, for example, AWT, 2:42 (May 3, 10, 1874).

5. On AW's election as a delegate, see ibid., 2:35 (October 28, 1873); Worcester *Evening Gazette,* October 29, 1873. The activities of the convention and the list of delegates can be found in *New National Era and Citizen,* November 27, December 4, 11, 18, 1873. Clark's speech is in ibid., December 18, 1873.

6. AWT, 2:33 (August 1, 1873).

7. Ibid., 2:36 (November 6, 1873).

8. Worcester *Evening Gazette,* February 17, 1874.

9. On the founding of Worcester's Household of Ruth, Post No. 27, see AWT, 8:80 (October 25, 1895); Boston *Advocate,* March 13, 1886; Chas. H. Brooks, *The Official History and Manual of the Grand United Order of Odd Fellows . . . ,* 131.

10. Worcester contained 599 black or mulatto residents in 1875 and they accounted for slightly more than 1 percent of the city's total population of 49,317. See Bureau of Statistics of Labor, *The Census of Massachusetts, 1875,* vol. 1, 55.

11. See AWT, 2:49 (December 1, 17, 1874); Worcester *Evening Gazette,* November 28, December 2, 17, 1874; Boston *Globe,* December 5, 7, 16, 17, 1874.

12. AWT, 3:55 (February 11, 1875); Worcester *Evening Gazette,* February 10, 1875.

13. Yet the overall crime rate for blacks remained low. At the time of the 1880 census, only 3 of the 145 inmates in the jail were black. For similarly low percentages almost a decade earlier, see Worcester *Evening Gazette,* January 10, 1871; January 6, 1872.

14. Worcester *Daily Spy,* January 1, 1861, January 12, 1865; Worcester *Evening Gazette,* October 28, 30, 1869, March 11, 12, 1873, February 8, September 18, 1875, January 11, 1876, May 31, 1879.

15. AWT, 2:53-55 (March 11, 14, 1874). Worcester's black residents also sent a small delegation to represent them at the Boston services. See Worcester *Evening Gazette,* March 14, 1874.

16. Worcester *Evening Gazette,* September 4, 1873, October 29, 1874; AWT, 2:68 (October 13, 1874).

17. On Citizens Party tickets, see AWT, 2:146 (December 12, 1874), 164 (October 4, 1872), 172 (December 5, 1872); on prohibitionist candidates, see ibid., 2:196-97 (November 5, 1873), 198 (December 10, 1873), 64 (September 10, 1874); 3:133 (December 13, 1876), 167 ([October 1877]); 5:85 (December 10, 1884).

18. Ibid., 2:64 (September 10, 1874).

19. Ibid., 2:67 (October 8, 1874).

20. Ibid., 2:67-70 (October 14, 28, 30, 1874).

21. Ibid., 2:70-71 (October 4, 1874). (AW erred in this date as the election was in November, not October, 1874.) For similar sentiments on the meaning of Reconstruction by black Republicans, see Richard Greener to Isaiah [Wears], February 22, 1876, box 8B, folder 1, and Isaiah C. Wears, Note Book, 67-69, 106-15, n.d. [1890s], box 9G, folder 3, LG.

22. Franklin P. Rice, "The Life of Eli Thayer," ch. 37, 4-5, FPR.

23. Bureau of the Statistics of Labor, *Census of Massachusetts, 1875,* 1:55; Massachusetts, *Thirteenth Annual Report of the Bureau of Statistics of Labor,* 165, 174. The estimate of black voters is based on an examination of the city's black population from the 1880 federal census manuscript returns. Of a population of 756, 41.3 percent were age twenty or below, and more than half of those twenty-one or older were female—both categories that prohibited electoral participation. Including those who were illiterate, less than 25 percent of the black population was eligible to vote.

24. Massachusetts, *Thirteenth Annual Report of the Bureau of Statistics of Labor,* 165; Robert J. Kolesar, "Politics and Policy in a Developing Industrial City," 316. The Boston *Pilot* is cited in Dale Baum, *The Civil War Party System,* 94-95.

25. AWT, 2:70 (October [November] 4, 1874).

26. Douglass, "Speech Before Mass Meeting of Colored Republicans of the District of Columbia, Mar. 14, 1876," 5 [microfilm, reel 15], FD-LC.

27. Worcester *Evening Gazette,* September 3, 1874.

28. William Still, *An Address on Voting and Laboring . . . ,* especially 5-11; Harry C. Silcox, "The Black 'Better Class' Political Dilemma,"

51-52. For a broader treatment of the changing relationship between the Democratic party and black Americans, see Lawrence Grossman, *The Democratic Party and the Negro.*

29. See, for example, Elizabeth Williams to William Still, March 24, 29, 1874; M.A.S. [Canthy] to William Still, May 11, 1874, both in box 2G, folder 18, LG; Silcox, "Black 'Better Class' Political Dilemma," 51-52. Almost thirty years later, a black plumber wrote Still's daughter upon her father's death and praised him for his independent leadership in leaving the Republican party when it relinquished its firm defense of equality: "[H]e refused to follow the cry of race," Allen W. Turnage wrote in 1902, "that says though you slay me without cause, yet will I follow thee without compensation, even to the extent of giving my consent against others in thy name . . . he had no such loyalty as that. He stood for his race and right actions toward all men; he was not a man of two principles, one for the American Negro and an entirely different principle for the Philippine Islands." Allen W. Turnage to Ella Still, August 9, 1902, box 9G, folder 21, LG. AW did not record Still's death.

30. AWT, 2:42 (May 3, 10, 1874).

31. W. Still to Rev. W. S. Lowry, January 26, 1874, WSLB. See also Still to William D. Jones, June 5, 1873, to J. C. Price, June 12, 1873, to J. W. Somers, July 12, 1873, WSLB; and J. A. Newby to Wm. Still, March 11, 1874, box 9G, folder 18, LG. For additional discussion by contemporaries on the need to build black businesses, see Henry M. Minton, *Early History of Negroes in Business in Philadelphia*, 20; Andrew F. Hilyer, comp., *The Twentieth Century Union League Directory*, 104-6.

32. See Louis R. Harlan, *Booker T. Washington: The Making of a Black Leader, 1865-1901*, 254-55, 266-71; Harlan, *Booker T. Washington: The Wizard of Tuskegee, 1901-1915*, 15, 58, 89, 100, 104. On the emergence of the National Negro Business League in Worcester, see Booker T. Washington to Walter M. Coshburn, March 3, 1905, BTW; untitled clipping, January 10, 1906, vol. 18, 116, ASR.

33. Purvis to Parker T. Smith, February 22, 1867, box 2G, folder 14, LG.

34. AWT, 2:84-85 (December 31, 1874).

35. Ibid., 2:65 (September 14, 18, 1874); III:51 (January 11, 1875). For a discussion of the attacks on the elected Louisiana government, see E. Foner, *Reconstruction*, 542-55.

36. AWT, 3:51 (January 11, 1875). AW did not refer to Anthony Burns by name, but the context suggests that was the case he had in mind.

37. Ibid., 3:52 (January 11, 1875), 54, 57-59, 62-64 (January 29, February 24, 1875). For Congressman Hoar's report, see *Congressional Record*, 43rd Cong., 2d sess., vol. 3, 1647-52 (February 23, 1875); another detailed speech by Hoar on conditions in the South can be found in *Congressional Record*, 44th Cong., 1st sess., vol. 4, 5373-80 (August 9, 1876). See also George F. Hoar, *Autobiography of Seventy Years*, vol. 1, 254-61.

38. AWT, 3:59 (February 24, 1875).

39. Ibid., 3:56, 61 (February 6, March 19, 1875); Worcester *Evening Gazette*, March 19, 1875. On the history of the Civil Rights Act, see AWT, 3:56 (February 6, 1875), 60 (March 4, 1875); E. Foner, *Reconstruction*, 553-56; Alfred Avins, "Racial Segregation in Public Accom-

modations," 137–43; Alfred H. Kelly, "The Congressional Controversey over School Segregation, 1867–1875," 471–72, 481–82. Compare this meeting with the more ebullient tones of an earlier meeting of Worcester's black activists endorsing Sumner's original bill in Worcester *Evening Gazette,* February 20, 1872. On 1874 Democratic victories, see AWT, 2:70–72 (November 4, 1874); for Clark's speech, see *New National Era and Citizen,* December 18, 1873.

40. On the founding of King David Lodge, see AWT, 2:36 (November 6, 1873); Worcester *Evening Gazette,* November 6, 1873; Prince Hall Masons, *Proceedings of the Prince Hall Grand Lodge . . . 1873,* 4–5. For an account of the parade itself, see Worcester *Evening Gazette,* June 23, 24, 1875. AW comments on other Worcester men in the lodge in AWT, 8:48–49 (December 11, 1894). The earliest public reference I found concerning AW's role in the lodge noted his election as secretary; see Worcester *Evening Gazette,* December 6, 1878.

41. On the presentation of the petition, and the appointment of the Grand Lodge committee, see Free and Accepted Masons, *Proceedings, Grand Lodge . . . of the Commonwealth of Massachusetts,* 1868, 46. The petition, with its signatories, is reprinted as part of the committee's report in Free and Accepted Masons, *Proceedings, Grand Lodge . . . of the Commonwealth of Massachusetts,* 1869, 129–36; the quotes are cited on 133 and 136 respectively.

42. *Proceedings of the Prince Hall Grand Lodge . . . 1873,* 15–16; Prince Hall Masons, *Proceedings of the Prince Hall Grand Lodge . . . 1874,* 24–25; William H. Upton, *Negro Masonry . . . ,* 35.

43. AWT, 3:73–75 ([June 1875]).

44. *Proceedings, Grand Lodge . . . of the Commonwealth of Massachusetts,* 1869, 93; Free and Accepted Masons, *Proceedings, Grand Lodge . . . of the Commonwealth of Massachusetts,* 1870, 184, 461; Free and Accepted Masons, *Proceedings, Grand Lodge . . . of the Commonwealth of Massachusetts,* 1871, 177; [Montacute Lodge,] *By-Laws and List of Members . . . ,* 15, 31.

45. AWT, 3:66–67 (April 19, 1875).

46. Ibid., 3:66 (April 19, 1875).

47. Boston *Globe,* June 18, 1875; AWT, 3:71–72 (June 18, 1875).

48. AWT, 2:51–52 (March 4, 1874). There was at least one local black woman involved in these efforts, as Mrs. Allen Walker represented the A.M.E. Zion Church.

49. Ibid., 3:94 (November 24, 1875).

50. On the growth of the yearly revival, see Worcester *Evening Gazette,* August 29, 30, September 1, 1866, August 15, 1870, August 20, 1884; AWT, 3:85 (August 26, 1875), 163 (August 24, 1877).

51. AWT, 2:21 (August 19, 1872).

52. Galatians 3:13.

53. AWT, 3:85 (August 26, 1875).

54. See ibid., 1:n.p. (March 1858), and the discussion below.

55. See the record card for AW, section 37, number 427, dated July 19, 1875, at the office of Hope Cemetery, Worcester. The date of Harry's reinterment is not listed. It is possible that AW himself went to Philadelphia to retrieve the body that October and that the reburial occurred soon

after. AW traveled to Philadelphia on Wednesday, October 13; he did not note when he returned. On Sunday, October 17, Susan Beulah, a Philadelphia friend from the Lombard Street church, arrived in Worcester; the following Saturday, another member of her family arrived as well. As the temperature throughout October did not drop below 40° F., they may have come for the reburial. See AWT, 3:10 (October 13, 17, 23, 1875). It is possible that the grave site was as large as it was to provide space for some of Lizzie Webber's blood relatives. At least in 1926 a William H. Douglass, possibly a nephew of Lizzie's, was buried in the plot.

56. See AWT, 3:17–22 (May to October, 1876). For AW's entry on the centennial, see ibid., 3:115–16 (May 11, 1876); on Decoration Day in Worcester, 3:119–21 (May 30, 1876); on July Fourth, 3:124 (July 4, 1876); on Custer's defeat, 3:125 (July 7, 1876); and on Integrity Lodge, 3:126 (August 18, 1876).

57. Ibid., 3:121–22 (June 7, 1876), 123 (June 29, 1876).

58. Ibid., 3:127 (September 12, 1876), 129 (October 10, 1876).

59. Ibid., 3:130–32 (November 8, 9, 29, 1876). On this electoral crisis, see E. Foner, *Reconstruction,* 575–87.

60. AWT, 3:139–40 (March 2, 5, 1877).

61. Ibid., 3:143–44 (March 28, April 21, 1877).

10. The Kindness of Brethren

1. See AWT, 3:91 (October 27, 1875), 138 (January 13, 1877), 29 (May 29, 1877), 30 (June 27, 1877), 31 (July 18, 1877), 34 (October 5, 1877), 38 (February 28, 1878). The quote is taken from Willard to Thomas Dodge, September 8, 1883, case 3, folder DcE-1592, ASW.

2. AWT, 3:144 (April 21, 1877), 145 (April 21, 1877), 146 (May 11, 1877), 148 (May 21, 1877).

3. Ibid., 3:147 (May 11, 1877), 151–53 (May 29, 1877), 154 (May 31, 1877); on "Miss Von Hillern," see 3:147 (May 16, 1877), 154 (June 6, 1877).

4. On AW's reading habits, see ibid., 2:116 (May 5, 1871), 166 (October 23, 28, 1872), 172 (December 5, 1872), 73 ([1874]); 4:125 (September 11, 1880); V:102–9 (July 23, 1885); 7:88–90 (December 2, 1892), 110 (February 21, 1893), 142 (August 10, 1893); 9:158 (June 22, 1898 [clippings inserted]). On the holdings of the Worcester Free Public Library, see Worcester City Council, *1684–1884,* 143.

5. On the patent and growth of the firm through 1885, see Worcester *Evening Gazette,* June 7, 1876; William T. Hogan, *Economic History of the Iron and Steel Industry in the United States,* vol. 1:108–109; Charles G. Washburn, *Manufacturing and Mechanical Industries, of Worcester,* 39, 40; Waukegan (Ill.) *Daily Sun,* undated clipping, case 12, folder DcE-1569, ASW; Worcester City Council, *1684–1884,* 151, 163; AWT, 5:31 (January 18, 1886).

6. See Massachusetts, *Seventh Annual Report of the Bureau of Statistics of Labor . . . ,* 63, on working-class home ownership in Worcester County in 1875.

7. Arthur G. Warren, penciled note, undated, appended well after the fact to the letter of Willard to Thomas Dodge, September 8, 1883, case

3, folder DcE-1592, ASW. Warren, who was the first curator of the ASW collection in Worcester, before it was transferred to the Baker Library, Harvard University Graduate School of Business Administration, knew AW personally.

8. AWT, 3:155 (June 25, 1877). On the Molly Maguires, see Wayne G. Broehl, Jr., *The Molly Maguires;* Anthony F. C. Wallace, *St. Clair,* 320–66.

9. On this strike, see Robert V. Bruce, *1877,* and Nick Salvatore, *Eugene V. Debs,* ch. 2.

10. AWT, 3:158–60 (July 27, [July 30], 1877).

11. Ibid., 3:161 (August 1, 1877).

12. Ibid., 3:161–62 (August 1, 1877).

13. Worcester *Evening Gazette,* May 3, 1877.

14. AWT, 3:167 ([October 1877]).

15. Ibid., 3:167–68 (November 1, 8, December 12, 1877).

16. Worcester *Evening Gazette,* October 5, 1877.

17. AWT, 3:169 (January 1, 1878).

18. Wendell Phillips, *Who Shall Rule Us?,* 3; Worcester *Evening Gazette,* August 6, September 18, 1878. On Lichtman's activities on behalf of Butler in Worcester, see Worcester *Evening Gazette,* August 22, 1884. On Kearney, see Alexander Saxton, *The Indispensable Enemy.*

19. On Mobray in 1878, see Worcester *Evening Gazette,* November 1, 1878.

20. Ibid., October 25, 1878.

21. For an example of the honor accorded Butler by some black veterans, see the letter of Sgt. John D. Berry (Company C, Fifth Massachusetts Cavalry) to Benjamin F. Butler, December 10, 1872, BFB.

22. Worcester *Evening Gazette,* November 6, 1878; AWT, 3:176 (November 6, 1878). On Butler's political career, see Dale Baum, *The Civil War Party System,* 156–61, 184–91, 194–98, 206. For an evaluation by a political opponent, see George F. Hoar, *Autobiography of Seventy Years,* vol. 1, 329–363.

23. See the comments of G. W. Darden, a Kentucky delegate, in *Proceedings of the National Conference of Colored Men . . . 1879,* 25–26. I have been unable to locate the source of Darden's reference.

24. Frederick Douglass, "The Negro Exodus from the Gulf States," 10–12, 16–18; Nell Irvin Painter, *Exodusters,* 202–55; Isaiah C. Wears to John A. [Sendery], October 4, 1879, and "Remarks by I. C. Wears Before the U.S. Senate Committee on the Exodus 1880," mss., both in box 9G, folder 4, LG; Harry C. Silcox, "The Black 'Better Class' Political Dilemma," 3, 56–57. The official report of Wears's testimony can be found in U.S. Senate, *Report and Testimony . . . to Investigate the Causes of the Removal of the Negroes . . . ,* 46th Cong., 2d sess., 1880, S. Rept. 693, pt. 3, 151–60. For an early expression of this idea that freedmen and -women had no desire to come North, see the speech by Reverend Lunsford Lane, given in Worcester County in the late 1850s, as reported in William G. Hawkins, *Lunsford Lane,* 204–6. A related discussion of proposals to bring freed slaves into Massachusetts during the Civil War, and the firm opposition of most elected Republican officials, can be found in Worcester *Daily Spy,* October 31, 1862; June 27, 1863. For descriptions of Douglass's enormous miscalculation in assessing the inten-

tions of the white South, see Neil R. McMillen, *Dark Journey*, and Pete Daniel, *The Shadow of Slavery*.

25. *Proceedings of the National Conference of Colored Men . . . 1879*, 26; Painter, *Exodusters*, 213, 227, 245-47; Richard T. Greener, "The Emigration of Colored Citizens from the Southern States." See also George F. Hoar's speech to the Republican State Convention, held at Worcester, September 16, 1879, Box 6, GFH.

26. AWT, 4:104-5 (April 5, 1879).

27. On immediate postwar aid to southern blacks, see Worcester *Evening Gazette*, March 10, 1866; January 7, May 17, 27, June 10, September 27, October 26, 1867; February 3, 1868; September 20, 1869.

28. Ibid., April 27, May 9, 1879; E. L. Comstock to William Brown, December 24, 1880, folder 1, BF.

29. AWT, 4:100 (January 3, 1879), 100-101 (February 10, 1879), 112 (July 17, 1879), 119 (September 22, 1879).

30. Ibid., 4:102-3 (March 16, 1879), 103 (April 2, 1879), 109 (June 23, 1879), 118 (September 29, 1879).

31. Ibid., 4:1 (January 12, 1879); *Our Remembrancer*, 1:1 (October 1882) (this was the parish bulletin for Union Church).

32. AWT, 4:106-9 (May 5, 1879); Charles Hersey, *History of Worcester, Massachusetts*, 323-25.

33. AWT, 4:111 (August 12, 1879).

34. On Union Seminary during the 1860s, see Robert T. Handy, *A History of Union Theological Seminary in New York*, 25-46; George Lewis Prentiss, *The Union Theological Seminary in the City of New York*, 44-52, 65-70.

35. H. A. Stimson to "My Darling," July 24, 1880, box 7, HAS; New York *Herald-Tribune*, July 19, 1936.

36. Henry A. Stimson, *Death of General Custer*. . . . See also the autobiographical manuscript, untitled and handwritten, in the folder marked "biographical & genealogical," box 7, HAS, for further reflections by Stimson on Indian/white relations.

37. Stimson to Philip L. Moen, July 6, 1880; to "My Darling," July 19, 20, 24, 1880, HAS.

38. Untitled, undated newspaper clipping, box 7, HAS.

39. Prentiss, *Union Theological Seminary of the City of New York*, 35.

40. AWT, 4:22 (October 13, 1880).

41. See *Our Remembrancer*, 1:1 (October 1882); 1:4 (January 1884 [Stimson's "New Year Message"]); 1:5 (April 1884).

42. Worcester *Evening Gazette*, February 22, May 23, 1878; January 12, August 6, 7, 8, 1880.

43. Ibid., August 2, November 4, 1880.

44. Ibid., December 21, 23, 24, 1880; Massachusetts, *Eleventh Annual Report of the Bureau of Statistics of Labor*, 10-14. The workers lost the strike, took a 9 percent reduction in pay for their ten-hour shifts, and returned to work.

45. AWT, 4:13 (January 1, 1880).

46. Ibid., 4:22 (October 2, 1880).

47. On AW and the Odd Fellows Patriarchical Lodge No. 12, see Patriarchy Account Book, 12, GUOOF; Worcester *Evening Gazette*, August 18, 1876. For his involvement with the Masonic Mt. Zion

Commandery, see AWT, 5:36 (June 24, 1886), 6:17 (May 23, 1889); Prince Hall Masons, *Proceedings of the Prince Hall Grand Lodge . . . 1885,* 67; Prince Hall Masons, *Proceedings of the Prince Hall Grand Lodge . . . 1888,* 5, 12, 18; New York *Globe,* February 2, October 25, 1884; Boston *Advocate,* October 10, 1885; New York *Freeman,* October 10, 1885, January 30, February 20, June 26, July 3, 1886; Worcester *Evening Gazette,* June 24, 1886; New York *Age,* September 7, 1889.

48. There are no membership books extant for either of the two GUOOF lodges, the King David Lodge, or the Pythian Lodge in Worcester. The fraternalists whose characteristics are discussed in the following pages were identified from AW's chronicle, a close reading of the Worcester press and the black press in Boston and New York, and from the *Proceedings of the Prince Hall Grand Lodge . . .* from 1873 to 1904. It is, nonetheless, necessarily incomplete. Those identified were then correlated with Worcester's black population as reported in the manuscript returns for the 1880 federal census of the city, and this is the basis for the statistical data that informs the discussion in this section. Many of these men were members of more than one lodge but they are counted only once in this calculation.

I would like to thank Eileen Driscoll, Tim Nolan, and Rafael Olazagasti for leading this neophyte into the intricacies of SAS and other computer applications that enabled me to analyze Worcester's black residents—and for leading me out as well!

49. The gender composition of Worcester's black population can be followed in Secretary of the Commonwealth, *Abstract of the Census of Massachusetts, 1865,* 126; Bureau of Statistics of Labor, *The Census of Massachusetts: 1875,* vol. 1, 55; Bureau of Statistics of Labor, *The Census of Massachusetts: 1885,* vol. 1, pt. 1, 203; Bureau of Statistics of Labor, *Census of the Commonwealth of Massachusetts: 1895,* vol. 2, 214–15. Only the 1895 census gives the ages.

50. These racial categories were frequently assigned in a highly subjective, if not arbitrary, manner, and it is impossible at this remove to account for possible errors. AW's listing as mulatto, however, is consistent with his military enlistment records from 1864.

51. For a discussion of black Boston's occupational structure in the postbellum years, see Elizabeth Hafkin Pleck, *Black Migration and Poverty,* 82–83, 122–60. Among the fifty-four Worcester lodge members for whom occupational data for 1880 is available, seventeen were skilled (nine born in former slave states), seven were semiskilled (five born in former slave states), and ten were in personal or domestic service (two born in slave states).

52. For comments on the differences between Odd Fellows and Masons, see Theodore Hershberg and Henry Williams, "Mulattoes and Blacks," 423; W. E. B. DuBois, *The Philadelphia Negro,* 222–24; Allan H. Spear, *Black Chicago,* 107; David M. Katzman, *Before the Ghetto,* 147–50; Kenneth L. Kusmer, *A Ghetto Takes Shape,* 97–98.

53. In the absence of information concerning salaries or other income, these comparisons must be tentative. AW and George H. Scott, for example, were both listed among the unskilled; yet each had relations with white elites that significantly improved their economic standing. Simi-

larly, barbers, although listed as skilled workers, encountered periodic bouts of unemployment; and their economic standing when employed often fluctuated between that of a small entrepreneur who hired others and being hired themselves. The census returns list 311 black residents who reported their occupations in 1880.

54. Of the 121 couples (i.e., those designated in the 1880 federal census as head of household and wife, residing at the same address), 71 percent of the marriages occurred between two northern- or two southern-born individuals. Seventeen percent were between southern-born men and northern-born women; in 10 percent the women were northern-born and the men from the South. There was a smattering of cases (four couples in all) where one spouse was from the West Indies (both black men), England, or Africa (the latter two both black women). Of the 120 couples identifiable by race in the census, 83 percent (100 couples) married black to black or mulatto to mulatto. Ten black men married mulatto women; three mulatto men married black women; and there were a handful of interracial marriages: three mulatto and three black men married white women, while one black woman married a white man.

55. The analysis here is based on the larger sample of 126 men in these lodges, and not just the 54 for whom detailed material is available in the 1880 federal census. See above, note 48.

56. Waller, a fifty-year-old black laborer in 1880, was born in Delaware, married a New York–born black woman, and lived at 42 Abbott Street, a single-family house, with three children, ages thirteen to seventeen. See U.S. Bureau of Census, *Tenth Census of the United States*, manuscript schedules, Worcester, Mass., 1880, [microfilm] reel 568, Enumerator's District 900, Supervisor's District 60, 20.

57. AWT, 4:36 (December 1, 1881); Worcester *Evening Gazette*, November 26, 1881.

58. Charles Ledyard Norton, *A Handbook of Florida*, 80, 188–89; William H. Nulty, *Confederate Florida*, 200–201; William Watson Davis, *The Civil War and Reconstruction in Florida*, 232, 299–300, 304; Frank Parker Stockbridge and John Holliday Perry, *Florida in the Making*, 252.

59. C. A. Hentz to "Brother," February 23, 1868, as quoted in Jerrell H. Shofner, *Nor Is It Over Yet*, 265; see also "Rambler," *Guide to Florida*, 86–95; Sidney Lanier, *Florida*, 127–28; Owen Nox, *Southern Rambles*, 76; Stockbridge and Perry, *Florida in the Making*, 252–53; Harriet Beecher Stowe, *Palmetto-Leaves*, 265; Branch Cabel and A. J. Hanna, *The St. Johns*, 245.

60. T. Frederick Davis, *History of Jacksonville, Florida . . .* , 160; U.S. Bureau of Census, *Tenth Census of the United States*, vol. 1, *Statistics of the Population of the United States*, 54, 119. Some in Worcester did get the "Florida fever"; see the report of the excursion of local white real estate investors in Worcester *Evening Gazette*, March 22, 1884.

61. Silvia Sunshine, *Petals Plucked from Sunny Climes*, 52.

62. Worcester *Evening Gazette*, November 26, 1881; U.S. Bureau of Census, *Tenth Census*, vol. 1, *Population*, 385. The town of Palatka was too small for the census to provide a racial breakdown of the residents. On the county's political history between 1865 and 1890, see Shofner, *Nor Is It*

Over Yet, 88, 142; W. W. Davis, *Civil War and Reconstruction in Florida,* 471 fn., 494 fn.; Edward C. Williamson, *Florida Politics in the Gilded Age, 1877–1893,* 68, 92, 96, 126; New York *Freeman,* February 5, April 16, May 28, 1887. For a detailed account of the Reconstruction era by a former slave and political activist, see John Wallace, *Carpetbag Rule in Florida.*

63. Julien de Nazarie and [ ] Wells, *Palatka Directory for the Year 1915,* 23–30; Jervis Anderson, *A. Philip Randolph,* 33; Prince Hall Masons, *Proceedings of the Prince Hall Grand Lodge . . . 1873,* 4–5. Reverend James Randolph was the father of A. Philip Randolph, the trade unionist and civil rights leader.

64. Putnam County *Journal,* as reprinted in the Worcester *Evening Gazette,* May 5, 1882.

65. On travel to Palatka, see "Rambler," *Guide to Florida,* 68–69, 82.

66. Worcester *Evening Gazette,* May 9, 1882.

67. AWT, 4:41 (May 3, 1882).

11. Common Ground

1. AWT, 4:161, 162 (December 9, 25, 1882). On AW's relationship with Charles F. A. Francis, a "colored Special messenger" to the Republican governor and grand master of the Prince Hall Masons, see ibid; Boston *Advocate,* October 10, 1885; Prince Hall Masons, *Proceedings of the M. W. Prince Hall Grand Lodge . . . 1888,* 12.

2. AWT, 4:163 (January 18, 1883).

3. Ibid., 4:167 ([between February and April 1883]).

4. Ibid., 4:168–91 ([between February and April 1883]).

5. Ibid., 4:196–99 ([April 1883]).

6. Ibid., 4:200–202 ([April 1883]).

7. See William E. Nelson, *The Fourteenth Amendment,* 193–96, for a discussion of the Supreme Court's 1883 decision in the *Civil Rights Cases;* see W. Fitzhugh Brundage, *Lynching in the New South,* 7–8, for figures on lynching and mob violence nationwide, and 105–6, 140–42, for more detailed data on Georgia and Virginia, respectively.

8. AWT, 4:69–72, 72–73 (May 21, 25, 1883).

9. Ibid., 4:76–77 (July 16, 1883).

10. Lewis Hayden to John D. Long, June 17, 1883, JDL. See also George L. Ruffin to John D. Long, December 26, 1883, box 13, JDL.

11. See Worcester *Evening Gazette,* October 18, 20, 1883; Worcester *Daily Spy,* October 13, 16, 1883; New York *Globe,* October 13, 1883. For an account of the sharp political debate between black Republicans and black Democrats, in which Isaac Mason and Edward Gimby represented black Republican Worcester at the Boston meeting, see New York *Globe,* September 22, 29, 1883.

12. Worcester *Evening Gazette,* October 27, 1883; Worcester *Daily Spy,* October 31, 1883.

13. T. H. Henderson to Hon. B. F. Butler, January 27, 1884, BFB. Information on Henderson is taken from U.S. Bureau of Census, Tenth Census of the United States, manuscript schedules, Worcester, Mass., 1880, [microfilm] reel 567, Enumerator's District, 881, 30. In 1880 he was listed as a baggage master, while Waples was not listed at all. Hen-

derson included the clipping from the Worcester *Daily Times* in his letter. For other reports on black Democrats in 1883, see Worcester *Evening Gazette*, October 18, 1883; New York *Globe*, October 27, November 3, 1883. AW knew Henderson—at least he commented on and probably attended Henderson's funeral at Bethel Church in 1900; see AWT, 9:199 (April 2, 1900).

14. AWT, 4:79 (November 7, 1883); Worcester *Evening Gazette*, November 7, 1883; Worcester *Daily Spy*, November 7, 1883.

15. AWT, 4:80 (November 19, 1883). Blacks in other northern cities and in San Francisco focused on patronage positions as well, implicitly comparing themselves with white immigrants as competing interest groups. See Douglas Henry Daniels, *Pioneer Urbanites*, 50–51. For a critique of the idea that immigrants and blacks experienced the American social structure in similar fashion, see Thomas Lee Philpott, *The Slum and the Ghetto*.

16. Worcester *Evening Gazette*, June 28, July 1, 17, 18, 22, 23, 25, August 1, 2, 22, 26, 27, September 2, 3, 4, 10, 11, 12, October 1, 3, 4, 11, 21, 22, 25, 1884; AWT, 5:7 (July 23, 1884), 13 (September 18, 1884), 14 (October 3, 1884), 15 (November 3, 1884), 71 (June 6, 1884), 72 (June 11, 1884). For an analysis of late-nineteenth-century popular political activity, see Michael E. McGerr, *The Decline of Popular Politics*.

17. Worcester *Evening Gazette*, November 3, 1884; New York *Globe*, November 8, 1884.

18. The People's Party and the Prohibitionist Party also fielded candidates.

19. Worcester *Evening Gazette*, November 5, 6, 1884. For AW's political evaluation, see AWT, 5:82–84 ([November 5, 1884]), 85 (December 10, 1884), 86 (n.d.).

20. For population figures in 1880 and 1885, see U.S. Bureau of Census *Tenth Census of the United States*, vol. 1, *Statistics of the Population of the United States*, 395, 420, 536–37, and vol. 18, *Report on the Social Statistics of Cities*, 335; Bureau of Statistics of Labor, *The Census of Massachusetts: 1885*, vol. 1, pt. 1, 7, 203, 294–95, 562–63.

21. On the Sixteen Associates, see AWT, 5:8 (August 12, 1884); New York *Globe*, August 23, September 6, 1884; New York *Freeman*, November 22, 1884, January 31, February 14, November 7, 1885, January 16, 1886. On the Unknown Club, see New York *Freeman*, February 28, March 7, 1885. On the B.P.T. Club, see New York *Globe*, September 13, 1884; New York *Freeman*, March 7, 1885; Boston *Advocate*, February 6, 1886.

22. See New York *Globe*, April 12, July 12, 1884; New York *Freeman*, March 7, 28, September 12, October 17, 1885, February 13, March 20, 1886.

23. New York *Globe*, July 19, 1884. I have not been able to determine whether Mary Laws was any relation to the William Laws AW knew from Charles Wurts's home or whether she was from Philadelphia's black Presbyterian circles. She was born in Pennsylvania.

24. Boston *Advocate*, July 18, 1885.

25. See the efforts of Henry Henderson to establish his own store as described in the Worcester column of the New York *Freeman*, April 11,

June 27, August 20, October 31, 1885. See also D. T. Oswell's complaints about the lack of support his orchestra received from black residents in New York *Globe,* February 9, 1884; New York *Freeman,* April 11, 1885.

26. On Scott, see John A. Sherman, "Neighbor's Affidavit," April 28, 1893 in Scott's file, RG15.

27. Information on William Baker can be found in New York *Freeman,* November 28, 1885. For comments about other black workers at Washburn and Moen, see ibid., October 31, November 28, 1885, October 30, November 6, 27, 1886; Boston *Advocate,* November 6, 1886; AWT, 7:8 (August 25, 1892). This estimate of the adult black male workforce was derived by using the percentage of black and mulatto men over age nineteen (the only age noted in the 1885 state census) in Worcester County and applying it to the totals for black and mulatto men in the city of Worcester for the same year; see Bureau of Statistics of Labor, *The Census of Massachusetts: 1885,* vol. 1, pt. 1, 203, 294–95. On the size of Washburn and Moen's workforce in 1886, see AWT, 5:31 (January 18, 1886). In contrast by 1928, when Washburn and Moen had been absorbed into the giant United States Steel trust, only one black worker was employed. See Ella L. Vinal, "The Status of the Worcester Negro," 26–32.

28. In May 1885, "a large delegation of colored people" feted Reverend Simmons at his home on Plymouth Street "to thank him for labors in their behalf, and presented him with $25 in cash in token of their esteem." Worcester *Evening Gazette,* May 23, 1885.

29. Blacks in Worcester File, untitled clipping, March 30, 1887, and Mount Olive Baptist Church File, untitled clippings, February 14, 25, 1885, June 25, 1888, June 21, 1891, September 11, 1896, December 11, 1920, WHM; Worcester *Evening Gazette,* February 24, May 23, 1885; New York *Freeman,* March 26, April 2, 1887. Membership figures for 1885–1900 can be found in Worcester Baptist Association, *Minutes . . . ,* published annually, See also the Minutes of the Worcester Baptist City Mission Board, 7 (April 14, 1885), 13 (September 15, 1885), 57 (January 11, 1887), 62 (January 15, 1887), 66 (May 10, 1887), 78 (March 13, 1888), 119–20 (December 16, 1890), 122 (February 10, 1891), 130–31 (September 15, 1891), 131–32 (September 24, 1891), 133–34 (November 2, 1891), ANTS.

30. The material for this section has been mainly culled from the local newspapers, 1861–1900.

31. For examples of these activities, see Worcester *Evening Gazette,* October 18, 1867, May 22, 1884, March 12, April 4, May 25, 1885, November 12, 1887; New York *Globe,* January 13, May 26, June 9, 1883, September 13, 1884; New York *Freeman,* March 7, 1885, January 9, 23, February 13, 1886.

32. Worcester *Evening Gazette,* March 29, 1876, January 9, October 8, 1884; New York *Age,* January 14, 1888. On the protracted struggle of Bethel to retire the debt on its property on Laurel Street, which ultimately failed, see Blacks in Worcester File, untitled clipping, May 23, 1878, WHM; Worcester *Evening Gazette,* February 22, May 23, 1878, January 12, 1880, March 23, 1882, June 9, July 16, 19, 28, 1884; New York *Globe,* June 14, July 26, October 4, 1884.

33. Worcester *Evening Gazette,* January 18, 1881, February 11, 1897; Boston *Advocate,* September 5, 1885; New York *Freeman,* June 5, August 28, 1886.

34. New York *Freeman,* April 18, 1885; February 13, April 3, 1886.

35. Worcester *Evening Gazette,* March 9, 1874; January 4, 12, 1882.

36. Ibid., October 23, 1884; New York *Globe,* October 4, 1884.

37. The data for this section has been taken from the local newspapers. By church affiliation, the known members consist of: Bethel⁻71 (45 men, 26 women); Zion⁻31 (18 men, 13 women); Mt. Olive (later John Street Baptist)⁻31 (23 men, 8 women).

38. Worcester *Evening Gazette,* February 4, 1884. Four years later, when Jennie Oswell married, among her wedding gifts was "a silver salver from Mrs. Amos Webber." See New York *Age,* January 7, 1888.

39. New York *Age,* April 19, May 10, 1884; Worcester *Evening Gazette,* May 2, 1884.

40. There is no breakdown of Worcester's wards by race in the 1880 federal census. The 1875 Massachusetts census does provide such an analysis, and it also gives the percentage, by ward, of the Irish-born. In 1875, the Second Ward contained 121 blacks, 20 percent of black Worcester but less than 3 percent of the ward's total population. Between 1875 and 1880, the black population of the city grew by 26 percent, while the city's population increased by 18 percent. In this section I have used the 20 percent figure from 1875 to estimate the ward's black population in 1880. Twenty years later, when the total black population of the city had reached 1,104 individuals, the Second Ward remained the residence of 19 percent of black Worcester. See Bureau of Statistics of Labor, *The Census of Massachusetts: 1875,* vol. 1, 55, 294, 728; U.S. Bureau of Census, *Tenth Census,* vol. 1, *Population,* 211; Massachusetts Bureau of Statistics of Labor, *Twenty-first Annual Report,* 134–35; Massachusetts *Bureau of Statistics of Labor, Thirty-fourth Annual Report,* 234–35.

41. The evidence for this residential cluster is taken from the Tenth Census, manuscript schedules, 1880 [microfilm]. The streets contiguous to Liberty were Glenn, Newport, Palmer, and Edwards; those within three blocks included Reservoir, Elliott, Laurel, Prospect, Hanover, and Carroll. On the concept of residential clusters, see Olivier Zunz, *The Changing Face of Inequality.*

42. Much of the housing in Worcester was (and remains) made up of triple-deckers, buildings containing three apartments that ran the length of the house, with the first and second floors the more spacious of the flats. For a brief discussion, see Roy Rosenzweig, *Eight Hours for What We Will,* 31, 41.

43. Worcester *Evening Gazette,* June 16, 1884. On baseball in black Worcester, see New York *Freeman,* June 27, 1885, August 21, 28, 1886, May 7, 21, September 3, 1887; New York *Age,* December 3, 1887. In some instances political and religious activism merged with such activities. The black community in Elmira, New York, celebrated August 1, 1884, with a public parade that began from that city's Bethel and Zion churches. When the large crowd assembled, including delegations from New York City, Syracuse, Utica, and Ithaca, New York, and Philadelphia, the Emancipation Proclamation was read and J. R. Lynch, the black

Mississippi politician, spoke. The crowd then watched as the Ithaca Fearless beat the Elmira Casino in a "match game of ball." This in turn was followed by a ball and dance or, for many, a visit to "the [roller] skating rink that has just been opened to accomodate the colored people of the city." New York *Globe*, August 16, 1884.

44. Boston *Advocate*, February 13, 1886.

45. On AW and the Knights of Pythias see AWT, 5:32 (February 22, 1886), 42 (December 8, 1886); 6:17 (May 9, 1889); Worcester *Evening Gazette*, February 23, 1886, May 11, 1889; New York *Freeman*, December 18, 1886.

46. The dates for the papers were: New York *Globe*, 1880–1884; *Freeman*, 1884–1887; *Age*, 1887–1914, when Fortune severed his relationship with the paper. The *Age* continued to publish, however. See Emma Lou Thornbrough, *T. Thomas Fortune*, 39, 78–79, 95–96, 307–21, 331–35, 341–42.

47. For Hood's signed reports, see New York *Globe*, January 6, 1883, to November 8, 1884. The *Freeman* carried the reports without signature. Information on Hood is taken from the Tenth Census, manuscript schedule, 1880.

48. Boston *Advocate*, October 17, 1885; July 16, November 6, 1886.

49. New York *Freeman*, November 7, 1885; Boston *Advocate*, October 3, 10, 1885.

50. On racism in the national GAR, see Wallace Evans Davies, "The Problem of Race Segregation in the Grand Army of the Republic"; Mary R. Dearing, *Veterans in Politics*, 411–20.

51. Boston *Advocate*, September 26, 1885; New York *Freeman*, August 20, 1885. The veterans present at the first meeting of the association were George Bundy, Alexander F. Hemenway, Alexander H. Johnson, and AW. On the December 1884 meeting, see New York *Freeman*, August 20, 1887.

52. New York *Freeman*, January 2, May 22, 1886; Boston *Advocate*, January 30, February 13, 1886. For an account of William Dupree's career in the two decades following the Civil War, see New York *Freeman*, March 14, 1885.

53. AWT, 5:35 (May 28, 1886); Boston *Advocate*, June 5, 1886; New York *Freeman*, June 5, 1886; Worcester *Daily Telegram*, May 28, 29, 1886; Worcester *Evening Gazette*, May 27, 28, 29, 1886.

54. Boston *Advocate*, June 5, 1886.

55. On railroad engineers and firemen as cultural "heroes," see Nick Salvatore, *Eugene V. Debs*, ch. 1–3.

56. On Robert Small, see Leon F. Litwack, *Been in the Storm So Long*, 51, 101, 178; Eric Foner, *Reconstruction*, 28, 72.

57. The text of Hallowell's speech is taken from Worcester *Evening Gazette*, May 29, 1886. A similar version, with slightly different excerpts, can be found in Worcester *Daily Telegram*, May 29, 1886. A shortened account, penned by "D D" [i.e., Amos Webber], can be found in Boston *Advocate*, June 5, 1886. For further criticism of the railroad brotherhoods for their racial exclusiveness, see New York *Age*, October 11, 1890.

58. Boston *Advocate*, June 5, 1886; Worcester *Daily Telegram*, May 29, 1886; Worcester *Evening Gazette*, May 29, 1886. Two days later Boston's black veterans, organized into the Robert G. Shaw Veterans Association,

decorated the graves of Crispus Attucks, the black Bostonian who was the first to give his life in the struggle for American independence, Charles Sumner, and General E. N. Hallowell, the colonel's brother. See Boston *Globe,* June 1, 1886.

59. Boston *Advocate,* June 5, 1886. AW's full commentary on the reunion in his chronicle was: "Re=union of Colored Veteran, (54, 55*th* Regiment, & 5*th* Cavalry." See AWT, 5:35 (May 28, 1886).

60. See Boston *Advocate,* August 1, 8, October 10, 1885, for AW's role at this time.

61. AWT, 5:36 (June 24, 1886); Worcester *Evening Gazette,* June 24, 1886; Boston *Advocate,* June 26, 1886; New York *Freeman,* June 26, July 3, 1886. The Latin inscription translates as: "In this sign you shall conquer."

62. Worcester *Evening Gazette,* June 25, 1886.

63. Professor Tony Fels was very helpful in developing my understanding of the nature of fraternalism as a religious belief system.

64. Worcester *Evening Gazette,* June 25, 1886.

12. For the Race

1. At this point AW referred the reader back to his discussion of the New York City railroad strike of 1,600 workers two weeks earlier, which he attributed to terrible working conditions, including fourteen-hour days and "certain oppressive rules enforced by timers, Starters, and Other petty officials." See AWT, 5:128 (March 13, 1886).

2. Ibid., 5:129 (March 26, 1886). On the Gould strike, see Ruth A. Allen, *The Great Southwest Strike,* passim.

3. On Worcester's nonunion atmosphere, see Roy Rosenzweig, *Eight Hours for What We Will,* passim. On the labor movement in the city, see Worcester *Evening Gazette,* February 22, March 12, May 21, 26, 1886; New York *Freeman,* May 8, 22, 1886.

4. Worcester *Evening Gazette,* March 4, 6, 8, 1886; New York *Freeman,* January 15, 1887. For a sense of the varied, often contradictory experience of blacks with labor organizations nationally, see New York *Freeman,* January 26, 1884; February 14, 1885; March 6, 20, 27, September 11, October 16, December 11, 18, 1886; January 15, February 12, August 13, 1887.

5. Worcester *Evening Gazette,* March 12, 1886.

6. Similar suspicions were expressed by a black observer of Baltimore's 1886 Labor Day parade. See New York *Freeman,* September 11, 1886.

7. AWT, 5:141 (July 12, 1887). On a related topic, AW approved of the execution of those convicted of the Haymarket bombing in Chicago; see ibid., 5:51 (November 11, 1887). On the bombing and trial, see Paul Avrich's superb book, *The Haymarket Tragedy.* For AW's comments on other labor strikes, see AWT, 6:116 (April 7, 1888), 158 (February 5, 1889).

8. AWT, 5:153 (November 27, 1887).

9. See Boston *Globe,* August 1 (evening edition), August 2 (regular and evening extra editions), 1887; *The Benevolent Banner* (North Topeka,

Kans.), August 6, 1887; New York *Freeman,* February 5, August 6, 1887; Joseph T. Glatthaar, *Forged in Battle,* 262.

10. Boston *Globe,* August 3, 1887; Hartwell's speech is reported in ibid., August 2, 1887 (regular edition).

11. AW's pension history can be found in AW, "Declaration for an Original Invalid Pension," April 9, 1888; "Surgeon's Certificate, Amos Webber," December 10, 1890; AW, "Invalid Pension," July 5, 1890, April 23, 1894; AW, "Pensioner Dropped," April 22, 1904; Lizzie Webber, "Widow's Pension," September 19, 1904, all in AW file, RG15. AW recorded information concerning his pension, especially payments received and forms signed, frequently throughout his chronicle after 1890. See, for example, AWT, 7:30 (June 8, 1894), 39 (September 14, 1894); 8:9 (June 4, 1895), 27 (December 4, 11, 1896); 9:3 (March 10, 1898), 24 (December 4, 8, 1899), 30 (June 5, 13, 1900), 45 (September 10, 1901), 51 (March 4, 10, 1902), 65 (May 16, 20, 1903), 69 (September 24, 1903).

12. On the campaign for the pension, and the provisions of the 1890 bill, see Mary R. Dearing, *Veterans in Politics,* 397–401; Wallace Evans Davies, *Patriotism on Parade,* 166–84; Stuart McConnell, *Glorious Contentment,* 143–53. For the national membership figures, see J. Worth Carnahan, *History of the Easel-Shaped Monument . . . ,* 18.

13. For Post 10, see Grand Army of the Republic, *Journal of the Fifteenth Annual Session of the National Encampment . . . ,* 774; Grand Army of the Republic, *Journal of the Sixteenth Annual Session of the National Encampment . . . ,* 935; untitled clipping, [May 1886,] vol. 3, GAR-WHM; Franklin D. Tappan, *The Passing of the Grand Army of the Republic,* 2, 20, 67, 116; Worcester *Evening Gazette,* February 10, 1897.

14. On black members in Post 10 in 1896, see William L. Robinson, comp., *Roster of George H. Ward Post, No. 10 . . . ,* 13–39; the list of the Post's members is reprinted in Edward P. Kimball, ed., *Brinley Hall Album and . . . Post 10 Sketch Book,* 347–60. The forty-seven black veterans were identified through these lists, military and pension files, and local newspaper reports. Some also joined other groups. Alexander F. Johnson was a member of Encampment 83, Union Veteran Legion in 1894; see *Union Veteran Legion, Encampment No. 83* n.p. AW attended at least one meeting of the Union Veterans Union; see AWT, 8:31 (April 10, 1897). The membership lists for the Union Veterans Union in Worcester are available in box 6, folder 5, COW. Kimball, *Brinley Hall Album,* 85–89, offers brief comments on both of these organizations.

15. These figures are compiled from the pension files of Worcester-area black veterans available in RG15.

16. On these deaths see, in the order mentioned, AWT, 5:51 (September 10, 1887), 49 (July 7, 1887), 54 (December 8, 1887); 6:1 (January 16, 1888), 17 (May 5, 1889), 36 (December 14, 1890), 39 (March 19, 1891).

17. See ibid., 6:17 (May 10, 24, 1889), 172 (untitled clipping, September 19, 1889), 178 (August 30, 1889).

18. Ibid., 6:164–66 (April 8, 18, 1889). For other contemporary accounts of Hayden's life, which AW may have used in his own entry, see New York *Age,* April 13, 1889; John C. Rand, comp. *One of a Thousand,* 294–95. Fuller accounts of Hayden's life can be found in James Oliver Horton and Lois E. Horton, *Black Bostonians,* passim; John W.

Blassingame, ed., *The Frederick Douglass Papers,* 1st ser., vol. 2, 444n; Stanley J. Robboy and Anita W. Robboy, "Lewis Hayden," passim.

19. On Dupree, see New York *Freeman,* March 14, 1885; on Busby, see *The Guardian,* December 20, 1902. On the Equal Rights Association in Worcester, see [Massachusetts Citizens Equal Rights Association,] *Constitution and By-Laws of Worcester Branch . . . ,* 3, 5, 7, 8; New York *Age,* September 21, 1889, December 27, 1890, December 26, 1891. For the celebration of the Emancipation Proclamation, see New York *Age,* December 6, 1890; Worcester *Evening Gazette,* January 1, 2, 3, 1891. Worcester was not unique in this celebration of emancipation more than twenty-five years after the formal proclamation. Philadelphia organized a large meeting the following year (see the leaflet, "Proclamation of Liberty," box 4G, folder 22, LG), while in Kansas the black communities of Nicodemus, Topeka, and Ottawa commemorated the anniversary of West Indian emancipation, with direct reference to their own American experience, during the 1880s—see *Western Cyclone* (Nicodemus), July 8, 1886; *The Benevolent Banner* (North Topeka), August 6, 1887.

20. AWT, 6:77–79 (April 24, 1891).

21. Ibid., 6:90 (October 17, 1891).

22. Ibid., 1:11 ([June 1859]).

23. Ibid., 6:149–50 (November 6, December 10, 1888); 7:82 (November 8, 1892).

24. Ibid., 7:88–90 (December 2, 12, 1892).

25. Ibid., 7:121 (May 1, 1893).

26. Ibid., 6:54–55 (December 18, 1890); Robert M. Utley, *The Lance and the Shield,* 291–307.

27. AWT, 6:55 (December 25, 1890).

28. Ibid., 7:55 (March 4, 11, 1892); Worcester *Evening Gazette,* March 4, 5, 8, 11, 1892.

29. AWT, 7:74 (July 14, 1892), 83 (November 20, 22, 1892). On Berkman and his associate, Emma Goldman, who also lived in Worcester (they ran an ice cream parlor before the Homestead strike), see Richard Drinnon, *Rebel in Paradise,* 42–43.

30. AWT, 7:197–198 (June 25, July 5, 1894), 199 (July 7, 11, 1894). On this major strike, see Nick Salvatore, *Eugene V. Debs,* ch. 5–6. AW never commented on national GAR commander John G. B. Adams's speech in September 1894, when Adams blamed immigrants for the recent strike and urged all Civil War–era veterans to publicly applaud the soldiers who broke the Pullman strike. Adams, a resident of Lynn, Massachusetts, suggested GAR members invite these soldiers to the post to assure them "that the soldiers that were are in full sympathy with the soldiers that are, and will support them in the discharge of their duties to the fullest extent." See [Grand Army of the Republic,] *Roll of Twenty-eighth National Encampment . . . ,* 44, 47–48.

31. AWT, 7:157 (November 3, 1893).

32. Ibid., 7:159–60 (December 2, 1893), emphasis in original; see also Daniel Alexander Payne, *Recollections of Seventy Years.*

33. On Rice, see AWT, 8:95 (March 2, 1896).

34. Tappan, *Passing of the Grand Army,* 26–27. On the role of the camp-fires, see McConnell, *Glorious Contentment,* 170–85. AW had attended

campfires before, as a member of the post; but black veterans never actively participated until 1896. See AWT, 2:34 (September 26, 1873).

35. AWT, 8:113 (June 18, 1896), 130 (September 26, 1896). On the election of 1896, see Michael E. McGerr, *The Decline of Popular Politics,* 138–45; Louis W. Koenig, *Bryan,* 221–51.

36. Worcester *Evening Gazette,* October 31, 1896. AW estimated the Washburn and Moen contingent at 3,000. See AWT, 8:25 (October 31, 1896).

37. AWT, 8:134 (November 9, 10, 1896); Worcester *Evening Gazette,* November 4, 1896.

38. AWT, 8:147 (March 2, 1897), 150 (January [March?] 2, 1897), 153–154 (April 16, 1897), 160 (June 1, 1897), 168 (August 25, 1897).

39. Ibid., 8:143 ([February 1897]), 151 (March 24, 1897), 153 (April 10, 1897).

40. Ibid., 8:158 (May 15, 1897), 162 (June 25, 1897), 155 (April 15, 1897).

41. Ibid., 8:143 ([February 1897]).

42. Ibid., 8:142 (February 13, 1897).

43. Ibid., 8:169 (August [September] 7, 1897).

44. Ibid., 8:29 (February 25, 1897).

45. Ibid., 8:37 (October 1, 31, 1897).

46. On these deaths, see ibid., 7:11 (November 10, 1892), 19 (July 2, 1893); 8:4 (January 5, 1895), 17 (February 16, 1896). See also untitled clippings, October 28, 1896 (on Alexander F. Hemenway), ASR.

47. AWT, 9:167 (August 27, 1898), 191–92 (October 12, 13, 1899). See also untitled clipping, August 27, 1898, ASR.

48. On *Plessy* v. *Ferguson,* see Charles A. Lofgren, *The Plessy Case,* passim. The reference to Justice Brown is on 174.

49. Women's Progressive Club, *Constitution and By-Laws,* n.p.

50. Undated form letter, Lucy Stone Club, LSC; Boston *Globe,* July 30, 31, August 2, 1895. Information on the club movement in Massachusetts can be found in Charles H. Wesley, *The History of the National Association of Colored Women's Clubs,* 13–14, 184–95.

51. Worcester *Evening Post,* July 19, 1900.

52. See the records of Mrs. Eunice Deboise (1801–1876), who had been "at service most of her life, a great part of it in Boston & Worcester," and who was a resident of Boston's Home for Aged Colored Women the last decade of her life, in HACW. Mortality statistics for Massachusetts children, black and white, between 1880 and 1900 can be found in Massachusetts Bureau of Statistics of Labor, *Thirty-fourth Annual Report,* 265. Estimates of life expectancy for black Americans born "in the middle quarters" of the nineteenth century are discussed in Douglas C. Ewbank, "History of Black Mortality and Health Before 1940," 105.

53. See, for example, Secretary's Records, 1:n.p. (April 11, November 13, December 14, 1904); 2:n.p. (January 9, 1911), ACP.

54. Ibid., 1:n.p. (February 8, April 11, May 10, July 12, October 13, November 13, 1904), ACP; *The Guardian,* December 20, 1902.

55. See AWT, 9:74 (February 29, 1904), 231 (September 23, 1903). The untitled clipping on Hanna, dated February 16, 1904, was inserted at the back of the volume.

56. On AW's death and funeral, see Amos Webber, Probate File #33734, CPRW; AW, Death Certificate [copy], AW file, RG15; untitled clipping, March 24, 1904, ASR; Worcester *Spy*, March 25, 28, 1904; Worcester *Evening Post*, March 25, 28, 1904; AW Record Card, section 37, number 427, Hope Cemetery, Worcester.

57. Secretary's Records, 1:n.p. (May 10, September 12, 1904), ACP. On Philip W. Moen's death, see Worcester *Evening Post*, September 13, 1904.

Epilogue

1. See William S. McFeely, *Frederick Douglass*, 81, 92, 103, 154.

2. See Lizzie Webber, "Affidavit," April 1, 1904, in AW's file, RG15.

3. "He was a member of no church," AW's obituary read. See Worcester *Spy*, March 25, 1904.

4. See the interview in Worcester *Sunday Telegram*, January 29, 1984.

BIBLIOGRAPHY

Manuscripts

The manuscript collections used in the notes are listed in the pages preceding the notes. While all contributed to my knowledge of northern black life in the nineteenth century, the following were absolutely indispensable for this study of Amos Webber and his world: the American Steel and Wire Collection, including Webber's nine-volume chronicle, at the Baker Library, Harvard University Graduate School of Business Administration; the Leon Gardiner Collection at the Historical Society of Pennsylvania; the Grand United Order of Odd Fellows Archives in Philadelphia; the Brown Family Papers at the American Antiquarian Society; the Association of Colored Peoples Record Books, in the personal possession of Mr. Stanley Gutridge of Worcester, Massachusetts; and the rich service and pension records of black veterans in the National Archives, Washington, D.C.

Besides those listed at the beginning of the notes (pp. 327–330), the following collections provided necessary historical background and were invaluable to my research:

Allen, William F. Civil War Correspondence, Historical Society of Pennsylvania, Philadelphia.

Armstrong, William. Diaries, 1866–1888, Historical Society of Pennsylvania, Philadelphia.

Banks, Nathaniel P. Correspondence, American Antiquarian Society, Worcester.

Blake, Franklin. Papers, American Antiquarian Society, Worcester.

Boutwell, George Sewall. Papers, Library of Congress, Washington, D.C.

Bruce, John E. Collection, Schomburg Center for Research in Black Culture, New York Public Library, New York City.

Carruthers, George North. Papers, Library of Congress, Washington, D.C.

Chase, Horace. Papers, New Hampshire Historical Society, Concord, N.H.

Colegrave, Frank. Collection, American Antiquarian Society, Worcester.

Coleman, Henry. Papers, Schomburg Center for Research in Black Culture, New York Public Library, New York City.

Draper, William Franklin. Papers, Library of Congress, Washington, D.C.

Earle, Edward. Papers, American Antiquarian Society, Worcester.

Fleetwood, Christian A. Papers, Schomburg Center for Research in Black Culture, New York Public Library, New York City.

Hawkes, Doctors J. M. and Esther. Papers, Library of Congress, Washington, D.C.

Herron, Francis Jay. Papers, New-York Historical Society, New York City.

Holloway, Houston Hartsfield. Papers, Library of Congress, Washington, D.C.

Jones, John Griffith. Papers, Library of Congress, Washington, D.C.

Lewis-Neilson Papers. Historical Society of Pennsylvania, Philadelphia.

Library Company Alphabetical Series. Library Company of Philadelphia in Historical Society of Pennsylvania, Philadelphia.

Littleton, Stephen F. Diaries, American Antiquarian Society, Worcester.

Mann, Horace. Papers, Massachusetts Historical Society Library, Boston.

Masonic Grand Lodge, Free and Accepted Masons of Massachusetts. Collection, Grand Lodge, Boston.

Miscellaneous American Letters and Papers, Schomburg Center for Research in Black Culture, New York Public Library, New York City.

Moen Family. Papers, American Antiquarian Society, Worcester.

Olin, William Milo. Papers, Massachusetts Historical Society Library, Boston.

Phillips, Wendell. Letters, American Antiquarian Society, Worcester.

Rush, Benjamin. Papers, Library Company of Philadelphia in Historical Society of Pennsylvania, Philadelphia.

Schomburg Clipping File (microfiche). Schomburg Center for Research in Black Culture, New York Public Library, New York City.

Shell, Elbridge. Papers, Massachusetts Historical Society Library, Boston.

Southard Family. Papers, New-York Historical Society, New York City.

Twichell, Ginery. Papers, Library of Congress, Washington, D.C.

Unger, Charles W. Collection, Historical Society of Pennsylvania, Philadelphia.

Wilson, Henry. Papers, Library of Congress, Washington, D.C.

Worcester Public Library. Collection, Worcester Room, Worcester Public Library, Worcester.

Young Men's Republican Committee. Papers (Worcester), Massachusetts Historical Society Library, Boston.

Newspapers and Magazines

Anglo-African Magazine. New York, 1859.

Army and Navy Journal. Washington, D.C., 1863–1868.

The Benevolent Banner. North Topeka, Kans., 1887.

Boston *Advocate.* Boston, 1885–1887.

Boston *Evening Transcript*. Boston, 1884, 1889.

Boston *Globe*. Boston, 1872–1890.

Bucks County *Intelligencer*. Doylestown, Pa., 1874.

The Colored American. Washington, D.C., 1899–1900.

The Colored Patriot. Topeka, Kans., 1882.

The Guardian. Boston, 1902–1904.

The Liberator. Boston, 1848, 1855–1860.

The Masonic Truth. Boston, 1883–1885.

New Era. Washington, D.C., 1870.

New National Era. Washington, D.C., 1870–1873.

New National Era and Citizen. Washington, D.C., 1873–1874.

New York *Age*. New York, 1887–1895.

New York *Freeman*. New York, 1884–1887.

New York *Globe*. New York, 1883–1884.

New York *Times*. New York, 1870–1896.

The Old Guard. Worcester, 1886–1889.

Our Remembrancer. Worcester, 1882–1884.

Pennsylvania *Freedmen's Bulletin*. Philadelphia, 1865–1866.

Philadelphia *Evening Bulletin*. Philadelphia, 1855–1860.

Philadelphia *Public Ledger*. Philadelphia, 1855–1860.

The Press. Philadelphia, 1864–1865.

Western Cyclone. Nicodemus, Kans., 1886–1888.

Worcester *Daily Spy*. Worcester, 1861–1865, 1882–1885.

Worcester *Daily Telegram*. Worcester, 1886–1890.

Worcester *Evening Gazette*. Worcester, 1865–1904.

Worcester *Evening Post*. Worcester, 1900.

Worcester *Sunday Telegram*. Worcester, 1889–1892.

The World. New York, 1872.

Government Documents

Boston. *Report of the Minority of the Committee of the Primary School Board, on the Caste Schools of the City of Boston; With Some Remarks on the City Solicitor's Opinion*. Boston, 1846.

Massachusetts. [*Second*] *Report of the Massachusetts Bureau of Statistics of Labor, Embracing the Account of Its Operations and Inquiries from March 1, 1870, to March 1, 1871*. Boston, 1871.

———. *Seventh Annual Report of the Bureau of Statistics of Labor, With an Appendix Containing a History of the Bureau, and of Labor Legislation in Massachusetts*. Boston, 1876.

———. *Ninth Annual Report of the Bureau of Statistics of Labor*. Boston, 1878.

———. *Eleventh Annual Report of the Bureau of Statistics of Labor*. Boston, 1880.

———. *Thirteenth Annual Report of the Bureau of Statistics of Labor*. Boston, 1882.

———. *Eighteenth Annual Report of the Bureau of Statistics of Labor*. Boston, 1887.

————. *Nineteenth Annual Report of the Bureau of Statistics of Labor.* Boston, 1888.

————. *Twenty-first Annual Report of the Bureau of Statistics of Labor.* Boston, 1891.

————. *Twenty-ninth Annual Report of the Bureau of Statistics of Labor.* Boston, 1899.

————. *Thirty-first Annual Report of the Bureau of Statistics of Labor.* Boston, 1901.

————. *Thirty-second Annual Report of the Bureau of Statistics of Labor.* Boston, 1902.

————. *Thirty-third Annual Report of the Bureau of Statistics of Labor.* Boston, 1903.

————. *Thirty-fourth Annual Report of the Bureau of Statistics of Labor.* Boston, 1904.

————. *Thirty-fifth Annual Report of the Bureau of Statistics of Labor.* Boston, 1905.

Massachusetts Bureau of Statistics of Labor. *The Census of Massachusetts: 1875.* 3 vols. Boston, 1876.

————. *The Census of Massachusetts: 1885.* 3 vols. Boston, 1887.

————. *Census of the Commonwealth of Massachusetts: 1895.* 2 vols. Boston, 1897.

————. *Census of the Commonwealth of Massachusetts: 1905.* 4 vols. Boston, 1909.

Massachusetts Office of Adjutant-General. *Record of the Massachusetts Volunteers, 1861–1865.* 2 vols. Boston, 1868–1870.

————. *Massachusetts Soldiers, Sailors, and Marines in the Civil War.* Norwood, Mass., 1933.

Massachusetts Secretary of the Commonwealth. *Abstract of the Census of the Commonwealth of Massachusetts, Taken with Reference to Facts Existing on the First Day of June 1855. With Remarks on the Same.* Boston, 1857.

————. *Statistical Information Relating to Certain Branches of Industry in Massachusetts, for the Year Ending May 1, 1865.* Boston, 1866.

————. *Abstract of the Census of Massachusetts, 1865: With Remarks on Same, and Supplementary Tables.* Boston, 1867.

Massachusetts State Senate. Senate Document No. 1. *Address of His Excellency John A. Andrew, to the Legislature of Massachusetts, January 9, 1863.* Boston, 1863.

————. Senate Document No. 1. *Address of His Excellency John A. Andrew, to the Legislature of Massachusetts, January 6, 1865.* Boston, 1865.

————. Senate Document No. 2. *Valedictory Address of His Excellency John A. Andrew, to the Two Branches of the Legislature of Massachusetts, January 4, 1866.* Boston, 1866.

————. Senate Document 3. *Address of His Excellency Alexander H. Bullock, to the Two Branches of the Legislature of Massachusetts, January 6, 1866.* Boston, 1866.

————. Senate Document 1. *Address of His Excellency Alexander H. Bullock, to the Two Branches of the Legislature of Massachusetts, January 4, 1867.* Boston, 1867.

———. Senate Document 1. *Address of His Excellency Alexander H. Bullock, to the Two Branches of the Legislature of Massachusetts, January 3, 1868.* Boston, 1868.

———. Senate Document 1. *Valedictory Address of His Excellency Alexander H. Bullock, to the Two Branches of the Legislature of Massachusetts, January 7, 1869.* Boston, 1869.

Philadelphia County Prison. *The First Annual Report of the Inspectors of the Philadelphia County Prison, Made to the Legislature, February 1848.* Harrisburg, Pa., 1874.

———. *The Sixth Annual Report of the Inspectors of the Philadelphia County Prison, Made to the Legislature, February 1853.* Philadelphia, 1853.

———. *The Eleventh Annual Report of the Inspectors of the County Prison, Made to the Legislature, February 1858.* Philadelphia, 1858.

United States Army, Quartermaster General's Office. *Roll of Honor: Names of Soldiers Who Died in Defence of the American Union, Interred in the Eastern District of Texas; Central District of Texas; Rio Grande District, Department of Texas; and Corpus Christie, Texas.* Washington, D.C., 1866.

United States Census Office. *Fifth Census; Or, Enumeration of the Inhabitants of the United States. 1830. To Which Is Prefixed, a Schedule of the Whole Number of Persons Within the Several Districts of the United States, Taken According to the Acts of 1790, 1800, 1810, 1820.* Washington, D.C., 1832.

———. Fifth Census of the United States, manuscript schedules, Bucks County, Pa., 1830 [microfilm].

———. *Compendium of the Enumeration of the Inhabitants and Statistics of the United States, as Obtained at the Department of State, from the Returns of the Sixth Census, by the Counties and Principal Towns, Exhibiting the Population, Wealth and Resources of the Country.* Washington, D.C., 1841.

———. *Statistics of the United States of America, as Collected and Returned by the Marshalls of the Several Judicial Districts, Under the Thirteenth Section of the Act for Taking the Sixth Census; Corrected at the Department of State. June 1, 1840.* Washington, D.C., 1841.

———. *Sixth Census or Enumeration of the Inhabitants of the United States, as Corrected at the Department of State, in 1840.* Washington, D.C., 1841.

———. Sixth Census of the United States, manuscript schedules, Burlington County, N.J., and Bucks County, Pa., 1840 [microfilm].

———. Seventh Census of the United States, manuscript schedules, Philadelphia County, Pa., 1850 [microfilm].

U.S. Bureau of Census. *Population of the United States in 1860; Compiled from the Original Returns of the Eighth Census.* Washington, D.C., 1864.

———. Eighth Census of the United States, manuscript schedules, Philadelphia County, Pa., 1860 [microfilm].

———. *Ninth Census of the United States.* Vol. 1, *The Statistics of the Population of the United States.* Washington, D.C., 1872.

————. *Ninth Census of the United States*. Vol. 2, *The Vital Statistics of the United States*. Washington, D.C., 1872.

————. *Ninth Census of the United States*. Vol. 3, *The Statistics on the Wealth and Industry of the United States*. Washington, D.C., 1872.

————. *Tenth Census of the United States*. Vol. 1, *Statistics of the Population of the United States*. Washington, D.C., 1883.

————. *Tenth Census of the United States*. Vol. 2, *Report on the Manufactures of the United States*. Washington, D.C., 1883.

————. *Tenth Census of the United States*. Vol. 18, *Report on the Social Statistics of Cities*. Washington, D.C., 1886.

————. Tenth Census of the United States, manuscript schedules, Worcester County, Mass., 1880 [microfilm].

————. *Negro Population, 1790–1915*. Washington, D.C., 1918 (reissue, Westport, Conn., 1968).

U.S. Congress. *Congressional Record*. 43rd Cong., 2d sess., 1875. Vol. 3.

————. *Congressional Record*. 44th Cong., 1st sess., 1876. Vol. 4.

————. House. *Mis. House Document No. 44, Civil Rights. Memorial of National Convention of Colored Persons, Praying to Be Protected in Their Civil Rights.* 43rd Cong., 2d sess., 1873.

————. Joint Committee on Reconstruction. *Report of the Joint Committee on Reconstruction*. 39th Cong., 1st sess., 1866. 4 parts.

————. Senate. *Report and Testimony of the Select Committee of the U.S. Senate to Investigate the Causes of the Removal of the Negroes from the Southern States to the Northern States*. 46th Cong., 2d sess., 1880. S. Rept. 693, 3 parts.

U.S. Department of War. *The War of the Rebellion: A Compilation of the Official Records of the Union and Confederate Armies*. 4 ser., 130 vols. Washington, D.C., 1880–1902.

United States Office of the Adjutant-General. *Official Army Register of the Volunteer Force of the United States Army for the Years 1861, 62, 63, 64, 65*. 8 vols. Washington, D.C., 1867.

Worcester. *Worcester City Directory*. Worcester, 1861–1904.

Worcester City Council. *1684–1884. Celebration of the Two Hundredth Anniversary of the Naming of Worcester, October 14 and 15, 1884*. Worcester, 1885.

Minutes and Proceedings

Foner, Philip S., and George E. Walker eds. *Proceedings of the Black State Conventions, 1840–1865*. Vol. 2. Philadelphia, 1980.

————. *Proceedings of the Black National and State Conventions, 1865–1900*. Philadelphia, 1986.

Grand Army of the Republic. *Proceedings of the First to Tenth Meetings 1866–1876. (Inclusive) of the National Encampment, Grand Army of the Republic, with Digest of Decisions, Rules of Order and Index*. Philadelphia, 1877.

————. *Journal of the Fifteenth Annual Session of the National Encampment,*

Grand Army of the Republic, Held at Indianapolis, Ind., June 15th and 16th, 1881. Philadelphia, 1881.

———. *Journal of the Sixteenth Annual Session of the National Encampment, Grand Army of the Republic, Held at Baltimore, Md., June 21, 22, 23, 1882*. Lawrence, Mass., 1882.

———. *Journal of the Nineteenth Annual Session of the National Encampment, Grand Army of the Republic, Portland, Maine, June 24th and 25th, 1885*. Toledo, Ohio, 1885.

———. *Roll of Twenty-eighth National Encampment, Grand Army of the Republic, Pittsburgh, Pa., September 12th and 13th, 1894*. N.p., n.d.

Masons, Free and Accepted. *Journal of the Proceedings of the M.W. Grand Lodge of the Ancient and Honorable Fraternity of Free and Accepted Masons, of the State of New Hampshire*. Manchester, N.H., 1868.

———. *Journal of Proceedings of the M.W. Grand Lodge of the Ancient and Honorable Fraternity of Free and Accepted Masons of the State of New Hampshire*. Manchester, N.H., 1869.

———. *Journal of Proceedings of the M.W. Grand Lodge, Ancient and Free Accepted Masons, of the State of New Hampshire*. Manchester, N.H., 1870.

———. *Journal of Proceedings of the M.W. Grand Lodge, Free and Accepted Masons of the State of New Hampshire*. Concord, N.H., 1871.

———. *Proceedings, Grand Lodge of the Most Ancient and Honorable Fraternity of Free and Accepted Masons, of the Commonwealth of Massachusetts*. Boston, 1865.

———. *Proceedings, Grand Lodge of the Most Ancient and Honorable Fraternity of Free and Accepted Masons, of the Commonwealth of Massachusetts*. Boston, 1866.

———. *Proceedings, Grand Lodge of the Most Ancient and Honorable Fraternity of Free and Accepted Masons, of the Commonwealth of Massachusetts*. Boston, 1867.

———. *Proceedings, Grand Lodge of the Most Ancient and Honorable Fraternity of Free and Accepted Masons, of the Commonwealth of Massachusetts*. Boston, 1868.

———. *Proceedings, Grand Lodge of the Most Ancient and Honorable Fraternity of Free and Accepted Masons, of the Commonwealth of Massachusetts*. Boston, 1869.

———. *Proceedings, Grand Lodge of the Most Ancient and Honorable Fraternity of Free and Accepted Masons, of the Commonwealth of Massachusetts*. Boston, 1870.

———. *Proceedings, Grand Lodge of the Most Ancient and Honorable Fraternity of Free and Accepted Masons of the Commonwealth of Massachusetts*. Boston, 1871.

———. *Proceedings of the Grand Lodge of the Most Ancient and Honorable Fraternity of Free and Accepted Masons of the Commonwealth of Massachusetts*. Boston, 1872.

———. *Proceedings of the Grand Lodge of the Most Ancient and Honorable Fra-*

ternity of Free and Accepted Masons of the Commonwealth of Massachusetts. Boston, 1873.

———. *Proceedings of the Grand Lodge of the Most Ancient and Honorable Fraternity of Free and Accepted Masons of the Commonwealth of Massachusetts.* Boston, 1874.

———. *Proceedings of the Grand Lodge of the Most Ancient and Honorable Fraternity of Free and Accepted Masons of the Commonwealth of Massachusetts.* Boston, 1875.

———. *Proceedings of the Most Ancient and Honorable Fraternity of Free and Accepted Masons of the Commonwealth of Massachusetts.* Boston, 1876.

———. *Proceedings of the Most Ancient and Honorable Fraternity of Free and Accepted Masons of the Commonwealth of Massachusetts.* Boston, 1877.

———. *Proceedings of the Most Ancient and Honorable Fraternity of Free and Accepted Masons of the Commonwealth of Massachusetts.* Boston, 1878.

———. *Proceedings of the Most Ancient and Honorable Fraternity of Free and Accepted Masons of the Commonwealth of Massachusetts.* Boston, 1879.

Masons, Prince Hall. *Proceedings of the Prince Hall Grand Lodge of the Most Ancient and Honorable Fraternity of Free and Accepted Masons, Located at Boston, in the Commonwealth of Massachusetts, for the Year 1873.* Boston, 1874.

———. *Proceedings of the Prince Hall Grand Lodge of Free and Accepted Masons, Located at Boston, in the Commonwealth of Massachusetts, for the Year 1874.* Boston, 1875.

———. *Proceedings of the Prince Hall Grand Lodge of Free and Accepted Masons, Located at Boston, in the Commonwealth of Massachusetts, for the Year 1875.* New Bedford, Mass., 1876.

———. *Proceedings of the Prince Hall Grand Lodge of Free and Accepted Masons, Located at Boston, in the Commonwealth of Massachusetts, for the Year 1876.* New Bedford, Mass., 1877.

———. *Proceedings of the Prince Hall Grand Lodge, of the Most Ancient and Honorable Fraternity of Free and Accepted Masons, Located at Boston, in the Commonwealth of Massachusetts, for the Years 1877–78–79–80.* Boston, 1881.

———. *Proceedings of the Prince Hall Grand Lodge, of the Most Ancient and Honorable Fraternity of Free and Accepted Masons, Located at Boston, in the Commonwealth of Massachusetts, for the Year 1881; A.L., 5881.* Boston, 1882.

———. *Proceedings of the Prince Hall Grand Lodge, of the Most Ancient and Honorable Fraternity of Free and Accepted Masons, Located at Boston, in the Commonwealth of Massachusetts, for the Year 1882; AL 5882.* Boston, 1883.

———. *Proceedings of the Prince Hall Grand Lodge, of the Most Ancient and Honorable Fraternity of Free and Accepted Masons, Located at Boston, in the Commonwealth of Massachusetts, for the Year 1883–4: A.L. 5883–4.* Boston, 1885.

———. *Proceedings of the Prince Hall Grand Lodge, of the Most Ancient and Honorable Fraternity of Free and Accepted Masons, Located at Boston, in the Commonwealth of Massachusetts, for the Year 1885: A.L. 5885.* Boston, 1886.

————. *Proceedings of the Prince Hall Grand Lodge, of the Most Ancient and Honorable Fraternity of Free and Accepted Masons, Located at Boston, in the Commonwealth of Massachusetts, for the Year 1886: A.L. 5886.* Boston, 1887.

————. *Proceedings of the Prince Hall Grand Lodge, of the Most Ancient and Honorable Fraternity of Free and Accepted Masons, Located at Boston, in the Commonwealth of Massachusetts, for the Year 1887: A.L. 5887.* Boston, 1888.

————. *Proceedings of the M.W. Prince Hall Grand Lodge, of the Most Ancient and Honorable Fraternity of Free and Accepted Masons, Located at Boston, in the Commonwealth of Massachusetts, for the Year 1888: A.L. 5888.* Boston, 1889.

————. *Proceedings of the M.W. Prince Hall Grand Lodge of the Most Ancient and Honorable Fraternity of Free and Accepted Masons from the State of Massachusetts, Located at Boston, 1898.* Boston, 1899.

————. *Proceedings of the Annual Communication of the M.W. Prince Hall Grand Lodge, Free and Accepted Masons of Massachusetts, Located at Boston, 1899.* Boston, 1900.

————. *Proceedings of the M.W. Prince Hall Grand Lodge, Free and Accepted Masons of Massachusetts, Located at Boston 1900.* Boston, 1901.

————. *Proceedings of the Most Worshipful Prince Hall Grand Lodge Free and Accepted Masons of Massachusetts, Located at Boston, 1901.* Boston, 1902.

————. *Proceedings of the Most Worshipful Prince Hall Grand Lodge, Free and Accepted Masons of Massachusetts, Located at Boston, 1902–1903.* Boston, 1904.

————. *Proceedings of the Most Worshipful Prince Hall Grand Lodge Free and Accepted Masons of Massachusetts, Located at Boston, 1904.* Boston, 1905.

Minutes and Proceedings of the First Annual Convention of the People of Colour, Held by Adjournments in the City of Philadelphia, from the Sixth to the Eleventh of June, Inclusive, 1831. Philadelphia, 1831.

Minutes and Proceedings of the Third Annual Convention, for the Improvement of the Free People of Colour in These United States, Held by Adjournments in the City of Philadelphia, from the 3d to the 13th of June Inclusive, 1833. New York, 1833.

Minutes of the Fifth Annual Convention for the Improvement of the Free People of Colour in the United States, Held by Adjournments, in the Wesley Church, Philadelphia from the First to the Fifth of June, Inclusive, 1835. Philadelphia, 1835.

Minutes of the State Convention of Coloured Citizens of Pennsylvania, Convened at Harrisburg, December 13th and 14th, 1848. Philadelphia, 1849.

National Equal Rights League. *Proceedings of the First Annual Meeting of the National Equal Rights League, Held in Cleveland, Ohio, October 19, 20, and 21, 1865.* Philadelphia, 1865.

Pennsylvania Anti-Slavery Society. *Fourteenth Annual Report . . . by Its Executive Committee, October 7, 1851. With the Proceedings of the Annual Meeting.* Philadelphia, 1851.

Pennsylvania Equal Rights League. *Proceedings of the State Equal Rights' Conven-*

tion, of the Colored People of Pennsylvania, Held in the City of Harrisburg, February 8th, 9th, and 10th, 1865, Together with a Few of the Arguments Presented Suggesting the Necessity for Holding the Convention, and an Address of the Colored State Convention to the People of Pennsylvania. Philadelphia, 1865.

Presbyterian Church. *Minutes of the General Assembly of the Presbyterian Church in the United States of America: With an Appendix.* Philadelphia, 1830.

————. *Minutes of the General Assembly of the Presbyterian Church in the United States of America: With an Appendix.* Philadelphia, 1844.

Proceedings of the Civil Rights Mass. Meeting Held at Lincoln Hall, October 22, 1883. Washington, D.C., 1883.

Proceedings of the Colored National Convention, Held in Rochester, July 6th, 7th and 8th, 1853. Rochester, N.Y., 1853.

Proceedings of the Colored National Convention, Held in Franklin Hall, Sixth Street, Below Arch, Philadelphia, October 16th, 17th and 18th, 1855. Salem, N.J., 1856.

Proceedings of the Connecticut State Convention of Colored Men, Held at New Haven, on September 12th and 13th, 1849. New Haven, Conn., 1849.

Proceedings of the National Convention of Colored Men, Held in the City of Syracuse, N.Y., October 4, 5, 6, and 7, 1864; with the Bill of Wrongs and Rights, and the Address to the American People. Boston, 1864.

Proceedings of the National Convention of the Colored Men of America, Held in Washington, D.C. on January 13, 14, 15, and 16, 1869. Washington, D.C., 1869.

Proceedings of the National Conference of Colored Men of the United States, Held in the State Capitol at Nashville, Tennessee, May 6, 7, 8 and 9, 1879. Philadelphia, 1879 (reissue, 1969).

Proceedings of the National Emigration Convention of Colored People; Held at Cleveland, Ohio, on Thursday, Friday and Saturday, the 24th, 25th and 26th of August, 1854. Pittsburgh, Pa., 1854.

Worcester Baptist Association. *Minutes of the Worcester Baptist Association, Held with the Greenville Baptist Church, Leicester, Mass., Wednesday and Thursday, October 7 and 8, 1885.* Worcester, 1885.

————. *Minutes of the Worcester Baptist Association, Held with the Northboro Baptist Church, Wednesday and Thursday, October 6 and 7, 1886.* Worcester, 1886.

————. *Minutes of the Worcester Baptist Association, Held with the West Sutton Baptist Church, Wednesday and Thursday, October 5 and 6, 1887.* Worcester, 1887.

————. *Minutes of the Worcester Baptist Association, Held with the Baptist Church in Spencer, Massachusetts, on Wednesday, Oct. 10, 1888.* Worcester, 1888.

————. *Minutes of the Worcester Baptist Association, Held with the Dewey Street Baptist Church, Worcester, Mass., on Wednesday, Oct. 9, 1889.* Worcester, 1889.

————. *Minutes of the Worcester Baptist Association, Held with the Baptist Church, East Brookfield, Mass., on Wednesday, Oct. 8, 1890.* Worcester, 1890.

————. *Minutes of the Worcester Baptist Association, Held with the Lincoln Square Baptist Church, Worcester, Mass., on Wednesday, Oct. 7, 1891.* Worcester, 1891.

————. *Minutes of the Worcester Baptist Association, Held with the Main Street Baptist Church, Worcester, Mass., on Wednesday, Oct. 5, 1892.* Worcester, 1892.

————. *Minutes of the Worcester Baptist Association, Held with the Webster Baptist Church, Webster, Mass., on Wednesday, Oct. 4, 1893.* Worcester, 1893.

————. *Minutes of the Worcester Baptist Association, Held with the Westboro Baptist Church, Westboro, Mass., on Wednesday, Oct. 10, 1894.* Worcester, 1894.

————. *Minutes of the Seventy-sixth Anniversary of the Worcester Baptist Association, Held with the Central Church, Southbridge, Mass., Wednesday, October 9, 1895.* Worcester, 1895.

————. *Minutes of the Worcester Baptist Association, Held with the First Baptist Church, Worcester, Mass., on Thursday, Oct. 8, 1896.* Worcester, 1896.

————. *Minutes of the Seventy-ninth Anniversary of the Worcester Baptist Association, Held with the First Baptist Church, Grafton, Mass., Thursday and Friday, October 6 and 7, 1898.* Worcester, 1898.

————. *Minutes of the Eightieth Anniversary of the Worcester Baptist Association, Held with the Pleasant Street Baptist Church, Worcester, Mass., Thursday and Friday, October 5 and 6, 1899.* Worcester, 1899.

————. *Minutes of the Worcester Baptist Association, Held with the Baptist Church, North Uxbridge, Mass., on Thursday and Friday, Oct. 11 and 12, 1900.* Worcester, 1900.

Books and Articles

Abbe, Cleveland. "Memoir of William Ferrell, 1817–1891." In National Academy of Sciences, *Biographical Memoirs.* Vol. 3, 265–309. Washington, D.C., 1895.

Abbott, Richard H. "Massachusetts and the Recruitment of Southern Negroes, 1863–1865." *Civil War History* 14, no. 3 (September 1968): 197–210.

Abdy, Edward S. *Journal of a Residence and Tour in the United States of North America, from April, 1833, to October, 1834.* 3 vols. London, 1835.

Abzug, Robert H. *Passionate Liberator: Theodore Dwight Weld and the Dilemma of Reform.* New York, 1980.

Address to the Coloured People of the State of Pennsylvania. Philadelphia, 1837.

Allen, Ruth A. *The Great Southwest Strike.* Austin, Tex., 1942.

Allen, Walter. *Governor Chamberlain's Administration in South Carolina: A Chapter of Reconstruction in the Southern States.* New York, 1888.

Anderson, Jervis. *A. Philip Randolph: A Biographical Portrait.* New York, 1973.

Anderson, Reverend Matthew. *Presbyterianism. Its Relation to the Negro. Illustrated by the Berean Presbyterian Church, Philadelphia, with Sketch of the Church and Autobiography of the Author.* Philadelphia, 1897.

Angell, Stephen Ward. *Bishop Henry McNeal Turner and African-American Religion in the South*. Knoxville, Tenn., 1992.

Appeal of Forty Thousand Citizens, Threatened with Disfranchisement, to the People of Pennsylvania. Philadelphia, 1838.

Ashcraft, Allan C. "Texas in Defeat: The Early Phase of A.J. Hamilton's Provisional Governorship of Texas, June 17, 1865, to February 7, 1866." *Texas Military History* 8, no. 4 (1970):199–219.

Asher, Reverend Jeremiah. *An Autobiography, with Details of a Visit to England, and Some Account of the History of the Meeting Street Baptist Church, Providence, R.I., and of the Shiloh Baptist Church, Philadelphia, Pa*. Philadelphia, 1862.

Avins, Alfred. "Racial Segregation in Public Accommodations: Some Reflected Light on the Fourteenth Amendment from the Civil Rights Act of 1875." In *Civil Rights in American History: Major Historical Interpretations*, edited by Kermit L. Hall, 136–68. New York, 1987.

Avrich, Paul. *The Haymarket Tragedy*. Princeton, N.J., 1984.

Bacon, Benjamin C. *Statistics of the Colored People of Philadelphia*. 2d ed. Philadelphia, 1859.

Bailyn, Bernard. "The Index and Commentaries of Harbottle Dorr." *Proceedings of the Massachusetts Historical Society* 85 (1973):21–35.

Banneker Institute. *The Celebration of the Eighty-third Anniversary of the Declaration of American Independence*. Philadelphia, 1859.

Barber, John W., and Henry Howe. *Historical Collections of the State of New Jersey; Containing a General Collection of the Most Interesting Facts, Traditions, Biographical Sketches, Anecdotes, etc. Relating to Its History and Antiquities, with Geographical Descriptions of Every Township in the State*. New York, 1846.

Barr, Alwyn. *Black Texans: A History of Negroes in Texas, 1528–1971*. Austin, Tex., 1973.

Bassler, R. E., ed. *Military Masonic Hall of Fame, 1975: First One Hundred*. N.p., 1975.

Batchelor, Alex. R. *Jacob's Ladder: Negro Work of the Presbyterian Church in the United States*. Atlanta, 1953.

Battle, J. H., ed. *History of Bucks County, Pennsylvania: Including an Account of Its Original Exploration; Its Relation to the Settlements of New Jersey and Delaware; Its Erection into a Separate County, Also Its Subsequent Growth and Development, with Sketches of Its Historic and Interesting Localities, and Biographies of Many of Its Representative Citizens*. Philadelphia, 1887 (reissue, 1985).

Baum, Dale. *The Civil War Party System: The Case of Massachusetts, 1848–1876*. Chapel Hill, N.C., 1984.

Bearse, Austin. *Reminiscences of Fugitive-Slave Law Days in Boston*. Boston, 1880.

Beath, Robert B. *History of the Grand Army of the Republic*. New York, 1888.

Beatty, Bess. *A Revolution Gone Backward: The Black Response to National Politics, 1876–1896*. Westport, Conn., 1987.

Bell, Howard Holman. *A Survey of the Negro Convention Movement, 1830–1861.* New York, 1969.

Bell, Marion L. *Crusade in the City: Revivalism in Nineteenth-Century Philadelphia.* Lewisburg, Pa., 1977.

Berlin, Ira, ed. *The Black Military Experience.* Freedom: A Documentary History of Emancipation, 1861–1867, 2d ser. New York, 1982.

Bernstein, Iver. *The New York City Draft Riots: Their Significance in American Society and Politics in the Age of the Civil War.* New York, 1990.

Betts, John R. "The Negro and the New England Conscience in the days of John Boyle O'Reilly." *Journal of Negro History* 51, no. 4 (October 1966): 246–61.

Bilotta, James D. "A Quantitative Approach to Buffalo's Black Population of 1860." *Afro-Americans in New York Life and History* 12, no. 2 (July 1988): 19–34.

Binder, Frederick M. "Pennsylvania Negro Regiments in the Civil War." *Journal of Negro History* 37, no. 4 (October 1952):383–417.

Bird, F. W. *Review of Gov. Banks' Veto of the Revised Code on Account of Its Authorizing the Enrollment of Colored Citizens in the Militia.* Boston, 1860.

Blassingame, John W., ed. *The Frederick Douglass Papers.* 1st ser., 3 vols. New Haven, Conn., 1979–1985.

———. *Slave Testimony.* Baton Rouge, La., 1977.

Blight, David W. *Frederick Douglass' Civil War: Keeping Faith in Jubilee.* Baton Rouge, La., 1989.

Blockson, Charles L. *The Underground Railroad in Pennsylvania.* Jacksonville, N.C., 1981.

Bodnar, John E., ed. *The Ethnic Experience in Pennsylvania.* Lewisburg, Pa., 1973.

Boromé, Joseph A. "The Vigilant Committee of Philadelphia." *Pennsylvania Magazine of History and Biography* 92, no. 3 (July 1968):320–51.

Bostic, Corrine. *Go Onward and Upward! An Interpretive Biography of the Life of Miss Sarah Ella Wilson.* Worcester, n.d.

Bowditch, Charles P. "The War Letters of Charles P. Bowditch." *Massachusetts Historical Society Proceedings* 57 (1923–1924):414–95.

Boyd, William H. *Boyd's Philadelphia City Business Directory, to Which Is Added a Co-Partnership Directory, (the Partners and Special Partners Therein, Obtained from Reliable Sources).* Philadelphia, 1858.

Boyer, Arthur Truman, comp. *Brief Historic Sketch of the First African Presbyterian Church of Philadelphia, Pa. Along with Rev. Wm. Catto's History and Discourse, from 1807–1940.* Philadelphia, 1944.

Bristol, Reverend D. W. *The Odd Fellows' Amulet: Or, The Principles of Odd Fellowship Defined; the Objections to the Order Answered; and Its Advantages Maintained.* Auburn, N.Y., 1852.

Broehl, Wayne G., Jr. *The Molly Maguires.* Cambridge, Mass., 1964.

Brooke, John L. *The Heart of the Commonwealth: Society and Political Culture in Worcester County, Massachusetts, 1713–1861.* New York, 1989.

Brooks, Chas. H. *The Official History and Manual of the Grand United Order of*

Odd Fellows in America, a Chronological Treatise of the Origin, Growth, Government and Principles of the Order: The Duties of the Various Officers in Every Branch of Odd Fellowship with Directions for Laying Cornerstones, Holding Thanksgiving Services, Dedicating Lodges, Cemeteries, Churches, Halls, and Other Public Edifices; Forms of Petitions, Reports, Charges, Appeals, Etc. Philadelphia, 1902.

Brown, Ira V. *The Negro in Pennsylvania History.* University Park, Pa., 1970.

Brown, William Wells. *The Negro in the American Rebellion: His Heroism and His Fidelity.* Boston, 1867.

Browning, James B. "The Beginnings of Insurance Enterprise Among Negroes." *Journal of Negro History* 22, no. 4 (October 1937):417–32.

Bruce, Robert V. *1877: Year of Violence.* Chicago, 1959 (reissue, 1970).

Brundage, W. Fitzhugh. *Lynching in the New South: Georgia and Virginia, 1880–1930.* Urbana, Ill., 1993.

Bryant, William Cullen II, ed. "A Yankee Soldier Looks at the Negro." *Civil War History* 7, no. 2 (June 1961):133–48.

Buckmaster, Henrietta. *Let My People Go: The Story of the Underground Railroad and the Growth of the Abolition Movement.* New York, 1941.

Bucks County Society for the Promotion of Temperance. *First Annual Report ... Presented at Doylestown, April 24th, 1832.* Doylestown, Pa., 1832.

Bullock, Penelope L. *The Afro-American Periodical Press, 1838–1909.* Baton Rouge, La., 1981.

Butler, Benjamin F. *Speech upon the Campaign Before Richmond, 1864, Delivered at Lowell, Mass., January 29, 1865.* Boston, 1865.

"The Butman Riot. October 30, 1854." *Proceedings of the Worcester Society of Antiquity,* 1 (1878; published Worcester, 1879):85–94.

Bywater's Philadelphia Business Directory and City Guide, for the Year 1850. Philadelphia, 1850.

Cabel, Branch, and A. J. Hanna. *The St. Johns: A Parade of Diversities.* New York, 1943.

Campbell, Georgetta Merritt. *Extant Collections of Early Black Newspapers: A Research Guide to the Black Press, 1880–1915, with an Index to the Boston "Guardian," 1902–1904.* Troy, N.Y., 1981.

Campbell, Randolph B. *A Southern Community in Crisis: Harrison County, Texas, 1850–1880.* Austin, Tex., 1983.

Carnahan, J. Worth. *History of the Easel-Shaped Monument and a Key to the Principles and Objects of the Grand Army of the Republic and Its Co-workers.* Chicago, 1893.

———. *Manual of the Civil War and Key to the Grand Army of the Republic and Kindred Societies.* Washington, D.C., 1899.

Carnes, Mark C. *Secret Ritual and Manhood in Victorian America.* New Haven, Conn., 1989.

Carter, Solon A. "Fourteen Months' Service with Colored Troops." In *Civil War Papers: Read Before the Commandery of the State of Massachusetts, Military Order of the Loyal Legion of the United States.* Vol. 2, 155–79. Boston, 1900.

Cass, Donn A. *Negro Freemasonry and Segregation: An Historical Study of Preju-*

dice Against American Negroes as Freemasons, and the Position of Negro Freemasonry in the Masonic Fraternity. Chicago, 1957.

Catto, Rev. William T. *A Semi-Centenary Discourse, Delivered in the First African Presbyterian Church, Philadelphia, on the Fourth Sabbath of May, 1857: With History of the Church from Its First Organization: Including a Brief Notice of Rev. John Gloucester, Its First Pastor.* Philadelphia, 1857.

Cawelti, John G. *Apostles of the Self-Made Man: Changing Concepts of Success in America.* Chicago, 1965.

Chamberlain, Daniel H. "Reconstruction in South Carolina." *Atlantic Monthly* 87 (April 1901):473–84.

Chandler, Alfred D. *The Visible Hand: The Managerial Revolution in American Business.* Cambridge, Mass., 1977.

Clark, Dennis. "Urban Blacks and Irishmen: Brothers in Prejudice." In *Black Politics in Philadelphia,* edited by Miriam Ershkowitz and Joseph Zikmund II, 15–30. New York, 1973.

Clark, Peter H. *The Black Brigade of Cincinnati: Being a Report of Its Labors and a Muster-Roll of Its Members; Together with Various Orders, Speeches, etc. Relating to It.* Cincinnati, Ohio, 1864.

Cogley, Thomas S. *History of the Seventh Indiana Cavalry Volunteers, and of the Expeditions, Campaigns, Raids, Marches and Battles of the Armies with Which It Was Connected . . . and of the Capture, Trial, Conviction and Execution of Dick Davis the Guerrilla.* La Porte, Ind., 1876.

Cohen's Philadelphia City Directory, City Guide, and Business Register for 1860. Philadelphia, 1860.

Colyer, Vincent. *Report of the Services Rendered by the Freed People to the United States Army, in North Carolina, in the Spring of 1862, After the Battle of Newbern.* New York, 1864.

Committee of Merchants. *Report of the Committee of Merchants for the Relief of Colored People, Suffering from the Late Riots in the City of New York.* New York, 1863.

Commons, John R., et al. *History of Labour in the United States.* 2 vols. New York, 1918.

Cooper, Frederick. "Elevating the Race: The Social Thought of Black Leaders, 1827–50." *American Quarterly* 24, no. 5 (December 1972):604–25.

Cornish, Dudley T. *The Sable Arm: Negro Troops in the Union Army, 1861–1865.* New York, 1956.

———. "The Union Army as a School for Negroes." *Journal of Negro History* 37, no. 4 (October 1952):368–82.

Cravens, John N. "Felix 'Zero' Ervin: Louisiana Negro Slave and East Texas Freeman." *East Texas Historical Journal* 10, no. 2 (Fall 1972):125–30.

Credentials of William Lloyd Garrison, Esq. from the Managers of the New England Anti-Slavery Society and the Free People of Colour. N.p., 1833.

Crowninshield, Benjamin W. *A History of the First Regiment of Massachusetts Cavalry Volunteers.* Boston, 1891.

Curry, Leonard P. *The Free Black in Urban America, 1800–1850: The Shadow of the Dream.* Chicago, 1986.

Custer, Elizabeth B. *Tenting on the Plains or General Custer in Kansas and Texas.* New York, 1887.

Dana, James D. "Memoir of Arnold Guyot, 1807–1884." In National Academy of Sciences, *Biographical Memoirs.* Vol. 2, 309–47. Washington, D.C., 1886.

Daniel, Pete. *The Shadow of Slavery: Peonage in the South, 1901–1969.* Urbana, Ill., 1972.

Daniels, Douglas Henry. *Pioneer Urbanites: A Social and Cultural History of Black San Francisco.* Philadelphia, 1980.

Daniels, John. *In Freedom's Birthplace: A Study of the Boston Negroes.* New York, 1914 (reissue, 1968).

Davies, Wallace Evan. *Patriotism on Parade: The Story of Veterans' and Hereditary Organizations in America, 1783–1900.* Cambridge, Mass., 1955.

———. "The Problem of Race Segregation in the Grand Army of the Republic." *Journal of Southern History* 13, no. 3 (August 1947):354–72.

Davis, Susan G. *Parades and Power: Street Theater in Nineteenth-Century Philadelphia.* Philadelphia, 1986.

Davis, T. Frederick. *History of Jacksonville, Florida and Vicinity, 1513 to 1924.* Gainesville, Fla., 1925 (reissue, 1964).

Davis, William W. H. *The History of Bucks County, Pennsylvania, from the Discovery of the Delaware to the Present Time.* Doylestown, Pa., 1876.

Davis, William Watson. *The Civil War and Reconstruction in Florida.* New York, 1913.

Day, Sherman. *Historical Collections of the State of Pennsylvania; Containing a Copious Selection of the Most Interesting Facts, Traditions, Biographical Sketches, Anecdotes, etc. Relating to Its History and Antiquities, Both General and Local, with Topographical Descriptions of Every County and All the Larger Towns in the State.* Philadelphia, 1843.

Dearing, Mary R. *Veterans in Politics: The Story of the G.A.R.* Baton Rouge, La., 1952.

Dedication of the Soldiers' Monument at Worcester, Massachusetts, July 15, A.D. 1874. Worcester, 1874.

Delany, M[artin] R. *The Origin and Objects of Ancient Freemasonry; Its Introduction into the United States, and Legitimacy Among Colored Men. A Treatise Delivered Before St. Cyprian Lodge No. 13, June 24th A.D. 1853–A.L. 5853.* Pittsburgh, Pa., 1853.

de Nazarie, Julien, and [ ] Wells. *Palatka Directory for the Year 1915.* Palatka, Fla., 1915.

Derr, Mark. *Some Kind of Paradise: A Chronicle of Man and the Land in Florida.* New York, 1989.

Dillon, Richard. *Burnt-Out Fires.* Englewood Cliffs, N.J., 1973.

Dizikes, John. *Opera in America: A Cultural History.* New Haven, Conn., 1993.

Douglas, Ann. *The Feminization of American Culture.* New York, 1977.

Douglass, Frederick. *My Bondage and My Freedom.* New York, 1855 (reissue, 1968).

————. "The Negro Exodus from the Gulf States." *Journal of Social Science* 11 (May 1880):1–21.

————. *Oration, Delivered in Corinthian Hall, Rochester, July 5, 1852.* Rochester, N.Y., 1852.

Douglass, Reverend William. *Annals of the First African Church, in the United States of America, Now Styled, the African Episcopal Church of St. Thomas, Philadelphia.* Philadelphia, 1862.

Drinnon, Richard. *Rebel in Paradise: A Biography of Emma Goldman.* Boston, 1961 (reissue, 1970).

Drummond, A. M. *The Union Army. A History of Military Affairs in the Loyal States 1861–65—Records of the Regiments in the Union Army—Cyclopedia of Battles—Memoirs of Commanders and Soldiers.* 8 vols. Madison, Wis., 1908.

DuBois, W. E. B. "The Black Vote of Philadelphia." In *Black Politics in Philadelphia*, edited by Miriam Ershkowitz and Joseph Zikmund II, 31–39. New York, 1973.

————. *The Philadelphia Negro: A Social Study.* New York, 1899 (reissue, 1967).

————. *The Souls of Black Folk.* New York, 1903.

Dumenil, Lynn. *Freemasonry and American Culture, 1880–1930.* Princeton, N.J., 1984.

Dunlap, Thomas. *Address . . . to the People of Colour, at the Exhibition of the Mary-Street Public School, at Bethel Church, in the City of Philadelphia, Nov. 16, 1825.* Philadelphia, 1825.

Dusinberre, William. *Civil War Issues in Philadelphia, 1856–1865.* Philadelphia, 1965.

Dyer, Frederick H. *A Compendium of the War of the Rebellion.* Vol. 3, *Regimental Histories.* New York, 1959.

Eckert, Ralph Lowell. "Antislavery Martyrdom: The Ordeal of Passmore Williamson." *The Pennsylvania Magazine of History and Biography* 100, no. 4 (October 1976):521–38.

Eddy, T. M. *The Patriotism of Illinois. A Record of the Civil and Military History of the State in the War for the Union, with a History of the Campaigns in Which Illinois Soldiers Have Been Conspicuous, Sketches of Distinguished Officers, the Roll of the Illustrious Dead, Movements of the Sanitary and Christian Commissions.* 2 vols. Chicago, 1866.

Edelstein, Tilden G. *Strange Enthusiasm: A Life of Thomas Wentworth Higginson.* New York, 1970.

Edwards, Alba M. *Alphabetical Index of Occupations by Industries and Social-Economic Groups, 1937.* Washington, D.C., 1937.

Elliott, Claude. "The Freedmen's Bureau in Texas." *Southwestern Historical Quarterly* 51, no. 1 (July 1952):1–24.

Ely, Melvin Patrick. *The Adventures of Amos 'n' Andy: A Social History of an American Phenomenon.* New York, 1991.

Emilio, Luis F. *History of the Fifty-Fourth Regiment of Massachusetts Volunteer Infantry, 1863–1865.* Boston, 1891.

Ershkowitz, Miriam, and Joseph Zikmund II, eds. *Black Politics in Philadelphia.* New York, 1973.

Evans, Clement A., ed. *Confederate Military History.* 12 vols. Atlanta, 1899.

Ewbank, Douglas C. "History of Black Mortality and Health Before 1940." In *Health Policies and Black Americans,* edited by David P. Willis. New Brunswick, N.J., 1989.

Farley, Reynolds. *Growth of the Black Population: A Study of Demographic Trends.* Chicago, 1970.

Ferguson, Charles W. *Fifty Million Brothers: A Panorama of American Lodges and Clubs.* New York, 1937.

Finch, John. *Travels in the United States of America and Canada.* London, 1833.

Finkelman, Paul. "*Prigg v. Pennsylvania* and Northern State Courts: Anti-Slavery Use of a Pro-Slavery Decision." *Civil War History* 25, no. 1 (March 1979):5–35.

———. "The Protection of Black Rights in Seward's New York." *Civil War History* 34, no. 3 (September 1988):211–34.

Fishel, Leslie H., Jr. "The Negro in Northern Politics, 1870–1900." *Mississippi Valley Historical Review* 42, no. 3 (December 1955):466–89.

———. "Repercussions of Reconstruction: The Northern Negro, 1870–1883." *Civil War History* 14, no. 4 (December 1968):325–45.

Fisher, Sidney George. *A Philadelphia Perspective. The Diary of Sidney George Fisher Covering the Years 1834–1871.* Edited by Nicholas B. Wainwright. Philadelphia, 1867.

Fletcher, Stevenson Whitcomb. *Pennsylvania Agriculture and Country Life, 1640–1840.* Harrisburg, Pa., 1950.

Foner, Eric. *Free Soil, Free Labor, Free Men: The Ideology of the Republican Party Before the Civil War.* New York, 1970.

———. *Reconstruction: America's Unfinished Revolution, 1863–1877.* New York, 1988.

Foner, Philip S. "The Battle to End Discrimination Against Negroes on Philadelphia Streetcars: (Part I) Background and Beginning of the Battle." *Pennsylvania History* 40, no. 3 (July 1973):261–92.

———. "The Battle to End Discrimination Against Negroes on Philadelphia Streetcars: (Part II) The Victory." *Pennsylvania History* 40, no. 4 (October 1973):355–80.

Ford, Worthington Chauncey, ed. *A Cycle of Adams Letters, 1861–65.* 2 vols. Boston, 1920.

Foster, George G. *New York by Gas-Light and Other Urban Sketches.* Edited, with an introduction, by Stuart M. Blumin. Berkeley, Cal., 1990.

Fox, Charles Barnard. *Record of the Service of the Fifty-Fifth Regiment of Massachusetts Volunteer Infantry.* Cambridge, Mass., 1868.

[Fox, John.] *Opinion of the Honorable John Fox, President Judge of the Judicial District Composed of the Counties of Bucks and Montgomery, Against the Exercise of Negro Suffrage in Pennsylvania.* Harrisburg, Pa., 1838.

Francis, Russell E. "The Religious Revival of 1858 in Philadelphia." *Penn-*

sylvania Magazine of History and Biography 70, no. 1 (January 1946): 52–77.

Franklin, John Hope. *George Washington Williams: A Biography*. Chicago, 1985.

Fredrickson, George. *The Black Image in the White Mind*. New York, 1971.

———. *The Inner Civil War*. New York, 1965.

Freedley, Edwin T. *Philadelphia and Its Manufacturers: A Hand-Book Exhibiting the Development, Variety, and Statistics of the Manufacturing Industry of Philadelphia in 1857. Together with Sketches of Remarkable Manufactories: And a List of Articles Now Made in Philadelphia*. Philadelphia, 1859.

Friedman, Lawrence M. *A History of American Law*. 2d ed. New York, 1985.

Furness, William Eliot. "The Negro as a Soldier." In *Military Essays and Recollections: Papers Read Before the Commandery of the State of Illinois, Military Order of the Loyal Legion of the United States*. Vol. 2, 457–87. Chicago, 1894.

Furstenberg, Frank F., Jr., Theodore Hershberg, and John Modell. "The Origins of the Female-Headed Black Family: The Impact of the Urban Experience." In *Philadelphia: Work, Space, Family, and Group Experience in the Nineteenth Century: Essays Toward an Interdisciplinary History of the City*, edited by Theodore Hershberg, 435–54. New York, 1981.

Gara, Larry. "William Still and the Underground Railroad." In *The Making of Black America: Essays in Negro Life and History*, edited by August Meier and Elliott Rudwick. Vol. 1, 327–35. New York, 1969.

[Garnet League.] *Ceremonies at the Reception of Welcome to the Colored Soldiers of Pennsylvania, in the City of Harrisburg, Nov. 14th, 1865, by the Garnet League: Together with the Report of the Committee of Arrangements, and the Resolutions of Vindication by the Garnet League, Defining Its Position with Reference to the Pennsylvania State Equal Rights League*. Harrisburg, Pa., 1866.

Gatewood, Williard B., Jr. "Aristocrats of Color: South and North. The Black Elite, 1880–1920." *Journal of Southern History* 54, no. 1 (February 1988):3–20.

Geffen, Elizabeth M. "Violence in Philadelphia in the 1840's and 1850's." *Pennsylvania History* 36, no. 4 (October 1969):381–410.

George H. Ward Post. *Comrades of Geo. H. Ward Post, No. 10, G.A.R. Department of Massachusetts, Worcester*. Worcester, 1870.

Gerber, David A. "Peter Humphries Clark: The Dialogue of Hope and Despair." In *Black Leaders of the Nineteenth Century*, edited by Leon F. Litwack and August Meier, 173–90. Urbana, Ill., 1988.

Gibbs, Mifflin W. *Shadow and Light: An Autobiography*. New York, 1902 (reissue, 1968).

Gillett, Rev. Charles Ripley, comp. *Alumni Catalogue of the Union Theological Seminary in the City of New York, 1836–1926*. New York, 1926.

Glatthaar, Joseph T. *Forged in Battle: The Civil War Alliance of Black Soldiers and White Officers*. New York, 1990.

Gloucester, Rev. S[tephen] H. *A Discourse Delivered on the Occasion of the Death of Mr. James Forten, Sr. in the Second Presbyterian Church of Colour of the City of Philadelphia, April 17, 1842, Before the Young Men of the Bible Association of Said Church.* Philadelphia, 1843.

Gordon, George H. *A War Diary of Events in the War of the Great Rebellion, 1863–1865.* Boston, 1882.

Gordon, Thomas F. *A Gazetteer of the State of New Jersey.* Trenton, 1834.

———. *A Gazetteer of the State of Pennsylvania.* Philadelphia, 1832.

Gorn, Elliott. *The Manly Art: Bare-Knuckle Prize Fighting in America.* Ithaca, N.Y., 1986.

Grand Army of the Republic. *Rules and Regulations for the Government of the Grand Army of the Republic, as Revised and Adopted in National Encampment, Washington, D.C., May 11 and 12, 1870.* Boston, 1870.

———. Post 10. *The Drummer Boy: Official Programme.* Worcester, 1892.

[Grand United Order of Odd Fellows.] *Fourth Quarterly Circular of the Sub-Committee of Management.* Philadelphia, 1882.

———. *Fourth Quarterly Circular of the Sub-Committee of Management.* Philadelphia, 1883.

———. *Fourth Quarterly Circular of the Sub-Committee of Management.* Philadelphia, 1884.

———. *General Laws Now in Force for the Government of the Grand United Order of Odd Fellows in America and Jurisdiction.* Washington, D.C., 1925.

Gravely, William B. "The Dialectic of Double-Consciousness in Black American Freedom Celebrations, 1808–1863." *Journal of Negro History* 67, no. 4 (Winter 1982):302–17.

Green, Alfred M. *Letters and Discussions on the Formation of Colored Regiments, and the Duty of the Colored People in Regard to the Great Slaveholders' Rebellion in the United States of America.* Philadelphia, 1862 (reissue, 1969).

Greenberg, Brian. *Worker and Community: Response to Industrialization in a Nineteenth Century American City, Albany, New York, 1850–1884.* Albany, N.Y., 1985.

Greener, Richard T. "The Emigration of Colored Citizens from the Southern States." *Journal of Social Science* 11 (May 1880):22–35.

[Greenfield, Elizabeth Taylor.] *The Black Swan at Home and Abroad: Or, A Biographical Sketch of Miss Elizabeth Taylor Greenfield, the American Vocalist.* Philadelphia, 1855.

Grimké, Archibald H. "Anti-Slavery Boston." *New England Magazine* 3 (1890–1891):441–59.

Grimké, Charlotte Forten. *The Journals of Charlotte Forten Grimké.* Edited by Brenda Stevenson. New York, 1988.

Grossman, Lawrence. *The Democratic Party and the Negro: Northern and National Politics: 1868–92.* Urbana, Ill., 1976.

Gubert, Betty Kaplan. *Early Black Bibliographies, 1863–1918.* New York, 1982.

Guralnick, Stanley M. "Geology and Religion Before Darwin: The Case of Edward Hitchcock, Theologian and Geologist (1793–1864)." In *Science in America Since 1820,* edited by Nathan Reingold, 116–30. New York, 1976.

Gurney, Joseph John. *A Journey in North America, Described in Familiar Letters to Amelia Opie.* Norwich, Eng., 1841.

Guthrie, James M. *Camp-Fires of the Afro-American; Or, The Colored Man as a Patriot, Soldier, Sailor and Hero, in the Cause of Free America: Displayed in Colonial Struggles, in the Revolution, the War of 1812, and in Later Wars, Particularly the Great Civil War—1861–5, and the Spanish-American War—1898: Concluding with an Account of the War with the Filipinos—1899.* Philadelphia, 1899.

Guyot, A[rnold Henry]. "Memoir of James Henry Coffin, 1806–1873." In National Academy of Sciences, *Biographical Memoirs.* Vol. 1, 257–64. Washington, D.C., 1877.

Hall, Kermit L., ed. *Civil Rights in American History: Major Historical Interpretations.* New York, 1987.

Hallowell, Norwood P. *The Negro as a Soldier in the War of the Rebellion.* Boston, 1897.

Hallowell, N. P., III. *Selected Letters and Papers of N. P. Hallowell.* Peterborough, N.H., 1963.

Hamilton, J. G. De Roulhac, and Rebecca Cameron, eds. *The Papers of Randolph Abbott Shotwell.* 3 vols. Raleigh, N.C., 1931.

[Hamilton, Thomas.] *Men and Manners in America.* 2 vols. Philadelphia, 1833.

Hanchett, Catherine M. "George Boyer Vashon, 1824–1878: Black Educator, Poet, Fighter for Equal Rights—Part One." *Western Pennsylvania Historical Magazine* 68, no. 3 (July 1985):205–20.

———. "George Boyer Vashon, 1824–1878: Black Educator, Poet, Fighter for Equal Rights—Part Two." *Western Pennsylvania Historical Magazine* 68, no. 4 (October 1985), 333–50.

Handy, Robert T. *A History of Union Theological Seminary in New York.* New York, 1987.

Hargrove, Hondon B. *Black Union Soldiers in the Civil War.* Jefferson, N.C., 1988.

Harlan, Louis R. *Booker T. Washington: The Making of a Black Leader, 1856–1901.* New York, 1975.

———. *Booker T. Washington: The Wizard of Tuskegee, 1901–1915.* New York, 1983.

Harrison, Eliza Cope, ed. *Philadelphia Merchant: The Diary of Thomas P. Cope, 1800–1851.* South Bend, Ind., 1978.

Hawkins, Reverend William G. *Lunsford Lane; Or Another Helper from North Carolina.* Boston, 1863.

Hayden, Lewis. *A Letter from Lewis Hayden, of Boston, Massachusetts, to Hon. Judge Sims, of Savannah, Georgia.* Boston, 1874.

———. *Masonry Among Colored Men in Massachusetts.* Boston, 1871.

Headley, P. C. *Massachusetts in the Rebellion. A Record of the Historical Position of the Community, and the Services of the Leading Statesmen, the Military, the Colleges, and the People in the Civil War of 1861–65.* Boston, 1866.

Heard, John T. *An Address Delivered Before the Grand Lodge of Masons in Massachusetts, on the Occasion of the Dedication of Freemason's Hall, in Boston, Dec. 27, 1859, with an Appendix.* Boston, 1860.

Hersey, Charles. *History of Worcester, Massachusetts. From 1836 to 1861. With Interesting Reminiscences of the Public Men of Worcester.* Worcester, n.d.

Hershberg, Theodore. "Free Blacks in Antebellum Philadelphia: A Study of Ex-Slaves, Freeborn, and Socioeconomic Decline." In *Philadelphia: Work, Space, Family, and Group Experience in the Nineteenth Century*, edited by Theodore Hershberg, 368–91. New York, 1981.

———. "A Tale of Three Cities: Blacks, Immigrants, and Opportunity in Philadelphia, 1850–1880, 1930, 1970." In *Philadelphia: Work, Space, Family, and Group Experience in the Nineteenth Century*, edited by Theodore Hershberg, 461–91. New York, 1981.

———, ed. *Philadelphia: Work, Space, Family, and Group Experience in the Nineteenth Century: Essays Toward an Interdisciplinary History of the City.* New York, 1981.

Hershberg, Theodore, and Henry Williams. "Mulattoes and Blacks: Intra-Group Color Differences and Social Stratification in Nineteenth-Century Philadelphia." In *Philadelphia: Work, Space, Family, and Group Experience in the Nineteenth Century*, edited by Theodore Hershberg, 392–434. New York, 1981.

Higginson, Thomas Wentworth. *Massachusetts in the Army and Navy During the War of 1861–65.* 2 vols. Boston, 1896.

Hilyer, Andrew F., comp. *The Twentieth Century Union League Directory, Colored Washington.* Washington, D.C., 1901.

Hine, Darlene Clark. *Black Women in America: An Historical Encyclopedia.* Brooklyn, N.Y., 1993.

Hoar, George F. *Autobiography of Seventy Years.* 2 vols. London, 1904.

Hobsbawm, E. J. *The Age of Revolution, 1789–1848.* New York, 1962.

Hogan, Rev. William T., S.J. *Economic History of the Iron and Steel Industry in the United States.* 5 vols. Lexington, Mass., 1971.

Holt, Thomas. *Black over White: Negro Political Leadership in South Carolina During Reconstruction.* Urbana, Ill., 1979.

Horton, James Oliver. *Free People of Color: Inside the African American Community.* Washington, D.C., 1993.

———. "Generations of Protest: Black Families and Social Reform in Ante-Bellum Boston." *New England Quarterly* 49, no. 2 (June 1976):242–56.

———, and Lois E. Horton. *Black Bostonians: Family Life and Community Struggle in the Antebellum North.* New York, 1979.

An Inquiry into the Condition and Prospects of the African Race in the United States: And the Means of Bettering Its Fortunes. Philadelphia, 1839.

Jacobs, Donald M. "The Nineteenth Century Struggle over Segregated Education in the Boston Schools." In *Civil Rights in American History: Major Historical Interpretations*, edited by Kermit L. Hall, 423–32. New York, 1987.

———. "William Lloyd Garrison's *Liberator* and Boston's Blacks, 1830–1865." *New England Quarterly* 44, no. 2 (June 1971):259–77.

Jacobs, Walter W., Jr. "Churches of the Black Communities in Bucks County." *Bucks County Genealogical Society Newsletter* 7, no. 4 (Summer 1988):53–55.

James, William. "Oration." In Boston City Council, *Exercises at the Dedication of the Monument to Colonel Robert Gould Shaw and the Fifty-Fourth Regiment of Massachusetts Infantry, May 31, 1897.* Boston, 1897.

Johnson, Robert Underwood, and Clarence Clough Buel, eds. *Battles and Leaders of the Civil War.* 4 vols. New York, 1887.

Johnson, Dr. William Henry. *Autobiography of Dr. William Henry Johnson.* Albany, N.Y., 1900.

Jones, Robert. *Fifty Years in the Lombard Street Central Presbyterian Church.* Philadelphia, 1894.

Katzman, David M. *Before the Ghetto: Black Detroit in the Nineteenth Century.* Urbana, Ill., 1975.

Keiley, A. M. *In Vinculis: Or The Prisoner of War, Being the Experience of a Rebel in Two Federal Pens, Interspersed with Reminiscences of the Late War, Anecdotes of Southern Generals, Etc.* New York, 1866.

Kelley, William D. *The Conscription. Also Speeches of the Honorable W. D. Kelley, of Pennsylvania, in the House of Representatives, on the Conscription; the Way to Attain and Secure Peace; and on Arming the Negroes. With a Letter from Secretary Chase.* Philadelphia, 1863.

Kelly, Alfred H. "The Congressional Controversy over School Segregation, 1867–1875." In *Civil Rights in American History: Major Historical Interpretations,* edited by Kermit L. Hall, 457–83. New York, 1987.

Kimball, Edward P., ed. *Brinley Hall Album and . . . Post 10 Sketch Book.* Worcester, 1896.

Kirkland, Edward Chase. *Charles Francis Adams, Jr., 1835–1915: The Patrician at Bay.* Cambridge, Mass., 1965.

Kiser, Clyde Vernon. *Sea Island to City: A Study of St. Helena Islanders in Harlem and Other Urban Centers.* New York, 1932 (reissue, 1967).

Koenig, Louis W. *Bryan: A Political Biography of William Jennings Bryan.* New York, 1971.

Kohlstedt, Sally. "A Step Toward Scientific Self-Identity in the United States: The Failure of the National Institute, 1844." In *Science in America Since 1820,* edited by Nathan Reingold, 79–103. New York, 1976.

Kusmer, Kenneth L. *A Ghetto Takes Shape: Black Cleveland, 1870–1930.* Urbana, Ill., 1976.

Lane, Roger. *Roots of Violence in Black Philadelphia, 1860–1900.* Cambridge, Mass., 1986.

———. *William Dorsey's Philadelphia and Ours: On the Past and Future of the Black City in America.* New York, 1991.

Lanier, Sidney. *Florida: Its Scenery, Climate, and History. With an Account of Charleston, Savannah, Augusta, and Aiken, and a Chapter for Consumptives.* Philadelphia, 1875.

Lapsansky, Emma Jones. "Friends, Wives, and Strivings: Networks and Community Values Among Nineteenth-Century Philadelphian Afroamerican Elite." *Pennsylvania Magazine of History and Biography* 108, no. 1 (January 1984):3–24.

———. " 'Since They Got Those Separate Churches': Afro-Americans and Racism in Jacksonian Philadelphia." *American Quarterly* 32, no. 1 (Spring 1980):54–78.

Laurie, Bruce. *Working People of Philadelphia, 1800–1850.* Philadelphia, 1980.

Lawrence, Vera Brodsky. *Strong on Music: The New York Music Scene in the Days of George Templeton Strong, 1836–1875.* Vol. 1, *Resonances, 1836–1850.* New York, 1988.

Lea, Tom. *The King Ranch.* 2 vols. Kingsville, Tex., 1957.

Leach, Frank Willing. *The Wurts Family.* Philadelphia, 1931.

Lebergott, Stanley. *The Americans: An Economic Record.* New York, 1984.

Lee, B. F., Jr. "Negro Organizations." *Annals of the American Academy of Political and Social Science* 49 (September 1913):129–37.

Lee, Rev. John W. *A Brief Sketch of the Presbyterian Church in the United States of America Among Negroes, Especially During the Last Fifty Years.* N.p., 1913.

Levesque, George A. "Boston's Black Brahmin: Dr. John S. Rock." *Civil War History* 26, no. 4 (December 1980):326–46.

———. "Inherent Reformers—Inherited Orthodoxy: Black Baptists in Boston, 1800–1873." *Journal of Negro History* 40, no. 4 (October 1975): 491–525.

Levine, Lawrence W. *Highbrow/Lowbrow: The Emergence of Cultural Hierarchy in America.* Cambridge, Mass., 1988.

Levy, Leonard W., and Harlan B. Phillips. "The Roberts Case: Source of the 'Separate but Equal' Doctrine." In *Civil Rights in American History: Major Historical Interpretations,* edited by Kermit L. Hall, 582–90. New York, 1987.

Lewis, David Levering. *W. E. B. Du Bois: Biography of a Race, 1868–1910.* New York, 1993.

Lightfoot, Billy Bob. "The Negro Exodus from Comanche County, Texas." *The Southwestern Historical Quarterly* 46, no. 3 (January 1953):407–16.

Litwack, Leon F. *Been in the Storm So Long: The Aftermath of Slavery.* New York, 1979.

———. *North of Slavery: The Negro in the Free United States, 1790–1860.* Chicago, 1961.

———, and August Meier, eds. *Black Leaders of the Nineteenth Century.* Urbana, Ill., 1988.

Lofgren, Charles A. *The Plessy Case: A Legal-Historical Interpretation.* New York, 1987.

Logan, Rayford W., and Michael R. Winston. *Dictionary of American Negro Biography.* New York, 1982.

Lothrop, Charles H. *A History of the First Regiment Iowa Cavalry Veteran Volunteers, from Its Organization in 1861 to Its Muster out of the United States Service in 1866. Also a Complete Roster of the Regiment.* Lyons, Iowa, 1890.

Lubbock, Francis Richard. *Six Decades in Texas, Or Memoirs of Francis Richard Lubbock, Governor of Texas in War-Time, 1861–63: A Personal Experience in Business, War, and Politics.* Austin, Tex., 1900.

Lux et Veritas—Light and Truth, or the Origin of Ancient Freemasonry, Among Colored Men, in the State of Delaware. Wilmington, Del., 1856.

Lyell, Sir Charles. *Travels in North America, Canada, and Nova Scotia, with Geological Observations.* 2 vols. London, 1845–1855.

Lyght, Ernest. *Path of Freedom: The Black Presence in New Jersey's Burlington County, 1659–1900.* Haddonfield, N.J., 1978.

McConnell, Stuart. *Glorious Contentment: The Grand Army of the Republic, 1865–1900.* Chapel Hill, N.C., 1992.

McCormick, Richard P. "William Whipper: Moral Reformer." *Pennsylvania History* 43, no. 1 (January 1976):23–48.

McElroy's Philadelphia Directory for 1850: Containing the Names of the Inhabitants, Their Occupations, Places of Business, and Dwelling Houses; Also a List of the Streets, Lanes, Alleys, the City Offices, Public Institutions, Banks, Etc. Philadelphia, 1850.

McElroy's Philadelphia City Directory for 1855: Containing the Names of the Inhabitants, Their Occupations, Places of Business, and Dwelling Houses; Also a List of the Streets, Lanes, Alleys, the City Offices, Public Institutions, Banks, Etc. Philadelphia, 1855.

McElroy's Philadelphia Directory for 1856: Containing the Names of the Inhabitants, Their Occupations, Places of Business, and Dwelling Houses; Also a List of the Streets, Lanes, Alleys, the City Offices, Public Institutions, Banks, Etc. Philadelphia, 1856.

McElroy's Philadelphia Directory for 1857: Containing the Names of the Inhabitants, Their Occupations, Places of Business, and Dwelling Houses; Also a List of the Streets, Lanes, Alleys, the City Offices, Public Institutions, Banks, Etc. Philadelphia, 1857.

McElroy's Philadelphia City Directory for 1858: Containing the Names of the Inhabitants, Their Occupations, Places of Business, and Dwelling Houses; Also a List of the Streets, Lanes, Alleys, the City Offices, Public Institutions, Banks, Etc. Philadelphia, 1858.

McElroy's Philadelphia City Directory for 1859: Containing the Names of the Inhabitants, Their Occupations, Places of Business, and Dwelling Houses; Also a List of the Streets, Lanes, Alleys, the City Offices, Public Institutions, Banks, Etc. Philadelphia, 1859.

McElroy's Philadelphia City Directory for 1860: Containing the Names of the Inhabitants, Their Occupations, Places of Business, and Dwelling Houses; Also a List of the Streets, Lanes, Alleys, the City Offices, Public Institutions, Banks, Etc. Philadelphia, 1860.

McElroy's Philadelphia City Directory for 1861. Philadelphia, 1861.

McElroy's Philadelphia City Directory for 1862. Philadelphia, 1862.

McElroy's Philadelphia City Directory for 1863. Philadelphia, 1863.

McElroy's Philadelphia City Directory for 1864. Philadelphia, 1864.

McFeely, William S. *Frederick Douglass.* New York, 1991.

———. *Grant: A Biography.* New York, 1982.

McGerr, Michael E. *The Decline of Popular Politics: The American North, 1865–1928.* New York, 1986.

McLoughlin, William G. *Revivals, Awakenings, and Reform: An Essay on Religion and Social Change in America, 1607–1977.* Chicago, 1978.

McMillen, Neil R. *Dark Journey: Black Mississippians in the Age of Jim Crow.* Urbana, Ill., 1989.

McNealy, Terry A. "Sources for Black Genealogy in Bucks County." *Bucks County Genealogical Society Newsletter* 5, no. 1 (Fall 1985):4–5.

MacPherson, James M. *Battle Cry of Freedom: The Civil War Era.* New York, 1988.

———. *The Negro's Civil War: How American Negroes Felt and Acted During the War for the Union.* New York, 1965.

———. "Wartime." *New York Review of Books.* April 12, 1990, 33–35.

———, ed. *Battle Chronicles of the Civil War.* 6 vols. New York, 1989.

Magill, Edward H. "When Men Were Sold, Reminiscences of the Underground Railroad in Bucks County and Its Managers." In *A Collection of Papers Read Before the Bucks County Historical Society,* vol. 2, 493–520. Riegelsville, Pa., n.d.

Martin, Tony. "Race Men, Bibliophiles, and Historians: The World of Robert M. Adger and The Negro Historical Society of Philadelphia." In *Rare Afro-Americana: A Reconstruction of the Adger Library,* edited by Wendy Ball and Tony Martin, 1–55. Boston, 1981.

Martin, Waldo. *The Mind of Frederick Douglass.* Chapel Hill, N.C., 1984.

Marty, Martin E. *Pilgrims in Their Own Land: 500 Years of Religion in America.* New York, 1984.

Marvin, Abijah P. *History of Worcester in the War of the Rebellion.* Worcester, 1880.

Mason, Isaac. *Life of Isaac Mason as a Slave.* Worcester, 1893.

[Massachusetts Citizens Equal Rights Association.] *Constitution and By-Laws of Worcester Branch of Massachusetts Citizens Equal Rights Association.* Worcester, 1891.

May, Henry. *The Enlightenment in America.* New York, 1976.

Meagher, Timothy J. " 'Why Should We Care for a Little Trouble or a Walk Through the Mud': St. Patrick's and Columbus Day Parades in Worcester, Massachusetts, 1845–1915." *New England Quarterly* 58, no. 1 (March 1985):5–26.

Meier, August. "Negro Class Structure and Ideology in the Age of Booker T. Washington." *Phylon* 23, no. 3 (1962):258–66.

———, and Elliott Rudwick, eds. *The Making of Black America: Essays in Negro Life and History.* 2 vols. New York, 1969.

Memoir of the Pilgrimage to Virginia of the Knights Templars of Massachusetts and Rhode Island, May, 1859. Boston, 1859.

Memorial of Thirty Thousand Disfranchised Citizens of Philadelphia, to the Honorable Senate and House of Representatives. Philadelphia, 1855.

Merington, Marguarite, ed. *The Custer Story: The Life and Intimate Letters of General George A. Custer and His Wife, Elizabeth.* New York, 1950.

Minton, Henry M. *Early History of Negroes in Business in Philadelphia.* N.p., 1913.

Mitchell, Reid. *Civil War Soldiers.* New York, 1988.

[Montacute Lodge.] *By-Laws and List of Members of Montacute Lodge, A.F. and A.M., Worcester, Mass.* Worcester, 1897.

———. *The Commemoration of the Fiftieth Anniversary of Montacute Lodge, A.F. and A.M., 1858–1908.* Worcester, 1917.

Morgan, Edmund M. *American Slavery, American Freedom: The Ordeal of Colonial Virginia.* New York, 1975.

[Morning Star Lodge.] *By-Laws of Morning Star Lodge of Ancient, Free and Accepted Masons, Worcester, Mass.* Worcester, 1880.

Morris, Richard B. *Government and Labor in Early America.* New York, 1946 (reissue, 1965).

Moses, Wilson Jeremiah. *The Golden Age of Black Nationalism, 1850–1925.* New York, 1978.

Muraskin, William A. *Middle-Class Blacks in a White Society: Prince Hall Freemasonry in America.* Berkeley, Cal., 1975.

Murdock, Eugene C. *One Million Men: The Civil War Draft in the North.* Madison, Wis., 1971.

Murray, Andrew E. *Presbyterians and the Negro—A History.* Philadelphia, 1966.

Nash, Gary B. *Forging Freedom: The Formation of Philadelphia's Black Community, 1720–1840.* Cambridge, Mass., 1988.

Nason, Edward S. *A Centennial History of Morning Star Lodge.* Worcester, 1894.

Needles, Edward. *Ten Years' Progress: Or A Comparison of the State and Condition of the Colored People in the City and County of Philadelphia, from 1837 to 1847.* Philadelphia, 1849.

Nelson, William E. *The Fourteenth Amendment: From Political Principle to Judicial Doctrine.* Cambridge, Mass., 1988.

Nevin, Alfred, ed. *Encyclopedia of the Presbyterian Church in the United States of America: Including the Northern and Southern Assemblies.* Philadelphia, 1884.

Nevins, Allan, and Milton Halsey Thomas, eds. *The Diary of George Templeton Strong.* 4 vols. New York, 1952.

Newcomb, Simon. "Memoir of Joseph Henry." In National Academy of Sciences, *Biographical Memoirs.* Vol. 5, 1–45. Washington, D.C., 1905.

Newton, H. A. "Memoir of Elias Loomis, 1811–1889." In National Academy of Sciences, *Biographical Memoirs.* Vol. 3, 213–52. Washington, D.C., 1895.

North, Thomas. *Five Years in Texas; Or, What You Did Not Hear During the War from January 1861 to January 1866. A Narrative of His Travels, Experiences, and Observations in Texas and Mexico.* Cincinnati, Ohio, 1871.

Northrup, Solomon. *Twelve Years a Slave.* Auburn, N.Y., 1853.

Norton, Charles Ledyard. *A Handbook of Florida.* New York, 1890.

Nox, Owen. *Southern Rambles: Florida.* Boston, 1881.

Nulty, William H. *Confederate Florida: The Road to Olustee.* Tuscaloosa, Ala., 1990.

Oblinger, Carl D. "Alms for Oblivion: The Making of a Black Underclass in Southeastern Pennsylvania, 1780–1860." In *The Ethnic Experience in Pennsylvania,* edited by John E. Bodnar, 94–119. Lewisburg, Pa., 1973.

———. "In Recognition of Their Prominence: A Case Study of the Economic and Social Backgrounds of an Ante-Bellum Negro Business and Farming

Class in Lancaster County." *Journal of the Lancaster County Historical Society* 72 (1968):65–83.

O'Brien's Philadelphia Wholesale Business Directory and Circular for the Year 1850. Philadelphia, 1850.

Odd Fellows, Independent Order of. *1844–1894: Fiftieth Anniversary of Worcester Lodge, No. 56, I.O.O.F.* Worcester, 1896.

———. *Odd Fellows Directory and Guide, Contains a Complete List of Odd Fellow Lodges in New England.* Boston, 1887.

Oehser, Paul H. *Sons of Science: The Story of the Smithsonian Institution and Its Leaders.* New York, 1949.

Offenberg, Richard S., and Robert Rue Parsonage, eds. *The War Letters of Duren F. Kelley, 1862–1865.* New York, 1967.

O'Flynn, Thomas F. *The Story of Worcester, Massachusetts.* Boston, 1913.

Oldmixon, John W. *Transatlantic Wanderings: Or A Last Look at the United States.* London, 1855.

Painter, Janice L. "Looking Back: The Blacks in Bucks County." *Bucks County Panorama* 18, no. 11 (November 1976):34–37, 62–65.

Painter, Nell Irvin. *Exodusters: Black Migration to Kansas After Reconstruction.* New York, 1977.

Paludan, Phillip Shaw. *"A People's Contest": The Union and Civil War, 1861–1865.* New York, 1988.

Parker, Inez Moore. *The Rise and Decline of the Program of Education for Black Presbyterians of the United Presbyterian Church U.S.A., 1865–1970.* San Antonio, Tex., 1977.

Patterson, Orlando. "Toward a Study of Black America: Notes on the Culture of Racism." *Dissent* 36, no. 4 (Fall 1989):476–86.

Payne, Bishop Daniel Alexander. *Recollections of Seventy Years.* New York, 1888 (reissue, 1968).

Pearson, Henry Greenleaf. *The Life of John A. Andrew: Governor of Massachusetts, 1861–1865.* 2 vols. Boston, 1904.

Pease, William H., and Jane H. Pease. "Antislavery Ambivalence: Immediatism, Expediency, Race." In *The Making of Black America: Essays in Negro Life and History,* edited by August Meier and Elliott Rudwick, vol. 1, 302–14. New York, 1969.

[Pennsylvania Anti-Slavery Society.] *The Arrest, Trial, and Release of Daniel Webster, Fugitive Slave.* Philadelphia, 1859.

Pennsylvania Society for the Promotion of the Abolition of Slavery. *The Present State and Condition of the Free People of Color, of the City of Philadelphia and Adjoining Districts.* Philadelphia, 1838.

Petrin, Ronald A. *French Canadians in Massachusetts Politics, 1885–1915: Ethnicity and Political Pragmatism.* Philadelphia, 1990.

Phillips, Rev. Henry L. *Church of the Crucifixion, Philadelphia, Pa., Semi-Centennial, May 1847–May 1897: A Historical Discourse.* Philadelphia, 1897.

Phillips, Wendell. *Who Shall Rule Us? Money, or, The People?* Boston, 1878.

Philpott, Thomas Lee. *The Slum and the Ghetto: Neighborhood Deterioration and Middle-Class Reform, Chicago, 1880–1930.* New York, 1978.

Pierson, William Whately, Jr., ed. *Whipt'em Everytime: The Diary of Bartlett Yancey Malone.* Wilmington, N.C., 1987.

Pleasants, Henry, Jr., and George H. Straley. *Inferno at Petersburg.* Philadelphia, 1961.

Pleck, Elizabeth Hafkin. *Black Migration and Poverty: Boston, 1865–1900.* New York, 1979.

Pollard, Edward A. *The Last of the War.* New York, 1866.

Porter, Dorothy B. "The Organized Educational Activities of Negro Literary Societies, 1828–1846." *Journal of Negro Education,* 5, no. 4 (October 1936):555–76.

Porter, Kenneth W. "Negroes and Indians on the Texas Frontier, 1834–1874." *Southwestern Historical Quarterly* 53, no. 2 (October 1949):151–63.

Prentiss, George Lewis. *The Union Theological Seminary in the City of New York: Historical and Biographical Sketches of Its First Fifty Years.* New York, 1889.

Preuss, Arthur, comp. *A Dictionary of Secret and Other Societies.* St. Louis, Mo., 1924 (reissue, 1966).

Price, Edward. "The Black Voting Rights Issue in Pennsylvania, 1780–1900." *Pennsylvania Magazine of History and Biography* 100, no. 3 (July 1976): 356–73.

[Princeton Theological Seminary.] *Necrological Reports and Annual Proceedings of the Alumni Association of Princeton Theological Seminary, 1875–1889.* Princeton, N.J., 1891.

The Prologue and Constitution of the Sisterhood of Good Angels; and the By-Laws of St. Luke's Society, of Said Sisterhood. New Haven, Conn., 1856.

Quarles, Benjamin, ed. *Blacks on John Brown.* Urbana, Ill., 1972.

[Quinsigamond Lodge.] *Charter and By-Laws of Quinsigamond Lodge, of Ancient, Free and Accepted Masons, Worcester, Mass.* Worcester, 1881.

Raboteau, Albert J. "Richard Allen and the African Church Movement." In *Black Leaders of the Nineteenth Century,* edited by Leon Litwack and August Meier, 1–20. Urbana, Ill., 1988.

"Rambler." *Guide to Florida.* Gainesville, Fla., 1875 (reissue, 1964).

Ramsdell, Charles William. *Reconstruction in Texas.* New York, 1910.

Rand, John C., comp. *One of a Thousand: A Series of Biographical Sketches of One Thousand Representative Men Resident in the Commonwealth of Massachusetts, A.D. 1888–'89.* Boston, 1890.

Redkey, Edwin S., ed. *A Grand Army of Black Men: Letters from African-American Soldiers in the Union Army, 1861–1865.* New York, 1992.

Reese, James V. "The Early History of Labor Organizations in Texas, 1838–1876." *Southwestern Historical Quarterly* 72, no. 1 (July 1968): 1–20.

Register of Trades of the Colored People in the City of Philadelphia and Districts. Philadelphia, 1838.

Reingold, Nathan, ed. *Science in America Since 1820.* New York, 1976.

————. *Science in Nineteenth-Century America: A Documentary History.* New York, 1964.

Rhees, William Jones, comp. *The Smithsonian Institution: Documents Relative to Its Origin and History, 1835–1899.* 2 vols. Washington, D.C., 1901.

Rice, Franklin P., ed. *The Worcester of Eighteen Hundred and Ninety-Eight.* Worcester, 1899.

Richards, Leonard L. *"Gentlemen of Property and Standing": Anti-Abolition Mobs in Jacksonian America.* New York, 1970.

Richter, William L. "The Army and the Negro During Texas Reconstruction, 1865–1870." *East Texas Historical Journal* 10, no. 1 (Spring 1972):7–19.

————. "Spread-Eagle Eccentricities: Military-Civilian Relations in Reconstruction Texas." *Texana* 8, no. 4 (1970):311–27.

Rickard, James H. "Service with Colored Troops in Burnside's Corps." *Soldiers and Sailors Historical Society of Rhode Island, Personal Narratives.* 5th ser., no. 1. Providence, R.I., 1894.

Ripley, C. Peter, ed. *The Black Abolitionist Papers.* Vol. 5, *The United States, 1859–1865.* Chapel Hill, N.C., 1992.

Ripley, Edward H. "Final Scenes at the Capture and Occupation of Richmond, April 3, 1865." In *Personal Recollections of the War of the Rebellion,* edited by A. Noel Blakeman, 472–502. New York, 1907.

Robboy, Stanley J., and Anita W. Robboy. "Lewis Hayden: From Fugitive Slave to Statesman." *New England Quarterly* 46, no. 4 (December 1973): 591–613.

Roberts, Rev. Edward Howell, ed. *Biographical Catalogue of the Princeton Theological Seminary, 1815–1932.* Princeton, 1933.

Robinson, Rev. Edgar Sutton, ed. *The Ministerial Directory of the Ministers in "The Presbyterian Church in the United States" (Southern), and in "The Presbyterian Church in the United States of America" (Northern), Together with a Statement of the Work of the Executive Committees and Boards of the Two Churches, with the Names and Location of their Educational Institutions and Church Papers.* 2 vols. Oxford, Ohio, 1898.

Robinson, William L., comp. *Roster of George H. Ward Post, No. 10, Department of Massachusetts, Grand Army of the Republic.* Worcester, 1896.

Rockwell, Alfred P. "The Tenth Army Corps in Virginia, May 1864." *Papers of the Military Historical Society of Massachusetts* 9 (1912):265–99.

Rollin, Frank A. *Life and Public Services of Martin R. Delany, Sub-Assistant Commissioner Bureau of Refugees, Freedmen, and of Abandoned Lands, and Late Major 104th U.S. Colored Troops.* Boston, 1883.

Rorabaugh, W. J. *The Craft Apprentice: From Franklin to the Machine Age in America.* New York, 1986.

Rosenberger, Lyle L. "Black Suffrage in Bucks County: The Election of 1837." *Bucks County Historical Society Journal* 4 (Spring 1975):28–36.

Rosenzweig, Roy. *Eight Hours for What We Will: Workers and Leisure in an Industrial City, 1870–1920.* New York, 1983.

Roy, Thomas Sherrard. *Stalwart Builders: A History of the Grand Lodge of Masons in Massachusetts, 1733–1970.* Boston, 1971.

Ruchames, Louis. "Race, Marriage, and Abolition in Massachusetts." In *Race Relations and the Law in American History: Major Historical Interpretations*, edited by Kermit L. Hall, 279–302. New York, 1987.

Sadie, Stanley, ed. *The New Grove Dictionary of Music and Musicians*. 20 vols. London, 1980.

Salvatore, Nick. *Eugene V. Debs: Citizen and Socialist*. Urbana, Ill., 1982.

———. "Two Tales of a City: Nineteenth Century Black Philadelphia." *Dissent* 38, no. 2 (Spring 1991):227–35.

Sanborn, F. B. "The Virginia Campaign of John Brown." *Atlantic Monthly* 36 (December 1875):704–21.

Saunders, Prince. *An Address Delivered at Bethel Church, Philadelphia; on the 30th of September, 1818. Before the Pennsylvania Augustine Society, for the Education of People of Colour*. Philadelphia, 1818.

Saxton, Alexander. *The Indispensable Enemy: Labor and the Anti-Chinese Movement in California*. Berkeley, Cal., 1971.

Scharf, J. Thomas, and Thompson Westcott. *History of Philadelphia: 1609–1884*. 3 vols. Philadelphia, 1884.

Schermerhorn, William E. *The History of Burlington, New Jersey, from the Early European Arrivals in the Delaware to the Quarter Millennial Anniversary, in 1927, of the Settlement by English Quarters in 1677*. Burlington, N.J., 1927.

Schor, Joel. *Henry Highland Garnet: A Voice of Black Radicalism in the Nineteenth Century*. Westport, Conn., 1977.

Schouler, William. *A History of Massachusetts in the Civil War*. 2 vols. Boston, 1868–1871.

Scott, Anne Fiore. "One Woman's Experience of World War II." *Journal of American History* 77, no. 2 (September 1990), 556–62.

Second African Presbyterian Church. *The Report of the Board of Trustees . . . for the Year 1842*. Philadelphia, [1843].

Sefton, James E. *The United States Army and Reconstruction, 1865–1877*. Baton Rouge, La., 1967.

Sernett, Milton C. *Black Religion and American Evangelicalism: White Protestants, Plantation Missions, and the Flowering of Negro Christianity, 1787–1865*. Metuchen, N.J., 1975.

Shannon, Fred Albert. *The Organization and Administration of the Union Army, 1861–1865*. 2 vols. Cleveland, 1928.

Shaw, James. "Our Last Campaign and Subsequent Service in Texas." *Soldiers and Sailors Historical Society of Rhode Island, Personal Narratives*. 6th ser., no. 9. Providence, R.I., 1905.

Shofner, Jerrell H. *Nor Is It Over Yet: Florida in the Era of Reconstruction, 1863–1877*. Gainesville, Fla., 1974.

Shook, Robert W. "The Federal Military in Texas, 1865–1870." *Texas Military History* 6, no. 1 (Spring 1967):3–53.

Silcox, Harry C. "The Black 'Better Class' Political Dilemma: Philadelphia Prototype Isaiah C. Wears." *Pennsylvania Magazine of History and Biography* 113, no. 1 (January 1989):45–66.

———. "Delay and Neglect: Negro Public Education in Antebellum Philadelphia, 1800–1860." *Pennsylvania Magazine of History and Biography* 97, no. 4 (October 1973):444–64.

———. "Nineteenth Century Philadelphia Black Militant: Octavius V. Catto (1839–1871)." *Pennsylvania History* 44, no. 1 (January 1977):53–76.

Singletary, Otis A. *Negro Militia and Reconstruction.* Austin, Tex., 1957.

[Sisterhood of the Good Angels.] *The Prologue and Construction of the Sisterhood of the Good Angels; and the By-Laws of St. Luke's Society, of Said Sisterhood.* New Haven, Conn., 1856.

"Sketch of James Pollard Espy." *Popular Science Monthly* 34 (April 1889): 834–40.

Sklar, Kathryn Kish. *Catherine Beecher: A Study in American Domesticity.* New Haven, Conn., 1973.

———. *Florence Kelley and the Nation's Work.* New Haven, Conn., 1995.

Slotkin, Richard. *The Fatal Environment: The Myth of the Frontier In the Age of Industrialization, 1800–1890.* New York, 1985.

Smith, Anna Bustill. "The Bustill Family." *Journal of Negro History* 10, no. 4 (October 1925):638–44.

———. "A Communication." *Journal of Negro History* 10, no. 4 (October 1925):645–47.

Smith, H. P., and W. S. Rann, eds. *History of Rutland County, Vermont, with Illustrations and Biographical Sketches of Some of Its Prominent Men and Pioneers.* Syracuse, N.Y., 1886.

Smith, James L. *Autobiography, Including, Also, Reminiscences of Slave Life, Recollections of the War, Education of Freemen, Cause of the Exodus, Etc.* Norwich, Conn., 1881.

Smith, Timothy L. *Revivalism and Social Reform in Mid-Nineteenth Century America.* New York, 1957.

Smith, William Farrar. "Butler's Attack on Drewry's Bluff." In *Battles and Leaders of the Civil War,* edited by Robert Underwood Johnson and Clarence Clough Buel, vol. 4, 206–12. New York, 1887.

Society of Friends. *A Statistical Inquiry into the Condition of the People of Colour, of the City and Districts of Philadelphia.* Philadelphia, 1849.

Southern, Eileen. *The Music of Black Americans: A History.* 2d ed. New York, 1983.

Southwick, Albert B., ed. *The Journals of Stephen C. Earle, 1853–58.* Worcester, 1976.

Spear, Allan H. *Black Chicago: The Making of a Negro Ghetto, 1890–1920.* Chicago, 1967.

Sprague, A. B. R. *Address of General A. B. R. Sprague, Grand Commander, Department of Mass. G.A.R. Delivered at the Annual Meeting of the Department in Worcester, January 20, 1869.* Boston, 1869.

Sprogle, Howard O. *The Philadelphia Police, Past and Present.* Philadelphia, 1887.

Stampp, Kenneth. *America in 1857: A Nation on the Brink.* New York, 1990.

———. *And Then the War Came: The North and the Secession Crisis, 1860–1861.* Baton Rouge, La., 1950.

Staton, James T. *Lectures of the Three Degrees of the Grand United Order of Odd Fellows.* Manchester, Eng., 1899.

Stearns, Frank Preston. *The Life and Public Services of George Luther Stearns.* Philadelphia, 1907.

Steinberg, Allen. *The Transformation of Criminal Justice: Philadelphia, 1800–1880.* Chapel Hill, N.C., 1989.

Stephenson, Mary Harriet. *Dr. B. F. Stephenson, Founder of the Grand Army of the Republic. A Memoir, by His Daughter.* Springfield, Ill., 1894.

Stern, Philip Van Doren. *Soldier Life in the Union and Confederate Armies.* Bloomington, Ind., 1961.

Stevens, Albert C. *The Cyclopaedia of Fraternities: A Compilation of Existing Authentic Information . . . of More Than Six Hundred Secret Societies in the United States.* Detroit, 1907 (reissue, 1966).

Stewart, James Brewer. *Wendell Phillips: Liberty's Hero.* Baton Rouge, La., 1986.

Still, Mary. *An Appeal to the Females of the African Methodist Episcopal Church.* Philadelphia, 1857.

Still, William. *An Address on Voting and Laboring, Delivered at Concert Hall, Tuesday Evening, March 10th, 1874.* Philadelphia, 1874.

———. *The Underground Rail Road.* Philadelphia, 1872.

Stimson, [Reverend] Henry A. *Death of General Custer, and the Indian Problem.* [Minneapolis, Minn., 1876.]

Stockbridge, Frank Parker, and John Holliday Perry. *Florida in the Making.* New York, 1926.

Storey, Brit Allan, ed. "An Army Officer in Texas, 1866–1867." *Southwestern Historical Quarterly* 72, no. 2 (October 1968):242–52.

Stowe, Harriet Beecher. *Palmetto-Leaves.* Gainesville, Fla., 1873 (reissue, 1968).

The Stranger's Guide in Philadelphia to All Public Buildings, Places of Amusement, Commercial, Benevolent, and Religious Institutions, and Churches, Principal Hotels, etc., Including Laurel Hill, Woodlands, Monument, Odd-Fellows', and Glenwood Cemeteries. With a Map of the Consolidated City and Numerous Illustrations of the Principal Buildings. Philadelphia, 1861.

Stuckey, Sterling. *Slave Culture: Nationalist Theory and the Foundations of Black America.* New York, 1987.

Sunshine, Silvia [Abbie M. Brooks]. *Petals Plucked from Sunny Climes.* Gainesville, Fla., 1880 (reissue, 1976).

Swift, David E. *Black Prophets of Justice: Activist Clergy Before the Civil War.* Baton Rouge, La., 1989.

Talbot, Edith Armstrong. *Samuel Chapman Armstrong: A Biographical Study.* New York, 1904.

Tappan, Franklin D. *The Passing of the Grand Army of the Republic.* Worcester, 1939.

Taylor, Frank H. *Philadelphia in the Civil War, 1861–1865.* Philadelphia, 1913.

Taylor, Susie King. *Reminiscences of My Life: A Black Woman's Civil War Memoirs.* Edited by Patricia W. Romero and Willie Lee Rose. New York, 1902 (reissue, 1988).

Thornbrough, Emma Lou. *T. Thomas Fortune: Militant Journalist.* Chicago, 1972.

Thornton, Mary Lindsay, ed. "The Prison Diary of Adjutant Francis Atherton Boyle, C.S.A." *North Carolina Historical Review* 39, no. 1 (Winter 1962): 58–84.

Toll, Robert C. *Blacking Up: The Minstrel Show in Nineteenth-Century America.* New York, 1974.

Toney, Marcus B. *The Privations of a Private.* Nashville, Tenn., 1905.

Trotter, James M. *Music and Some Highly Musical People: Containing Brief Chapters on I. A Description of Music. II. The Music of Nature. III. A Glance at the History of Music. IV. The Power, Beauty, and Uses of Music. Following Which Are Given Sketches of the Lives of Remarkable Musicians of the Colored Race. With Portraits and an Appendix Containing Copies of Music Composed By Colored Men.* Boston, 1880.

Tucker, David M. *Black Pastors and Leaders: Memphis, 1819–1972.* Memphis, Tenn., 1975.

Turner, Edward Raymond. *The Negro in Pennsylvania: Slavery—Servitude—Freedom, 1639–1861.* Washington, D.C., 1911.

Turp, Dr. Ralph K. "Burlington: The Colonial Capital." *South Jersey Magazine* 9, no. 2 (Spring 1980):14–21.

Twain, Mark. *Pudd'nhead Wilson.* San Francisco, 1968.

Ulle, Robert F. "Popular Black Music in Nineteenth Century Philadelphia." *Pennsylvania Folklife* 25, no. 2 (Winter 1975–1976):20–28.

Union Benevolent Association. *Eighteenth Annual Report of the Executive Board, and of the Ladies' Board of Managers of the Union Benevolent Association.* Philadelphia, 1849.

———. *Nineteenth Annual Report of the Executive Board, and of the Ladies' Board of Managers of the Union Benevolent Association.* Philadelphia, 1850.

———. *Report of the Ladies' Branch of the Union Benevolent Association. For the Months of October, November, December, January, and February, 1839–40.* Philadelphia, 1840.

[Union Veteran Legion.] *Union Veteran Legion, Encampment No. 83.* Worcester, 1894.

Union Veterans Union. *Roster, Massachusetts Department, Union Veterans Union, —Also—Gen. William S. Lincoln Command No. 18.* Worcester, 1895.

Upton, William H. *Negro Masonry, Being a Critical Examination of Objections to the Legitimacy of the Masonry Existing Among the Negroes of America.* Cambridge, Mass., 1902.

Utley, Robert M. *The Lance and the Shield: The Life and Times of Sitting Bull.* New York, 1993.

Veney, Bethany. *The Narrative of Bethany Veney, a Slave Woman.* Worcester, 1889.

Vlasek, Dale R. "The Economic Thought of E. Franklin Frazier." *American Studies* 20, no. 2 (Fall 1979):23–40.

Voorhis, Harold Van Buren. *Negro Masonry in the United States.* New York, 1940.

Walker, Clarence E. *A Rock in a Weary Land: The African Methodist Episcopal Church During the Civil War and Reconstruction.* Baton Rouge, La., 1982.

Walker, John C. "Reconstruction in Texas." *Southern Historical Society Papers* 24 (1896):41–56.

Walker, Joseph A., Jr. *Black Square and Compass: 200 Years of Prince Hall Freemasonry.* N.p., 1979.

Wall, Caleb A. *Reminiscences of Worcester from the Earliest Period, Historical and Genealogical, with Notices of Early Settlers and Prominent Citizens, and Descriptions of Old Landmarks and Ancient Dwellings, Accompanied by a Map and Numerous Illustrations.* Worcester, 1877.

Wallace, Anthony F. C. *St. Clair: A Nineteenth-Century Coal Town's Experience With a Disaster-Prone Industry.* New York, 1987.

Wallace, Ernest. *Charles De Morse: Pioneer Statesman and Father of Texas Journalism.* Paris, Tex., 1985.

———. *Texas in Turmoil.* Austin, Tex., 1965.

Wallace, John. *Carpetbag Rule in Florida: The Inside Workings of the Reconstruction of Civil Government in Florida After the Close of the Civil War.* Jacksonville, Fla., 1888.

Walton, Clyde C., ed. *Private Smith's Journal: Recollections of the Late War.* Chicago, 1963.

Warner, Robert A. "Amos Gerry Beman—1812–1874, a Memoir on a Forgotten Leader." *Journal of Negro History* 22, no. 2 (April 1937):200–219.

Warner, Sam Bass. *The Private City: Philadelphia in Three Periods of Its Growth.* Philadelphia, 1968 (reissue, 1986).

Washburn, Charles G. *Manufacturing and Mechanical Industries, of Worcester.* Philadelphia, 1889.

Washburn, R. M. *Smith's Barn: "A Child's History" of the West Side, Worcester, 1880–1923.* Worcester, 1923.

Washington, Booker T. *The Future of the American Negro.* Boston, 1899.

———. *Up from Slavery.* In *Three Negro Classics,* edited by John Hope Franklin. New York, 1965.

Weigley, Russell F. *Philadelphia: A 300-Year History.* New York, 1982.

Weisberger, Bernard A. *They Gathered at the River: The Story of the Great Revivals and Their Impact upon Religion in America.* New York, 1958.

Wesley, Charles H. *The History of the National Association of Colored Women's Clubs: A Legacy of Service.* Washington, D.C., 1984.

White, Rev. William P., and William H. Scott. *The Presbyterian Church in Philadelphia. A Camera and Pen Sketch of Each Presbyterian Church and Institution in the City.* Philadelphia, 1895.

Williams, George W. *History of the Negro Race in America, from 1619 to 1880. Negroes as Slaves, as Soldiers, and as Citizens, Together with a Preliminary Consideration of the Unity of the Human Family, an Historical Sketch of Africa, and an Account of the Negro Governments of Sierra Leone and Liberia.* 2 vols. New York, 1883 (reissue, 1969).

Williams, Loretta J. *Black Freemasonry and Middle-Class Realities.* Columbia, Mo., 1980.

Williams, Richard E. *Called and Chosen: The Story of Mother Rebecca Jackson and the Philadelphia Shakers.* Metuchen, N.J., 1981.

Williamson, Edward C. *Florida Politics in the Gilded Age, 1877–1893.* Gainesville, Fla., 1976.

Wills, Gary. *Lincoln at Gettysburg: The Words That Remade America.* New York, 1992.

Willson, Joseph. *Sketches of the Higher Classes of Colored Society in Philadelphia.* Philadelphia, 1841.

Wilson, Joseph T. *The Black Phalanx: A History of the Negro Soldiers of the United States in the Wars of 1775–1812, 1861– 65.* Hartford, Conn., 1888.

Winch, Julie. *Philadelphia's Black Elite: Activism, Accommodation, and the Struggle for Autonomy, 1787–1848.* Philadelphia, 1988.

Winks, Robin W. *The Blacks in Canada: A History.* New Haven, Conn., 1971.

Women's Progressive Club. *Constitution and By-Laws.* Worcester, 1898.

Woodlin, Reverend Joshua. *The Masonic National Union; A History of the Origins of Ancient Freemasonry Among the Coloured Citizens, in the United States of America.* Burlington, N.J., 1855.

Woodson, Carter G., ed. "Letters of Negroes, Largely Personal and Private." *Journal of Negro History* 11, no. 1 (January 1926):62–214.

Woodward, Samuel B. "Early Charitable Organizations of Worcester." *Worcester Historical Society Publications* 1, no. 7 (new ser., April 1934): 391–402.

Wooten, Dudley G., ed. *A Comprehensive History of Texas, 1685 to 1897.* 2 vols. Dallas, 1898 (reissue, 1986).

Yacovone, Donald. "The Transformation of the Black Temperance Movement, 1827–1854: An Interpretation." *Journal of the Early Republic* 8 (Fall 1988):281–97.

Yerkes, Harman. "Anti-Slavery Days—Experience of Fugitives." In *A Collection of Papers Read Before the Bucks County Historical Society,* vol. 3, 504–12. Riegelsville, Pa., n.d.

Zochert, Donald. "Science and the Common Man in Ante-Bellum America." In *Science in America Since 1820,* edited by Nathan Reingold, 7–32. New York, 1976.

Zunz, Olivier. *The Changing Face of Inequality: Urbanization, Industrial Development, and Immigrants in Detroit, 1880–1920.* Chicago, 1982.

Unpublished Work

Brown, Thomas I. "Sociological Study of the Colored Population of Worcester." Master's thesis, Clark University, 1914.

Cheagle, Roslyn V. "The Colored Temperance Movement: 1830–1860." Master's thesis, Howard University, 1969.

Gordon, Alan Ira. "Political Elites in Worcester, Massachusetts (1855–1860)." Master's thesis, Clark University, n.d.

Gutridge, Stanley Holmes. "Women, Men, Progress: A History of the Association of Colored Peoples in Worcester, Massachusetts." N.d.

Kolesar, Robert J. "Politics and Policy in a Developing Industrial City: Worcester, Massachusetts, in the Late Nineteenth Century." Ph.D. diss., Clark University, 1987.

Spencer, Edna P. "What Color Is the Wind?" Master's thesis, Clark University, 1985.

Swan, Paul R. "Personal Histories of Worcester's Social and Industrial Leaders with Certain Sociological Interpretations." Master's thesis, Clark University, 1929.

Vinal, Ella L. "The Status of the Worcester Negro." Master's thesis, Clark University, 1929.

Vincent, Bernard. "Masons as Builders of the Republic: The Role of Freemasonry in the American Revolution." 1986.

INDEX

NOTE: Italicized page numbers refer to picture captions.

ABOUT THE AUTHOR

NICK SALVATORE grew up in Brooklyn, New York. He received his B.A. from Hunter College in the Bronx (now Lehman College), a division of the City University of New York, and his M.A. and Ph.D. from the University of California at Berkeley. He is currently a professor of American history at Cornell University's School of Industrial and Labor Relations. His previous books include an abridged edition of Samuel Gompers's *Seventy Years of Life and Labor* and *Eugene V. Debs: Citizen and Socialist,* for which he received the Bancroft Prize in 1983 and the John H. Dunning Prize in 1984. He lives in Ithaca, New York.